STUCK ON ME:
MISSING YOU

STUCK ON ME: MISSING YOU

LARRY A. BUGEN, PHD

ACFEI Media
Springfield, Missouri

Stuck on Me: Missing You

ACFEI Media
2750 E. Sunshine
Springfield, MO 65804

ISBN: 978-0-9822121-3-4

Printed in the United States. First printing February 2011

DEDICATION

To Claire, Erik, Jessica and Ryan
To Family and Friends
To Clients

And you can tell everybody this is your song
It may be quite simple but now that it's done
I hope you don't mind
I hope you don't mind that I put down in words
How wonderful life is while you're in the world.

Elton John [*Your Song*]

Praise for Dr. Bugen's books:

Dr. Bugen is a master at weaving empirical science with fascinating stories, all presented in clean categories and compelling prose. To be certain, this book will be an asset to pastors or religious leaders of any stripe, as we tread the turbulent waters of understanding and dealing with narcissistic persons, and strive to check those tendencies in ourselves.

Reverend Merrill Wade • Rector, St. Mathews Episcopal Church • Austin, Texas

A must read! Compelling stories and a strong message show us how to move beyond self-absorption to find acceptance and love.

Psychologist Kate Ludeman, Ph.D. • Author, Radical Change, Radical Results • President, Worth Ethic Corporation

In a world of imperfect and broken relationships, Larry Bugen once again explores the heart of intimacy and calls us to go beyond our self-absorption and cherish the love in our lives.

Psychologist Janis Abrahms Spring, Ph.D. • Author, *How Can I Forgive You*

The book argues convincingly that healthy acceptance of one's own imperfections serves as a prerequisite and catalyst for generous love and acceptance of intimate others. Larry Bugen brings new depth of understanding to what it means to love oneself and others constructively – accepting imperfection in a way that inspires mutual encouragement.

Psychologist Douglas Snyder, Ph.D. • Professor and Director of Clinical Training
Department of Psychology - Texas A&M University • Author: *Getting Past the Affair*

Narcissism exists on Wall Street, in politics, in our assault on the environment – but change must come from within. Dr. Bugen gives us guidance in this book.

Jim Hightower • Former Texas Agricultural Commissioner • Best selling author, radio commentator • Editor of the *Hightower Lowdown*

An inspirational blend of Larry's personal stories, contemporary songwriting and encyclopedic knowledge from over 30 years of professional counseling...Larry Bugen dispenses antidotes to our self-absorption that allows us to come out on top when not feeling "OK."

Sandi Aitken • Benefits Manager • Freescale Semiconductor

A book for everyone. Dr Bugen gives us a glimpse of narcissism in self, community, and leadership. He invites us to learn cognitive behavioral skills, punctuated by metaphor, and sage wisdom, leading us to a final existential sense of grace. A beautiful undertaking for the human spirit... Live, Love and Learn....

Luniece Obst M.Ed, LPC, BCPC, • Executive Advisory Board • American Psychotherapy Association

ACKNOWLEDGMENTS

I would like to thank my immediate family for all their support throughout the years this project has gestated, been transformed, and finally been delivered in this final form. Claire, without you, I would never have had the experience of love that has sustained me and helped me grow as a person. You are my muse, my best friend, and most of the ideas in this book would not have been possible without you. Erik and Jessica, each of you have taught me to cherish the *Six Gifts* I describe in this book, most notably humility, compassion, and sacrifice. Most importantly, through each of you, I understand why creation is perhaps the most profound human experience. I cherish each of your journeys in life. Ryan, thank you for all the Sunday dinners, swimming, and photography that have helped sustain me when I've needed to recharge my batteries.

No endeavor this grand could be sustained without the many words of encouragement of friends and extended family. Without mentioning your names (for fear I would forget someone quite special), let me thank you all with one heartfelt smile and hug. To my colleagues, David Clemons and Kavita Murthy, I particularly appreciate your reading of certain chapters and turning my head around to see better perspectives when I most needed a lobotomy.

A special tribute must be extended to the ever-gracious Kathleen Niendorff, publishing consultant and literary agent. This book was originally entitled "I'm Not OK, You're Not OK, But That's OK" and was intended to be a book about imperfection. With Kathleen's wisdom and literary guidance, I was able to broaden the scope of my writing well beyond imperfection itself. Kathleen's enthusiasm about narcissism as a concept blended beautifully with my need to write about love once again. The integration of these concepts, *narcissism* and *love*, would not have occurred without her. Moreover, Kathleen actively marketed the book and has meticulously read and reread the manuscript, delicately offering suggestions as needed, without offending my weary soul along the way.

I would also like to express much gratitude to my friend and colleague, Luniece Obst, who has offered sage advice and inspired feedback to me for a number of years. As a Board Member of the American Psychotherapy Association, it was Luniece's idea to offer this project to APA. Thanks to her extraordinary ability to yoke stakeholders together, we were able to find a wonderful home for ***Stuck On Me...Missing You***. Thank you as well to APA's Editor in Chief, Chris Powers, and graphic designers Christeen Clark and Cary Bates for such an appealing layout and design. And to Eve Chenu, the illustrations are magnificent.

Table of Contents

Introduction 1

SECTION I: NARCISSSISM REFLECTED 15
    Chapter 1: Self-Absorption's Slippery Slope 17
    Chapter 2: The Naked Truth About Narcissism 29
    Chapter 3: Our False Self and Our True Self 41
    Chapter 4: The Seven Deadly Sins 55

SECTION II: THE ROOTS OF NARCISSISM 69
    Chapter 5: The Roots of Narcissism — Nature 71
    Chapter 6: The Roots of Narcissism — Nurture 85
    Chapter 7: The Roots of Narcissism — Leadership 99
    Chapter 8: The Roots of Narcissism — Psychotherapy 113
    Chapter 9: The Roots of Narcissism — Religion 127

SECTION III: LOVE'S SANCTUARY 145
    Chapter 10: Our Need for Attachment 147
    Chapter 11: Romantic Love 163
    Chapter 12: Disenchantment 177
    Chapter 13: Mature Love 193
    Chapter 14: Self-Assessment 205

SECTION IV: THE SIX GIFTS 217
    Chapter 15: Humility 221
    Chapter 16: Forgiveness 235
    Chapter 17: Acceptance 249
    Chapter 18: Compassion 263
    Chapter 19: Sacrifice 277
    Chapter 20: Vision 291

References 308

INTRODUCTION

The paradox of our time in history is that we have taller buildings but shorter tempers; wider freeways, but narrower viewpoints. We spend more, but have less. We buy more, but enjoy less. We have bigger houses and smaller families; more conveniences, but less time. We've been all the way to the moon and back, but have trouble crossing the street to meet a new neighbor; we build more computers to hold more information, but we communicate less and less.

— *George Carlin*

Sometimes I cannot see very far beyond my own needs. Perhaps you do as well.

I faced such a dilemma on a recent safari. As my wife, Claire, and I prepared to embark on our wild African adventure, I was informed that the luggage weight limit, per person, was **10 kilograms** – a scrawny 22 pounds for both checked and carry-on bags!

"Ridiculous, absurd," I bellowed.

My camera equipment alone weighed 22 pounds. Any reasonably bright person would clearly choose black, metallic camera bodies over drab, long-sleeved safari shirts, baggy pants, and winter garb for the Southern Hemisphere. Deluding myself for five minutes, I actually thought that I could get by with one pair of silk underwear and one safari shirt, for two weeks, in three South African countries.

Being resourceful, not to mention self-absorbed, a second option quickly came to mind. I could selfishly manipulate Claire into stowing most of my clothes in her bag. Surely 34 years of marriage at the time entitled me to this kind of spousal support. Despairingly, I soon realized that her bag topped the scales at 20 pounds without our toiletries.

I was doomed.

Compulsively I weighed everything I "needed" for the trip over and over again, only to realize with utter frustration that it weighed in at 30 pounds. Oh, for God's sake, who would even notice?

"This wasn't even close to being fair. Dripping wet I weigh 175 pounds compared to some of the big boys on this trip weighing well over 230. Surely I was entitled to my 10 pounds overage, WASN'T I?

After driving myself mad with this dilemma I finally found peace when I begrudgingly surrendered my 8-pound tripod from my bag. Twenty-two pounds at last. Somehow, I reasoned, I would find a way to steady my shots with a tiny beanbag that I would fill with Kalahari sand. Giving up a camera support for a serious photographer is the equivalent of chopping off one's legs. Yet, I believed this was the proper thing to do even though a self-serving, seductive voice inside my head lured me into the temptation of looking out for number one.

The real issue here had little to do with my creature comforts or photographic necessities. What truly mattered were the lives of 10 people, each of whom would be boarding small, six-seater, Cessna 206s on four different occasions throughout the trip. If each of us, on our own terms, decided that we were entitled to bend the rules – in our own behalf – one good headwind would be the final arbiter in the matter, with a decision none of us might like, or remember! Small planes do crash with excess loads, an abhorrent truth which gripped our Austin community within two days of our return.

Without acknowledging the tacit web which bound us to one another, each of us had to wrestle with a universal question:

Do I love me at the expense of thee?

Destiny often peers out from the underbelly of adventure. Who would have imagined that 10 relative strangers, gathering together for an African safari, would become so bound to one another? Together, we coped with airline incompetence and Serengeti incontinence as we bounced in open Land Rovers. We held our collective breaths as elephants postured, trumpeted, and then charged. We broke bread, toasted savannah sunsets and collectively found bladder relief together in the Bush as well. As last light beckoned, we spun tales with the locals, harmonized together by each evening's camp fire, and bid each other adieu with a sip of Amarula, an after-dinner liqueur.

We found value in one another – in a collective "we-ness". In a whispered breath, reminiscent of Marcus Aurelius, I was learning to "accept the things to which fate binds you, and to love the people with whom fate brings you."

We're here for one very good reason: to learn how to love one another.

This is not easy at a time in our evolution when "me-ness" absorbs us so fully. We are intoxicated with ourselves. Just listen to the myriad of coffee orders at Starbucks and you'll get the picture. Personally, I just settle for my triple, non-fat, half-caffeinated, half-sweetened, extra hot, venti latte, with a touch of vanilla and soy!

Our lifetimes are overflowing with opportunities to learn how to love. At the core, we will discover that sacrifice for the good of others defines our human evolution. We're not there yet.

Selfish genes and narcissistic preoccupations, whether religious or secular, are threatening to wipe us off the face of the planet. Self-expansion may be killing us.

Somehow, we must learn to surrender into something greater than just our selves.

I could have remained a stranger on this African safari. Surely friendship and caring were not part of the ticket price for this journey. At some level, I was merely chasing elephant dung. Yet, the allure of potentially special people called to me. A simple decision regarding a tripod served as a litmus test for virtue, for integrity, and yes, for love. So I left my eight-pound tripod at home for the sake and well being of community. For a moment at least, the promise of budding relationships lifted me out of my own self-absorbed reverie. Only in moments like these do we have an opportunity to probe the pastors query, "What, on earth, are you here for?" Surely, not just to please myself.

What a strange thing to do for strangers!

Illness Is A Wakeup Call

Much of my life has been filled looking for external markings of success.

I've seen others clamor for such fullness. We spend lifetimes defining it and then seeking it. Too often, abundance is seen as concrete – wood, metal or glass. A puffed up home in the suburbs, a suped up Mustang under wraps in the garage, a pregnant six-figure salary with stock options, frequent flyer miles, plasma TVs, or an MP3 player make our day. Sometimes we add a little flesh to the mix: A new husband, a new wife, 15-inch bulging biceps, breast implants and a full penis, and we're all set for a good life.

Our happiness often seems to be based on things we can easily count rather than on things that matter the most.

Prior to the age of 60, an eight-pound tripod was part of this external madness for me. Two weeks after the age of 60 a diagnosis of prostate cancer changed all of this. Suddenly, a full penis and a full life were very much in jeopardy for me. In a tearful blink of the eye, I was catapulted into an overnight frenzy. Traumatized by a diagnosis I had only treated in others, I sank to the floor, shaken and horrified by what lie ahead. All I could ponder was the power of the word cancer. Both my parents had died from cancer and my mind immediately flashed back to sorrowful and painful days where helplessness and grief had become unwelcome guests in my life. Now, almost forty years later, cancer was to be my battleground as well.

In a cosmos, infinitesimally huge and expanding, my life suddenly shrunk. How many breaths would I have left to breathe? How many warm hugs were left to be held? How many more sunsets were left to behold? In a universe where longevity is measured in billions of light years, my life's brevity, measured in autumnal seasons, was painfully clear. The only thing I cared about was living.

Fear, as illuminating as an electrical storm, awakened me. I thought:
My breath
The warmth of a fire in the hearth;

Hugs which will soothe;
And yet,

The whispers of a death denied,
A life fully tried.
Echoes of a life gone by
Call to me.
Yes it is true:
One day, I will die.

A routine yearly physical, accompanied by a routine blood screen, accompanied by a routine PSA – to rule out prostate cancer – revealed a sudden elevation, termed velocity rate, in one year. A digital exam necessitated a biopsy which then necessitated surgery to remove a cancerous prostate. In what seemed liked milliseconds, I found myself anesthetized and fatefully in the hands of a two million dollar robot whose task it was to sever my bladder, remove a diseased organ from my body, and suture me back together again. This laparoscopic surgery was hardly an intimate act.

Visualize a cold 300-pound robot, engineered with metallurgic brilliance, hovering over my unconscious body – entering my most sacred haven – to probe, to lasso, and to remove an alien mass. This life-giving dance of intimacy, performed by this 21st century automaton of modern medicine, was of course guided by a gifted surgeon with a beating heart and warm hands – who, unceremoniously enough, sat 20 feet away from me! This surgeon's eyes never met mine as he peered at "his work" through a camera inserted in my belly by my metallic new best friend.

When I awakened my entire life seemed upside down.

There were no lurid sexual fantasies to stimulate me or sumptuous meals to tempt me. There were no Rocky Mountain trails to challenge me, half marathons to tire me, or mile swims to mellow me. There were no rooms to redecorate or purchases to invigorate. There were no clients to heal or books to reveal. Now the fullness of my life was to be measured by the cc's of urine in a catheter bag. Simple abundance never seemed so clear.

I struggled in those early hours of discovery and recovery. I needed help in a way that I had never needed it before. My longtime friend Dick Orton, a deacon and spiritual director, came through for me. This, as always, was an honorable challenge for a devout Catholic preaching, reaching to an expatriate Jew. I recorded his words on my voice mail as he quoted Henri Nouwen each day, every day, as I approached surgery. These were the last words I heard before "going under":

God I am afraid to open my clenched fists;
Who will I be when I have nothing else to hold onto?
Who will I be when I stand before you with empty hands?
Help me to gradually open my hands and discover that I am not what I own, but

What you want to give me;
And what you want to give me is love, unconditional, everlasting love.
And what am I holding in my clenched fists?
I don't know where you're leading me.
I don't know what the next day, week, or year will look like.
But as I try to keep my hands open, I trust that you will put your hand in mine and
Bring me home.[1]

What is it that I hold onto? Life, yes! Most of us do. What else? Perhaps a parade of p-words: *power, prestige and possessions.* These are not merely words to many of us – they are lifelong pursuits. I know each of them intimately and have spent countless years chasing one or the other.

Graciously, cancer changed this.

Awakening from surgery I knew more than ever that it was the relationships in my life that mattered most. I treasured the presence of Claire, Erik, our son, and Jessica, our daughter. I embraced extended family and cherished friends as well. Somehow, I knew that there is no endeavor more worthy, no element of happiness more pivotal, and no life experience more misunderstood than this thing we call love. Most of us don't even know what love is. We can't love…because we never learned how:

* Have you learned how to distinguish romantic love from mature love…how to distin guish passion from intimacy from commitment?

* Have you learned how to distinguish the illusions of your beliefs and expectations from the reality of your lovers and your lives?

* Have you learned how to view disenchantment as a natural, inevitable process in relationships…an opportunity to learn and grow?

* Have you learned how to cope successfully with adversity or do you grab for quick fixes instead that trap you in a cycle of continuing pain and frustration?

* Have you learned the nine intimacy styles that can enrich any love relationship?

* Have you learned that each partner in any love relationship must be willing to cultivate *Six Gifts* in order for the relationship to endure?

Many of us never learned these things because our parents – our source of nurture – never learned them. They simply didn't know how to show us a mature, loving, adult relationship. Not did they know how to give us the kind of parental love we needed in order to experience what mature love feels like. They couldn't help it…but we can.

This book regales love as our greatest life journey and shows the way.

I believe that each of us inherently needs, even hungers for, secure relationships in our lives. These warm, comforting, and predictable bonds may be with a spouse, a larger community of caring souls, or a Higher Power. Within them we often find healing warmth, personal renewal, and shelter from life's inevitable storms. Yet, many of us jettison relationships that were once the center of our hearts? Why?

Often the heartache of being in a relationship, or leaving one, is based on the same need – the lifelong need to find a secure/loving connection with another. This need doesn't go away. We are prewired to need someone who can value us, nurture us, and protect us. It is this lack of emotional comfort, nurture, and safety that prompts so many of us to move on in search of that someone special who will meet these needs.

When our secure connections become threatened or compromised we often turn against or away from one another, rather than toward one another? We learn to give up on love. Many of us seem programmed to turn away from one another in order to pursue our own self-interests. This pursuit of self-interests can become intoxicating. When this spiral inward occurs we sometimes forsake the counterbalancing gift of love. What's worse is that once we learn to withdraw or angrily lash out we tend to repeat these actions in subsequent relationships, diminishing our chances of finding secure love even more. This book explores how to turn toward one another as we honor our self-interests as well.

In the chapters ahead I will underscore our inherent need for stable and secure love bonds throughout our lives. *Six Gifts* will also be presented which enable us to value those we love in everlasting ways. The *Gifts* are: humility, forgiveness, compassion, acceptance, sacrifice, and vision. Lasting love would not be possible without these gifts.

So why do many of us resist giving these gifts once there is a disconnect?

Mirror, Mirror On The Wall

Do you think of yourself as a caring person – someone who wants to love and care for others? Most of us do. Most people want to be more humble, forgiving, compassionate, accepting, sacrificing, and envisioning. What is getting in the way?

Perhaps you've had a person close to you, say a spouse, tell you that you're "self-centered." Strangely enough, that's really normal in our society now, as the title of this book suggests: *Stuck on Me: Missing You*. Now we're getting to the heart of the matter. Many of us simply get too distracted looking inward, not outward. We create patterns of living which satisfy our personal hunger for power, prestige, and possessions rather than our hunger for love.[2] There are three reasons that almost all of us fall into a "self-centered" trap and miss out on finding the love we need to flourish:

I. Our genes (nature) – Our genes, Mother Nature, are ruthlessly selfish. This gene selfishness will usually give rise to selfishness in individual behavior. We, the people, are merely "survival machines" for individual selfish genes, which are archaically programmed to do whatever is needed to survive. Indeed, natural selection favors genes that control their survival machines. We are controlled by our own self-absorbed genes – a very humbling reality!

II. Our upbringing (nurture) – In our need to find a perfectly divine partner, we usually find instead an imperfect human being who will frustrate us repeatedly over the years. Fantasy meets reality. Intricately entwined within the fabric of that person, not to mention ourselves, resides an "inner child of the past." We carry this homunculus of raw emotion and memories with us wherever we go. This "inner child" often bears the wounds of earlier life experiences and selfishly pulls us into stagnating thoughts, feelings and behavior that can stifle the best of relationships.

III. The materialistic world we live in (culture) – In our culture, "me-ness" trumps "we-ness," and love gets distorted. We pass each other by, absorbed by self-indulgent schedules, encased within luxurious cars, and obsessed by the next major purchase. Our culture has also instilled a belief that each of us is entitled to a full life with a perfect partner. This entitlement has evolved into a right to shed. When the magic wears off our commitments, the chemical high recedes, and the illusions shatter, we feel pain. Where did our happiness go? So we hire big guns to divide all that is external and has value – our estates, our children, even our pets! We shed. The end game becomes self-absorption – what's best for me.

This relentless tide of nature, nurture, and culture often distracts us from love.

In her recent book, *Generation Me*, psychologist Jean Twenge asserts that the American culture has seemed to shift in its emphasis on the rights of "self" as more important than "duty." This change has influenced both attitudes and personality traits of individuals, which in turn has influenced differences among the generations.[3]

It's a wonder that any of us can escape the "self-centered" trap and learn the way to more happiness. As we will learn in the chapters ahead, even our political leaders, our therapists, and our religious institutions have been unable to protect us from ourselves – from this relentless, self-centered tide which threatens to drown out our capacity to love one another.

The key to our happiness is to value the *Six Gifts* of love beyond all other things. Life is about connections we make with one another. Nothing matters more. Hopefully we can do this without having a life-threatening illness provide a wake-up call. Dr. Sue Johnson, one of the leaders in our field of relationship counseling, says it quite well.

"Today, we can no longer afford to define love as a mysterious force beyond our ken. It has become too important. For better or worse, in the twenty-first century, a love relationship has become the central emotional relationship in most people's lives."[4] Yet, the three "self-centered" traps block this from happening. This book examines how.

For instance, let's take a moment to look at our image-conscious culture.

I overheard three women at lunch yesterday. One woman, talking about her stressful day, stated "I'd be more relaxed today, y'all, if my nanny had arrived on time, the air conditioning repairman wasn't late, and if I didn't have this problem with my body image. Lousy genes! A wrinkle here, a varicose vein there – it is pure hell! I even gained two pounds over the holidays. You guys know what I'm talking about! Can y'all believe I have to work out three hours a day just to maintain? If I didn't build in sauna time, I'd be going absolutely nuts!"

Not that I was looking, y'all, but this woman was a perfect size 3!

I say, just send this gal to Kosovo for a week and she'll be happy with every pound she has! We are mesmerized by body images reflected in mirrors, self images reflected in who we are, and ego images reflected in what we own and who we know. Self image does correlate with happiness, but we have distorted the looking glass.

This young woman mirrors our society's obsession with itself – with image.

Just like the warnings on cigarettes, I believe that self-inhalation can kill you and your relationships.

How we appear to others, once a luxury, has now become a life necessity. As a culture, we have always celebrated the virtuous and the grandiose. Stars and starlets, heroes and heroines, warriors and conquerors have always had the attraction of the Magnetic North Pole. Now, however, we are seeing a phenomenon for the first time in human history. As a people, we are now celebrating the morose, the imperfect, and the flawed – but only from a distance. The Magnetic South Pole seems to have its own flux.

As a culture we have taken human frailty and held it up for public scrutiny.

Occasionally this occurs in healthier, more seasoned arenas such as the Catholic Church, where personal testimonials allow an opportunity for personal/parish renewal and growth in spiritual life during shared Christ Renews His Parish (CHRP) weekends. More commonly however, this same scrutiny of human flaws and imperfections is also occurring on Oprah, Jerry Springer, and Ellen DeGeneres. If Bob Newhart can't remedy personal problems in a humorous way, Dr. Phil is prepared to use a jackhammer to reveal neurotic seams and undercurrents.

Many of us simply become too afraid to reveal ourselves in this meat market.

For the first time in our Western history we are reveling in the morose as well as the grandiose. It is "OK" to be "not OK" if you are chum which feeds the sharks and voyeurs. Inglory now matches up well with vainglory on the playing fields of life! From a distance, we are glued to our television sets, People Magazine, and journalistic trash such as Star Magazine. Mental illness becomes a mockery as we see with Brittany Spears. We are mesmerized watching Nicole Richie and Reese Witherspoon go down in flames. What daytime media and the paparazzi don't ingest in their feeding frenzy, Judge Judy is willing to flay for us on the carcass that remains. Speaking of carcass, it's even "OK" to be obese and the Biggest Loser – if you end of up winning.

We love imperfection – from a distance. We just can't live with it.

How can we love if we are too afraid to reveal imperfection?

What image do you live with – grandiose or morose? Either may reflect self-absorption or narcissism. If you are grandiose how do you see yourself? Are you the VP of operations, the architect of it all? Are you the parent with lots of children, large and small? Or, are you the "chosen one," blessed by a supreme being to be the righteous one – above the fray? As many of us know, the fear of imperfection often drives us to appear greater than we actually are!

In contrast, are you the moribund alcoholic whose career has failed or are you the divorcee whose marriage has derailed? Are you the depressed investor whose fortunes have waned? Are you the evangelist whose reputation is defamed? Or, are you the woman I heard whose body is shamed! Be you saint or sinner, ebullient or depressed, grandiose or morose, self-absorption entraps you. You become self-centered and you are now less available to others, temporarily casting love into a distant galaxy where it must be retrieved.

We cannot make love happen until we understand our self-absorption.

Through A Psychologist's Eye

I am a psychologist, with my own privileged views of the world. I see uncompromising self-absorption virtually every hour I am in session. When my door closes I hear the desperate pleadings of everyday people who are feverishly caught up with their own life agendas. These agendas often ignore the needs of others tragically. Some people become tsunamis, propelled by seemingly alien forces, that obliterate the lives of family and friends previously held so close to the heart.

What do I hear? I hear stories of self-absorption. I see us out of balance.

I hear of the nationally ranked triathlete, Ed, who immersed himself in a tortuous schedule of running, swimming and cycling which began at 5:00 a.m. and might not end until 8:00 p.m. A runner's high was his siren call. This guy's routine would begin most mornings by seductively spooning his wife, getting "a little nookie," and then furtively slipping out the door. Somehow, amidst all this blood, sweat, and tears, Ed managed to attend to his career duties as an accountant but somehow lost sight of his children! While peaking in his high performance gear and finding personal success, this guy managed to forget that his children went to bed by 7:30 each weekday evening. It wasn't until Ed's self-absorbed running shoes were dragged into therapy by his wife that he realized he had left a few things behind at the starting line. Ed was out of balance.

Self-absorption is my greatest obstacle as a therapist.

I hear of the multimillionaire who doted upon himself with the purchase of Porsches, Jaguars, and a smorgasbord of Jeeps and convertibles for just the right "occasion." Just like his father, Bill impulsively bought whatever he wanted, got sloshed whenever he wanted, and spontaneously disappeared to Vegas – with whomever he wanted. His wife and adult children mattered not as he disappeared for Christmas, New Year's, and birthdays, always leaving behind a "personal" check for indulgences the rest of the family might have. The closest anyone got to Bill, emotionally, was when a buddy put a drunken arm around him in some godforsaken honky-tonk, and sang an off-key verse of "He's a jolly good fellow!" Therapy lasted four sessions with this guy before he "no-showed" me and his wife TWICE – never to return. A diagnosis of bipolar disorder, a history of childhood neglect, an abuse of legal and illegal medication, and a bottomless pit of greenbacks all blended into a lethal potion for Bill. Bill was out of balance.

I hear of the young Vanderbilt-degreed entrepreneur, Sonja, gifted in so many ways, who accepted a position in Dallas with a startup technology company. While opportunity knocked on her door in Austin, Texas, this brilliant upstart accepted the seductive offer to make "big bucks" in a short time. She was angry that her husband could not understand. Yes, she had only been married a year, and, yes, her longest relationship – among many – had lasted only one year, but surely her self-assured partner would get it! An inner voice, easily drowning out the protests of a lonely and broken-hearted mate, urged her to boldly go for the gold. Sonja was actually married to her cell phone, lap top, and Wall Street financials. These accoutrements followed her wherever she went. Ski slopes, theaters, and restaurants were not off limits. When her brother traveled 1,000 miles to be with her, she brushed him off talking gibberish about deadlines and corporate zeal. Now, one year later, we find her insatiably bent on her Dallas position fulltime, full of resentment that her husband hungers for her presence, and aromatically innocent of any guilt given the romantic triangle she has established with a colleague. Meeting me in therapy for the first time, she bemoaned, "Surely people can understand that I am not well-suited for commitment. And what's wrong with that?"

Sonja was out of balance.

Prior therapists had not helped this couple. Sonja had "fired" the one therapist who seemed to be getting through. Then there was the other therapist! Both remembered her because she seemed to bias their decision to end their marriage. That therapist commented that "Once you're this far gone, there's no coming back" and "Partners needn't struggle to this extent."

Self-absorption ripples throughout our friendships, work groups, and business dealings. Just recently, I bumped into an old friend whom I hadn't seen for six years. Wanting to catch up, I invited her to meet me for coffee after work. Pausing, to scroll through her iPhone, she gingerly accepted my invitation on the condition that I would be satisfied with the 20 minutes she would make available between her workout with her "personal" trainer and the kneading her sculpted body would receive from her "personal" massage therapist. Somehow, the word personal had lost its meaning as I chose to sip my latte alone.

Each of these atrophied souls – the triathlete, the millionaire, the entrepreneur, and the sculpted diva – has a challenge. Each, to be fully human must shed a superficial skin, face their temporary nakedness, and learn to value an enduring connection to others which kindles the very essence of life. Surely each can sacrifice a little me, for thee!

Rather than fulfill their commitments to others, each of them cut and run. Rather than do the necessary work required to become a healthier person, each created Disney Worlds where they expected to be princes and princesses. A world of entitlements was born. And this very unstable world became a house of cards.

Each one of them crossed a line from self-interest to self-indulgence. This self-indulgence often appears as narcissism in today's society.

Narcissism is an   [1] uncompromising self-absorption, which
                   [2] alienates others, while
                   [3] compromising the ultimate good of all.

Each of these individuals is [1] self-absorbed, [2] alienates others, and [3] compromises the ultimate good of all. In a real sense their self-absorption drains life out of the very relationships that should be nurtured to flourish. Each of these individuals glories in self-acceptance, self-affirmation, self-appreciation, self-assertiveness, self-concept, self-discipline, self-efficacy, self-enlightenment, self-esteem, self-fulfillment, self-discovery, self-responsibility, and self-validation.

Each also reflects self-deception, self-destruction, and certainly self-absorption!

Each, without knowing, desperately needs a greater force – call it love – to see beyond one's self. My friend, the Reverend Ray Burchette, captures this well:

> He drew a circle that left me out,
> Heretic, rebel, a thing to flout;
> But love and I had a will to win;
> We drew a circle that took him in.[5]

Each of us is pulled by opposing forces which must be reconciled continuously throughout our lives. "Narcissism" and "Love" may be two of the most important. Disenchantment, a force I described in *Love and Renewal*, is the pain we feel as we attempt to chart a course between these two poles. While painful, this is a journey which defines our very humanity and the true heroes in this epoch journey are those who teach us how to love and bring us back to center. Once I define love in the chapters ahead I will offer *Six Gifts* which I hope will help each one of us in all our relationships.

The Room of Doom

I write this book as a person who struggles with life forces. A perpetual tug of war seems to exist for me, too. There are times when I yearn for more, yet there are other times when I celebrate life as it is; there are times when I obsessively do my own thing; and there are other times when my love and devotion to my family, Claire, Erik and Jessica, has no bounds.

Am I the cancer patient or the cancer survivor? Am I the person dying or the person surviving? Am I a creative spirit, forever seeking or am I a wounded veteran, stuttering and quivering. In truth, I am all the above. But I have learned from my illness not to be enamored by either pole, either end of an endless continuum. No label captures, no image prevails. More than anything experiences sustain me.

Soren Kierkegaard has suggested, "While life can only be understood from the past, it must be lived forwards." I realize that too much time obsessing about my past is not a good thing, no matter the number of insights gleaned. I must feel the freedom of living life forward – no matter the time I think I have left. I must be able to appreciate my abundance, as well as the life flow of solicitude. This is not always easy, as my clients have taught me for over 35 years!

My clients often appear to be stuck in what I describe as a "room of doom." Each is consumed by pride and possessions on the one hand, or depression and helplessness on the other. Even when we seem to be making wonderful progress, an invisible, magnetic charge seems to pull them right back into the "old stuff."

The Room of Doom actually exists as a huge 30 by 30 foot eddy, river-right, in Westwater Canyon along the Colorado River, as I discovered on a raft trip with our son Erik. The careless rafter, drifting too far right, will be sucked into a side canyon existing only as a powerful, slurping, man-eating vortex. Once inside this hellhole one is destined to helplessly float in a clockwise, circular motion, seemingly forever. Ironically, the apparently doomed traveler must look to the very source of his peril for hope: the way in is the same way out!

I will never forget my own experience in this canyon. One force, the eddy, seems to trap and control a person for eternity – just as self-absorption might do. Yet, simultaneously, flowing alongside this "room of doom" is the abundance, the promise of love, and the mighty splendor of the meandering river itself. There are two ways out of this mess. Six rafters can, by harnessing their energy and mustering their will, paddle harder and harder until there is enough momentum to literally thrust them out of the eddy, through a narrow "birth canal" and into the welcoming flow of the river. A second way out is to rely on another raft of thrill seekers who would throw a line as the river's current whipped them by. By grasping the line, the "room of doomers" are drawn out of their plight.

The first solution represents "willpower" as a force contra force. Without the will to free ourselves from walled-off isolation, not to mention internalized fears and anger, we will always stay *Stuck on Me Missing You*. Scarcity will always preempt abundance. Life teaches us that we must sometimes paddle very hard for that which is to be cherished. The second solution represents the power of love over narcissistic isolation. When we tether ourselves to one another, particularly when vulnerable, intimacy flourishes.

The trouble with you and me, my friend, is that we have grown distant from one another. We don't reach out. We don't know our neighbors three doors down, we have moved far away from our extended families, and we are deserting our nuclear families. The vision of lasting love is fast becoming a fading star.

In an expanding universe, a collapse inward – towards an insatiable ego – is not the answer.

There is a battle going on; and it is not in divorce court. It is a battle to persevere in our relationships, to reclaim lost love, to want what we have, and to take what we are given. Today, for the first time in history, more women in the United States are living singly – outside the crucible of marriage.

I recognize that much of what underscores our lives is an unrelenting sense of being lost, incomplete and wounded. In our own "rooms of doom" we are continually haunted by three huge questions:

Who am I in this world?
What do I need to exist?
Who will heal my broken heart?

In response, we seek union to combat the loneliness, we seek a world of one thousand things to hide our pain, and we seek healers and shamans to comfort a wounded self. We want to be saved, fulfilled and healed – often in the same relationship we call love. This very brokenness can be a catalyst for love if we cultivate the *Six Gifts*.

This ache for union is so primal that famed theologian Henri Nouwen once expressed his lament in never finding it during his lifetime as a celibate priest. "The…struggle to find some-one to love me is still there; unfulfilled needs for affirmation…remain alive in me…I experience deep sorrow that I have not become who I wanted to be, and that the God to whom I have prayed so much has not given me what I have most desired."[6]

Henri Nouwen struggled. You and I struggle. Life is struggle, both within and without; but we'll win if we don't give in. Singer Keith Whitley struggled:

I fought with the devil
Got down on his level,
But I didn't give in,
So he gave up on me![7]

Henri Nouwen never gave in. He held on to the hope in the redeeming power of faith, love and community. "I know that the longer I live, the more suffering I will see and that the more suffering I see, the more sorrow I will be asked to live. But it is this deep human sorrow that unites my wounded heart with the heart of humanity. It is this mystery of union in suffering that hope is hidden."[8]

Nouwen teaches us that our brokenness is healthy, human, and even a beautiful bless-ing. In one of his favorite scenes from Leonard Bernstein's *Mass*, the priest is "lifted up by his people…carrying a glass chalice. Suddenly, the human pyramid collapses, and the priest comes tumbling down. His…glass chalice falls to the ground and is shattered. As he walks slowly through the debris…the priest notices the broken chalice. He…says, "I never realized that broken glass could shine so brightly."[9]

We are special when we are accepted for who we are. We are blessed when we are ac-cepted for who we are not.

We learn to either love imperfectly or to live life alone.

It is my hope that we can learn to see our imperfections as broken glass that shine brightly in our lives. Let's not hide them. Let's not run from brokenness in our relationships. It is my hope that brokenness opens hearts. It is my hope that struggle renews and that forgiveness heals. It is my hope that each of us will see that love is perfectly imperfect – just the way it is supposed to be.

This book explores how the power of love transforms pride into humility, resentment into forgiveness, blind ambition into acceptance, indifference into compassion, self-indulgence into sacrifice, and self-defeating habits into vision – the glory of ego gratification with the glory of loving connectedness with others. These *Six Gifts* ensure that love maintains its stature as the quintessential human experience.

NARCISSISM REFLECTED

We waver back and forth, to and fro, as a rocking horse does during the playful seasons of our youth. One moment we are able-bodied, jogging 30 miles per week; the next moment we find ourselves under a two-million dollar robot having a cancerous prostate taken out. One moment we find ourselves enraptured by the songs of the muse we hold so dearly in our arms, only to find months later that we have been entwined by Medusa herself. Life fluctuates this way: one moment we bask in abundance; the next we struggle and bemoan a scarcity that rivets us to the Cross.

In this first section we will attempt to do four things. First, I will describe the progressive, slippery slope from self-interest to self-absorption to narcissism. This spiral inward, when seen in family members, can be quite painful to endure. Second, I will then define "narcissism" with the help of the "Emperor's New Clothes," a tale that is all too revealing about the human condition. Third, since each of us will be self-absorbed at times, I will propose a normal continuum upon which we waver for an entire lifetime. Finally, for those of you who feel spared by this reflective onslaught, I will call upon Pope Gregory who had the cosmic wisdom to rank the seriousness of the Seven Deadly Sins by the degree to which each blighted the concept of love: *Pride, Envy, Anger, Sloth, Avarice, Gluttony,* and *Lust.*

Each of the Seven Deadly Sins represents an expression of love that, somehow, has gone badly. Over 1400 years ago Pope Gregory had the sense to know that narcissism as a life force, if played out to an extreme, could tarnish its polar opposite, love; that is, self-absorption could compromise our capacity to care for and to love one another. This was absolutely brilliant. By the time you complete Section One, you will either be growing comfortable with the idea that self-absorption can cascade into a narcissism which blurs our capacity to love or you will have used the paper this book is printed on as kindling to keep your house warm. Hopefully, it is the former, and with that acceptance you buy into my definition of narcissism as well:

> Narcissism is **1** uncompromising self-absorption, which
> **2** alienates others, while
> **3** compromising the ultimate good of all.

CHAPTER 1

Self-Absorption's Slippery Slope

Everything is farther away now than it used to be; it is twice as far to the corner, and they've added a hill I've noticed. I've given up running for the bus; it leaves faster than it used to. It seems to me they're making steps steeper than in the olden days, and have you noticed the smaller print they're using in the newspapers? There is no sense in asking anyone to read aloud; everyone speaks in such a low voice that I can barely hear them. And the material in clothes is getting so skimpy, especially around the waist and hips. Even people are changing; they are so much younger than they used to be when I was their age. On the other hand, people my own age are so much older than I am. I ran into an old friend the other day and she had aged so much that she didn't even recognize me. I got to thinking about the poor thing while I was combing my hair this morning, and while I was doing that I happened to glance at my reflection and you know what? They don't even make good mirrors anymore![1]

—The Way It Is
James T. Simpson

Defining life moments exist for each of us.

One needn't be looking in the mirror to notice them. Whether we call these moments epiphanies, crisis points, or transitions does not matter. What does matter is the fact that some life force uproots us from the familiar, and we are somehow never the same. Suddenly, or gradually, a flat expanse appears hilly and mirrored reflections appear cracked. I have had such moments – some quite profound.

One of those was a dreary, rain-soaked day in August of 1971. My mother was to be released from Allentown State Hospital where she had been a patient for only three days. On this day in August I received a call from the chief psychiatrist who informed me that my mother had informed him that I had requested – no, insisted – that she be released to my care.

"I agreed to what!" I moaned.

"Your mother appears to be stable enough to be released from our hospital. In numerous consultations with staff she has enthusiastically described a plan that you "proposed" in which she will live with you and your wife, Claire."

I cringed and felt like fainting! "But Dr. Stein, I haven't a clue about any of this, feel totally overwhelmed and am only 23 years old. I just got married. What am I supposed to do?"

"Uh, well, uh, uh, hold on, well, uh, let me get back to you on this, Larry," came words that trailed off into a black hole. I had been engulfed by this black hole for years.

This most recent hospitalization followed her fifth, or perhaps sixth, suicide attempt with barbiturates. My sister, my father, and I had been painfully traumatized by suicide attempts, hospitalizations, and mother's chronic depression for years. Our tears and anger often cascaded into a more stagnant pool of numbness and helplessness. Our efforts as a family, not to mention the professional community, failed to make a difference with Mother. I am frustrated to this day whenever I must confront these same feelings of helplessness within myself as I face clients whose own stagnation reminds me of my mother's.

Mother's chaotic flailing at life competed with her equally desperate desire to die. Both her reality and her coping suffered immensely. When elated, she proclaimed herself to be Miss Bronx, USA, or a New York State ice-skating queen. In reality, mother grew up in squalor and neglect, seldom ice-skated, and, by the age of 20, found herself grieving the death of her fiancé who died as a pilot in 1944 in the European theater. One year later, on the rebound, she settled for my father, a milquetoast of a man, who would eventually be emasculated even further. This move from the ravages of New York City to the bucolic town of Easton, Pennsylvania, would be mother's illusory escape from the gnarled roots of her past.

By the age of 31, personal neglect of her health had left her with full upper and lower dentures, a bleeding ulcer, migraine headaches, and a heating pad for chronic lower back pain. When not in a depressive stupor, her broken dreams would erupt into screams of outrage that would eventually drive most family and friends into underground bunkers.

Over the years we all had learned to hide from her anger, placate when possible, and deftly walk on eggshells. Conflict avoidance was a major survival skill. Mother was known for her rage. No one was safe. As I literally hid under covers at night, I knew that the postman, milkman, neighbors, relatives, schoolteachers, and of course my father and sister, were at more risk from her than the Pentagon from North Korea.

That bleak day in August was complicated by several other life forces. First, Claire and I had been married for less than one year and were trying to establish our own beginning.

Second, my father had died two months earlier from a brain tumor, which tragically had been inoperable. My mother's fragile mental health was hard to compete with. In fact, during his protracted illness Mother would attempt suicide on two occasions. On one particularly horrific night, I was to sit alone in ER, not knowing which of my parents would live or die – Dad on 2 North, Mom on 2 South.

So, with the deftness of Houdini, Mother had convinced the psychiatric staff that she was to be released into our care. Our newlywed apartment in Philadelphia was to become her new outpatient mental health clinic. The fact that Claire and I had not been informed of this ploy was incidental - OUR needs and wants irrelevant. We were neither seen nor heard by my mother.

In effect, my mother had set up a no-win scenario. On the one hand I could accept the ruse and go along with her desperate manipulation. The hospital staff would be duped, my mother's hapless dependency sustained, and I would live the lie. On the other hand, for the first time in her life, as well as mine, I could call her on her selfish exploitation of the situation. I could hold the line against her, setting a firm limit, and choose the painful truth.

I chose the truth on that August day. In an emotionally tormented moment, reminiscent of the famous line in the sand at the Alamo, I told my mother that I loved her – always had, and always would – but the time had come to embrace the fullness which life held for me. My home would not become a psychiatric ward. While I would continue to actively support her psychological and psychiatric needs, I would no longer sacrifice my personal life in order to absorb her emotional pain. I told Mother that I was committed to my new life with Claire and that living with us would not be an option for her.

The hospital staff was so informed. In a surprise compromise, the psychiatrist allowed my mother's release to her own aging mother who lived in the Bronx, New York. This was akin to sending a Russian defector back to the Soviet Union. Not a good idea. Claire and I were to provide "limousine" service nonetheless.

As Claire, my mother, and I approached Pellam Parkway and Whiteplains Road on this bleak day, we could all hear the sound of the overhead subway, see the endless rows of drab tenement brownstones, and smell the stench of garbage piled high in the alleyways sandwiched between those dreary buildings. I will never forget the wretched awkwardness fermenting as we drove these final few blocks. Finding no one home at my grandmother's apartment and, in one final force de resistance, Mother directed me to drop her off at a corner luncheon counter. After many protests, I acceded to her request.

This final manipulation on Mother's part had its impact. How could a loving son leave his depressed mother tragically alone in a dilapidated corner store, in the midst of a vast concrete jungle, where anonymity breeds so much loneliness? If there is a stronger sentiment than guilt and shame, I felt it. I called my grandmother to confirm she was on her way home.

Then I left.

As Claire and I drove away from my mother, who vacuously peered from an isolated table within, I began to cry. Turning the car keys over to Claire I sank into a grief-stricken womb for the next two hours as we drove to Claire's home on Long Island where a saner family waited with a thick farmer's market sirloin steak, and a cheap bottle of Rose.

What appeared to be my mother's Waterloo actually served as her Battle of the Bulge. After spending but one night in the primordial muck that fashioned her, Mom left New York City. In a classic Honey Ann Bugen move, she said goodbye to her mother, directed a cabbie to drive her 200 miles to her home in Easton, Pennsylvania, whereupon she wrote a check to both the cabbie and a local apartment complex, once more ready to flail at living.

This ordeal, this moment in time, was to become what the French call our "baptism of solitude." Our healing had begun, as I will reveal in the chapters ahead. A dramatic shift was underway. Each of us was to discover the "secret of the Sahara" according to Paul Bowles:

> *You leave the gate of the town behind you, pass the camels lying there, and go up into dunes, or out onto the hard, stony plain alone. It is a unique sensation, and it has nothing to do with loneliness, for loneliness presupposes memory. Here, in this wholly mineral landscape lighted by stars like flares, even memory disappears. Nothing is left but your own breathing and the sound of your heart beating. A strange, and by no means pleasant, process of reintegration begins inside you, and it remains to be seen whether you will fight against it, and insist on remaining the person you have always been, or whether you will let it take its course. For no one who has stayed in the Sahara for awhile is quite the same as when he came.[2]*

I'll never know how much my mother was transformed by her stay in the Sahara. She died in 1973. There were no more suicide attempts and her depression, by all accounts, seemed to lift. Sadly, it was not her mental demons that became her demise but a rapid and fatal last round with acute myeloblastic leukemia. I sat and held her during these last two weeks of life, wondering how the toxicity of her overdoses might have compromised her immunity and hastened her death.

She had just begun to celebrate, and nurture, my sister's pregnancy. Baby books yoked Shelly and Mom together and a precious crib was purchased for the imminent birth of Lisa. Love, as a life force, had begun to spring forth. Mother had begun to think of others beside herself. The needs of Shelly and Lisa had begun to loom larger than her own misery. Not bad for a mother who had often screamed to a shattered daughter, "Why on Earth did I ever have you?" The cruelty of stormy nights often becomes a faint whisper with the dawn of a new day. Thankfully, it is these faint whispers that Shelly remembers.

A triangle of narcissism, scarcity, and superficial materialism had imprisoned my mother. While these three life forces pulled and tugged at her over time, her life was primarily built upon a narcissistic preoccupation with scarcity as a life force. Often, she sunk into self-absorbed reverie. She brooded endlessly about what was missing in her life. Not enough love, not enough status, not enough money, not the right husband, and not enough dreams fulfilled. A glass half empty would be an understatement. The barren landscape of her life resembled Mount St. Helens following its last eruption.

A brief narcissistic fling at material abundance offered little succor. She shocked the community when she purchased a bright orange Ford Mustang in 1964. The fact that she never drove this supped up 286 hp power plant mystified others even more. This is often true with external abundance. That which glitters brightly often fades quickly.

My mother's perpetual struggle with life certainly was evident to others. Few would say she led a happy life. And fewer still would say she was healthy, in any sense of the word. Yet, amidst this doom and gloom, she occasionally blossomed. And when she did, the world stood still. For just a moment, often the briefest of moments, she cast forth a glow of iridescent radiance, of extraordinary beauty, that took your breath away. It was in these moments I learned an important life lesson:

Hope is the light that lifts the spirit from darkness.

The Slippery Slope

There was something not right, not normal, about Mom. Anger, helplessness, and a hopeless despair kept her trapped in a "room of doom." Mom was morose. Her only exit from this inner, depressive whirlpool seemed to be prescription drugs, suicide attempts, and an occasional extravagant purchase. Yet, through it all, I somehow sensed I was loved and cherished. To this day I hold dearly those moments, as brief as they were, when a warm hug, a beaming smile and an apple cake greeted me when I arrived home. Somehow, I thought that we were OK, as mother and son, even though she was not.

While my mother's clinical, depressive state was chronic, clearly diagnosable, and abnormal, most of us do not present our imperfect selves so clearly and so tragically. I know that where she ended up is not where her journey began. No single day signaled the forthcoming landslide. There was a progression – from a time when her needs and self-interests were reasonable, even reachable – to a time of hopeless despair. In this hollow space Mom lived only in her head instead of the hearts of those who loved her.

There was a time, however brief, when she may have been satisfied with what life had given her. Certainly there were stories of celebration and joy, when a handsome soldier returning home from V-E Day met a strikingly beautiful woman from the Big Apple where together they began their courtship. There was a time, however blurred, when two newlyweds began to build a family, buy their first home, and enjoy budding friendships with neighbors down the street. There was a time when self-interests overlapped – creating one mosaic – until the beginning of a terrible slide inward gripped Mom. There was a time when healthy attachments underscored my mother's life:

* There was a time when mom sought out a cherished love bond.
* There was a time when mom sought a secure connection.
* There was a time when mom sought emotional comfort, nurture, and warmth.
* There was a time when mom felt safe, secure, and protected.
* There was a time when mom sought out affirmation that she mattered–that she was special.
* There was a time when mom felt cherished and valued for who she was.
* There was a time when mom felt she had a buffer from life's inevitable hurts and pain.

* There was a time when mom felt held and reassured.

* There was a time when mom felt renewed when life had drained her dry.

This need for loving union certainly underscores healthy self-interest. To survive and thrive most of us want a secure attachment in life. There was a time when my mother did as well. Most relationships begin with an affirming vow that these needs are satisfied in enough abundance to last a lifetime. This is the Promised Land where two lovers share a common footing to face all that lies ahead.

There is a time when self-interests are perfectly normal, well within bounds, and are woven beautifully into the lives of others.

There is a time when healthy self-interest reflects an affirming "yes" to who we are as we invest energy in one's genuine true Self. We become emotionally available to others, productive members of society, and enjoy maintaining relationships with a diversity of adults. We learn to be humble, to laugh at our selves, and to accept our imperfections as part of our living architecture. We seek to create a contribution which is uniquely ours and to leave an imprint in the hearts of others that eternally echoes that our time here has made a difference. We experience a full kaleidoscope of emotions that are woven into the lives of others, we learn to separate what's real from fantasy, and learn to celebrate our joys and accomplishments in a way that blossoms into healthy self-esteem.

Often, however, we cross a line into the land of self-absorption, then narcissism.

In this land of distorted vision normal needs and self-interests morph into something very distant, something out of reach, often not with a bang but with a whimper. This happened to my mother. Somehow, she stopped trying to connect. Others in her life became blurred vestiges of the past. In her world of disturbed thoughts, anguished feelings, and harsh criticisms Mom drifted farther and farther away from her once-cherished hopes and dreams – eventually distancing from each of us as well.

Author Sandy Hotchkiss says it very well in her wonderful book, *Why Is It Always About You?* "The narcissist we recognize as unhealthy is someone who, no matter what age, has not yet fully developed emotionally...This person lacks a realistic sense of Self and an internalized system of values – apart from unmitigated self-interest – that guides behavior."[3]

It is often difficult to know where the line separating self-interests vs. self-absorption exists, or for that matter self-absorption vs. narcissism.

The threshold is one of degree: unbridled self-interest gradually becomes self-absorption; unbridled self-absorption gradually becomes narcissism – either grandiose or morose. There often are noticeable patterns which mark the transitions however. This is where we gasp and wonder what forces might possibly explain such actions. Hotchkiss helps us identify telltale signs when this drift evolves (devolves) into narcissism[4]:

Shamelessness – Shame is the terrible pain we feel within when we discover that we are personally flawed, somehow imperfect in the deepest of ways. My mother had a great deal of shame. Unlike guilt which relates more to what we did wrong, shame holds us captive because *we* are wrong. We are bad, we have fallen short, and we have disappointed others around us. We learn to hide shame. As Hotchkiss points out, "We first experience shame in the eyes of our mother or primary attachment figure, when, starting around the age of one, we bring her our excitement and, instead of sharing our pleasure, she scowls and says, 'No!' Her unexpected disapproval shatters the illusion of power and importance that is how we see ourselves at that early age." To know love we must ultimately share our shame.

With shame, we begin to slide into a wounded self.

Magical Thinking – In an effort to avoid the humiliation of our shame we look for ways to launch ourselves into a brighter, better, bigger, and more beautiful image – an image that easily compensates for the deeper feelings of inadequacy which lurk within. The fear that one is not enough, that one is defective or insignificant, drives the narcissist mad. The resulting drive state creates a self-absorbed inner world of distortions and a life filled with intoxicating exaggerations. Narcissists are forever hiding their diminished feelings about themselves in the hope that others will see instead their glittering fantasy being staged each day. According to Hotchkiss, "Their challenge is to find a way to stay pumped up inside in order to hold harsh realities at bay." To know love we must be real.

With magical thinking, we slide into a distorted sense of self.

Arrogance – The challenge for the narcissist is to stay emotionally attached in a world where both strengths and weaknesses are tolerated within oneself as well as others. This normal capacity is intolerable for the narcissist. Instead, we notice an intolerant person who is often critical, demeaning, and painfully judgmental of others. By diminishing others, the narcissist is self-absorbed, indeed consumed, by a need to taint the perceived status of others in order to distance from her own personal sense of shame. "The persona that many narcissists present to the world often comes across to others as "superiority complex." But behind the mask of arrogance is a fragile internal balloon of self-esteem that is never satisfied with being good or very good – if they are not *better than*, then they are worthless." To know love we must connect at the heart, life's equal playing field.

With arrogance, we slide into living life on a pedestal made out of sand.

Envy – Often the feelings of arrogance and superiority morph into something much more sinister – envy. It is the eyes of envy which look maliciously upon others. When the narcissist's attempt to achieve superiority fails – which it must – an internal state of emergency exists. Now, to feel good about oneself it becomes necessary to bring others down. This is where contempt comes in. "The intent, usually quite unconscious, is to soil the other enough so that the narcissist, by comparison, is restored to the superior position. There may be awareness of feelings of disdain, but the feeling of envy will be adamantly denied. To admit to envy would be to acknowledge inferiority, which no good narcissist would ever do." To know love we must embrace rather than debase one another.

With envy, self-absorption slides into endless yearning and craving.

Entitlement – If you have ever been in a relationship with a narcissist you know that your needs matter little compared to theirs! Mutuality and reciprocal giving are distant concepts for the self-absorbed narcissist who truly believes that others exist merely to meet and greet his every need. Caught up in their own entitlement feelings most narcissists don't even see that others have needs, let alone meet them. "Children whose infantile fantasies are not gradually transformed into a more balanced view of themselves in relation to others never get over the belief that they are the center of the universe. Such children may become self-absorbed "entitlement monsters," socially inept and incapable of the small sacrifices of Self that allows for reciprocity in personal relationships." To know love we must embrace the needs of others in proportion to our own.

With entitlement, self-absorption slides into grandiosity.

Exploitation – Love implores us to know what our loved ones' know, to know what they feel, and to know what they are going through. To compassionately know someone this deeply requires empathy. Narcissists seem to lack this capacity. Driven by seemingly endless needs the narcissist lives her life exploiting others for personal gain. People are often used and discarded, disregarding their feelings or interests completely. "Driven by shame and prone to anger and aggression, the narcissist never develops the capacity to identify with or even to recognize the feelings and needs of others…Others are not seen as separate entities but rather as extensions of Self, there to do the narcissist's bidding." To know love we must know one another from the inside out.

With exploitation, self-absorption slides into self-justification.

Bad Boundaries – While each of us is hardwired to need union with others, to feel secure within the embrace of caring and loving bonds, there is a time to honor separateness. While we need to belong, each of us also needs space from one another. We have personal feelings, private thoughts, and a physical presence which is ours to keep safe. When self-absorption reigns, respect for boundaries usually slides. For the narcissist, wary of being known too deeply, there may be rigid boundaries and anxious preoccupation keeping others out – thereby missing out on the blessing of intimacy. For others, painfully enmeshed in a relationship with a narcissist, there is usually the total collapse of boundaries. In these relationships, narcissists are not able to recognize others as separate beings rather than self-serving extensions of themselves. To know love we must embrace separateness and union simultaneously.

With bad boundaries, the self-absorbed obliterate the existence of others.

My mother refused to be present at our wedding unless she approved of the "house of worship." Our wedding became her wedding. This collapse of boundaries between what was hers vs. ours was one of many signs of a slide from self-interest to something much darker. As the beginning of this chapter chronicled, her attempt to live with us during our first year of marriage was certainly self-interest gone wild. Where was Mom's other-directedness, her sacrifice for, her empathy with our needs? For Claire, who witnessed Mom at the end of her journey, it is hard to fathom a time when a more gracious balance existed between Mother's needs and my own. Was there truly a time when self-absorption did not taint her capacity to love?

I would like to believe there once was such a time, before the slide.

Balance, Bandwidths, and Homeostasis
Life is a balancing act.

Much of what we take for granted actually fluctuates regularly along an invisible continuum, usually well within normal limits. Our blood pressure continuously strains upward when a deadline approaches or languidly dips downward as a palette of evening colors in the sky greets us on the way home from work. Of course there is an optimal range, even finite numbers that are desirable for our optimal health. The usual reported numbers for blood pressure are 120 systolic over 80 diastolic, but every health care professional knows these numbers are not static. They go up and down as our vascular system absorbs our daily trials and tribulations – just as a shock absorber helps to stabilize an automobile bouncing along our nation's byways.

We waver back and forth, to and fro, as a rocking horse does during the playful seasons of our youth. One moment we find ourselves enraptured by the songs of the muse we hold so dearly in our arms only to find months later that we have been entwined by Medusa herself. Life fluctuates this way: One moment we bask in abundance; the next we struggle and bemoan a scarcity that rivets us to the Cross.

My mother's continuum was hardly invisible and certainly not optimal.

Her unbalanced life story raged through our household like tsunami tidal waves. What I now know as a psychologist is that my mother's brain chemistry was out of balance. Today, I realize that my mother had a chemical imbalance. Important oceanic fluids in her brain, such as serotonin and dopamine, were seriously outside normal limits. Some of the reasons for this imbalance were biological, or endogenous, while others were psychological or situational. Sadly, psychopharmacology at that time didn't afford us the options we have available today.

In this chapter we have seen how far we can slide outside a normal bandwidth. It is at these times that we appear abnormal and out of balance. Intellectual prowess, crowning life achievements, and cultural heroics cannot protect us from "flipping out," from slipping outside clearly normal pathways for living. In fact, intellectual prowess, crowning life achievements, and cultural heroics may actually just be another form of flipping out – a sign of narcissism.

We don't even need to be awake to be outside the bounds of normalcy. Betting that weary but wealthy baby boomers are willing to put their money on a good night's sleep, mattress companies are fluffing up their selections of "ultra-luxe" beds that retail for more than many cars or super grandee boats. With a heart-stopping price approaching $50,000 a Swedish manufacturer has recently launched the Vividus bed, which means "full of life", or was that "full of oneself!"

Slips outside the bounds of normalcy can even occur with today's astronauts, such as Lisa Marie Novak. The once-smiling face of this 10-year veteran for NASA was in stark contrast with the mug shot of her that appeared in the nation's press on February 7th, 2007. Mrs. Novak, we learned, had driven 900 miles from Houston, Texas to Florida in an apparent attempt to murder a woman who appeared to be a rival for the affections of a fellow astronaut, William Oefelein.

Mrs. Novak was so self-absorbed, so tunnel-visioned, in her mission to get to this Florida airport, that she wore diapers all the way so that she would not have to waste time making pit stops. It was this same determined, intellectual efficiency which had previously contributed to her reaching a space station, orbiting our planet, where she had adeptly operated the arm of a multi-million dollar robot months before. Now, instead of reaching for the stars, we find Mrs. Novak in disguise, possessing a steel mallet, a knife, pepper spray, 4 feet of rubber tubing, latex gloves, and garbage bags with some very bad thoughts racing through her mind. The intoxication of romantic love can be cruel.

This is clearly not the "right stuff" image that national heroes appear to symbolize. Something went awry for Astronaut Novak. Healthy homeostatic forces, which had been psychometrically assessed and reassessed countless times, suddenly loosened their grip. A perfect storm of passion, jealousy and mania spun her 20-year marriage into a tailspin, catapulted her valedictorian career into ruins, and tragically severed her obsessed mind from the loving heart which previously had embraced the collective welfare of her three children and family. Where were they on her radar screen?

Initial speculations from psychiatrists suggested bipolar disorder, even a brain tumor. Other observers, perhaps numbed by the commonality of love triangles, simply wrote her off as being human, disassociating her from gods and goddesses who somehow would be incapable of manifesting such madness. Once again, we are reminded of Robert Johnson's edict that "Whenever we put someone on a pedestal, we put them out of human reach." Human frailty has a way of piercing the loftiest images imaginable. On this sad day in February, Astronaut Novak hit the ground in a freefall.

Normal continuums are awfully hard to define at times.

We are reminded that a very fine line exists between a relentless uncompromising pursuit of one's career goals and a maniacal obsession, which crash lands into a Challenger-like disaster, even murder. While we can easily pigeonhole Mrs. Novak's crazed behavior as self-absorbed, it is my intention to emphasize that any obsession, even socially desirable ones, lead us into the pit of self-absorption – a sanctuary where each of us battles to find balance between a life lived for our own good vs. someone else's good! Mrs. Novak's behaviors were clearly outside the norms, but how about the rest of us?

This notion of normalcy is not easy in a time when people like Barack Obama and Jane Fernandes were each rejected for being outside acceptable limits – too far outside the bandwidth of acceptable norms. Senator Obama, during his presidential campaign, had been critiqued for "Not being Black enough"! The American-born son of a black father from Kenya and a white mother from Kansas, Obama was derided by many Black Americans for not embodying the experiences of most African-Americans whose ancestors endured slavery, segregation, and the bitter struggle for civil rights.

Jane Fernandes, the beleaguered president-elect for Gallaudet College in 2007, was ridiculed by the student body and faculty for "Not being deaf enough"! Mrs. Fernandes was raised reading lips and did not learn American Sign Language until she was in graduate school at the University of Iowa. Months after she was nominated to lead the country's premier liberal arts university for the deaf, we find protesters camped out by the front gates of the Northeast Washington D.C. campus demanding a new search for president with a fair process.

Even though each represented potential presidential pedigree, each was rejected for different reasons. Barack Obama had not "suffered" enough as a Black man to be "OK" in the eyes of some, while Jane Fernandes was not "disabled" enough to qualify as a real deaf person in the eyes of some. Somehow, their very normal self-interests were seen by some as not aberrant enough. What a strange world we live in. How many ghetto experiences would it take to convince some constituents that Obama understands cultural diversity, and how many years of immersion within a deaf community from birth would it take for Fernandes to qualify as deaf?

What kind of wounded self-absorption, even narcissism, are we asking for?

I've seen this pattern over and over in other ways. I've seen bereaved parents reject grief groups because they were not exclusively groups of grieving parents. I've seen bereaved parents of children who committed suicide reject grief groups that were not exclusively "SOS" groups, (i.e., survivors of suicide). I've seen Orthodox Jews reject other Jews who were not Orthodox. I've seen evangelical Christians reject other Christians who were not fundamental enough in their beliefs.

What does all this mean? Not black enough. Not deaf enough. Not normal or righteous enough. Somehow, as a people, we are in a struggle to find a place where acceptability is grasped but not at the expense of vicissitude.

It is our variance which defines our normalcy.

It is our capacity to waver, to fluctuate, and to be different which defines our normalcy. Without a capacity to embrace diversity, to cherish dissimilitude, to honor contrast, and to forgive one another's deviations from the norm, we are doomed. Our hope for a more compassionate human condition lies in our ability to see ourselves for who we really are – different. Fluctuations outside the norms are just as normal as adherence to the norms. There is room for deviancy, even self-absorbed narcissism, so long as we acknowledge it. This redemptive process begins with "humility," the first of the *Six Gifts*, as we will see in Chapter 15.

CHAPTER 2

The Naked Truth About Narcissism

Once upon a time there lived a vain emperor whose only worry in life was to dress in elegant clothes. He changed clothes almost every hour and loved to show them off to his people.

Word of the Emperor's refined habits spread over his kingdom and beyond. Two scoundrels who had heard of the Emperor's vanity decided to take advantage of it. They introduced themselves at the gates of the palace with a scheme in mind.

"We are two very good tailors and after many years of research we have invented an extraordinary method to weave a cloth so light and fine that it looks invisible. As a matter of fact it is invisible to anyone who is too stupid and incompetent to appreciate its quality..."

...Well, you know the rest of the story: the Emperor's endless need for adoration lures him into the ruse by the two tailors. After paying them a bag of gold in exchange for their promise to create a masterpiece, he sends them on their way. Later in the story we learn that the Emperor feels like fainting when he checks on his creation only to find that he can't see the vibrant colors or feel the fine cloth between his fingers. Stunned, he realizes he cannot admit this, for then he too would be considered stupid and incompetent. Yet, all the townspeople have heard about his new clothes and want to see them. Putting his doubts aside the Emperor agrees to bring his nakedness to the people where only the stupid and incompetent wouldn't notice his fine threads…As we fast forward, we eventually find the Emperor being applauded by everyone in the community who had gathered to witness this special regal procession. As he passes by:

> *Everyone said, loud enough for the others to hear: "Look at the Emperor's new clothes. They're beautiful!"*
>
> *"And the colors! The colors of that beautiful fabric! I have never seen anything like it in my life." They all tried to conceal their disappointment at not being able to see the clothes, and since nobody was willing to admit his own stupidity and incompetence, they all behaved as the two scoundrels had predicted.*
>
> *A child, however, who had no important job and could only see things as his eyes showed them to him, went up to the carriage.*
>
> *"The Emperor is naked," he said.*
>
> *"Fool!" his father reprimanded, running after him. "Don't talk nonsense!" He grabbed his child and took him away. But the boy's remark, which had been heard by the bystanders, was repeated over and over again until everyone cried:*
>
> *"The boy is right! The Emperor is naked! It's true!"*
>
> *The Emperor realized that the people were right but could not admit to that. He thought it better to continue the procession under the illusion that anyone who couldn't see his clothes was either stupid or incompetent. And he stood stiffly on his carriage, while behind him a page held his imaginary mantle.*

As this children's story by Hans Christian Andersen[1] reveals, the Emperor cannot accept his obvious nakedness. He knew that the people were right but could not admit to that. Why? Perhaps, he is afraid. After all, he panicked and felt like fainting. Or perhaps he is held captive by pride and vanity. He changed clothes almost every hour and loved to show them off to his people. Or perhaps the pain of his basic insecurities requires him to compensate by pretending to be superior and arrogant. Your highness, this cloth will be woven in colors and patterns created especially for you. Perfectionism forces him underground. Nobody could find out he was stupid and incompetent. As we will see, narcissists hide their true colors.

Intimacy is possible only when we share our true nakedness with one another.

Fear. Pride. Vanity. Arrogance. Perfectionism. The Emperor pretends to live his life on a pedestal, but in reality he finds himself anxious, embarrassed, and humiliated like the rest of us. Even after being reduced to his most fundamental birthday suit he is unable to "humbly" accept his very humanness. Instead…he stood stiffly on his carriage, while behind him a page held his imaginary mantle. He would never admit that he has aggressive tendencies, lustful fantasies, or that he farts in the middle of the night!

As a psychologist I am clinically trained to diagnose the Emperor as a possible narcissist since he displays:

a) A grandiose sense of self-importance

b) Preoccupation with fantasies of unlimited success, power, brilliance, or beauty

c) Exhibitionism, i.e., needing constant attention or admiration

    d) A lack of empathy or ability to recognize how others truly feel

    e) A sense of entitlement or special favors

    f) Interpersonal exploitativeness, i.e., taking advantage of others in order to indulge one's
       desire for self-aggrandizement

    g) Relationships which vacillate between over idealization and devaluation

The Emperor could scarcely control himself. Imagine that the Emperor was an only child of royalty. As the first-born male, his royal family treated him as the next entitled one to the Kingdom. He was pampered, indulged, and spoiled. Instead of tinker toys he played with elephant tusks, which he hoarded in castle turrets. Instead of sleeping on grass smelling of cow dung, he slept on goose down pillows bordered in fur. Instead of earthen mugs scraped from riverbanks, he drank from the finest blown glassware of the time.

Things distracted the Emperor from life's real treasures.

Imagine that every wish was his command. He desired four Arabian horses to ride and he received them. He yearned for entertainment at bedtime – instead of hugs. No problem. Court jesters and gypsies were his nighttime delight.

    He learned that he could receive without giving in return. He learned that material goods would replace human good. He could acclaim prominence without effort. An inner world of emotional tidal pools seemed not to exist. He knew nothing of responsibility to others and nurtured no one. He lived an isolated life with few friends. Each year, on his birthday, the entire countryside was required to celebrate, but no intimate friends existed to share in Baskin & Robbins ice cream or Entenmann's coffee cake. Have you ever met the Emperor?

> *The Emperor lives among us. He is Max from Boston, twice divorced, retired on disability benefits, pays three different women to provide sexual favors, and does nothing for anyone else, or his community. A life of self-indulgence, at the expense of his insurance company, hallmarks his life. When friends visit, they are offered sexual favors regardless of their marital status. Should a friend decline an offer, they are entertained with Max stories which glorify the "services" he receives as well as his abundant life of leisure, leisure, and more leisure. From what I can tell, this is "social security" at its worst!*

While I cannot say that the Emperor, or Max for that matter, exists in each of us, I can say that narcissistic tugs do occur. Our "baby boomer" homes are four times the size of our parents' homes. A preoccupation with self underscores our boomer lives. Concern over appearance, social standing, sexual fulfillment, or life achievement consumes each one of us at one time or another. If narcissism can be sliced into such "normal" aspects of humanity, what can be so wrong with narcissism, or for that matter, humanity itself?

    How do we get out of balance?

    If narcissism is "normal," what life events or conditions drive us to the extreme? When does this normal preoccupation with ourselves shift and ignite a neglect of the needs of others? What gets us out of balance in our slide from normal self-interest to self-absorption and finally to narcissism. How do we ensure that this preoccupation with ourselves does not alienate others while compromising the ultimate good? How do we avoid an upside down mortgage when we become prisoners to unpaid debt? What does it mean to be in balance and what are the essential life forces that constitute balance?

How do we know narcissistic features when we see it? Well, let's look around:

* * I see it in the woman who flicked her cigarette butt out her car window, oblivious to the city employee who would eventually have to sweep it up.
* * I see it in the compulsive body builder who humiliates and belittles his girlfriend for expecting a romantic dinner on the eve of her 30th birthday.
* *I see it in the sexually obsessed husband who continues to secretly seek out pornographic internet sites despite his wife's painful pleading to come to bed.
* * I see it in the father who walks out on his wife and three children so that he can have "more space" to pursue his career and his lover.
* * I see it in the chronically depressed homemaker who lies in her bed hours each day while her eldest daughter cares for the needs of the other children.
* * I see it in the attorney who required a receptionist, i.e., a person who receives another, to literally open her door for her and turn on her light each morning so that her entry is smooth and effortless.
* * I see it in the father, who, upon giving his son four truck tires as a graduation present, then billed him for these same tires one month later.

A narcissist will break your heart. It's just a matter of time.

I see "arrogance," "entitlement," and "lack of empathy" in the above examples. Do you? Unless we learn to balance preoccupation with our selves with the needs of another we are destined to be miserable souls who create misery in the lives of countless others. Why do we make it so difficult to experience relationship with one another, whether it is lovingly with a soul mate for life, respectfully with a stranger in a coffee shop, or with a wider swath of humanity.

Balancing "we-ness" with "me-ness" can be quite challenging.

The Myth of Self-Fulfillment

At no time in the history of mankind have we been so narcissistically consumed and duped by our own illusion of specialness. We walk around with cell phones blaring in therapy offices, churches, concert halls and bedrooms. Do we believe that God, or one of eight billion people on the planet, is about to break through our cosmic insignificance and comfort us? Darwin, now 200 years later, is at best confused and at worst having nightmares about the goings on down here! Much of the evolution of narcissism exploded into being in the 60's with the "free speech movement," "love ins," the drug culture, the sexual revolution, and so-called human potentialists.

Psychiatrist Irvin Yalom[2] describes the 60's as a time when there was a focus on hedonism ("if it feels good, do it"), on anti-intellectualism (which considers any cognitive approach as "mind-fucking"), on individual fulfillment ("doing your own thing," "peak experiences"), and on self-actualization (a belief in human perfectibility). A devotee of the time, Gestalt therapist, Fritz Perls, said it best:

I do my thing and you do your thing.
I am not in this world to live up to your expectations.
And you are not in this world to live up to mine.
You are you, and I am I.
And if by chance we find each other, it's beautiful.
If not, it can't be helped.[3]

The "me generation" has exploded into a tragic life form, which exists in a "mirrored reality" – seeing only ourselves – that avoids responsibility to one another. How can relationships last with this tripe? We started the Twentieth Century troubled by Freud's notion that we are deterministically governed by primal urges such as sexuality and aggression. At least we had a cultural Puritanism at the time to help buffer some of these forces. Now we have ended the Twentieth Century with few cultural restraints, spawning migratory patterns, a dramatic loss of ritual in our lives, and a soaring divorce rate. We now experience a frightening anomie in which the values of our society no longer have much personal relevance or meaning to us individually. We are so alone!

At times, many of us can appear narcissistic. We can be demanding, whiny creatures who now use lawyers to buttress our entitlements. Give me what I want or I'll sue your ass! Look at some of these scenarios reported in various newspaper articles:

* ✳ An outraged woman, with her children in tow, demanded to see the "real" dinosaurs as advertised by Marine World Africa in Vallejo, California. After all, she had not paid good money only to see "fake ones." **[Grandiosity]**

* ✳ A father threatened to sue the Pointe Hilton Squaw Peak Resort in Phoenix because his child had swallowed too much pool water. Financial compensation would calm these stormy seas, right? **[Exploitativeness]**

* ✳ A guest at the Lanesborough hotel in London called downstairs at 3 a.m. and demanded an immediate change in the curtains in his room. He simply did not like them – they were changed. **[Entitlement]**

＊ Spaghetti delivered by room service at the Wyndham Hotel in Puerto Rico was sent
back by a guest who said he had ordered it for his dog – and that his dog liked it cooked
al dente. **[Entitlement and special favors]**

Our passion for self-fulfillment goes far beyond the satisfaction of basic needs. We are drawn
into a blinding vortex we often call the pursuit of glory. What better example than the Olympic pursuit for gold. The glitter of gold blinds us. We worship athletes with the superhuman
strength and speed necessary to bring the gold home.

What is curious is how we malign other cultures for being excessive in their pursuit of
glory – of grandiosity. We blanch at the dismissive manner in which the Russian coach refuses
to kiss his athletes after their less-than-perfect performance. Or we condemn the Chinese
training method of removing children as young as three years old from their homes while
submitting them to rigorous training programs. If they see their parents once in six months,
they're lucky. Why? The pursuit of glory! While we might condemn this portrait of ambition
in other cultures I actually see this daily in our own culture. Surely the 60-70 hour per week
executive, technocrat, or physician is not too different in his or her neglect of family. When is
abundance abundant enough?

**When the pursuit of glory becomes yoked to perfection we are flirting with psychic
disaster.**

Such is the case of swimmer Jenny Thompson, who captured a staggering cache of gold in three
Olympic Games – seven – more than any American woman in any sport. She also became the
most decorated U.S. woman Olympian ever when she tied with teammate Dara Torres to
capture a bronze medal in the 100-meter freestyle in Australia. Yet, there was no celebration
for Ms. Thompson. Athletes and broadcasters throughout the Olympic village felt compassion
for her since she had been unable to win gold in any individual event – only relays! Thus she
had not really proven herself as an individual. In some bizarre, distorted way, Jenny had fallen
short and failed. In her final opportunity to win an individual gold she could only tie for third
(in the world!) with Dara Torres.

In an effort to halt the media's insane obsession with both glory and perfection, Jenny
Thompson mused, "It's time to stop looking at what I don't have and time to look at what I
do have." Each of us, like Jenny Thompson and the Emperor, must massage the underbelly of
our lives. We must look inward and try to accept our imperfect uniqueness. This has been our
quest, maybe our cultural obsession, for much of the previous century. As we do so, we will
find that the pursuit of glory is a precarious teeter-totter.

The Missing 10 Degrees
Narcissism and glory always reflect the missing pieces of our lives.

We are haunted by the incompleteness of our lives. Sometimes we are motivated by it;
sometimes we succumb to it. Surely each of us knows this as scarcity. If we are thirsty or hun-

gry, we seek out water or food. If we need attention from others, we spend thousands of dollars on our homes or at Macy's. If we are confused, we seek answers. If we lose our job, we obsess until we find another. If the Wall Street collapse decimates our 401(k) we strategize until we secure a new retirement nest. If life seems meaningless, we seek a purpose for living. Most of these missing puzzle pieces in our lives are quite obvious. But the real source of incompleteness may lie far below the surface, yet cause endless ripples, even tidal waves, for years and years.

We are biologically wired to notice the missing ten degrees. We try to fill what's empty. If a circle is broken we perceptually seek to complete it. A circle has 360 degrees. If one tiny segment is missing, we don't notice the fullness of the completed line segment – say 350 degrees. We immediately fixate on the missing ten degrees. Since a state of tension now exists, we are compelled, often consumed, with a need to replenish the missing ten degrees. Gestalt psychologists have recognized this for half a century and call this need closure. This seems to be true of our lives as well. We seek to complete what is incomplete about our lives – an existential nightmare given the inevitability of death.

The missing ten degrees spawns many stepchildren: awareness begets craving, then obsessions, and then self-addiction. It is helpful to turn to Aristotle for help in understanding this progression in our lives. Aristotle describes four planes of existence, each of which has churned up our lives for thousands of years:

1) *The Physical* – How do I relieve the primal tensions within my body?
2) *The Emotional* – How do I mend a broken heart?
3) *The Cognitive* – How do I achieve all I was meant to be?
4) *The Spiritual* – How do I find meaning and purpose in a larger cosmos?

Our narcissistic obsessions are inextricably woven around these four tacit questions of living. We are driven by [1] bodily tensions, [2] emotional hunger, [3] blind ambitions, and [4] eternal reverence. These are DRIVERS. We are motivated to relieve bodily tension – e.g. an orgasm; sooth emotional pain – e.g., be warmly held; achieve personal ambitions – e.g., have a large, well-appointed home; and create a lasting imprint – e.g. leave a legacy. Many of us have all the above, but there is a difference between having these and being consumed by them. Self-absorption reflects the latter.

Narcissistic preoccupation is unavoidable, but it can be a blessing or curse.

On a **physical** level, we seek an end to craving. This explains satiety and the satisfaction of a "want." We feel full at the completion of a meal, we feel bliss in the afterglow of lovemaking, and we feel relief when our bladders have emptied. An end to a tension state of hunger, sexual desire, and urgency is welcomed. In fact, we may not be able to focus on anything else in our lives until these tension states are resolved. The missing ten degrees can be quite distracting. There is a reward system in the brain which is activated when a person does what is necessary to survive, such as eating. We feel pleasure, and whatever we did to create this pleasure is reinforced, providing positive feedback to keep us doing what we were doing. Unfortunately, this same process occurs when we abuse drugs, licit or illicit. By increasing the levels of neurotransmitters in the cortex, such as dopamine and glutamate, drugs bring pleasure. This leads to an addictive process of needing more and more substance to maintain the pleasure and to end the pain associated with the craving.

On an **emotional** level, we seek union. This is what Mother Nature intended. However, our need for attachment and closeness can create a hunger in its own right if we feel deprived. Indeed, those of us who did not receive enough parental warmth, affection, and attention in childhood may find ourselves desperately longing for connection throughout our adult years. Even when our partners seem to be providing so much for us, the neediness of so many years of neglect may create a hunger so insatiable that the pain of yearning never subsides. We may feel worthless, empty, and alone in spite of abundance around us. When this happens we may become preoccupied with being depressed or seeking validation outside our genuine love bonds – our marriages.

On a **cognitive** level, we seek fruition. As a species we are blessed with a capacity to remember the past, enjoy the present, and anticipate the future. It is this last gift which launches dreams and aspirations to be all that we can be and to have all that we can imagine. We are often blinded by these dreams: they become narrow tunnels of light casting everything else in our lives into darkness. Whenever we get too caught up in our own importance and our own successes, self-absorption may deny others their opportunity to be seen or appreciated. Entitlement or grandiosity then becomes a prism.

Finally, on a **spiritual** level, we seek wholeness. To be at one with ourselves, with God, and with the universe is a sacred happening. This once was described as "God breathing with us," by my dear friend, Reverend Chuck Meyer. Whether this quest is driven by a fear of death or a longing for integration, we know we have arrived when total acceptance resonates throughout our being. We accept the universe as it is, and "know" that we are similarly embraced. The path to wholeness requires a journey inward and may also blur our focus on all that abounds in our external world.

Narcissism can breed havoc within any of these realms. The prayerful, meditating spiritualist, who lives an ascetic life while ignoring the needs of his family, is no different from the philandering wife who flits surreptitiously into the night. If we live our lives focused only on our missing pieces – physical, cognitive, emotional, or spiritual – what can we know of love?

Let's take a look at Bill who has it all – or so it seemed: a loving wife, two vibrant and joyful children, two black Labrador retrievers, and three posh homes in ideal settings around the country. Before he inherited his money, he had attended one of the finest prep schools in the country which served as a launching pad for an Ivy League school in the East. A golf membership at the Country Club, Porches, and Jaguars would all seem to define a life of abundance. Right? Wrong!

Bill was addicted to alcohol, women, and gambling. The abundance of money in his life belied the real scarcity and insecurity which lurked beneath his bravado. Free tickets on

Southwest Airlines, luxurious accommodations in Vegas, and a carte blanche with escort services were enough to fool his friends, but not his family. While his addictions drew him to tinsel town, his wife and children knew that a chemical imbalance, genetically fueled by his father's blood line, drove Bill to altered states and lacquered dates. But, like so many others, he was addicted not just to chemicals but also to a false image of himself which insatiably drove him away from the very essence of what he truly needed – the love of his family.

Too distracted by his temporary highs, Bill refused to pause in life, or in therapy, to understand his manic states, his physical addiction, or his childhood history of neglect and abandonment. Like the Emperor, Bill had never been physically held as a child. He had never been emotionally comforted when afraid. His father traveled on business trips rather than see his school play or football games. Neither parent showed up at his high school graduation. A Mediterranean cruise had trumped that.

Bill never shed a tear about any of the above. After all, his father hadn't made his millions by feeling sorry for himself. And his mother had told him, "Men feel with their hands, not their head or heart!" So, a fix – attention from friends, sexual flings with other women, or a line up his nose – provided comfort for Bill. The sound of a slot machine in Vegas provided more relief than the love and compassion waiting for him back home. He had never learned to turn toward such comfort as a child and, sadly, he refused to learn as an adult.

A pattern of avoiding pain spun into a lifestyle of addictions all intended to fill a void. Rather than do the work needed to rebalance his life in a healthier way, Bill allowed the neon lights of Vegas to distract him. Bill became addicted to the short term superficial solutions which physical pleasure afforded him. While narcissism is a normal life force in all of our lives, it can override all other forces. When this happens, we become addicted to our own self-image, our own mirror image. We saw this with the Emperor as well. As is true with other licit and illicit substances, Bill literally needed more and more of himself in order to feed the very image he had created.

Within all addiction there is an avoidance of pain. Many people live out their lives addicted to substances or life styles in order to avoid feeling the inevitable pain of life struggles. Altered states trump reality states. Suffering and imperfection are part of our journey and within the belly of all pain, as in the story of Jonah and the whale, lie both salvation and redemptive power of love. Instead of feeling the heat – being transformed – we often live our lives coldly detached from one another. Bill fits that pattern.

A preoccupation with the missing pieces of our lives leads to preoccupation with the totality of our lives.

Self-preoccupation, self-interest, self-fulfillment, self-esteem, self-determination, and the holy grail of self-aggrandizement – self-actualization – become altered states that blind us to what exists around us. We get lost in self-reverie. We become consumed by what is missing OR what is glistening – by the morose, or by the grandiose!

The risk, of course, is that we can alienate others, or compromise the good of all!

Va Bene – Go Well!

I hope you still feel small when you stand by the ocean.
When one door closes, I hope one more opens.
I hope you give faith a fighting chance.
And when you get the choice to sit it out or dance, I hope you dance.[4]
> – Lee Ann Womack

The "missing ten degrees" invites us to have faith, to dance, and to "go well!"

Our Type A, palm-piloted, narcissistically driven lifestyles cannot be denied forever. However, with the right lightening strike, we do mellow. We awaken. We learn to appreciate *people*, not possessions; we learn to cherish *love*, not power; and we learn to value *time*, not money. Just listen to those three words: *People love time!* Ironically, we think more about time when we seem to have less of it. But this is true of everything that we value, especially the unrelenting human need for attachment, intimacy, and love. Connection with others, with humankind, is a life force, a human life force, which unifies every separate soul and every disparate nation on earth.

To appreciate the "gift of life" we must "go well" in life!

But what does it mean for us to "go well"? And what would we, when we are self-absorbed, have to give up getting there? If love is truly the antidote for narcissism we must eventually open our hearts and find someone to love. What would it take for us to finish unfinished business, so that we can open our eyes, so that we can consciously see – really see – what we have? Why does it sometimes take the "end of life" to say and mean the five things that my friend, Chuck Meyer, recommended to many of us in the weeks before he died: **Forgive me! I forgive you! Thank you! I love you! Good-bye!**

Forgive me! This is the second of the *Six Gifts*. There is something wrong with us, as individuals, and as a whole. But this is OK. This is where we meet. We find each other in the abyss between perfection and imperfection. It is in this abyss that we find intimacy, love, and acceptance. Deeper intimacy is often accompanied by what one friend calls a "post confessional blush." We don't get closer to one another when lying on a chaise lounge in the Bahamas with Bain de Soleil all over our perfect bodies. This may feel good, but real intimacy requires getting below the epidermal layer. In his piece, *Anthem*, Leonard Cohen is very clear:

Ring the bells that still can ring,
Forget your perfect offering.
There is a crack in everything.
That's how the light gets in.[5]

I forgive you! No human relationship can continue, or be renewed, without the gift of forgiveness. When we are hurt by those we love the most, a very natural tendency is to withhold forgiveness. This is called resentment. Resentments are memories, not feelings, so we can actually "decide" to forgive someone, even when the bastards don't deserve it. Now, that's a Gift! Forgiveness is truly more of a Gift to you because the bearer of the resentment is always in more pain than the person who created it.

Resentment is often about narcissism, while forgiveness is about love. After all, the narcissist is "entitled" to his angry feelings since s/he has been "wounded" and is "entitled" to a better, more fulfilling life! Let's be careful here. Anger is not an entitlement. Sometimes we do get less than we deserve, sometimes more, and sometimes we get just what we deserve. While some people are not worthy of being forgiven, we may "want" to forgive more often than we do. Oftentimes there is much more at stake. If we never learn to forgive, we will never be able to answer the pastor's query: What on Earth are you here for". To be fully human, to know love, we must forgive.

Thank you! We are drawn to the incompleteness of our lives – to the missing piece. We often are blindsided by circumstances that spotlight what's missing: a child disappoints us, a salary increase doesn't materialize, or a class reunion leaves us high and dry. Like dealing with an out-of-focus lens, we usually do a simple attitude adjustment, count our blessings and move on in gratitude.

A deeper gratitude exists, however. Circumstances are irrelevant. Our joy is based on total "acceptance" of life – the good, the bad and the ugly. Acceptance is the third of the *Six Gifts*. We rejoice because we are able to! Our existence is enough. We breathe into the present moment. We accept all the twists and turns without judging them too harshly. This gratitude for life is similar to unconditional love where our appreciation is not determined by circumstances and outcomes. Just being a part of a cosmic, living architecture is enough. As we awake each day, we hear a voice in the back of our minds say "Wow." And we say in return, "Thank you."

Appreciation for what we have is often blurred by a greater need for what we want. Marriage, unfortunately enough, has become the 21st Century's scapegoat for these unmet needs. As we will see in Chapter 11, romantic love has become the genie in the bottle for most of us who live in the West. Encouraging narcissistic partners in couple's therapy to say "Thank you" or "I appreciate" or "You're enough for me!" is Herculean at best. Solicitude finds value in what exists, be it life itself, or the bountiful abundance provided to us. As the poet Henry Alford expresses:

> *Come, ye thankful people, come.*
> *Raise the song of Harvest-home;*
> *All is safely gathered in,*
> *Ere the winter storms begin.*[6]

I love you! Karl Menninger, the renowned psychiatrist from Kansas, once remarked, "Love cures people: both the ones who give it and the ones who receive it." To say "I love you" is one of the greatest blessings afforded to another. We cannot say these words enough.

Just as "the gift of life" balances "the fear of death," the force of narcissism is balanced by love.

Why are these words so hard to say for some? "I love you."

Can you remember the first time you said these words? Was it with flowers in your hand? Was it beneath her bedroom window as rain began to fall? Was it just after a moment of ecstasy? Was it haltingly shared as a flashlight shone through the car windshield and a baton tapped quickly on the window?

Later, when the flush of romantic love gives way to mature love, we might remember saying these words differently. Do you remember whispering these words softly as a loved one was whisked into an emergency room at your local hospital or at the end of a long-distance phone call to a long-time friend? Mature love teaches us that love is more about the "other" than the "self." We are reminded of Erich Fromm's definition of love as "care, concern, and solicitude." Solicitude means to have the interests of the "other" at heart. This mutuality is a steep learning curve for a narcissist. When we say "I love you," we are transcending the personal realm in order to celebrate the interpersonal realm. While solicitude may embrace both realms, love poignantly nurtures only one.

Goodbye! David Brower, hero emeritus of the Sierra Club, has repeatedly delivered what he considers to be "the Sermon." He usually invites listeners to consider the six days of Genesis as a figure of speech for what has in fact been four and a half billion years! According to Brower, a day in this formulation equals something like seven hundred and fifty million years, and thus all day Monday and until Tuesday noon creation was busy getting the earth going. Life began Tuesday noon, and the "beautiful, organic wholeness of it" developed over the next four days. At 4 p.m. Saturday, the big reptiles came. Five hours later, the reptiles were gone. At three minutes before midnight, man appeared. At one-fortieth of a second before midnight, the 20th Century beckoned.[7]

We, as a species, have only been here for a fraction of a second and we, as individuals, will be gone in even less time. We can choose to live this nanosecond unconsciously like the Emperor or, more consciously, with wondrous appreciation for the brief opportunity we have been given to celebrate life, embrace its abundance, and to love one another.

Thank you, goodbye, and va bene – "Go well, my friend."

CHAPTER 3

Our False Self and Our True Self

A little old lady gets onto a crowded bus and stands in the front of a seated young girl. Holding her hand to her chest, she says to the girl, "If you knew what I have, you would give me your seat." The girl gets up and gives her seat to the old lady.

It is very hot and the young girl takes out her fan and starts fanning herself. At which point the little old lady looks up and remarks, "If you knew what I have, you would give me that fan." The girl gives her the fan too.

Fifteen minutes later the woman gets up and says to the bus driver, "Stop, I want to get off here." The bus driver tells her that he has to drop her off at the next corner, for safety reason, not in the middle of the block. With her hand across her chest, she vehemently says to the driver, "If you knew what I have, you wouldn't hesitate. You would drop me off right here!"

The bus driver pulls over in the middle of the block and opens the door to let her out. As she's walking out of the bus, he can't help but ask her, "Madam, what is it you have?" Without blanching for a moment, the old woman looks irreverently back over her shoulder and nonchalantly replies, "CHUTZPAH".

Do you detect a smidgen of narcissism here?

Chutzpah is a Yiddish word, originating from the ancient Hebrew word huspah, meaning supreme self-confidence, nerve, or gall. This little old lady helps us see that this supreme confidence can actually come across as aggressive boldness – as a kind of "in-your-face-I'm-taking-care-of-me" attitude.

Have you met people like this who wantonly disregard the needs of others?

Chutzpah isn't always displayed in such an obnoxious way. A second way to look at chutz-pah much less obnoxiously is to view it as "risk-taking," not as rudeness or disrespect for others. For instance, if you are waiting in line at a concert and Madonna walks by, you have chutzpah if you hoist your three-year-old on your shoulders, begin singing one of her hits, and offer your program to her for an autograph. Assertiveness often requires that we take care of our own needs without violating the needs of others. The kind of aggressiveness trickling out of this "little old lady" is quite another matter.

The little old lady exists everywhere. We find her slicing in and out of traffic lanes on American highways, we read about her capitalizing on insider trading, and we are jolted by her corporate greed within the tobacco industry as she hides the truth about the harmful effects of smoking.

Personal gain at the expense of others taints the water supply of humanity, seducing the unwary into selfish acts.

Chutzpah shows up in divorce court. We see the little old lady in Lionel Richie's estranged wife Diane who, according to newsprint headlines, stated that she did not want her $300,000 per month lifestyle affected by their impending divorce. Having had nine full time staff members to maintain the plants, detail the cars, care for the pool, and groom the dog, Mrs. Richie supposedly requested of the court that she be granted:

* $15,000 per month for clothing
* $3,000 per month for dermatology
* $1,000 per month for laser hair removal
* $600 per month for massages
* $5,000 per month for jewelry, and
* $20,000 per year for plastic surgery

Mrs. Richie has cohones and an expensive image to maintain.

Remember that healthy self-care or self-interest is normal. Mrs. Richie seems to have crossed a line here: first into self-absorption, and now into the mirrored darkness of narcissism.

There are two ways to understand a person who devolves into narcissism.

At one extreme, narcissism reflects a kind of "false self," an inflated self at that, designed to impress the world around us. Our self esteem is based on illusion – a house of cards built upon qualities which we really don't possess.

At the other extreme, narcissism reflects a "true" self esteem which is built upon qualities which we really do possess. A genuine intelligence, creative spirit, athletic prowess, or inspi-rational leadership is possessed in spades. Moreover, these qualities are felt to be true by those who know us best. Here's the kicker though:

Both the "false self" and the "true self" can manifest as narcissism.

You might think that only the "false self", a self-esteem built upon qualities we really don't possess, would be narcissism. Puffing ourselves up with expensive homes, cars, and a $300,000 per month expense account is most likely a desperate attempt to look good on the outside when we feel miserable on the inside.

But here's the confounding parallel: I also believe that self-esteem, built upon qualities we really do possess can be narcissistic when the continued display of these qualities either (1) alienates others around us or (2) compromises the ultimate good of all. While Barry Bonds alienated 70 percent of baseball enthusiasts by puffing himself up on steroids, he genuinely did possess some incredible skills.

On the surface, all narcissism is about self reflection, whether true or false. This was the case with Narcissus who was so mesmerized by his own surface image in a pond that he tragically missed the calls of Echo, who repeatedly beckoned him. The narcissist usually misses the calling of those around him. Unable to hear, the narcissist may not even see others, let alone respond to them. Others are thereby alienated.

A great irony exists.

While narcissism is masked as outward image-making, it really is a collapse inward. The glitter of the outer jewelry only distracts us. Extreme narcissism is really being drunk on ourselves. We get sloshed on our obsessive thoughts, personal entitlements, and emotional hunger within. Our thoughts are distorted and our vision is poor. Denial is high and the needs of others are low. The more absorbed we are within – with what is missing, with what is scarce – the less attentive we are regarding others around us. We become prisoners, locked within our own desperate need to fill our selves, to be full of ourselves.

Sometimes this self-absorption is hard to see as self-absorption. This is often the case in which self-anointed, holier-than-thou, God-fearing saints judge the rest of us as wayward sinners. These folks believe that they have found the path to righteousness and castigate the rest of us imperfect souls daily. Their lofty self-righteousness is pompous, alienates most of us most of the time, and compromises the well-being of all. Refusing to go to a "friend's" wedding because she is not pure enough is enough to make one's blood boil! Underneath this pious persona lies a false self, hungry not just for salvation, but for love as well.

We are hard-wired for attachment, for proximity, for closeness. We began this vulnerable life journey needing someone – reaching out for someone. How can some of us end up so self absorbed that we appear hard-wired only to ourselves?

The "False" Self

Narcissism, at one extreme, is a desperate attempt to prove our worth.

At first glance, when most of us stare at our own reflections, we see the image we have created inwardly, and then projected outwardly, in the hope that others will think well of us. This is our self-image, that glossy portrait of self, which relates so strongly to our self-esteem. From our earliest years we become obsessed with our superficial preening among our peers and contemporaries – our image! "Mirror, mirror on the wall: who's the fairest of them all?" I am, of course.

This obsessive concern over image remains an inherent part of our daily quest until we're dead – or at least until we find validation in the soothing reflection of our own web page, or on Facebook, where surely one of six billion people will fawn over us. If the design of a web page is too complicated, we can simply slither behind some identity we have created in a chat room or 1-900 number. Or, if technology is overwhelming, we can put together a slam-dunk resume, which surely will glitter in the light of a curious readership. Or, if we are Warren Beatty, we can run for President.

The journalist Leonard Pitts sadly notes "The only thing sadder than people believing too deeply in an image is an image believing too deeply in itself."[1]

Narcissistic presence is very ethereal.

Image is only surface deep and easily blurs with the slightest ripple. We intuitively know that there is more to surface reflection than meets the eye. Emmy Lou Harris captures this quite well in one of her lyrics:

Beneath still waters,
There's a strong undertow.
The surface won't tell you,
What the deep water knows.[2]

We often believe that a narcissistic presence is a wholesome, self-assured one. This is far from the truth. Instead of a stable foundation built upon self-love, the narcissist more often feels unloved, unappreciated, and empty. A void exists at the very core of the narcissist's being. An obsessive and manipulative life script often results in a desperate attempt to fill the void.

"I must be sexy and attractive. See my youthful look, my six-pack gut, and the gorgeous women dangling from my arms." According to Susan Faludi, men have joined women in a "display culture" where they've become the equivalent of hood ornaments on a fancy car or mastheads on a sailing vessel – beautifully defined by bulging pectoral muscles, ripped abs, and the hairless torso of Italian marble statuary.[3]

"I must be important. My academic resume, from only 10 years of teaching, weighs 35 pounds, I serve on five Boards, my cell phone erupts 391 times a day, and I play golf with the lieutenant governor every leap year."

"I must be seen as exhilarating, as exciting! I drive a fast car, I dress in tantalizing and seductive clothing, I last five hours in bed without Viagra and I have multiple orgasms every Tuesday evening. The fact that my husband doesn't know about these sexual trysts is inconsequential. I feel alive."

Narcissism doesn't go awry – it is awry?

We must wonder how a healthy confidence becomes distorted, even clinically diagnosable. For some, it is a permissive, enabling upbringing which spoils and instills a sense of entitlement. For others, the pathway is a childhood void which turbo-charges these folks to continually seek affirmation seldom available as a child. Unconsciously, one thinks, if I didn't get attention, appreciation or affection as a child I surely don't want to miss out any longer. An imperative gets created. I must have it now. These are the wounds of childhood that fuel narcissistic behaviors.

Let's look deeper.

Karen Horney, M.D., helps us understand how the disturbances of childhood can set up narcissistic patterns throughout life. Horney states that, "the factor which contributes most fundamentally to the development of narcissistic trends appears to be the child's alienation from others, provoked by grievances and fears. His positive emotional ties with others become thin; he loses the capacity to love."[4]

"Others" for a child means mother, father, or caretaker. When a child experiences a distant emotional relationship with caregivers, anxiety creates a vacuum where love, security and comfort should have resided. Anxiety may consume a child who experiences the continued toxic presence of parents or the traumatic loss of parents through sudden death or hostile divorce.

Anxiety and fear are nasty emotions for a little tyke to deal with. We would like to believe that young children reach out to their parents with these emotions continuously. They don't. There is a time when young children, living with anxiety, reach a conclusion regarding those most dear to them. I can't count on you; I can't trust you; I won't turn to you anymore. Emotional ties become very thin, so thin that we often hang by a thread. When we are not experiencing the mutual sharing of love, we begin to lose our capacity to love.

Parents cripple our capacity to love in many ways according to Horney.

First, a parent might be exceedingly authoritative, expecting a child to be utterly obedient in all ways. "If you respect me, you will do as I say and command!" "I am in charge and know what is best for you." "Children are to be seen and not heard." God forbid I should have my own voice within such a family! In this scenario we learn to adopt our parent's standards: to comply, to repress, to hide, and to make peace in the face of fear. We stop being real.

Second, a parent might appear to be self-sacrificing for a child. "Don't you see what I have given up for you? Don't you see how different my life would be if I were not burdened with your care?" A tacit quid pro quo often exists whereby the child grows to understand that "You owe me, since I have given up so much for you." In this scenario we learn that guilt and manipulation are powerful forces which shape our response to the world. We stop being real.

Third, a parent may transfer their ambitions and unrealized goals to us, so that we may become what they weren't. Our parents thus live vicariously through us, cheering and yelling very loudly from the sidelines with every missed goal, basket, or reception. As a child we begin to get the idea that we are loved for imaginary qualities, i.e., our capacity to be a Michael Jordan, an embryonic genius, or a Madonna princess, rather than for being our true self. We stop being real.

Fourth, a parent might criticize and belittle such that a child lives in fear of being diminished and smaller than he already feels he is. Parents who threaten, judge, blame, label, name-call, and scream at a child paralyze a child. As a child we begin to get the idea that our own will, likes and dislikes, and feelings do not matter. We stop being real.

Fifth, a parent might prefer other siblings, making it quite clear that we don't measure up. In this case we are forever comparing our qualities to those of our brothers or sisters. To survive in such a family we may adopt a trait or characteristic which belongs to another sibling in order to be accepted by a parent. Or, more tragically, we might simply drop out, becoming the rebel who disowns both the family and our self. We stop being real.

The embers for a "false" self begin in these incipient moments in our lives. According to writer Hameed Ali:

> *Because our parents are usually so hopelessly out of touch with their own essential depths and have never experienced these qualities in themselves, they can't mirror them back to us. When a certain essential quality is not seen in us, or it's devalued, we tend to lose contact with it. This lost connection is experienced as a hole. It is an absence, a lack, a sense of something missing, and it literally feels like a hole. What happens is that we end up filled with holes. Most of us build our lives, usually unconsciously, around finding ways to avoid feeling these holes. What you fill the holes with are the false feelings, ideas, beliefs about yourself, strategies for dealing with the environment. These fillers are collectively called the personality, but after a time, we think that is who we are. After many losses of contact with who we are, we begin to take ourselves to be what we are not.[5]*

The impact of early parenting styles often shapes us like a river carving out limestone. We learn that in order to be liked, loved, or even accepted, we must be as others would want us to be. We become dependent upon opinions of others. While self esteem is partially dependent on the estimate of others, for the "false self," nothing but the estimate of others counts. Image becomes everything, and we stop being real.

For the narcissist, image is everything.

By creating a fantasy world in which he lives, the narcissist is a hero who comforts himself and compensates for not being affirmed, appreciated, or loved. If others do not love me, or respect me for who I really am, at least others are paying attention to me. For the narcissist with low self-esteem, illusions may indeed be life saving. These illusions about ourselves are so fragile however – so rickety – that they eventually must shatter. I remember this as a life guard in the Pocono Mountains at age 19.

A fellow by the name of Dick Kidder [no kidding!] was a life guard hired by management at this plush mountain resort. Dick was forever spinning tales about his prowess with women, his academic achievements in college, and his black belt in karate. One rainy day, with little to do on the waterfront, a group of guards began to chide Mr. Kidder into demonstrating his "stuff." After an hour of backpedaling, he relented to crushing a board with the edge of a hand – a simple task he had once claimed. With rain pouring down around us, Dick repeatedly smashed his hand against the brazen board of oak. With blood pouring down his hand, and the oak still standing tall, Dick bemoaned the fact that he had been up all that night with a stomach virus. Even Samson needs a good night sleep, we thought.

This narcissistic ruse ended dramatically enough the next week with a cry for help from a weary swimmer. As this frightened and fatigued woman flailed in the cold mountain lake water, she helplessly called out to Dick Kidder who fatefully was sitting in the life guard chair that day – only a few feet away. In turn, Dick Kidder helplessly called out to me as I approached from a nearby dock. Taking one look at Dick's helpless expression, I dove in quickly, swam the necessary 20 yards, and instinctively positioned a very grateful swimmer in a cross chest carry and brought her to safety.

An emergency debriefing with management that day necessitated a check on Mr. Kidder's credentials. A quick call to the American Red Cross center, which supposedly credentialed Mr. Kidder, revealed no such individual had ever taken a water safety class. Mr. Kidder, we discovered, was more than a kidder. He was a pathological liar who placed the lives of others in jeopardy in order to bolster a skeletal self-image. As Mr. Kidder packed his bags, his hand still swollen and bloodied from days before, a group of young men learned that personal aggrandizement can indeed be costly to oneself and others.

We have seen how low self esteem can morph into a fragile narcissism. Narcissism at this end of the continuum is built upon shaky pilings which eventually give way in a stormy sea – or perhaps a serene, mountain lake in the Poconos.

To better understand the "false self" we must explore deeper into its archaic roots.

Archaic Roots

The missing ten degrees for a "false self" is a life or death matter.

So far in this chapter we have been looking at how a "false self" copes with low self-esteem. In order to survive, the low self esteem person must compensate for what s/he is lacking inside by creating something grand on the outside. This is the grandiosity, the entitlement, and the glitter which comprise false abundance for many narcissists. We see this need for compensation in Mr. Kidder, Mrs. Richie, and the little old lady.

The "false self" must also protect against being discovered or being diminished any further. Therefore, the extreme narcissist is very emotionally reactive to any slight from another person which would appear to threaten his or her fragile self-worth – what little there is of it! After all, we must defend against losing what little we think we have. This is a very high stakes game played on a daily basis. This is where our archaic roots kick in.

Marion Solomon, author of *Narcissism and Intimacy*, describes "archaic" narcissism. She suggests that these individuals are characterized by [1] exquisite sensitivity to psychic injury, [2] great anxiety, [3] fear of being hurt or humiliated, and [4] defensive measures that affect relationships to various degrees. "The degree of early damage may cause narcissistically vulnerable people to misread or misunderstand the interaction with others; thus, they are more easily provoked to defensive reactions."[6]

If wounds are archaic, they are old, painful and a powder keg of explosives. Archaic narcissism, in this most extreme form, is always grounded in urgency: *Fulfill me! Comfort me! Understand me - NOW!!* There is a disturbance of balance here. Care for self almost always obliterates the need to care for others. Archaic narcissism is marked by a pattern of eruptive and destructive behavior, which occurs and reoccurs throughout a person's life. This extreme narcissist is trying to erase painful memories while filling up reservoirs that never received enough during the childhood years. Erasing painful memories sometimes erases the presence of those around us.

Tony, a compulsive body builder, is a case in point. Abandoned as a youth, Tony was addicted to alcohol, codeine, cocaine, and the steroids that helped define his bulging musculature. Of course there was a cost. Tony also experienced tachycardia, or a racing heart, which panicked both him and Sylvia, his wife, into three emergency room visits and two abnormal echocardiograms. When Tony was emphatically told to cut out the drugs, he ignored all medical advice as well as Sylvia's pleadings. Instead, he repeatedly turned to the mirrors in his fitness center where both men and women admired his steroid-driven build. When Sylvia cratered emotionally from his compensating lifestyle, Tony would archaically rage at her, claiming that she was a demanding bitch who would never entrap him in her web. The explosive level of his tirades could never be understood by looking merely at the situations which seemed to "trigger" them.

A typical discussion between Tony and Sylvia would sound something like this:

Tony, I feel very empty. I feel unimportant and devalued. I feel unheard and disrespected. I feel ignored and unloved. You expect others to do for you, but you rarely help. It takes weeks, even months, for you to do even the smallest chores. You seldom spend time with us as a family, and when you do, it is usually with regret and resentment. When we took our marriage vows, we should have become partners. Partners who value each others' opinions, who respect each others' values, who stand up for each other, who are sensitive to the other's feelings and needs, and who make a real effort to find time to know, understand, and to love each other.

And Tony shouts back:

SYLVIA, YOU'RE JUST LIKE THE OTHER LOW-LIFE SCUM IN MY LIFE. IT'S ALWAYS BEEN THIS WAY. NONE OF YOU UNDERSTAND HOW HARD I WORK – HOW HARD I HAVE TO WORK! WHO ELSE DO YOU THINK IS GOING TO KEEP OUR HOUSEHOLD RUNNING? PLUS, I'M CLOSE TO REALLY MAKING IT BIG. SINCE I AM PUTTING FOOD ON THE TABLE, COVERING MEDICAL BILLS AND PAYING ABSURD VET BILLS, THE LEAST YOUR LAZY ASS CAN DO IS COVER THINGS AT HOME!

Sylvia is living with someone who sees only his own pain, his own mission, and lives life to the beat of his own drum. Tony is mesmerized by his own body, works excessive hours, ignores his kids, demands much from others, chases the glory of fame and fortune, and seems unable to grasp that others have needs as well. There is no spirit of mutuality, no sense of sisterhood, here.

Tony not only compensates for his low self-esteem, he reacts violently toward his own wife when he feels threatened – just as he did his own mother many years before! The wounds of childhood can spawn "narcissistic vulnerability" according to Dr. Solomon. Then, in adult-hood – while under stress – some people will regress to levels of functioning that were typical of earlier life stages.

People with low self esteem really do not want to be alone. Instead these individuals have a desperate need to attach to others in order to feel complete or whole. At the archaic level, this need to attach is exaggerated to such an extent that the person often searches for an "idealized other." This is why romantic love often becomes the love of choice for the narcissist. There is an urgent need for fusion and a feeling of oneness which narcissists confuse with lasting love.

"False selves" and the archaically wounded are so busy compensating for an impoverished sense of self that they seem unable to connect with others in a more authentic or "true" way. Essentially they are not healthy enough to provide the *Six Gifts* of love described in the last sec-tion of this book. Being consumed by pain, obsessed with hiding, and frightened by intimacy these folks are not ready to be humble, forgiving, accepting, compassionate, sacrificing, or envisioning – qualities of the "True" Self.

Obsession with a broken self often blurs a path of wholeness towards others.

The "True" Self

I once had lunch with a physician friend who wanted to have lunch with me so he could dis-cuss a few issues. After reassuring me that he was content with life as he approached age 40, he still wondered about a few things:

> *It seems to me that 95 percent of my worth, as a person, comes from what I do as a physi-cian – not who I am as a person. Though I recognize that I am quite successful, make good money, and have a great reputation in the community, I am troubled by a realization that, aside from my professional role, I personally do not have other ways to value myself.*

My friend's dilemma is no different from what each one of us faces on a continuing basis throughout our lives. By what formula, by what design, and by what criteria do we judge our worth as a person? How do we learn to care, value, and respect ourselves realistically? Nathaniel Branden reminds us that "There is no value judgment more important to man {kind} – no factor more decisive in his psychological development and motivation – than the estimate he passes on himself."

In a world of competing identities how do we "strut our stuff?" How do we show the world what we're made of? This is normal. Judith Viorst, in her wonderful book, Necessary Losses, captures this sense of a healthy self in the making quite well:

For there is a time in our life when we need to strut our stuff and groove on grandiosity,
when we need to be viewed as remarkable and rare, when we need to exhibit ourself in
front of a mirror that reflects our self-admiration, when we need a parent to function as
that mirror…. There is a time in our life…. when we need to be larger than life, a golden
self. And we need to believe that our actual self – the eager, jubilant, preening self we
reveal – is accepted, at least for a little while, as golden.[7]

So, what can be wrong with strutting our stuff?

Here's the rub. My physician friend stated that "95 per cent of my worth, as a person, comes from what I do as a physician." In order to feel good about himself my friend found it necessary to continue being immersed in the lives of patients – not only for their benefit, but his own. What about my friend's wife, or son, or daughter, or friends, or community service, or a personal soul life? In the words of author John Bradshaw, my friend was in danger of becoming a "human doing" rather than a "human being." My friend needed to weave his wonderful qualities and strengths into his life with others – friends and loved ones. He needed a broader canvas upon which to etch his specialness. Do you, like my friend, allow work roles to overly define who you are?

Achievement can become a hiding place for a wounded spirit.

My friend possessed a genuine self worth and esteem, fashioned out of prestigious schools of higher learning, board positions in the community, and a healthy upbringing. He possessed a confidence to speak out vehemently on health care issues – at times creating political conflicts in the wake. He had been blessed with adoring parents, each of whom possessed a robust identity of their own. As parents they would easily pass any test which measured effective parenting. They paid attention, they listened, and they hugged. While they had succeeded in maintaining enduring bonds with each of their children, my friend had somehow gotten off track in his own life.

A far more serious example of taking healthy self esteem too far was the triathlete mentioned in the Introduction of this book. He truly was a physical marvel. Chiseled like an Adonis, conditioned like a fine tuned Harley, and persevering like a modern-day Sisyphus, he cast himself upon the competitive world with genuine self-worth and esteem. Sleek muscles, a vascular system that wouldn't quit, and a resting heart rate of 47 carried him great distances far from home!

He had been dragged into therapy by his wife because he worked out too much. Strangely enough he was too good at what he did and "needed" to maintain both his prowess and his image. He paid the highest price possible. Leaving at 5:00 a.m. and returning home at 8:00 p.m., this guy missed sunrise with his dog, lunch with friends, dinner with his wife, and bedtime with his kids. What's most shocking, of course, is that this Adonis thought all was well. Oh, that narcissistic pool, where we see only our own reflection can be so blinding.

Both my physician friend and the triathlete were in trouble. While both were blessed with inordinate capacities, stunning successes, and adoration from many, each found themselves mired in a self-image which colored too much of their landscape. Even though both "strutted their stuff" and "grooved on grandiosity" quite well, we are reminded once again that uncompromising self-absorption may alienate others while compromising the ultimate good of all. This even occurs when narcissism is built upon healthy self-esteem.

Call it chutzpah, or call it narcissism. Self absorption can kill our relationships.

40 Sacred Years

In life, a healthy tension is maintained between two powerful life forces: Care for self (identity) and care for others (relationship). Two core beliefs anchor this dynamic equilibrium between self and others:

If I do a good job taking care of me, I am freer to take care of you.
If I do a good job taking care of you, there will be plenty left for me.

A tension of opposites exists between these two life forces. There is also necessary loss. If I overindulge myself taking care of "me," there is less of me for thee. If I spend precious time taking care of you, there is less time for me. Unfortunately, many people who take care of others feel resentful that they must give up a piece of themselves.

Maintaining this delicate balance of self versus other is elusive to many of us.

From the beginning of our lives, most of us have experienced the force of others trying to map out our lives – to carve out a piece of our lives! Perhaps it was once a parent. Now, perhaps a spouse. For a teenager, such intrusions are an affront. "This is my life and I need to discover who I am!" Each one of us is a puzzle piece and must discover how we fit into a greater, more meaningful whole. Our "meaningful whole" is this dynamic yin/yang interplay between personal identity and personal relationships. If we live our lives intentionally, we can find the proper balance for both.

We are defined in part by our relationships, but our relationships are certainly defined by us as well. As Dr. Thomas Szasz once put it: "In the animal kingdom, the rule is eat or be eaten; in the human kingdom, define or be defined." If we were wounded during the wobbly innocence of childhood, we are at risk of developing and maintaining a fragile, wounded self – a self which doesn't know itself very well at all.

A fool went to the rabbi and said: "I know I'm a fool, Rabbi, but I don't know what to do about it. Please advise me what to do."

"Ah, my son!" exclaimed the rabbi, in a complementary way. "If you know you're a fool, then you surely are no fool!"

"Then why does everyone say I'm a fool?" complained the man.

The rabbi looked at him thoughtfully for a moment and said: "If you yourself don't understand that you're a fool," he chided him, "but only listen to what people say, then you surely are a fool." [8]

Only a fool would live without a personal identity.

Of course, only a narcissist would live without a love relationship. Life teaches us how to balance the two. We have only 24 hours in a day. We have fixed incomes, fixed schedules, fixed dispositions, and fixed life agendas. We have limited savings, limited resources, and limited options to draw upon. We have limited time. We must make choices. An equitable balance between "strutting our stuff" while meeting the needs of others can only be maintained over time with "sacrifice," one of the *Six Gifts* presented in chapter 19. It is possible to celebrate healthy ego and narcissistic strengths but only within the context of limitation and sacrifice.

We generally have 40 fruitful years to rise above our narcissistic inclinations.

Some people have many more; others have frightfully few. From the time most of us emerge from college – at age 22 – till the time some of us retire from work – at age 62 – we have five significant opportunities to expand beyond our own ego, our own self-absorption. *First*, we learn to be productive. *Second*, we create and maintain an enduring love with a significant other. *Third*, we procreate and learn to nurture children. *Fourth*, we learn to give to our communities. *Fifth*, we create a spiritual relationship with a higher power. Some of us learn to do all five quite well. For others, there is only struggle!

It is in these middle years – these golden 40 years – that we best serve the needs of others while fulfilling ourselves. I realize the spectrum from age 22 to 62 appears to be a capricious one. I certainly realize that many do not go to college and that the average number of years to graduate is five or more years these days. I also realize that close to 33% of all young adults end up moving back in with mom and dad by the age of 25 – and some never leave. Nonetheless, there must be some societal standard for launching oneself into adulthood, a time and a place where the "I want...," "Give me...," and "Buy me..." mentality of childhood and adolescence fades. There must be a time when young adults don't view older adults as breast extenders, who exist merely to give.

I realize that many people do not retire at 62 and that many "boomers" choose to continue working for many reasons. I also realize that it is common belief that the golden years are the giving years. Yet, at 62 we are empty nesters, downsizers, and almost qualifiers for Social Security. I also know the research findings that retirement at age 62 is hazardous to the health of men – too much time, not enough friends! Nonetheless, the sunset years past the age of 62 often represent a period when the average person turns inward to deal with aging, health care concerns, financial worries, and personal leisure or hygiene needs. This is often a time, being aware of time, to fulfill personal dreams heretofore unmet: e.g., travel, hobbies, even a second career.

For many, our golden years are focused more on bowel movements rather than protest movements, walking ability more than upward mobility, pill-popping more than thrill-stopping. The gray haired servant volunteering his or her way through the twilight years is a wondrous exception to the rule. Narcissism is even destined to rule the day in our latter days.

Seeing the absorbing ravages of old age is enough to wake up any baby boomer.

We, like our forbears, see the role reversals that come with aging parents. While my own parents didn't survive past the age of 50, I do see the turning inward for Sophie, Claire's mother. Her days of giving are no longer seen at Thanksgiving. Making lasagna for the family has morphed into making it to the bathroom in time. A once-doting grandmother now clings to her walker rather than a crib. Childhood rearing has now become anticipatory fearing. The Christmas shopping has ended and sudden falls have become frantic calls. Sadly, "How are you?" has become "What about me?" Independent living begets dependent living, which begets a desperate need for a secure hold on something, someone. Survival needs are, by definition, self-absorbing.

Sky is no longer the limit for someone losing ground.

We all know the feeling of losing ground. We needn't be 90 to experience the free fall. During these times of disharmony, each of us – like Sophie – must find that core within ourselves that calls to us….that core which beckons and resolutely declares, "I know who I am; I know who I love; and I love the way they fit together."

Ultimately we must ask if we have been as true to ourselves as others.

The Danish philosopher Soren Kierkegaard argued that the most common human despair was to be in despair at not choosing or willing to be oneself. I believe the ultimate despair lies in choosing to be someone other than oneself! Being special entails a process of being who we truly are, without the socially sanctioned need to hide behind masks. For my friend, the physician, all that was needed was a gentle reminder that it is here, in our love relationships, that we find our true selves… It is here that we become known for "who we are" rather than "what we do". It is here that we find safe harbor from the storms that life brings. It is here that we find refuge from ourselves and the havoc we wreak upon ourselves.

Life on a narcissistic continuum is balanced only when we are embedded in the lives of others.

Many forces upset this precarious balance. In the last chapter we explored how self-addiction, with all its obsessions and cravings, often denies love's bloom. In the next chapter, we will unveil what our philosophers and religious leaders have known about us for thousands of years – that the Seven Deadly Sins represent an expression of love that, somehow, has gone badly.

CHAPTER **4**

Seven Deadly Sins

THE TREES

There is unrest in the forest; there is trouble with the trees.
For the maples want more sunlight and the oaks ignore their pleas.
The trouble with maples,
{And they're quite convinced they're right}
They say the oaks are just too lofty and they grab up all the light.
But the oaks can't help their feelings if they like the way they're made
And they wonder why the maples can't be happy in their shade.
There is trouble in the forest and the creatures all have fled,
As the maples scream "oppression" and the oaks just shake their heads.
So the maples formed a union and demanded equal rights.
"The oaks are just too greedy. We'll make them give us light."
Now there's no more oak oppression for they passed a noble law,
And the trees are all kept equal
By Hatchet, Axe and Saw.[1]

The Seven "Deadly" Sins

While surfing the internet one day I happened upon Josef Rosenberg, who cynically opined that "People have always been immoral, shiftless, self-gratifying, shits. But for ages, human-kind struggled to find a conceptual system to operationalize their spiritual shortcomings. The challenge was formidable. The system had to be complex and inclusive enough to implicate a vast range of disgusting behavior, yet simple and memorable enough to inspire guilt in an illiterate peasant."[2] This system of spiritual shortcomings was the fourth century's equivalent of the Diagnostic and Statistical Manual of Mental Disorders (DSM) used by mental health professionals today.

Is this mere cynicism or a blast of harsh reality?

We can see that narcissism is indeed a life force, which can be pared down into bite-size categories inclusive enough to capture every man and woman. Cynics like Rosenberg easily believe that the Church, for centuries, has been able to parlay these normal characteristics of mankind and "market" them as "deadly sins." This certainly has enhanced the power of the Church in as much as every religion demands recurrent rituals to exact repentance for narcissistic outbreaks. Recurrent rituals would be needed for centuries to come in order to deal with shameful incrimination and guilt. The human species has been corralled for centuries in this way.

The point is clear enough. Clergy have known forever that our Achilles heel is self-gratification. Given its consummate authority and influence at the time, the Church long ago decided to categorize our "obsession with self" into neat cubbyholes. Doctoral degrees, knowledge of research design, and sophisticated factorial analyses were not required to pull this off.

Evagrius of Ponticus, a Greek, monastic theologian, got things fired up pretty well around 370 A.D. with his original list of eight offenses and wicked human passions, listing them in order of increasing seriousness: gluttony, lust, avarice, sadness, anger, acedia, vainglory, and pride. Acedia, from the Greek word "akedia," meant not to care, an early likeness to indifference and spiritual sloth. Evagrius believed the increasing severity in the list represented more and more fixation on self, with pride as the most egregious of all. There it is. Fixation on self! Narcissistic self-absorption! Pride is the ultimate psychic whirlpool which entrapped the Emperor, who was lured by the power of gold.

Evagrius' work stimulated a great deal of thinking and writing for centuries. In the late 6th Century, Pope Gregory the Great simplified the list to seven sins, subsuming vainglory into pride, acedia into sadness and adding envy. Eventually, sloth was substituted for the vague sin of sadness. Pope Gregory was able to classify the sins in such a way that they were able to describe a classification system of the normal perils of the soul in the most ordinary conditions of life.

One needn't be either evangelical or cynic to see the importance of understanding sin. Evagrius and Pope Gregory really got it.

They understood that each of us lives our lives with a hole in it, an empty place I have called the "missing ten degrees."

When we plumb these depths we find that the trappings of life fail us, leaving us desperately hungry for something else to fill the hollow. If we are blessed, if indeed our eyes are wide open, one day we may find the courage to look inward – deeply inward – to find that sliver of humanity which eternally and perhaps infinitely connects us to all things. Or, perhaps this is the place where sin corrupts and causes its upheaval and devastation – a place where slick Gucci handbags, Thierry Rabotin snakeskin shoes, and internet porn exist.

The real brilliance of the Seven Deadly Sins is that one did not have to be secluded in a monastery to envision these perils, because while they were often viewed as very serious cardinal sins by clergy a normal continuum existed that mirrored normal society. This banality, if you will, was captured well by Geoffrey Chaucer in his Canterbury Tales over 700 years ago. As we tune into the story lines of the Parson's Tale we hear about 1) excessive and extravagant spending of rubles on fashion and clothing, 2) the greediness of property owners, 3) the decadence of fine dining, 4) the deceit of merchants and retailers, 5) the neglect of children, 6) and the vainglory of humiliating a friend through gossip. Sound familiar? If you have watched any soap operas recently, you will find Chaucer's observations well documented throughout the "sinful" plots and storylines of today's society as well.

You may have noticed in your life that all of the Seven Deadly Sins are bound together like siblings in a dysfunctional family system. They are leashed together within an interlocking matrix that binds us for a lifetime. While many of us may display gluttony on one occasion, or excessive lust on yet another, deep within us lies an inherent potentiality or inclination to sin in all seven sinful ways. Repression is not an option. In this vein, the sins are similar to emotional states within us – vibrant limbic bursts which cannot be suppressed singularly without smothering an entire family of affective aliveness.

In an extraordinary move, Pope Gregory also had the cosmic wisdom to rank the seriousness of these seven sins by the degree to which each blighted the concept of love: Pride, Envy, Anger, Sloth, Avarice, Gluttony, and Lust. Essentially, the Seven Deadly Sins represent an expression of love that, somehow, has gone awry. Over 1400 years ago Pope Gregory had the sense to know that narcissism as a life force, if played out to an extreme, could tarnish its polar opposite: love. That is, self-absorption could compromise our capacity to care for and to love one another.

This was absolutely brilliant.

Pride, Envy, and Anger all represent a *perverted* love – that is, while pleasing or satisfying ourselves we cause harm to others. Sloth can be viewed as a *defective* love – love not given in proper measure. Avarice, Gluttony and Lust may be viewed as sins of *excessive* love – that is, as expressions of self-gratification that destroy one's capacity to love another. The first three are often viewed as "cold sins" because they can ruthlessly devalue and reject a sense of community with others. We hear the words, "I am," "I want," and "I hate" with the first three. The last three, because they at least capture some involvement with others, are often viewed as "warm" sins.[3]

The Church understood that sin has little to do with a pattern of behavior but rather a very basic existential attitude. This is the key to opening up our understanding even further. A fixation on oneself is nothing more than a collapse inward, which is the ultimate tragedy. For we human beings are intended, are wired, to be in relation to other human beings. This collapse inward is captured quite well by Shirley MacLaine in an interview with The Washington Post in 1977:

> The most pleasurable journey you take is through yourself...that the only sustaining love involvement is with yourself. When you look back on your life and try to figure out where you've been and where you are going, when you look at your work, your love affairs, your marriages, your children, your pain, your happiness — when you examine all that closely, what you really find out is that the only person you really go to bed with is yourself....The only thing you have is working toward the consummation of your own identity.[4]

Self identity! ME! ME! ME! MacLaine represents the egoism, the self-centeredness, the self-absorption that brings narcissism to a new level. She suggests that the people in our lives, not to mention love itself, are nothing more than a logical extension of our incessant need to aggrandize ourselves, to affirm our selves throughout an entire lifetime. What a painful loss of spirit, solicitude, and love.

In order to understand MacLaine's self-absorption, Christian writers remind us that humankind has "fallen" and ask that we understand this drama through the lives of Adam and Eve, who are made in the image of God, are sinless, and are set down in a perfect place. In a story line we know so well from Genesis 3:1-7, Eve succumbs to the serpent, Adam succumbs to Eve, and the forbidden fruit becomes an esophageal nightmare for eternity. We hear the seductive invocation from the serpent, "You will not die; for God knows that when you eat of it your eyes will be opened, you will be like God, knowing good and evil." And then, in the blink of a cosmic second, nakedness, guilt, and an exodus from Paradise become our destiny. This is the "Fall."

It behooves us to remember that not all of us are Christians. One needn't be a Christian to realize the secular importance of being able to draw a moral line. "Morality like art," says G.K. Chesterton, "consists of drawing a line somewhere."[5] Even nonbelievers must wrestle with the incessant, oceanic forces which beckon us – forces we call free will or responsible choice or just plane character.

Each of us fails and each of us falls.

There is optimism in the notion that once we accept our "sinful nature," and even perhaps our helplessness in eradicating this aspect of our nature, we are free to make choices which enhance our own integrity as well as our capacity to love. By accepting that we fundamentally are "not OK," we are at the horizon line where being "not OK" is "OK." Henry Fairlie states that, "To say that our natures are inclined to do evil is very different from saying that we are doomed to do evil. The first is a doctrine of hope and choice, the second a doctrine of despair and abdication."[6]

With hope in mind let's look inward at the Seven Deadly Sins.

Pride (vs. Humility)

Welcome to the mother load of all sins!

The Latin word for pride is superbia (sounds like suburbia, doesn't it!) which means "aiming at what is above." This quest to be "above" is the heart of the problem. Webster's dictionary defines pride as "an inordinate self-esteem," while the Oxford English Dictionary views pride as "...an unreasonable conceit of superiority....an overweening opinion of one's own qualities."

What can be wrong with this? Singer Jack Ingram echoed this sentiment quite well in an Austin Chronicle Interview in 2005: "Is it overly ambitious to look at what my heroes have accomplished and want the same? We have halls of fame all over this country. They erect those statues for a reason. It's so people can look at them and be inspired...I want to sell millions of records and play music for 50 years. I want to die that way. I don't want to work my ass off and not see the results I think I can. I believe I'm going to see the results. I do."

Well, Jack, while I do wish you much success, I'm not sure a statue or other forms of idolatry are in your interest or mine for that matter. Again I must remind us of Robert Johnson's warning that once we put someone on a pedestal we put them out of human reach. There is something inherently narcissistic about "towering" over others – be it stardom, kingdom, or martyrdom.

A tower is perhaps the most visual and common symbol or metaphor for Pride. A proud person primps and props himself up, and in doing so, sets himself apart from others. It is this separation from one's human brotherhood that makes Pride a "cold" vacuous sin. A prideful person seeks loftiness and inaccessibility. When we say that someone towers over us we believe that they are out of reach.

There even seems to be a universal "pride expression," according to researchers Jessica Tracy and Rick Robins at the University of California.[7] Their studies suggest that pride is one of the basic human emotions and actually serves an important social role. While there is not a unique smile to pride, there is a unique posture! The head tilts back, the chest puffs out, and the hands are often placed on one's hips or are raised high in the air as if one is crossing a goal line in football. This posturing is universal. We saw it in the bold public persona of George W. Bush, while children as young as four years old from East Africa are able to identify the pride expression correctly in their peers.

There is sometimes a thin line between a healthy pride, which is built upon healthy self-esteem, and an arrogant conceit which separates one from one's community. The first kind of pride can be productive while the second is clearly linked to narcissism. People demonstrating a healthy pride credit their behavior, their effort, for their success, while people demonstrating a more narcissistic pride, credit themselves.

The celebration of effort is "OK"; it is the glorification of a self that is "Not!" George O'Leary, the former Notre Dame coach, learned this the hard way. In a span of 86 hours O'Leary rose to the pinnacle of college coaching as the head coach for the iconic Fighting Irish, only to topple and fall from his towering perch once it was discovered that he had padded his resume to look good. Mr. O'Leary had stated that he played varsity football while an undergraduate at the University of New Hampshire and had received a master's degree as well.

By the time the Manchester Union Leader, a local press, got finished with Mr. O'Leary, we learned that no one could remember O'Leary's ever playing for the school, let alone lettering. And sadly, the master's degree was found to be a prop as well for an ego that only needed a willing audience to fester. The problem with George O'Leary, and perhaps most of us, is that once we create a prideful image of our selves we are often imprisoned by it. So why do we do it? What fuels this madness? Praise! Praise has become the modern day serpent which seduces us, beguiles us, and distorts us.

We have even been taught to believe that praising one's child is a good thing. By telling a child that he or she is "smart," "gifted," or "talented" we think that this constant praise is life-enriching by symbolically putting an angel on their shoulder, ensuring that they do not sell their talents short. Eighty-five percent of us think this is the right thing to do. Research by Carol Dweck has now revealed just the opposite effect.

Dweck and her Columbia University team found that giving kids the label of "smart" does not prevent them from underperforming; it might actually be causing them to underperform! When children who performed well at a task were told that they did well because they were "smart," they actually made a choice to do a less difficult task next. By comparison, when another group of children were told that they did well because they "worked hard," they chose a more difficult task next. This is why gifted children, for decades, have severely underestimated their own abilities.[8]

The prideful essence of all this research is that once we burden children with the crown of royalty, the robes of grandeur, or the pedestal of greatness it becomes too much to bear for many of them. These kids give up, go away, and throw in the towel. Why not? After all, this gift of praise really isn't intended for the child at all. Praise is really a gift that the prideful parent bestows upon him or herself. It is the prideful parent who regales at the knowledge that he or she is the progenitor of such an exceptional human being. It is this parental pride which burdens the lives of so many innocents by instilling a belief that one's ideal self should be greater than one's real self.

Envy (vs. Acceptance)

The look of envy is always about the eyes.

Catherine Zeta-Jones is an eye popper to most admirers. According to Dr. Toby G. Mayer, co-director of the Beverly Hills Institute of Aesthetic and Reconstructive Surgery, "She has sexy eyes. She's got great eyebrow position; the shape is fantastic; and you don't see a lot of her eyelid. She's open on the inner part of the eye, but the outer part is low. When you're young and that area is filled with plump skin, it looks attractive."[9]

Tunnel vision like this puts "keeping up with the Joneses" in a new light!

How many women have looked upon Catherine Zeta-Jones, not with joyful celebration and wonder, but with envy? The word envy comes from the Latin invidia, which means to "look maliciously upon" – to literally possess an "evil eye" toward another. Of all the sins, envy is considered by many to be the nastiest, most morbid, and most mean-spirited of all. Simply put, there just doesn't seem to be a happy ending with envy. Unlike the other sins, gratification seems elusive, leaving us endlessly tormented and yearning for what we don't have. We become self-absorbed over something that is missing, yet possessed by someone else we somehow admire.

Envy is all about grief.

We grieve over the "missing ten degrees." But envy is not merely a grieving over another's blessings; it is a grieving over that which is missing in oneself. This is the essence of envy as a sin. As Henry Fairlie states, "Merely to grieve that one does not have something that another has is not envy. It is a sin when the envious person wishes that the other did not have it, so that he himself might not suffer his imaginary disadvantage."[10] It is this imaginary disadvantage which drives us to do a myriad of crazy things.

Dermatologists refer to this "disadvantage," this misperception, this obsession, as body dysmorphia and make anywhere from $2,500 to $11,000 per procedure to deal with it. Vanity drives us into surgical gowns and outpatient clinics because we feel inadequate and believe we are disadvantaged. In 2005, 250,000 healthy women elected to enlarge their breasts with saline implants. Still others choose Botox, one of the most poisonous substances known, to smooth out any perceived "crevice" in the facial area. Thousands upon thousands of people, compensating for an imaginary disadvantage, allow a professional to fill a syringe with a highly diluted form of this killing agent.

This same culture woos men into using Viagra and other erectile enhancing drugs to boost tumescent egos and flagging self-esteem. Men have now become the equivalent of hood ornaments – with bulging pectoral and trapezius muscles, ripped abs, and hairless torsos of marble statuary. A culture, screaming inadequacy at us with banner headlines, often read, "Last longer in bed," "Satisfy better with bigger," or "Look better with less." Many men lie face down on message tables as cosmetologists rip strips of hair-removing wax off their backs in order to compete in an imaginary market place where we are "green with envy" over what others possess, how they look, or what they are able to do.

As with all the other sins, there is a continuum with envy. Where is the line that separates coloring one's hair vs. having a radical face lift, or where is the line which delineates braces for one's teeth from radical mandibular jaw reconstruction or breast augmentation? The trend toward narcissism is real and is still the culture that Ellen Goodman believes "is stacked against us."

At its worst, envy is a zero sum game. Somehow we believe that another person's happiness or success diminishes our own. We feel threatened, become self-absorbed about being "less than," and look for ways to tear them down, whether through gossip or good old-fashioned competition among equals in the market place. A pleasure center in our brain, the ventral striatum, even lights up with joy when we see envied others have a downfall. Sadly, the misfortunes of others are often our sweet taste of honey.

A fatal flaw lurks in a society where our goal is to pull others down, rather than pulling people up.

Anger (vs. Forgiveness)

On June 28th, 1997, heavyweight fighter Mike Tyson was disqualified for biting off a piece of Evander Holyfield's ear in their World Boxing Association title match at the MGM Grand Hotel Casino in Las Vegas, Nevada. Yes, iron Mike Tyson actually bit off another man's ear as cameras snapped away, capturing for eternity, an image of a man apparently gone mad. A Nevada boxing commission suspended him, a district attorney interviewed him, a doctor did a blood test on him, and Evander Holyfield wanted to sue him. All this commotion inside the ring led to a brawl outside the ring that left 40 people injured or hospitalized after fights broke out in restaurants, bathrooms, and VIP lounges.

What got into Iron Mike, the "baddest man of the decade"?

On June 14th, 1998 thousands of people came by foot, by jet, and by caravan to bury James Byrd, Jr., an open-hearted black man whose only crime was being black. His unimaginable, barbaric death behind a piston-powered, anger-fueled, whiplashing truck became an immediate wake-up call for a town, for a State, and for a country to examine its soul. How could a disabled man who always seemed to carry a song in his heart be dragged to his death by three white ex-convicts in Jasper, Texas – a small, tranquil setting of 7,800 townsfolk who had no history of racial tensions?

What sinister forces got into these three brutal men?

There is a buildup of tensions in each of the above dramas. Unseen forces lurk in very dark crevices. What are the forces that shape cruelty, racism, and retaliation? How does someone unknown become an irritant, then a frustration, then a source of anger, then a source of rage, and finally, a source of fury?

It is not the emotion of anger which is the sin. We all have limbic systems where anger, as a feeling, can be triggered. It is not the flash of lightning, the constriction of striated muscles, or the shattering clap of thunder which makes anger "sinful." Each of us can lose our temper – very justifiably at times when we feel powerless and sense a futility in getting our needs met. While anger can be viewed as a normal feeling, it is safe to say that it is the least intimate of all our feelings. Anger, more than any other emotion, alienates people and distances them from us.

I see it in my office every day. A line is crossed. Resentments that are stored up over time burst forth – creating outbursts that alienate others and compromise the well-being of all. It is this slow burn, the storing up of resentments, the obsessive rumination, and a compulsive seeking of revenge that crosses the line.

Perhaps there is something deeper than stored-up resentments which drive anger?

According to the journal, *Current Biology*, we may be hard wired for violence.[11] The March 2007 issue actually reported that chimpanzees have been observed making spears from branches in order to kill defenseless, nocturnal bush babies. Even the noted anthropologist, Dr. Jane Goodall, observed how brutal and calculatingly violent chimps could be as they hunted and killed monkeys for food. She even documented a four-year war between rival chimpanzee colonies. We must wonder, if chimps are hard wired for violence, are humans hard wired for war? Is it in our nature?

Nature not only hardwires us for anger, but reason as well.

Release from our self absorbed inner torment is possible only if we learn to forgive one another.

Each of us is capable of far more rational thought, more reasonability, and more forgiveness. Ironically, the refusal to forgive perpetuates resentment, and the true victim of resentment is always the one who refuses to forgive. Neither resentment nor forgiveness is a feeling. Both are willing choices. One leads us into the cauldron of anger, while the other guides us to freedom. They are akin to fire and water. The water will either put the fire out, or the fire will vaporize the water.

The choice is ours.

Sloth (vs. Compassion)

During the 1960's one murder case stood alone in its ability to shock this country. The victim was an ordinary young woman named "Kitty" Genovese, the 28 year-old daughter of Italian-American parents. What happened to Kitty Genovese that fateful night, what happened to all of American society that horrific night, would reverberate across the country for decades and generate a national soul-searching that continues to this day.

On March 13, 1964, Kitty Genovese had just parked her red Fiat in the Long Island Railroad parking lot which was a mere 20 feet from her New York City apartment door. As she locked her car door she noticed a man approaching her quickly from out of the shadows. In a matter of moments the man caught up with Kitty Genovese and proceeded to stab her to death over the course of an hour or more. It was not the gruesomeness of the crime that the country responded to but rather the lack of responsiveness by those living in the neighborhood that horrified so many.

Reportedly, 38 "witnesses" failed to call the police to save Kitty Genovese.

What accounted for this horrific apathy? Why didn't someone step up, take responsibility and call the police? Among the many psychological explanations for the "Kitty Genovese Syndrome" were the (1) bystander effect and (2) the diffusion of responsibility effect. The first theory speculates that as the number of bystanders increases, the likelihood of any one bystander's intervening decreases, while the second theory suggests simply enough that there is a decrease in the feeling of personal responsibility when one is in the presence of many other people. In the presence of many other people, it is more likely that any one individual will do nothing to help.

Among the Seven Deadly Sins the morbid inertia just described is referred to as Sloth, or Acedia in Greek, meaning literally, "no care." I don't care! Sloth is laziness, a kind of disengagement, by which we abstain, we move away from our commitment to love one another. We don't protect the heartfelt interests of one another. With Sloth we die a little bit each day. In the words of W. H. Tilman:

Strenuousness is the immortal path. Sloth is the way of death.

While Pride can be viewed as a narcissistic attempt to be more than human; Sloth can be understood as a narcissistic attempt to be less than human. If Pride seeks the coronation, Sloth seeks to escape the Kingdom. Sloth is about apathy, a state of indifference, which Henry Fairlie captures quite well:

> *I mind my own business! Live and let live! Nothing is worth getting very serious about, except one's own wants at the moment in one's own immediate environment. I'm Ok, you're Ok. So what reason is there to worry? It is the sin that believes in nothing, cares for nothing, seeks to know nothing, interferes with nothing, enjoys nothing, hates nothing, finds purpose in nothing, lives for nothing, and remains alive because there is nothing for which it will die.*[12]

Sloth is a paralysis. Like deer in the headlights, we are often blinded by our own agendas and mantras. We become paralyzed. It was this same paralysis that epitomized the hubris of many elitists who set sail on the Titanic in 1912. While some people acted heroically on that fateful day many others chose to watch "effortlessly" as many others drowned. In the words of columnist, Richard Cohen, "The sinking of the Titanic thus sank the romantic ideal of who we are and how we will behave when threatened. Whether on the ocean or on land, most chose not to hear the screams of the doomed. This is the greatest luck of all: the luck of selfishness. It is one, as the Titanic tragedy showed early in our century, that most of us have in abundance."[13]

Avarice (vs. Sacrifice)

Most Texas school administrators are not privileged enough to be driving a brand new Lincoln Navigator, purchased with public taxpayer money. Nor do most publicly funded schools spend thousands of taxpayer dollars at five-star hotels in Madrid and London. And most publicly funded schools are watching their pennies so carefully that electronic purchases at the Sharper Image would be out of the question. But then again, Dolores Hillyer was not a typical public school administrator here in Texas, nor was the Texas Academy of Excellence a typical school!

In August of 2004, Ronnie Earle, Travis County's District Attorney, decided to ask Ms. Hillyer some very difficult questions regarding the school's finances. Mr. Earle wanted to know why the Academy had become the first charter school to file for bankruptcy in Texas, why payroll checks were bouncing, why money deducted from teacher's paychecks for taxes and retirement funds was missing, and why a former landlord was chasing down hundreds of thousands of dollars from the school for illegally breaking a five-year lease. Mr. Earle was also curious about why a bank card used by the school showed $1,195.65 worth of expenses at the Sharper Image, $648.49 at Neiman Marcus and $470 for University of Texas athletic tickets. It turned out that Mr. Earle was not alone in his curiosity. The Texas Education Agency, which passed out about $340 million to 281 charter schools in 2004, also got their dander up!

What got into Ms. Hillyer?

Fast forward to 2006 and we'll find retired physician, Dr. Max Wells, apparently spending big money in Las Vegas. He had a "personal host," received free first class airfare, hotel suites, an Alaskan cruise, meals and shopping trips by several casinos. Within a matter of months, Dr. Wells was somehow able to gamble away $14 MILLION in various casinos. Rather than looking inward to examine himself, there really was only one course of action for Dr. Wells. He sued GlaxoSmithKline, a major drug company, which made the prescription drug he was taking for Parkinson's disease. Dr. Wells and his ace legal team had found evidence that the Mayo Clinic had documented 11 Parkinson's patients who developed compulsive gambling habits while taking Mirapex, To top it off, Dr. Wells also sued Mandalay, Treasure Island, Bellagio, Wynn Las Vegas, Las Vegas Sands, Harrah's, and Hard Rock Hotel. The lawsuit asserted that the casinos should have been aware of the Mayo study. For Dr. Wells and his ace legal team, it was the casino's responsibility to monitor appropriate gambling patterns of their clientele!

Do you sense an underlying force which may be at play here besides a deck of cards? Both Ms. Hillyer and Dr. Wells appear to have had an obsession regarding money. On the one hand, Ms. Hillyer had a yearning to spend what she didn't have while Dr. Wells spent too much of what he did have. Both lived lives distorted by the glitter of gold. Both soon learned that having an abundance of possessions or financial capital is not the same as having an abundant life. Both succumbed to the Midas touch and had their humanity compromised.

Research shows a zero correlation between money and happiness.

According to theologian, Mel Wheatley, the arithmetic of affluence should go something like this: if one barn makes a man ten percent happy, then it make sense that ten barns – or some equivalent – should make the same man one hundred percent happy. We know it doesn't work that way. Our 21st Century generations easily have ten times more than any preceding generation, and we certainly don't see more happiness.

Avarice is self-absorption in monetary terms and we are distorted by it. In the words of Henry Fairlie, "If one is too rich, one is never really in charge of one's life; the possessing has taken over."[14]

Gluttony (vs. Vision)
Typical of how he plays golf, John Daly holds nothing back in his book, *John Daly: My life In and Out of the Rough*. Daly candidly describes how he lost 60 pounds in college by smoking three packs of cigarettes and drinking a fifth of whisky a day. Lustful exploits involving his four wives are also "fleshed out" in his book. He even admits to losing somewhere between $50 million and $60 million during a 12-year run of heavy gambling, and owed $4 million to a variety of casinos until he won the 1995 British Open. Humbly enough, Daly also acknowledges "conduct unbecoming a professional," an admission that he does not exemplify the best of the Professional Golfers Association.

Yet he remains one of the most popular sports figures in America. People relate so well to Daly because his gluttonous flaws are our flaws. In some way he is every man and every woman. In an era when celebrities – indeed, all of us – attempt to hide anything that would be disparaging, every wrinkle beneath a face lift, Daly hides nothing.

Daly and many others put both their money and countless calories where their mouth is! In some cases this is a McDonald's-made-me-fat lawsuit as we saw in 2005 when two over-weight, self-absorbed New York teens realized that they weren't gluttonous, they were victims. After scarfing down McDonald's burgers and fries several times a week for years, these two young men, ramped up by their ace team of plaintiff attorneys, asserted that they were victims of corporate malfeasance because McDonalds deceives customers about its products.

How wide-spread is gluttony? Well, we now know that girls who have a high "body mass index" (BMI) as young as three years old enter puberty earlier as a result of this excess weight. Two-thirds of Americans are overweight, and Corpus Christi, Texas, is considered the fattest city in the United States with one third of its population considered "obese." Houston, we have a problem.

What's really going on here with all this eating and drinking and smoking?

There is pain, hollowness, and discomfort in life that we ought to be able to tolerate. In-stead we look for ways to minimize pain and maximize immediate pleasure. Food, alcohol, and other substances produce altered states which numb our feelings and distance us from everyone around us. Even boredom, which often is a deeper emptiness, can't be tolerated for very long. Instead of looking into the void within our lives, we buy and consume more and more to fill up the emptiness and give ourselves a sense of worth.

We are obsessed with both Craig Claiborne cook books and Jane Fonda diet books. Cook-ing, as a self-interest is one thing; but gluttony is another. It is our constant never-ending preoccupation with food that makes it a sin. People in our lives who are too steeped in thought about themselves seldom have the time or inclination to take much interest in others. Ironi-cally, the anorexic or bulimic person suffers from this same preoccupation. The eyes of both are fixated not just on the bathroom scales but rather on the mirror.

Psychologist Laura Park of the University of Buffalo has developed the appearance-based rejection sensitivity scale (ARS) that measures the extent to which people anxiously expect to be rejected by others based on their looks. In a 2007 study Park discovered that women in her sample not only avoided food, they avoided every meaningful relationship in their life – for fear of rejection. (15) These women lived each day, mired in obsessive self reproach, spiraling down-ward into a hellacious "room of doom." When these same women were taught to let in positive affirmations and to renew their closest relationships, they felt better about themselves.

So we see that any extreme regarding food intake, whether gluttony or restriction, actu-ally distances us from others. The driving force for both is a desperate and inordinate need for self-love. The irony, as we have seen with all the Seven Deadly Sins, is that our self-absorption removes us from the very love we crave.

Gluttony and Lust are the only sins that abuse something that is essential for our very sur-vival. It is right that they stand together for in neither do we truly see the object of our desire. Instead we are held captive only by the burning desire itself. It is to Lust that we now turn.

Lust (vs. Love)
Dateline, January 24, 2007: Israel's attorney general said Tuesday that he would charge Moshe

Katsav, President of Israel, with raping a former office assistant and sexually harassing three other employees in the President's office.

Dateline, November 4th, 2006: The Reverend Ted Haggard of Colorado Springs said Friday that he bought methamphetamine and received a massage from a male prostitute. Haggard, once president of the National Association of Evangelicals, wielded influence on Capitol Hill and condemned both gay marriage and homosexuality.

Dateline, November 18th, 2006: When Louis "Bill" Conradt put a bullet in his brain November 5th, he may have lost two lives. The first was a public life in Texas which included more than 20 years as a prosecutor in Kaufman and Rockwell counties. The second life was that of a "hidden" personality who used the internet at least once in an attempt to entice someone, he thought was a 13-year-old boy, into having sex.

Six patterns are evident in these tragic motifs. First, there is the element of risk, where lustful longing has no thoughts of consequences. Second, there is preoccupation, where lust has become a solitary, self-absorbed journey. We have moved from a Victorian age repression to a modern day obsession. Third, there is objectification, where lust transforms warm-hearted and soulful human beings into objects of desire. We lust for or after someone, not with someone. Fourth, there is temporality, where the half life of lust is measured in multiple orgasmic moments rather than relationship years. Fifth, there is the altered state, where lust and the pursuit of pleasure has usurped reason. Sixth, there is impersonalization where we can self-stimulate by a quick push of a button on a keyboard which searches millions upon millions of internet porn sites, each capable of triggering a quick release.

For President Katsav, the Reverend Haggard, and Prosecutor Conradt, lust took little pause in thinking through possible consequences. These heads of state were clearly not using the right cranial cavity. The thrill of the chase, the titillation of arousal, and the immediate joy of orgasmic release dominated their actions as well as their relationships, their careers — even their lives. While power corrupts, lust erupts and disrupts. Lust cares not about college transcripts, university diplomas, or reverence. Each of us, regardless of status or stature, is vulnerable to its siren call.

Just as the pursuit of excellence is not sinful, neither is intense passion, longing, or desire. These for sure are part of nature's blessings. So where is the line that distinguishes lust from love? Henry Fairlie once again helps us here:

> *Lust is NOT interested in its partners, but only in the gratification of its own craving, not in the satisfaction of our whole natures, but only in the appeasement of an appetite that we are unable to subdue. It is a form of self-emptying. Love has meaning only insofar as it includes the idea of its continuance....Love wants to enjoy in other ways the human being whom it has enjoyed in bed. In contrast, lust is always furtive. It dresses as mechanically as it undresses and heads straight for the door, to return to its solitude....Lust does not come with open hands and certainly not with an open heart. It comes only with open legs.*[16]

We are driven to lust by our genes, according to Richard Dawkins in *The Selfish Gene*. Lust is a genetic power plant that thrusts us into the continuous practice of sex – a direct consequence of a woman's concealed ovulation. We humans engage in sex on any day of the month not knowing if fertility awaits us. Sure we can say it's just for fun, but our genes know better. As we will learn in the next chapter: "The fundamental unit of selection and therefore of self-interest, is not the species, nor the group, nor even the individual. It is the gene, the unit of heredity."[17]

The sad news for men is that we think we're in control of the courtship/lusting process, but evolution has appointed a different master of ceremonies.

From an evolutionist point of view, not even the promiscuity aspect of lust is "sinful," it is natural. It is nature's calling. But nature alone does not control us. Each of us is capable of forming love bonds which convey true caring. We are capable of blending love with lust, like no other species on the planet. In Hebrew, the word yada means both "to know" and "to have sexual relations with." For our sexuality to be normal, we must create a sacred union between our longing and our knowing.

This blending of lust and love is the "mature covenant love" of Chapter Thirteen. Mature, covenant love is the crucible in which our "sinful nature" is revealed and healed. As we will see in the last section of this book, the *Six Gifts* are the tools we can learn to use in this redemptive process. Before we turn to these healing *Gifts*, however, we must first understand the roots of our self-absorption. It is time to explore nature, nurture, and culture.

THE ROOTS OF NARCISSISM

Our genes have a voice which must be heard. Can you imagine approaching our solar system's sun, sternly putting your hands on your hips, and asserting that the sun must stop hurling its billowing rays our way? We're too hot in the summer, and we would like a break! A little pompous, don't you think? The sun is an irrepressible force which won't burn out for many millions of years. This same tenacity is true of our genes. Their persistence, their obstinance, is what often makes therapy so difficult for me, not to mention my clients. Section Two of this book looks at the forces that shape our lives.

Like a mighty oak tree, each of us is fed by a narcissistic root system which encourages our growth – as well as our retardation; glorious blooms – as well as blighted decay; protective umbrage – as well as deciduous droppings. Simply stated, I have observed that nature, nurture, and culture conspire against us and forever flow into our narcissistic pool often making us appear "Not OK" in the eyes of our loved ones. I further believe that, within our culture, three of the most significant shaping forces are our leaders, our therapists/gurus, and our religious doctrines.

We will reveal the mysteries of how these five root systems influence our personal growth as well as our interpersonal health over a lifetime. *First*, the chapter on nature shows that survival of the fittest may not be very pretty. *Second*, in the chapter on nurture, it becomes clear that deep inside us, intricately entwined in the fabric of our being, resides an "inner child" who may torment us – as well as our partners – for years. *Third*, self-absorbed leaders are often too tunnel-visioned to see the wider swath before them. *Fourth*, the "self-love" movement, enmeshed in self-esteem building, may have blinded us. *Fifth*, I propose that "hope" is about vision, "religion" is about power, and "God" is about love.

In our culture, where "me-ness" trumps "we-ness," contemplation gets distorted. Love, as imperfect as it may be, is our answer – if we permit to be. Love, like out-stretched branches of the mighty oak, invite us to reach into the wondrous life-space around us to find meaningful connections. To begin, however, we must look downward, into the very roots which delivered us forth.

CHAPTER **5**

The Roots of Narcissim — Nature

Be warned that if you wish, as I do, to build a society in which individuals cooperate generously and unselfishly towards a common good, you can expect little help from biological nature. Let us try to teach generosity and altruism, because we are born selfish. Let us understand what our own selfish genes are up to, because we may then at least have the chance to upset their designs, something that no other species has ever aspired to.

Richard Dawkins is quite bold.[1] But then again you might expect this of someone who has sold over one million copies of his book, *The Selfish Gene,* in over twenty languages. Universal love, not to mention the welfare of the species as a whole, is out the window for Dawkins.

There is a war going on, and selfishness is winning out over altruism.

This war can be quite brutal. Blackheaded gulls nest in massive colonies which are often only a few feet apart. Baby chicks, when first hatched, are quite defenseless and quite easy to swallow. It is quite common for a gull to wait until a neighbor's back is turned, perhaps while it is off snatching a dinner meal for the family, and then pounce on one of the neighbor's chicks and swallow it whole. Why go to the hassle of going fishing when you can get good nutrition just a mouthful away?

And if you consider these greedy gulls a bit narcissistic, what do you think about female praying mantises who actually bite the heads off their male partners, often during the sex act itself. You would think she would wait at least until copulation is completed! But the loss of a head does not seem to throw the rest of his body out of kilter. In fact, once the male head is removed, certain inhibitory features of the nervous system are actually removed, and the male's performance is enhanced. At the very least, the female gets a bit more protein to be used during gestation as an added benefit.

Survival of the fittest is not very pretty.

It also is not very polite. Emperor penguins of the Antarctic can be somewhat cowardly. A stalemate is often observed as groupings of penguins stand around by the edge of the sea, waiting to see which one might chance a meeting with a voracious seal who has been dreaming of a penguin steak all night. If only one altruistic soul would dive in to check out the safety issue, he surely would win the hearts of many. But, no, this is not the program. With no guinea pig stepping up to the plate, the penguins are often seen trying to push one another into the gasping sea in order to rule out any potential blood baths.

We are observing natural selection in the examples above, and it follows that anything which has evolved by natural selection is, by definition, selfish. Evolution works by natural selection, and natural selection necessitates the differential survival of the fittest. But are we talking about the fittest individuals, the fittest races, the fittest species, or what? And to what extent do our own "fitness" needs compromise others?

For Dawkins the fundamental unit of selection, and therefore of self-interest, is not the species, nor the group, not even the individual. It is the gene, the unit of heredity. The argument in his book is that we, and all other animals, are machines created by our genes. "Like successful Chicago gangsters, our genes have survived, in some cases for millions of years, in a highly competitive world. This entitles us to expect certain qualities in our genes. I shall argue that a predominant quality to be expected in a successful gene is ruthless selfishness. This gene selfishness will usually give rise to selfishness in individual behavior."[2]

So people are merely "survival machines" for individual selfish genes, which are archaically programmed to do whatever is needed to survive.

Natural selection favors genes that control their survival machines. We are controlled by our self-absorbed genes – a very humbling reality! We are vessels which carry blueprints for generations to come.

Dawkins, like Sigmund Freud, was influenced greatly by Charles Darwin. Darwin's theory of evolution by natural selection (1859) is the key that has unlocked our understanding of an egocentric view of human nature. The basic assumption of Darwin is that any heritable trait which gives an individual any survival advantage will be selected in a population. Differential survival and reproduction over many generations ensures the continued presence of these traits.

For example, imagine that you are a finch flapping around in some glorious environment in which the primary food sources are nut-bearing trees and bushes. Each day you flap your wings twice and thank your lucky stars for the particular shape of your beak which has allowed you to fill your tummy on these succulent nuts. While you have been able to crack open these nuts and delicately remove the meat, your competitors, with less favorable beaks, have all but died out. Those genes which designed your beak are certain to be passed on to future generations.

Darwinian Theory implies that all animals, including human beings, are exclusively motivated by narcissistic self-interest. The theory of natural selection clearly suggests that individuals who behave selfishly are much more likely not only to survive, but to leave more offspring. Survival, in itself is necessary but not sufficient: we must also win sexually. Reproductive competition requires that we also survive at the game of love. Not surprisingly, our genes, and therefore our hormones, control this as well.

First, let's look at the survival variant. In order to survive we need our genes to regulate our bodies in adaptive ways. As an example, the genes that control the selection of sweat glands continue generation after generation for us Homo sapiens. Our very survival depends on our capacity to regulate our body temperatures so that we remain at roughly 98.6 degrees.

The reproductive variant is seen in the male peacock as he proudly struts about with a full and brilliant plumage in order to be selected by a female partner. Studies, in which a male's luxurious abundance is trimmed back, results in very lonely nights. A sparse plumage signals weakness and ill-health, and few opportunities for reproduction occur. Note the risk taking here. The male peacock, with all his colorful glory, is willing to risk the attention of potential predators just to get laid. Natural selection does indeed work in mysterious ways.

Well you must be wondering how blackheaded gulls, female praying mantises, Emperor penguins, and male peacocks have any relevance at all to people. Surely we, as a species, have evolved into enough complexity to sort out better choices than eating our spouses or pushing each other into seal-infested waters. Hmm, I wonder!

While I don't see finches, penguins, or blackheaded gulls in therapy I do see numerous clients who are driven by their own selfish genes. As a reminder, these genes serve one of two purposes — survival or reproduction. Let's briefly take a look at Roger, a wealthy dentist who pulled himself up by the bootstraps to make his way in the world.

Roger and Claire had been married for 17 years following a more-than-satisfying period of romantic love just after meeting their senior year in college. Roger had endeavored to become one of the area's outstanding dental professionals while Claire relished her time with their two children and their church. As I met them at the brink of their divorce I learned that Roger had been having an affair with a hygienist he had met at a local conference. Time with me was to be their "last ditch effort" before signing up the heavy hitters in family law.

I soon found out from Claire that Roger thoughtlessly brought his lover to the kids' soccer games, whereupon Claire would break out in hives. Roger seemed to thrive on insensitivity and self-absorption. He would often work until midnight — accumulating a secure nest egg, he would say. He refused to "baby-sit" for his own children while Claire was at church Tuesday evenings. Instead he hung out with his lover, always returning home minutes before Claire did. He told her that he worked much too hard to be burdened with kids in the evening. He mocked anything Claire cherished as her own, such as making pottery in her lay ministry role at church. Working together as a team around the house was impossible because he "always" seemed to get distracted by one thing or another. Ten plates would be spinning at once above his head. "Never would he complement or hug me," bemoaned Claire. "It is almost as if he doesn't see me!"

Three sessions deep into therapy Claire tearfully reported that Roger had asked for her ski clothes. She didn't need to ask why, but Roger offered an explanation anyway. "If you are not going to use them this ski season, I would at least like to get my money's worth by letting Godiva [his lover] use them next weekend in Aspen. Crushed, Claire seemed to sink into a despair which sucked the spirit out of her. How could Roger violate an agreement he had made to me and Claire not to see his lover during the course of therapy, let alone go skiing with her at a posh resort? It was almost as if he didn't see or hear us. [Narcissus, are you listening?]

I saw the sun setting very quickly on this couple.

When Claire refused to give him the ski clothes, he threw an all-too-familiar fit. After shredding curtains and impulsively threatening to humiliate Claire in front of the kids, Roger left the house and therapy as well. This volatility was not a surprise, I learned. Three years earlier an employee had filed a civil harassment suit against him because he had lambasted her in front of patients, violently slammed his fist on a table, telling her to "F...off" in front of three other staff members. Soon after that crisis was resolved, Roger – like his mother – was diagnosed as ADHD (Attention Deficit Disorder with Hyperactivity). A diagnosis of Narcissistic Personality Disorder was also suggested.

Most of us would agree that Roger's selfish genes are in full bloom. And, it's more than ADHD. Somehow, self-absorbed doesn't seem to be a strong enough adjective. But let's pause for a moment. Is it possible that his behavior is actually being driven by forces beyond his control? Is it possible that while his selfish behavior is abhorrent by societal standards, it actually is adaptive by evolutionary standards?

Are Roger's genes winning out over reason? Has love lost the battle here?

Survival of the Fittest

When Charles Darwin fashioned the term survival of the fittest he was not meaning your good looks or your degrees from an Ivy League university. For Darwin, it was more basic than that. He was counting your children. If your children grow up to have more children, you are "fit" according to nature. If you have more partners to have more children, you are fit according to nature. You have successfully passed your genes onto the next generation and, in terms of survival, you have won!

By these standards Roger has won as well. Roger already has two children and he is on his way to having more with his new lover. His new flame lures him in with all the charms that nature's courting rituals require. She must appear healthy so that Roger's genes "know" she will produce viable offspring. The ingredients are there: youth, dazzling eyes, clear skin, luxurious

hair, alabaster teeth, dynamic personality, and the visual Mecca for men – a supple and propor-
tionate body. These characteristics have been found to be alluring for men from the savannas
of Botswana to the highlands of Nova Scotia.

Indeed, if she meets the standards of Devendra Singh, a psychologist at the University of
Texas at Austin, Roger's lover also has a waist-to-hip ratio of 0.7. Singh has found that men
everywhere in the world find women with these dimensions to be sexually alluring. Natural
selection, he believes, has embedded this preference into the genes of every man because this
ratio suggests a fecund reproductive potential.

Roger's behavior with his lover is also being driven by a small molecule in the brain called
phenylethylamine, or PEA, which excites him, exhilarates him, infatuates him, elates him. and
turns him on to euphoria and romantic love. PEA is a natural stimulant, or amphetamine,
which literally revs up the brain. With the hydraulics of PEA powering him forward, Roger
and his lover are "ecstatic" – from the Greek word ekstasis – which originally meant "deranged." In many ways, Roger is actually "out of his mind," blinded by a montage of compelling images and sensations. There are citizens of this majestic global community, usually men,
who get absorbed chasing one PEA "high" after another. This altered state underlies affairs,
serial monogamy, and sexual addiction.

Roger and Claire had disclosed in therapy that their love-making had "fallen off the
charts." This signals an SOS to a primal part of the brain, that archaic residue controlled by
genes, which want to keep manufacturing carbon copies. During times like these, a desire for
novelty is sparked in order to maintain desire and arousal, both necessary conditions for the
delivery of sperm. When our partners are remiss, lovers can provide this novelty. Roger is no
doubt producing much more sperm these days with Godiva than he had been with Claire. This
pleases the gene machine while disturbing Claire, the kids, and the therapist!

As Helen Fisher describes in *The Anatomy of Love,* the sexes are intimately locked in a
mating ritual, endlessly adjusting their moves to complement those of each other.[3] Only in
tandem can either men or women reproduce and pass on the beat of human life. The question
is whether men like Roger have taken their quest to create offspring too far.

In our culture, Roger has selfishly abandoned a standard of care and devotion. Empathy
appears to be out the window. But is he "over the top" in the eyes of other cultures? "Hogamus,
higamus, men are polygamous" is an old ditty. Dr. Fisher reports that only 16 percent of the
853 cultures on record actually prescribe monogamy, in which a man is permitted only one
wife at a time. We, as a Western culture, are among these 16 percent. A whopping 84 percent
of all human societies permit a man to take more than one wife at once. But women don't
take this philandering of men without a response of their own. They are actively involved in
the mating dance themselves for the survival of their genes as well. Women, according to evolutionary biologists, are looking for men who possess material goods, valuable property, and
money. These belongings suggest to women that men have power, prestige, worldly success,
and certainly the ability to provide for the children. Donald Trump, not to mention the Emperor in Chapter 2, appears to have it made in the shade.

Evolutionary biologist Robin Baker believes that survival actually requires women to be instinctively clever in their reproductive styles. Dr. Baker states in his book *Sperm Wars* that "a good part of the sexual behavior of a female – even one who has no rational reason to distrust her long-term partner or to cheat on him herself – is driven at least in part by an urge to out-maneuver her partner and other males or to influence which male's sperm will have the best chance of succeeding in any competition she promotes."[4]

Why? Because, disturbing as this observation may be, past evolutionary imperatives have dictated that a female who promotes competition may better the chances of her offspring having good genes. Human females are the only species who actually conceal their ovulation. We men don't know when our partner is fertile. This means that a male must continually endeavor to keep his female partner "topped off" with his own sperm, as Baker puts it, in order to ensure that the offspring he might rear is actually his own. Rearing someone else's child may be the loving thing to do, but it is not what Mother Nature and Charles Darwin envisioned.

Sperm competition is so intense among primates, such as chimpanzees, that females often mate with every male in the band within minutes, filling their reproductive tracks with a diversity of donated matter. To compete in this kind of a high stakes game, male chimps evolved bigger testicles capable of producing more sperm.

The strategy by women is often referred to as "female choice" and suggests that women dramatically influence survival of the fittest genes. So we see that both men and women are actively engaged in a selfish struggle to perpetuate their genes. As Dr. Baker puts it, "Whether we know it or not, whether we want to or not, and whether we care or not, we are all programmed to try to win our generation's game of reproduction, to pursue reproductive success. Our successful ancestors have saddled us inescapably with the genetic instructions that tell us not only that we must compete, but also how to compete." This is true for sparrows, gibbons, and Roger and his lover.

Is it possible that natural selection is actually killing us?

While egoism and narcissism may win at survival, many of the survivors represent the walking wounded. Competitive drives and individualistic values have led to isolation, despair, loneliness, a sense of alienation, violence, discrimination, abuse toward women, and the murder of step-children. We are so isolated that national surveys often find that we Americans have few close friends and can't name our neighbors two doors down.

For Roger, this isolation and despair led to divorce.

Like many divorcing fathers I have seen, Roger cried only when he grieved for his children. He wavered only when he wondered if his children would "survive" the divorce and its aftermath. He fought for his visitation rights to be with his children – to nurture them and to protect them.

Roger wanted the best of both worlds. He wanted to spread his seed far and wide, extending his harem as far as our culture and his lifespan would allow. And yet, he wished to cherish everything he had created. His genes fought hard for every "survival machine" they occupied. This is the nature of Mother Nature.

Selfishness or altruism: Which dueling banjo will it be?

Rogers's dilemma is our dilemma. Which force will survive? Which aspect of human nature will "win" out? [1] temperament or character, [2] a desire for union or narcissistic pre-occupation, [3] surrender or autonomy, [4] communion or agency, [5] togetherness or individuality, [6] attachment or separation, [7] affection or power, [8] relationship or achievement [9] interpersonal relatedness or development of self, [10] narcissism or love. For me, there is no doubt that each of the above life forces must have their way.

A mature and robust identity requires the primordial soup we call relationship, and the development of healthy relationships requires the birth of a robust identity.

Let's sum up so far.

Our genes are driven to replicate themselves and to manifest themselves. I call these *succession* and *expression*. Offspring fulfills the first longing, while our persistent behavior patterns fulfill the second. Roger's Attention Deficit Hyperactivity Disorder (ADHD) was clearly expressed by his distractibility, impulsivity, and poor anger management. These annoying behaviors – these genes – were woven into the fabric of his life and had been present forever. Roger's mom was of the same cloth. It is now time to look at a third force that affects our lives. Genes also want to calibrate themselves when forces drive them out of balance. I will refer to this process as *restoration*.

Restoration reflects the comfort zones within which we live.

I grabbed the morning paper on the way to work a few years ago and found one headline particularly stunning: "The secret of happiness: It's in the genes." The brain appears to be wired for a set point for happiness. Each of us possesses a genetically determined mood level which moves up and down according to the vicissitudes of life. Just as the body rebounds to a set core body temperature of roughly 98.6 degrees or our blood sugars return to a normal range after eating half a cheese cake, we seem to return to a set happiness level following any life event.[5]

Selfishness, as a set point, means returning to what our genes know best.

Psychologist Edward Diener evaluated more than 30 survey studies in the United States and 42 other countries. His findings are surprising. "We find that for events like being promoted or losing a lover, most of the effect on people's mood is gone by three months, and there's not a trace by six months."[6] And, on the serendipity side, it's not much better. Those lucky souls who win huge sums of money in the lottery are no happier a year after their good fortune than they were before they struck gold. Even people with spinal cord injuries were able to rebound in spirits – to somehow return to a set point which existed before tragedy.

The University of Minnesota is home of the twin studies, where more than 2,300 sets of twins have been surveyed from 1936 to 1955. Researchers there also believe that people are likely born with a "contentment set point." When they explored the lives of 254 identical and fraternal twins, they found that a person's sense of well-being is largely inherited – be it depression or joy!

In fact, heredity appears to account for at least 50 percent of happiness. Dean Hamer is even more vehement about this.[7]

"How you feel right now is about equally genetic and circumstantial. But how you'll feel on average over the next ten years is fully 80% because of your genes."

These conclusions are sobering: If you are a twin, your happiness is better predicted by your twin's happiness than your socioeconomic status, your income, or your marital status. In other words, there is relatively little difference in well-being among identical twins no matter if your twin was reared with you or away from you!

Looking Deeper Into Our Nature

Behaviors we see as self-absorbed are often diminished physical conditions.

We know that many millions of us live our lives diminished in some physiological ways. Virtually all of mental illness and perhaps most of physical illness reflects our inability to restore deficits – mostly deficits that our genes have given us. When these low levels are corrected many of the expressed behaviors, which seemed so selfish, clear up. For example, each of the following diagnoses reflects an imbalance:

* Parkinson's disease = low dopamine
* Social phobia = low dopamine
* Childhood autism = low serotonin
* Chronic low back pain = low serotonin
* Obsessive/compulsive disorder = low serotonin
* Impulsive disorder = low serotonin
* ADHD = low serotonin
* Depression = low serotonin and low epinephrine

The brain functions as a result of chemical messengers. These messengers are neurons that attempt to talk to one another by releasing chemicals which produce signals. We call these chemical messengers neurotransmitters. Dopamine is an adrenaline-like neurotransmitter that controls bodily movements and emotional responses as well as our experience of pleasure or pain. Serotonin is another neurotransmitter which helps us resist impulses, plays an active role in depression, suicide, impulse disorders, and aggression.

We need our levels of neurotransmitters to be high enough in our midbrains to allow signals to be passed back and forth. You might think of these levels as a vast oceanic fluid. There is no way we are going to sail from Bar Harbor, Maine, to Portsmouth, England, without enough water in the Atlantic to get us there.

When these neurotransmitters are not at sufficient levels, a "selfish" craving occurs which is our attempt to restore balance from imbalance. Everything from eating disorders to alcohol addiction is related to restoration attempts. Eating disorders are associated with low estrogen, which in turn contributes to low dopamine. Scarcity cravings for carbohydrates, such as chocolates, reflect our need to fix what is broken – to fill what is running on empty. The use of cocaine, alcohol, or amphetamines increases our levels of dopamine, albeit in different ways. While amphetamines actually release more dopamine, cocaine actually blocks the use of dopamine by a process called "reuptake." Either way, we feel better after we have increased our level of dopamine.

I truly wish that psychotherapy could remedy these deficits, but it can't.

Nothing is more frustrating than two partners, in what's left of a love relationship, battling it out over and over again, blaming each other for what is nature's doing! Sometimes, in order to survive in our relationships we must be immersed in the very primordial gook that defines our essence. This takes a willingness to be vulnerable — a desire to truly understand oneself.

Instead of blaming our partners for our lack of happiness, we must look within!

Researchers, who look inside our brains, use evoked related potentials (ERPs), positron emission tomography (PETs), and electroencephalographs (EEGs) to reveal the mysteries of our genes. They have found a place in our brains where happiness actually has found a home — where the set point mechanism probably operates. This command central is located in the prefrontal lobes of our cerebral cortex.

These modern-day Houdinis have found that those of us with relatively more activity in the left prefrontal area enjoy more positive emotions. We get more pleasure out of life's more ordinary routines like making dinner and also report that we are more upbeat, energetic, and alert.

Those of us with more activity in the right prefrontal lobe have a different, more impoverished story to tell. We are more agitated, angry, aggressive, distressed and anxious. We are also more depressed, sinking into emotional ravines where pleasure and joy seem to be echoes of the past. Just in case you might think that these differences are conditioned or shaped by the environment, studies of infants reveal that abundance of activity in the left prefrontal cortex is established by the age of 10 months!

Research psychologist Richard Davidson has found that infants as young as 10 months, with more activity in the left prefrontal lobe, are less likely to cry when briefly separated from their mothers. Likewise, exuberance in three year olds holds up over time so that when they are studied at the age of seven these same children jump to pop bubbles blown over their heads. They laugh and hop all over the place according to Davidson. In contrast, fellow age mates — with more activity on the right side — barely got up on their tippy toes![8]

Our genes have created a bicameral brain with two uniquely different sides.

Two different states of being are reflected: One being "abundance", the other "scarcity." To view our lives as half empty is to miss an equal truth — that our lives are also half full, yet there is a tendency to focus on the emptiness. Our emotional inner life reflects this same duality. The National Advisory Mental Health Council has studied emotions and they have suggested that from a list of over 150 a dramatically reduced set of six emotional categories exist:

* Love   * Anger
* Joy   * Sadness
* Surprise   * Fear

This list can be reduced even further to two groups of emotions: You guessed it. We're back to positive and negative. This is our evolutionary baggage. As we have seen, the positive emotions are processed in the left hemisphere while the negative emotions are processed in the right hemisphere. Because positive and negative emotions are triggered in two very different brain systems, people often can feel both happy and sad at the same time!

Roger, as you recall from earlier in this chapter, had a high level of anger and negative emotions. This is often the case with Attention Deficit Disorder with Hyperactivity. ADHD is marked by symptoms of (1) hyperactivity, (2) inattention, and (3) impulsivity. We now know that ADHD consists of two distinct conditions: A disorder of disinhibition, where impulsivity rules, and one of deficits, where lack of focus and selective attention rule. Roger experienced both. Reduced development or functioning in the anterior brain contributes to the disinhibited type. Reduced development or functioning in the posterior brain contributes to problems with attention deficits. Roger's ADHD mind may have been nature's design, but he drove everyone else out of their minds.

Instead of understanding his own genetic patterns, Roger blamed Claire, and sought a remedy outside himself. He was no doubt triggering much activity in his right hemisphere and sought relief from the flood of negative feelings which threatened to engulf him. Godiva became his fix. And we know from research on addictions that there are also two very different parts of the brain which control "liking" and "wanting." The first system processes the *experience* of pleasure while the other processes the *pursuit* of pleasure. While most "street" drugs activate the positive "liking" emotions, addiction occurs as these same drugs activate the "wanting" system.

Roger, like so many others, responded to the call of these evolutionary forces. Any drug which reduces anxiety or other negative emotions tends to be "wanted". This craving is the nature of addictions and may account for why lovers like Godiva are desired. Sexual addiction is often the name we give this kind of pursuit. The infatuation "high" which Godiva no doubt represented temporarily appeased the sea of distress Roger floundered in. Of course, this lasted only a fortnight, leaving him and his family lost at sea.

A Gene Pool and Pull

I hope that I have challenged each of you to question the limits of free will in this chapter. The first part of this chapter has been directed to succession – our persistent struggle to survive and reproduce ourselves. The case study of Roger has been a profile in how our genes express themselves. In his case, his preoccupation with work, his distractibility, and his anger all reflect behaviors which push through so to speak. Finally, the discussion of "set-points" reveals the narrow bands which, like rubber bands, pull us back to a preset point after we have been stretched beyond our comfort zone. This is what I refer to as restoration.

Each of us may be humbled by these physical "givens" – wonderfully and uniquely created out of the fundament of life itself. Their presence, even obstinance, is what often makes therapy so difficult for me, not to mention my clients. These givens are neither good nor bad: they just are.

We often find it difficult to accept things as they are – the third *Gift*! We find it even more difficult to accept two apparently conflicting things as they are. This is true with nature and nurture. While the overt signs of nurture are often much easier to see – and complain about – we can no longer dismiss the powerful and covert pull of nature.

The cruel effects of an abusive parent upon a child's ultimate well-being are not difficult to see. This is nurture at its worst, and few of us are surprised to find such children depressed many years later following years of repeated tongue-lashings – debasement which leaves them bereft of self-worth or self-love. We will explore these sources of pain in the next chapter on nurture. What we've learned in this chapter however, is that the marks of nature can be more subtle.

The influence of genes is not seen on a daily basis, only on an evolutionary one.

We have seen that genes are the instructions – the marching orders – that direct our growth, our looks, and our actions – yes, even our selfish, narcissistic actions! Each of us has 70,000 pairs of these orders that instruct the cells in our bodies. A complete package of genes that defines a fish as a fish, a finch as a finch, and a human as a human is called a genome. We now know, thanks to the Human Genome Projects, that our genetic code is a compilation of 3.5 billion letters that scientists refer to as the Book of Life. The deconstruction of this "book of life" has resulted in a string of letters representing four protein substances that make up every gene: adenine, thymine, guanine and cystosine, which are referred to simply as A, T, G, and C. This sequence, MOST of which is shared by all living things, can now help us understand all aspects of human behavior, misbehavior and disease – even suicide – with surprising accuracy.

With survival as an end game, suicide is clearly not what our genes had in mind!

Yet, suicide is the ninth leading cause of death for adults and the third leading cause of death for adolescents according to the National Institutes for Mental Health. As complicated as suicide is to understand, geneticists have now linked a particular area of chromosome 2, one of the myriad of sites on the genome, with impulsivity and suicide. It is difficult to believe that this level of specificity can be achieved, but participants in a Johns Hopkins study with a history of both attempted suicide and bipolar disorder showed similarities in a certain area of the genome, DNA marker D2S1777, on a section of chromosome 2 referred to as 2p12![9]

Most of us will want to recoil at this level of specificity.

As we dizzily tilt backwards onto our heels, however, it is apparent that "Psychology will soon be transformed by both neuroscience and evolutionary psychology!" according to neuro-scientist Dr. Frans de Waal who addressed the American Psychological Association in 2001.[10] Because psychology came out of a more philosophical tradition, it has always maintained these dualisms of mind and body, human and animal, which biology cast aside long ago. Dropping those dualisms will allow psychology to develop a more nuanced view of human behavior.

Nature even controls our moods during the change of seasons.

It's not even possible to enjoy spring without some evolutionary biologist getting her dibs in. We come alive with spring blooms. We're flushed with joy and optimism as we bounce from one bluebonnet patch to another. Yet, could it be that this fresh bounce is merely the pull of genes – the power of biological changes – that are set in motion simply by fluctuations in sunlight? Could it be that springtime bliss is the direct result of sensors in the eyes that take note of when days get longer or shorter? If so, then we human beings are buoyed by the same seasonal hormonal changes that wake bears from winter hibernation and send chipmunks scurrying around for a bit of warm-weather love.

Is spring yet another opportunity to remind us that we are all animals "cut from the same evolutionary cloth"? Well, yes! We know that an area of the brain, called the hypothalamus, stimulates the nearby pineal gland, which regulates sleep patterns by releasing melatonin at night. In the fall, when darkness lasts longer, melatonin is secreted for longer periods. Because the hormone dulls activity, we mammals slow down, slumber more, and gain weight to survive the coming winter. In the spring, days lengthen, and melatonin is released for shorter periods. We mammals are rejuvenated, sleep less, mate more, and give birth in warm months when food is more plentiful.

So much for spring fever! It's not about self-absorbed me. It's about all of us.

Darwin's theory of evolution by natural selection, i.e., survival of the fittest, is gratifying to many of us because he demonstrated how simplicity could evolve into complexity and how seemingly random and unordered atoms might coalesce into more complex and meaningful patterns, until they "manufactured" people. Alfred Lord Tennyson captured the spirit of this unfolding humanity – this simplicity – quite well.

> *Once there was a fluid haze of light,*
> *That eddied into suns,*
> *Which wheeling cast the planets,*
> *Then the monster,*
> *Then the man.*[11]

We, as human beings are but a twinkle in the eye of evolution.

In these 23 words, Alfred Lord Tennyson tells a story that actually unfolded over the course of 14 billion years! Yet, our narcissism impales us on a stake which proclaims our supremacy above all other species. Is this prideful bravado "well-earned" in evolutionary terms? Hardly! When a chimp, named Clint, at the Yerkes National Primate Research Center in Atlanta, was compared to the human genome results, we learned that Clint shared a whopping 96 percent of our DNA! In fact the number of genetic differences between humans and chimps is ten times smaller than that between mice and rats!!

Perhaps most shocking of all, it has taken us only six million years to mutate from our closest relative, Clint. In a universe 13.6 billion years old, this is the time equivalent of a good belly laugh. These findings are so mind-blowing to geneticists like Frans de Waal, that he concludes that "Darwin wasn't just provocative in saying that we descend from the apes – he didn't go far enough!"[12]

As if being related to Clint the chimp isn't enough, the National Human Genome Research Institute announced in 2005 that humans and mice are cousins, each descended from a small mammal that split into two species toward the end of the Dinosaur era. Despite 75 million years of separate evolution, more than 90 percent of mouse genes have a functional equivalent in the human genome. Only about 300 genes – one percent of the 30,000 possessed by each mammal – have no obvious counterpart in the other's genome.

No doubt this is a time when nature, over nurture, is in full bloom. But let's be cautious nonetheless. The pendulum in the nature-nurture debate has swung very widely over the past century. Today, with the advent of genetics, we are certainly witnessing a very strong hereditary tidal wave. However, let's remember that nurture dominated the debate scene during the 1960's and the 1970's!

Genes only dictate where we begin our journeys, not our destinations.

Nature is clearly a powerful force. But so are environment, a healthy nurture, and a vibrant spiritual life. Most social and biological scientists today have abandoned the supremacy debate regarding nature vs. nurture. Clearly both are wrapped around each other within a cauldron of possibilities. What we must understand is how our genes are expressed within any given environment. It has been suggested that our genes dictate what exists within our walk-in closets, i.e., our pants, shirts, blouses etc. Our environments dictate, however, which of these apparel items we will actually choose to wear.

Let's be cautious with our current enthusiasm over current research findings, understanding that flip-flops have occurred with each generation and that our real goal is not picking a winner, but integrating both nature and nurture into our knowledge of human behavior. While DNA marker D2S1777 on chromosome 2 may help us to understand the impulsive, self-absorbed "nature" of bipolar disorder, an infinite palette of lifestyle choices exists for those so diagnosed.

Anotole France reminds us, "It is human nature to think wisely and act foolishly."

So, perhaps we can put our trust in nature, accepting the force fields that are shaping us, as well as the choice points we do have regarding the set points we're given. We don't need the Seven Deadly Sins to lift our spirits. Perhaps, it is as simple as a recipe for living recommended by Dr. David Lykken, author of the University of Minnesota twin studies: "Be an experimental epicure. A steady diet of simple pleasures will keep you above your set point. Find the small things that you know give you a little high – a good meal, working in the garden, time with friends – and sprinkle your life with them. In the long run, that will leave you happier than some grand achievement that gives you a big lift for a while."[13]

CHAPTER 6

The Roots of Narcissism – Nurture

In the arms of an angel
Fly away from here,
From this dark cold hotel room
And the endlessness that you fear,
You are pulled from the wreckage
Of your silent reverie,
You're in the arms of the angel
May you find some comfort there.[1]
    – Angel by Sarah Mclachlan

Margaux Hemingway sought comfort in the arms of an angel. Love beckoned her twice but, sadly, departed. Having no real home, she then traveled the world to find God and, ultimately, herself. Spiritual quests lured her first to Hawaii where she sought a "healer," next to India to find a guru, and then to Santa Monica to embrace the Agape Church of Religious Science. Finally, in the stillness of a summer evening, consumed by a vast loneliness, Margaux Hemingway took her own life – and perhaps found some comfort there.

    Hara Estroff Marano, editor at large for *Psychology Today*, captures Margaux's enigmatic persona quite well. "She was six feet tall in her bare feet – five foot twelve, she'd say – with such a remarkable face and such a radiant presence and such an alluring name that when she walked into a room, conversation left it. If she shook your hand, you might think your wrist was going to snap…With her long legs came great lungs, and you didn't hike with her, you gasped behind her. She started right at the top with the first million-dollar contract ever awarded a model. She wasn't even out of high school. She asked for none of it.[2]

On July 6, 1996, her ashes were buried in Ketchum, Idaho, in the shadow of a memorial to her grandfather Ernest Hemingway, arguably one of the twentieth century's most celebrated literary figures. Like her famous forebear, Margaux Hemingway took her own life, the fifth to do so in four generations of Hemingways, and on the eve of the thirty-fifth anniversary of her grandfather's death."

We'll never know what killed Margaux Hemingway. But we must wonder as all survivors do. Why would a beautiful woman, age 41, take her own life by acute Phenobarbital intoxication? Why would a famous actress, who just hours before, stood before a microphone singing songs in front of a chorus of 500 friends and wannabes, snuff out her own life? What kind of combination of upbringing and genes, of nurture and nature, could have contributed to perpetuating such a legacy of doom? We can only wonder, as Hara Estroff Marano wonders, "What underground spring, what vein of vulnerability, can run through a life and claim it in a bad second?"

Was Margaux Hemingway self-absorbed?

The nature of depression is such that it leaves many individuals in a state of self absorption. As a depressed actress, she presumably was even more self absorbed. But what combination of nurture and nature shaped this self-absorption? Like Bryce Canyon's eroded sandstone pinnacles, we are etched by forces around us as well as deep within us. This chapter will explore these forces. We do know that nature, with all its biogenic power, exerted a tectonic force upon Margaux's life and death:

* She was six feet tall. "Bigness" ran in the family – impacting body image.
* Margaux had been bulimic since adolescence.
* Biological depression and bipolar disorder affected many in the family.
* Five Hemingways in four generations committed suicide.
* Margaux was epileptic and had taken Phenobarbital since age seven.
* Margaux's sister, Joan, had been hospitalized many times since age 16.
* Margaux was dyslexic which impaired her ability to read.
* Margaux had a history of alcohol abuse and had gone to the Betty Ford Clinic in 1968.

More to the focus of this chapter, we know that nurture, with all its psychogenic power, also shaped Margaux:

* Margaux's father, by his own description, was a model of emotional detachment who would disappear for days at a time.
* Margaux was never close to her mother who lay dying in Idaho while Margaux was treated for alcoholism. Neither was available for the other.
* Margaux once described herself as a lost middle child that no one noticed.
* Margaux had no close emotional bonds with anyone in her family.

* Margaux's epilepsy was diagnosed at the age of seven, just after her parents had to endure the shame of her grandfather's suicide. Were they ashamed of her epilepsy as well, emotionally detaching even further?
* On the day of Ernest's death, when Margaux was only seven, her father learned that he and his brother had been cut out of the will – further detaching him from everyone.
* Sister Mariel was born prematurely four months after Ernest's death and after a very dangerous RH factor pregnancy. Mariel now became the focus of everyone's concern, leaving Margaux at age 7 floundering on her own.
* Margaux never graduated from high school because her dyslexia made reading and math difficult.

We also know that a catalyst often exerts a final fatal force upon a fateful moment. There were a number of such forces pressing upon Margaux Hemingway. Her career had plummeted over a period of two decades. She had taken personal bankruptcy and felt like a failure. She had taken sexually kinky B-movie roles to get by, and felt ashamed. Her younger sister Mariel had a soaring TV career. Margaux was continually exposed to the Liza Minnelli's of the world, and felt diminished by comparison. Finally, Margaux was aging at the margins of a profession that celebrates youth and tends to ignore women over the age of 40. At 41, she felt over the hill.

Margaux Hemingway had slipped below the surface and found herself drowning within her own pool of self-doubts and longing. How far along the self-absorption – narcissism continuum did Margaux waver? While a grieving public mourned the loss of an image, an icon, Margaux herself grieved the loss of something much deeper and more profound. She wept for what she lacked in life and could not find: a vibrant love where she could thrive with another. Depression, a dark force, had consumed that fertile space where love might have thrived. A wounded self, forged in the solitude of her youth, had tragically become her significant other.

What life forces, what nurture, might have helped to shape this wounded self?

The Missing 10 Degrees

Once again, I believe we are motivated by the incompleteness of our lives.

We do not notice the fullness of a circle that reflects 350 degrees. We notice, instead, the missing 10 degrees. Like a mountaineer hearing the faint calling of a far away valley, we live our lives responding to throbbing, incessant echoes – inescapable cries, an undeniable hunger that demands our attention consciously or unconsciously.

A voice calls to us: seek what you most need to find.

For most of us, this call, or missing 10 degrees, represents our unmet needs in life.

For Margaux Hemingway, the missing 10 degrees became her stuck place – a stultifying silence where loneliness, not love, flourished. How badly scarred did she consider herself? Scarcity, rather than abundance, ruled her psyche. Her famous name, her voice, her stunning beauty, her sultry sensuality, and her striking presence mattered not. Instead she was haunted by that abyss within each of us – that gnawing void – which moans, "I am not the right height." "I am not beautiful enough." "I am not smart enough." "I am not successful enough." "I am not loved enough." I AM NOT ENOUGH! Each of these incessant echoes doubtless trapped her in a hellacious room of doom for decades.

When narcissism calls to us, we hear only its voice. The siren call!

Where do these voices arise from? How do the missing 10 degrees keep us stuck in self-absorption? What can go so wrong in our early upbringing? Why do we so easily get hurt or angry in our relationships? Why do so many of us fear intimacy and avoid commitment because of these underground fissures?

This chapter will delineate six parenting patterns which, in the best of worlds, create a healthy basis for intimacy and love. In the worst of worlds, these six parenting patterns create a veritable symphonic chamber of hell. You will have an opportunity to answer six questions which reveal these inner worlds to you. First, however, we must embrace a basic assumption:

> *Psychological wounds, suffered in childhood, may leave indelible imprints – an undeniable hunger – which can influence our relationships for the rest of our lives. These imprints may forever be engraved into our personalities or etched into our character structure. They are often the missing 10 degrees.*

Oh, how dear these early years are! How difficult can it be for a parent to lift himself up – out of his own bliss or misery – and reach out to an infant, child, or young adult? How difficult can a hug, a smile, a pat on the back be? How difficult can a moment in time, repeated many times, be?

Let's briefly look at one scenario:

> *A woman, shopping in a food store, stops to pluck an item off the shelf. With her, nestled comfortably in one corner of the food cart, lies her three-month-old infant. As she carefully places a bag of flour in the cart, a fast-paced businessman stops in his tracks to respond to the familiar cooing sounds emerging from the shortening, peanut butter, and bread. As he bends over to make better facial contact with this adorable child, he experiences a deja-vu of when his own children once uttered these same beguiling, universal sounds.*

For such a common life event, this situation is quite profound. Here we find a helpless three-month-old infant somehow getting more of a response out of a top level executive than his own subordinates sometimes do. Not bad for a fourteen-pound baby! This momentary blip in the universe is the fundament of what psychologists call attachment theory – the bond established between infant and parent which buffers the infant from risk and secures the child in its later development.

We are left to wonder how secure Margaux was in her bonds with her parents.

Healthy bonding leads to a "healthy attachment" where a splendid abundance between parent and child is celebrated. Secure comfort, warmth, and availability are present. Unfortunately, illness, death, divorce, and abandonment are traumas which impede healthy attachments later on in life. Behavioral studies consistently bear this out. Unhealthy bonding leads to "insecure attachment" where scarcity drives the child underground – a haven where either anxiety or ambivalence abounds.

Do you see how attachment is a two way street? Both infant and parent need to be very, very active in the interaction process leading to secure attachment. Nature takes care of this nicely for the infant. Such behaviors as "cooing," "smiling," and "visual following" are actually inborn, prewired signals designed to stop us in our tracks. Our infants are quite prepared from day one to influence us as unsuspecting parents – to elicit a response!

Our children are our calling. Do we hear them? Do we respond to them?

My mother's depression absorbed her, leaving me and my sister bereft of those sweet tendrils we needed to grow. Tendrils are filamentous organs a growing, climbing plant needs for attachment on a wall or tree trunk. I, like so many others, missed out on this secure attachment. My mother's darkness became the shadow my "wounded child" lived within.

As a therapist, I see this legacy daily. Recently, a divorced couple arranged for a one-session psychological consultation before bringing in the legal "big dogs" to fight it out. The issue, it appeared, was the ex-husband's insistence that it was his right to move to San Francisco with "his" child, leaving his ex-wife behind in Austin to lick her own wounds. After all, she deserved it since she had initiated the divorce to begin with – abandoning him painfully in the process. She tearfully protested his move, pleading with him to allow her and "their" son an opportunity to grow together with loving frequency.

During the session, a significant piece of the puzzle emerged. The ex-husband had been abandoned as a child by a father who left forever without a forwarding address. He just walked on the entire family. When I asked how he felt about this earlier abandonment, the ex-husband shrugged and said "That's just the way it is." Distanced from his own feelings of grief, his own wounds of childhood, his own responsibility, this man intended to distance from his wife and a hometown which had become tainted from the pain of a divorce. Wounds perpetuate wounds.

The Imprint of Childhood

Deep inside us, intricately entwined in the fabric of our being, resides an "inner child." We carry this inner child, this homunculus of raw emotion, with us wherever we go. Our illusions of the perfect partner are largely created by the experiences our inner child has had in relationships with our mothers, fathers, and other caretakers. There is a little Larry, a little Claire, a little you. The hurt and anger we express as adults are largely the unresolved pain of this little child within. Dr. Hugh Missildine said it very well almost a half century ago:

> *When two persons marry, they are "in love." This usually means that two adults...see in the opposite adult the promise of fulfillment of past longings. Then, either gradually or suddenly, each marital partner comes face to face with the "child of the past" of the other – the childish part of your spouse, the part that seems so unreasonable.*[3]

As adult lovers, we hope to find in one another the fulfillment of past longings. These longings arise from three fundamental human needs: 1) the need to belong, 2) the need for control over our lives, and 3) the need for affection. Dr. Bill Shultz, in his wonderful text, *The Interpersonal Underworld,* has taught us much about these needs. When we were children, if one or more of these needs was not met by our parents, we felt deeply angry or hurt. That angry or hurt child still lives within our adult bodies and minds, emerging years later when triggered by six patterns in our adult relationships:

  ✳ Too many demands or expectations
  ✳ Too little attention
  ✳ Too much imposed control, criticism, or manipulation
  ✳ Too little appreciation or approval
  ✳ Too much smothering or overprotection
  ✳ Too little affection

Ninety percent of our emotional reactions as adults typically have nothing to do with the immediate situation.

Instead, our anger and hurt often reflect the buried pain of childhood whenever our basic needs for belonging, control, and affection are frustrated. We may stew, brood, and self-absorb hopelessly over these unmet needs. In our quest to find a perfectly divine being, we usually find instead an imperfect human partner who will frustrate one or more of these needs over time. Some of us do not consciously brood over our lost childhoods: instead, we unconsciously react with the strike of a cobra.

Anger and hurt are not the only sequellae of childhood as Hank Williams Jr. tells us:

Lordy, I have loved some ladies
and I have loved Jim Beam;
and they both tried to kill me in 1973.
When that doctor asked me:
Son, how did you get in this condition?
I said "Hey, sawbones, I'm just carrying on
an old family tradition.[4]

Each of us has an old family tradition. The tap roots for scarcity in adulthood are always buried deeply in the fertile soil of childhood. We learn all about relationships during these early years. Sometimes we learn that others we need to depend on are not there for us. We learn what we need – and we learn what we don't need – from others:

  ✳ We *do* need enough attention. We *don't* need too many expectations.
  ✳ We *do* need enough appreciation. We *don't* need excessive criticism.
  ✳ We *do* need enough warmth. We *don't* need too much smothering.

Each day, in each hour of therapy, a client reveals an inner child of the past. This is particularly true in couple's therapy, which is the heart of my private practice. From the beginning I hear one partner blaming the other for their misery. "He treats me like crap." "She's never home on time." "He's always taking care of his own needs and ignoring mine." "She invests more in the children in one hour than she does in me for an entire year." Sound familiar? These are the words of adults but the emotions of wounded children. These emotions are tied to an Achilles heel, a place of vulnerability. As a therapist, it is my responsibility to shed light on this darkness.

Fear of intimacy or fear of commitment, in today's lingo, is really the frightened sanctuary created by a lonely child of the past.

Unrecognized early wounds often hide in the shadows.

Who goes looking for such wounds during the dawn of a budding relationship? Instead, we notice her legs, his eyes, her lips, his status, her degree, his aspirations, her social grace, his sense of humor, her ability to initiate, his interest in photography, or her interest in wilderness adventures.

Our early illusions – what I call "portraits of desire" – convince us that what we see is what we get. But it just isn't so. The attractive, bright, energetic lover we embrace in the light of today may also be the hurt and angry child of twilight past. If wisdom prevails we will learn to love both – the perfect illusion and the imperfect reality.

Identifying Your Inner Child of the Past

Unless you take the time to identify your inner child, you will not be able to understand why you get hurt, angry, resentful, withdrawn, or drink too much Jim Beam. You are very likely to continue blaming your partner – wrongly – for all the anger and hurt you feel. Though he or she may be responsible for 10 percent of it – by triggering it – you still have the responsibility to account for the other 90 percent. Your gene pool aside, such an accounting will require that you recall how your parents wounded you many years ago. What you learn will help you identify and understand the buttons or triggers that seem to set you off now – why you are so "Stuck on Me: Missing You!"

We are wounded by parents who are in some way extreme in their child rearing practices. I believe that parents can be extreme in any of the following six ways:

1) Parents may be extreme in providing ***too much inclusion*** by demanding or expecting too much. These parents are interested in imposing their values, their hopes, and their dreams upon you implicitly or explicitly. Your business becomes their business when they get too involved.

2) Parents may be extreme in providing ***too little inclusion*** by not paying attention to you. These parents may be too busy working, getting manicures, or being too depressed to find out what is happening in your world. They do not provide the undivided attention you need.

3) Parents may be extreme in providing *too much control* by being critical, manipulating, or overpowering. Criticism is a direct means of controlling, while manipulation is less direct. These parents may use very stern voice tones, threaten physical harm, or more subtly influence your every decision. You may consequently not feel accepted or encouraged.

4) Parents may be extreme in providing *too little control* by not appreciating your input or by not taking the time to really listen to what is going on with you. These parents are too laissez-faire and have no idea what you feel or really think about. If you have a stated or unstated need, it usually goes unnoticed. You may begin to sink into silence.

5) Parents may be extreme in providing *too much affection* by being smothering or over-protective. In the name of love, these parents are constantly warning you of all the dangers of the world, whether they be physical, biological, or interpersonal. As a result, you may have been restricted from doing many things you wanted to do.

6) Parents may be extreme in providing *too little affection* by not demonstrating love with hugs or saying "I love you." These parents may be cold, unfeeling, emotionally numb, or distant. Worse yet, some parents are emotionally and physically abusive, which scars us in so many ways.

With the above in mind, settle back comfortably in your chair. Recall a period of time when you were under the age of 18 growing up in your hometown or city. Be young for a moment in time. See yourself in the old neighborhood surrounded by the familiar scenes that filled your childhood years on a regular basis. What were Mom and Dad doing? Where were they? Were they happy? Were you happy? If a parent died, or a stepparent raised you, or some other caretaker raised you, consider substituting this person or persons for your mother or father. You may still be able to get a profile of your original "family tradition."

As you recall these early years, get an image of Mom in your mind.

As you drift back in time be aware that there often is a temptation to protect a parent when completing this exercise. Please remember that this is not intended to judge or condemn our parents. Often this was the best they could do given their upbringing and their life circumstances. In fact, by responding to these questions honestly, you will likely understand both yourself and your parents more deeply. So, keeping this image of Mom very vivid, respond to the following statements according to this scale:

	Not True	Somewhat True	Generally True	Usually True	Very True
1. Mom, you demand or expect too much from me.	1	2	3	4	5
2. Mom, you criticize, manipulate, or overpower me.	1	2	3	4	5
3. Mom, you smother or overprotect me.	1	2	3	4	5
4. Mom, you don't pay attention to me.	1	2	3	4	5
5. Mom, you don't listen to or appreciate my needs.	1	2	3	4	5
6. Mom, you are not affectionate. You don't hug or say "I love you."	1	2	3	4	5

Now, I would like you to do the same with an image of your father. Be young. Remember back many years if you need to. Experience your father as if you were a child once again:

	Not True	Somewhat True	Generally True	Usually True	Very True
1. Dad, you demand or expect too much from me.	1	2	3	4	5
2. Dad, you criticize, manipulate, or overpower me.	1	2	3	4	5
3. Dad, you smother or overprotect me.	1	2	3	4	5
4. Dad, you don't pay attention to me.	1	2	3	4	5
5. Dad, you don't listen to or appreciate my needs.	1	2	3	4	5
6. Dad, you are not affectionate. You don't hug or say "I love you."	1	2	3	4	5

I consider all "4" and "5" scores to be significant. Certain patterns may emerge from the above questions. **First**, some people feel anger in response to too much inclusion, control, or affection. It just seems to be human nature that we often get angry when others are demanding, controlling, or smothering us – then and now. **Second**, people usually feel hurt in response to too little inclusion, control, or affection. It is very painful when loved ones do not attend to us, listen to us, understand our needs, or hug us. This is where intimacy is experienced for the first time. **Third**, your inner child of the past is likely to erupt when any other person in the present is perceived to act in the same way our parents did many years before. **Fourth**, as people recall these early hurts and anger, they often tend to distort their recollections in extreme ways. We use words like *always* or *never* to describe these early experiences, as if there were few exception. We say to our partners, "Mom was *never* there for me – and neither are you!"

Two caveats apply to these observations: First, Harvard developmental psychologist, Jerome Kagan, reminds us that recall of past events is unreliable. "The correlation between reality and what people say is just 30 or 40 percent."[5] Secondly, being a hurt or angry child, or perhaps a child who fears abandonment, does not mean you expressed your hurt, anger, or fear. It often was not safe for you to do so as a child. Adult children of alcoholics know this quite well. Many parents will pulverize children who express intense emotions. In other families, there is always the threat of physical or emotional abandonment by parents if we express our pain too loudly. How fragile our homes can be! So we sadly grab our pillows, pull them over our heads to drown out the yelling in the other room, and then cry ourselves to sleep.

So Who's To Blame?

To sum up, I believe that both "nature" and "nurture" conspire to create lifelong imprints which dramatically influence our lives, especially our willingness to enter into and maintain love bonds. This chapter has explored nurture as an imprint and we have seen how the forces of inclusion, control, and affection can affect our desire for, or our avoidance of, intimacy. In the case of Margaux Hemingway we have seen the tragedy that can result, in part, because of these wounds.

Both marital satisfaction and marital dissatisfaction are largely predetermined before we ever meet our partners.

Is it really possible that early bonding experiences, or lack thereof, can shape so much? I believe that early life experiences shape many aspects of our adulthood experiences. This is certainly true with trauma. Most of us can easily grasp the tragic aftermath for a child whose parents died unexpectedly, or whose parents raped and sodomized them ruthlessly over the course of years. We can understand the wounds of a young Texas boy who grows up knowing that his own mother stoned his two siblings to death under the supposed command of God. We understand his bed-soaked nightmares, hesitancy to trust, and frightened rigidity when hugged. Abuse often leaves behind visual and visceral shards as we hear below from Connie, a client who experienced chronic verbal abuse, public humiliation, and abandonment from her mother over many years:

> It was bad enough that I couldn't get to my mother or have a good soothing mothering experience. But worse, I was left with an awful feeling, not of being unlovable, or hate-able, or detestable, but of being the jettisoned one. Perhaps being garbage conveys the idea a little, but not quite. Garbage was never human. I was, once; but then my humanity was stripped from me; all I was left with was being the one who was radically excluded, my existence denied. I experience this as a visceral sensation: being hurled away violently; then being a large glass container loudly fracturing into a million pieces. There is a feeling of impact, as if I was thrown against a wall violently, just before the sound of breaking glass. And with my mother, I couldn't get away.

The impact of childhood trauma is so significant to both the American Psychological Association and the American Psychiatric Association that there is a move a foot to develop a new diagnosis called "developmental trauma disorder" or DTD to be included in the Diagnostic and Statistical Manual of Mental Disorders V scheduled to be released in 2011. This need for a new diagnostic category recognizes the prevalence of repeated and serious traumas such as abuse, neglect, and caregiver impairment, whether from illness, alcohol or depression. No one

knows the number of children affected but one gauge is the number of children reported an-
nually to child protective services for abuse and neglect: 3,000,000!

Among the core symptoms of DTD are affect dysregulation, negative and cynical beliefs
one's life, and functional impairments in major areas of one's life, e.g. work. Affect dysregulation represents a wave of emotional flooding so intense that an individual often goes into "shut
down" mode when confronted with a reminder of the original trauma. Some mental health
professionals believe that parents who maltreat their children often are dysregulated themselves, a phenomenon known as "intergenerational transmission of trauma."

Most of us, thankfully, do not have to live through the horrors of abuse and psychotic
eruptions. The truth is that most of us do live lives of quiet desperation or at least pensive
wonderment; most of us have subtle wounds which are triggered by subtle reminders.

Many of us are Margaux Hemingways, without the glitter, without the drama, without
the gene pool, and without the tragic ending. We have reflex arcs which flare up when triggered. When our partners refuse to hold us, talk with us, or come home on time, we are reminded consciously or unconsciously of a mother whose career, depression, or self-indulgences
got in the way. We go limp. Our arms become flaccid. When a partner barks at us, critiques us,
or humiliates us, we are reminded of a father who emasculated us and robbed us of our power
and glory. Most of us, like rings of a tree, are left with permanent marks:

1) **Which define us,**
2) **Which we didn't create,**
3) **Which we are destined to reveal, and**
4) **Which we have an opportunity to heal – with the *Six Gifts*.**

You may remember the biblical story of Abraham and Isaac. If you were like me, you probably
heard this story of commitment and sacrifice from Abraham's perspective. Abraham, as God
requested, agreed to sacrifice his own son, Isaac, as a measure of his faith. God told Abraham to
take his son Isaac to the land of Moriah and offer him as a burnt offering. Obediently, Abraham
agreed to do so. Together, Abraham and Isaac went to the mountain-top where they searched for
wood whereupon they constructed an altar for the burnt offering. With the altar completed, Isaac
inquired where the customary sacrificial lamb might be! No doubt to his horror he is then told by
his father, Abraham, to lie down on the wood pyre where he would be sacrificed in place of the
lamb. Abraham tethered his arms and legs securely. Then, raising a sharpened knife high above
his head, Abraham prepared to slay his only beloved son. Just before the sacrifice could be made
God intervenes, telling Abraham to abandon this act of devotion. With his faith tested and his
mettle proven, Abraham is now told where to find a ram to sacrifice instead of his son.

But what of Isaac? What of his mental health and well-being? After all, he had thought
that his father loved him. What kind of loving father would kill his own son? Surely there could
be another sacrifice worthy of God's countenance! The Bible doesn't tell us so but Isaac had to
be a wounded young man after this painful life experience. Think about his losses. He lost his
innocence in this frightening moment when love could not provide a safe haven. He lost his

dignity as he lay weak and helpless beneath his father's knife. And he lost his trust in life's fairness and in human kindness. Would he ever allow himself to be so vulnerable again, to enter into a loving relationship again? Of course he did, marrying Rebekkah many years later.

Wounds can be overcome, however painfully.

The wounds we suffered as children may not have been as dramatic or as brutal as Isaac's – although I have seen worse. But most of us, perhaps all of us, were wounded in some way within our families during childhood. These wounds usually go relatively unnoticed until disenchantment tests our will to truly commit, our capacity to fully love. If we are wounded, this capacity is often impaired.

Lawyer Andrew Vachss thinks we have truly botched our jobs as parents. In his latest novel, *Safe House*, Vachss asserts that "Although we all believe our human species to be the highest point on the evolutionary scale, there is one critical area in which we do not represent an improvement upon our predecessors. This is a failure so fundamental, so critical, that our long-term survival is at stake…We are not protecting and preserving our own. Our notion of the human family as the safeguard of our species has not evolved. Instead, it has gone the opposite direction – it has devolved."[6]

The epidemic of "wounded" children has become so grave to David Lykken that he proposes a "parental licensure process"! Underlying this bid for licensure is a belief that prospective biological parents be expected to meet the same minimum requirements expected of persons wanting to adopt someone else's child. The most basic prerequisites would require that the parties be mature, married, and self-supporting, that they not be handicapped by substance abuse or by disabling mental illnesses, and that they have no prior convictions for crimes of violence."[7]

The tragedy of lousy parenting is not difficult to understand given the failure of many parents so honor their birth obligation. There are only three ways a child can be conceived. The first way is by *immaculate conception*. This is very rare. Second, a child can be desired as a *planned pregnancy*. In this case, parents dream their dreams of a family and recognize the sacrifices they are prepared to make along the way. This is increasingly becoming rarer because of the third option – *unwanted pregnancy*.

Think about these words: *Unwanted pregnancy! Unwanted!* According to Stanley Henshaw, there were 5.38 million pregnancies in 1994. "Excluding miscarriages, 49% of these pregnancies were unintended; 54% of these ended in abortion." (8) What are these children likely to face in life? Well, for some, there is nurturance and love because many people rise to the occasion, celebrate the gift of life, and respond to the call of the child. These children survive and flourish. Many other precious births, regrettably, are destined to become wounded children, whose parents are narcissistically chasing careers, six-figure salaries, job titles, Rolex watches, Porsches, gold medals in triathlons, notoriety in the community and orgasms! The lives of these resented children are often marked by insecure attachment, a term that reflects the strength of the emotional bond – or lack thereof – between parent and child.

But on the other hand…a la *Fiddler on the Roof*…how blameworthy are parents!

According to Judith Rich Harris, parents are getting a raw deal. Harris, who received an American Psychological Association scholarly award in 1998, asserts that parents have little influence over the long-term development of their child's personality. Harris believes that shared genes and a shared culture conspire to influence personality development in children far more than parents do. In particular, she believes that children are most influenced by their peers – the very people who tell them in classrooms, on soccer fields, or at parties just how well they are accepted. This seeking of peer approval is sacrosanct, requiring behavioral adaptations outside the home in order to be successful.

Harris's book, *The Nurture Assumption*, won her instant praise in 1998, landing her spots on the Today Show, *USA Today,* and a cover story in *Newsweek*.[9] She even won a prestigious scholarly award from the American Psychological Association, even though she is not a psychologist or a member of the APA! So where does all this leave us? Are we really creating disastrous consequences when we cut the apron strings too soon, assign too many chores, or miss too many Little League games?

Parenting, genes, and peers are **all** part of a developmental cocktail mix.

All three act in conjunction with one another and are influenced by one another. Over the years, it is true that many researchers have found that traits like impulsivity, aggression, thrill-seeking, neuroticism, and shyness are partly due to genes. "Partly" means anywhere from 20 to 70 percent. The other 30 to 80 percent reflects the very rich and diverse environments in a child's life. "Environment" means anything from a friend down the street, a college wrestling coach next door, an encounter with a bully in the 7th grade, to an awe-inspiring English teacher in high school.

Environment also includes parental contribution. Harris's intent, by her own admission, is to lessen the guilt of parents who did play Mozart in the nursery and still managed to rear difficult children who display aberrant and abhorrent behavior at times. Somehow, most of us must rise up out of our own ashes to become effective parents.

Each of us must find an inner beacon to become more than what we were given as children – to become more of what we were intended to be as adults.

Regardless of our gene pool, in spite of lousy parenting during our formidable years, each of us has a responsibility to rise above what our "givens" may be. Each of us has only a few *Living Years* to see more clearly as Mike and the Mechanics remind us:

Every generation
Blames the one before
And all of their frustrations
Come beating on your door.

I know that I'm a prisoner
To all my father held so dear
I know that I'm a hostage
To all his hopes and fears.
I just wish I could have told him
In the living years.[10]

CHAPTER 7

The Roots of Narcissism — Leadership

Deep in the bowels of Washington, hidden from public scrutiny and prying cameras, there is an illicit underworld where people are subtle, reasonable and interesting. I have occasionally been admitted to this place, the land of RIP (Reasonable in Private). I have been in the Senate dining room and heard senators, in whispers and with furtive glances, acknowledge the weaknesses in their own arguments and admit the justice of some of the other side's points. If it ever got out that they could think for themselves or often had subversive and honest thoughts they would be branded traitors to their party and uncertain champions for their cause. For politicians are not permitted to ply their trade in the land of RIP. In our democracy, all public business must be done in the land of SIPB (Self-Important Pathetic Blowhards)......In private, we have a decent leadership class. In public, it's rotten.[1]

Our leadership cannot rescue us from our own self-absorption because they are too caught up in their own. Our democracy regrettably takes decent individuals in private, churns them through a political tumbler which dilutes integrity, and spits them out as trumped up public puppets as David Brooks, from the New York Times, states above. This chapter, while recognizing that leaders are indeed the products of a narcissistic culture, examines how leaders create such cultures as well!

To be re-elected, each political leader must compromise an inherently healthy self to fuel a pseudo self created for the masses.

Why don't leaders, who are reasonable in *private*, become reasonable in *public*?

Why do personal agendas of leaders win out over public need? Image precludes honesty. Re-election trumps advocacy. Constituent earmarks and pet projects stifle the greater good. Trivial advantage and party favors usurp personal integrity. Wisdom falls prey to foolishness. Power obliterates compassion. Transcontinental cattle calls reign in resiliency. Pre-approved bromides engulf authenticity.

Kissing up to voters and one's party members expunges what we most long for in our elected officials: [1] *vision*, [2] *virtue*, and [3] *vehemence*. We need to be drawn forward by what we don't see, yet know is possible with vision. When Muhammad Yunus, winner of the 2006 Nobel Peace Prize, speaks of a world where there will be no passports, no visas, and no countries, that's vision. Granted, we're not very close to this reality, yet we need to be challenged. We need our heroes to speak up with vehemence, not silenced by a persona non grata. We need leaders with humility who are willing to acknowledge failures.

We need failures not afraid to be leaders – to be "OK" when they are not!

Most leaders are horrendous failures because they fail at what they are most expected to do – lead! Rather than lead, most leaders merely and meekly react. Each reflects back what their party triumvirates want to hear and what their constituents demand to hear. "Keep my taxes low!" "Keep the open pit coal mines going." "Keep the minorities out of our neighborhoods." Once a leader succumbs to group think, the will to think, at least out loud, is gone. Most powerful, image-minded leaders, intoxicated by their own self-importance, steeped in their own re-election fantasies, refuse to challenge their own points of view, let alone ours. Narcissism prevails, both theirs and ours!

It is refreshing to occasionally see exceptions, i.e. folks who speak up honestly.

Former Texas Agriculture Commissioner, Jim Hightower, believes we need to make noise. "I am rude enough to call this what it is: class war. A devastating class war is raging in America's countryside. The corporate media don't cover it, and you can bet that candidates of both major parties will studiously avoid any mention of it in this fall's congressional campaigns, because this is not a class confrontation in which the many are menacing the wealthy few...Rather, today's class assault has been initiated from the top – a ruthless war of attrition in which the wealthy few, from their bastions of privilege on Wall Street and in Washington, are lobbying bomb after bomb into the lives and communities of the many."[2]

Senator John McCain once reminded us that "You must be afraid to have courage. Suffering is not, by itself, courage. Choosing to suffer what we fear is!"[3] Courage is that exceptional moment in time, when political leaders somehow rise above their party affiliations, in order to forge a unity of proper attitude and action – when something deep within them strikes the flint of love, of honor, and duty. Getting past one's own self-interest is the key. In this highly polarized political climate we must hope for more.

Has Senator McCain's courage and integrity held up over time? According to Pulitzer prize-winning columnist, Leonard Pitts, the answer is a resounding "No!"

> *Senator McCain's integrity died recently when he told Newsweek magazine, "I never considered myself a maverick." How could he disavow himself of this quality [author's inclusion] when the word "maverick" was the subtitle of his 2003 memoir and his campaign plane, when he ran for president back in 1989, was dubbed Maverick. Once, integrity was his most attractive political trait, drawing smitten praise from political reporters and intrigued attention from voters sick of the same old, same old politicians who would bend like Gumby for the electorate's approval...Since being bested by George Walker Bush he has embraced right-wing religious extremists he had once condemned. And he reneged on a promise that he'd be open to repealing "Don't Ask, Don't Tell" if military leaders advised it. And went from opposition of offshore oil drilling to "Drill, baby drill!" And et cetera. These are not just changes of opinion we're talking about. They are betrayals of core principle. And while that might be politics as usual, there is a higher standard for the politician who has positioned himself as a man of uncommon integrity; a purveyor of straight talk in a nation hungry for same...McCain is hardly unique. Indeed, they have a name for people who change their opinions in order to win votes: politicians.[4]*

A winning ticket for leaders who choose to lead is vision, virtue, and vehemence.

Whether the topic is economic reform, global warming, equal opportunity, equal rights, or stem cell research, leaders have a responsibility to create a vision, join hands, and reach out to us. As a narcissistic culture, we need to be blessed with courageous peacemakers who encourage dialogue, rise above their limitations, and who lead us beyond our selves.

Sometimes, it's just very discouraging. Take 2010 "health care reform" for instance. Regardless of whether you're a Democrat or Republican, regardless of whether you support reform or not, partisan politics and self-interest permeates our psyches. We cringe as we hear about Senate Majority Leader Harry Reid offering a carrot to the final Senate holdout, Ben Nelson from Nebraska. With time running out, Reid offered to have the federal government pay for the expansion of Nebraska's Medicaid program in perpetuity! Of course, Senator Nelson signed the bill. Well, what about the other 49 states? Where's the mutuality here? Where's the collective spirit, the virtuous process, we all hoped for?

Even veteran U.S. Senators get fed up enough to leave Washington politics in the rear view mirror. In 2010, disenchanted Evan Bayh from Indiana bemoaned, "I no longer love congress; the American political system is "dysfunctional," riddled with "brain-dead partisanship" and permanent campaigning. Bayh argued that the American people needed to deliver a "shock" to Congress by voting incumbents out en masse and replacing them with people interested in reforming the process and governing for the good of the people, rather than deeppocketed special-interest groups."[5]

Regardless of where we look, well beyond the Washington Beltway, we see signs that narcissistic self-interest is usurping the needs of a greater good – in our marriages, in our families, in our neighborhoods, in our politics, in therapy offices and in our religious institutions. The id, ego, and superego of our personal constitutions have lost their triumvirate status. We are out of balance. Pleasure-seeking and ego gratification have trumped society's conscience. We have failed to find a measured bandwidth wherein one's self needs are properly balanced with another's needs.

It's one thing to find such self-absorption woven throughout the fabric of our psyches and societies; it is quite another to find it caricaturing our heads of state, our therapeutic remedies, and our most cherished religious rites. The present chapter explores leadership; the next two chapters represent two other of society's most favored ways of seeking balance in a catawampus world: psychotherapy and religion. Yet, each suffers from, and may contribute to, a prevailing narcissism that only serves to separate us further from each other.

It is time to dissect the cultures of *leadership, psychotherapy*, and *religion*.

Narcissus stared at his own reflection in a pond and learned nothing new. Once a politician falls in love with his or her own persona, expect the party line for the next four to six years. A mirrored reflection of one's own persona is nothing more than stagnation entrapping a frozen soul. This can be true of one's lover, one's therapist, or with one's presidential cabinet of muted teammates. We must hope for far more from out leaders, our therapists, and our spiritual guides.

We need inspirational mentors, honest critics, imperfect heroes, and irreverent reverends to drop their holy rocks into our illusory ponds so that we may wake up from our self-absorbed reveries.

What we find instead is that our national leaders, our cultural icons, and our athletic heroes not only mirror our own narcissism they go far beyond what we could do on our own. What's more sobering is that their narcissism can only exist in a world which mirrors back attention and approval, which then reinforces a continuation of the farce, as we saw with the Emperor's New Clothes.

This chapter explores the essence of leadership. We will consider a number of questions. **First**, how do we define effective leadership? **Second**, how does leadership, in general, fail us? **Third**, how do presidential politics, in particular, fail us? **Fourth**, how do we, as followers, allow a failed leadership to fail us? **Finally**, why do we love "gurus" as we do? [I offer my apologies to a Right Wing minority who by now have identified me as an enemy and long ago put down this book as annoying tripe.]

Effective Leadership

Sometimes our leaders get it right! Even a Pope and a Jew can get it right!

Several centuries ago, the Pope, as leader of the Christian World, decreed that all the Jews had to convert or leave Italy. There was a huge outcry from the Jewish community, so the Pope offered a deal. He would have a religious debate with the leader of the Jewish community. If the Jews won, they could stay in Italy. If the Pope won, they would have to leave.

The Jewish people met and picked an aged but wise Rabbi, Moishe, to represent them in the debate. Rabbi Moishe however refused, saying it was no use and the Jews might as well start packing. The people were distraught. Out of the weeping and wailing, a voice was heard. It was Yakel saying "I will do it!"

The people said "You Yakel? You are just a dumb schmuck. A putz! How could you, who cannot even read the Torah, possibly face the Pope in a debate?"

"It is either me or move," replied Yakel. So the people agreed.

However, as Yakel spoke no Italian and the Pope spoke no Yiddish, they all agreed that it would be a 'silent' debate. On the chosen day, the Pope and Yakel sat opposite each other for a full minute before the Pope raised his hand and showed three fingers. Yakel looked back and raised one finger!

Next the Pope waved his finger around his head. Yakel pointed to the ground where he sat.

The Pope then brought out a communion wafer and a chalice of wine.

Yakel pulled out an apple. With that, the Pope stood up and declared that he was beaten, that Yakel was too clever and that the Jews could stay.

Later the Cardinals met with the Pope, asking what had happened. The Pope said: "First I held up three fingers to represent the Trinity. He responded by holding up one finger to remind me that there is still only one God common to both beliefs. Then, I waved my finger to show him that God was all around us. He responded by pointing to the ground to show that God was also right here with us. I then pulled out the wine and wafer to show that God absolves us of all our sins. He pulled out an apple to remind me of the original sin. He had me beaten and I could not continue."

Meanwhile, the delirious Jewish community was gathered around Yakel. "What happened," they asked. "Well," said Yakel, "First he said to me that we had three days to get out of Italy, so I said to him, 'This is what I think of the idea! Then he tells me that the whole country would be cleared of Jews and I said to him. 'Mr. Pope, we're staying right here!'"

"And then what?" asked a woman.

"Who knows?" said Yakel. "He took out his lunch so I took out mine."

(Source Unknown)

Most of us reading this light-hearted tale of Yakel taking on the Pope would laugh at the notion that he possessed real leadership skills. Many of us, like his brethren, might just consider him a dumb schmuck, a putz! But there is more to this picture than meets the eye. Historically, psychologists tended to see leadership as an individual phenomenon. Since the field of psychology began with a heavy emphasis on tests and measurements, it was not unusual to search for a Holy Grail using various assessment instruments over the years; this, unfortunately, has led to a popularization of certain notions of leadership which quite frankly have been misleading.

The first misleading notion is that leadership can be viewed as a unique attribute of extraordinary individuals, of "Great Men." Yakel doesn't appear to do well here. All we need to do is examine a number of folks considered successful leaders and find the common thread. The implication here is that mere exposure to these exceptional, transformational figures is all that is needed for success. Viewing leadership as an individual phenomenon is nuts to established writers in the field like Warren Bennis, who believes that "the only person who practices leadership alone in a room is the psychotic."[6]

The second misleading notion about leadership suggests that the identified unique attributes are genetically endowed and are passed from one generation to another. Again, Yakel, being a dumb schmuck, doesn't appear to have arrived at his moment of destiny from fine lineage. The implication here is that these characteristics are immutable and not subject to influence from others. Both of these notions together have been called "trait-based" theories and were soundly rejected by behavioral scientists for 30 to 40 years because attribute analysis alone did not even come close to explaining the effectiveness of certain individuals.

Nonetheless, popularization of attributes continues today. Whether he adequately "walks the talk" or not, Senator John McCain's belief that effective leadership requires courage is a good example of unique attributes:

> *Courage is like a muscle. The more we exercise it, the stronger it gets. I sometimes worry that our collective courage is growing weaker from disuse. We don't demand it from our leaders, and our leaders don't demand it from us. The courage deficit is both our problem and our fault. As a result, too many leaders in the public and private sectors lack the courage necessary to honor their obligation to others and to uphold the essential values of leadership. Often, they display a startling lack of accountability for their mistakes and a desire to put their own self-interest above the common good. That means trouble for us all, because courage is the "enforcing virtue," the one that makes possible all the other virtues common to exceptional leaders: Honesty, integrity, confidence, compassion, and humility.[7]*

In short, leaders who lack courage aren't leaders.

Now here is where Yakel hits a homerun. Yakel was "a schmuck," "a putz," "couldn't read the Torah," and "couldn't speak Italian," but he had courage to represent his Jewish community. Deep down, Yakel knew that courage was the "enforcing virtue." He not only came prepared with his own lunch; he also arrived with vision, was inspired by virtue, and spoke with vehemence. And the Pope experienced him as an effective, courageous leader!

Where was the courage to say "It's my fault" or "I'm sorry, I did it" following the "intelligence failures" preceding the 911 attacks in New York? When "weapons of mass destruction" in Iraq were proven to be an exaggeration – or perhaps a lie – why did no one in senior administration have the courage to step up to be accountable, or punished? McCain wanted to know, and so do we!

We see this same lack of courage and integrity in corporate America with people like Leo Mullin, the former CEO of Delta Airlines. Mullin, like many other greedy CEO's, was committed only to his own self-interest and enrichment. In 2002, Mullin received a bonus of $1.4 million plus $2 million in stock, even as the airline was laying off thousands of employees. And what can we possibly say about those snake charmers at Enron who actually bragged about ripping off California taxpayers during that State's energy crisis. In the words of McCain himself, "Those traders weren't executives, but they were inspired to behave the way they did by the "me first" climate of self-aggrandizement that Enron leaders personified."

We have trivialized the concept of courage by dumbing it down.

We dilute the true meaning of courage when we suggest that it takes courage to reveal our deepest fears to a therapist, that it takes courage to escape a failing marriage, or that it takes courage to leave everything on the field after an exceptionally brutal athletic event.

These examples of self-disclosure, self-assertion, and self-aggression miss the real essence of courage – the capacity to overcome fear in order to sacrifice for a greater good. We must be willing to sacrifice our egos, even our careers, for that greater good. These are choices we must make, particularly if we work in Washington.

You must be afraid to have courage. It bears repeating to emphasize that suffering is not, by itself, courage. Choosing to suffer what we fear is. Courage is that exceptional moment in time, when we rise above our limitations, in order to forge a unity between conscience, fear, and action, when something deep within us strikes the flint of love, of honor, of duty, to make the spark that fires our resolve.

You cultivate courage by loving something more than your own well-being.

This is where we must leave "trait theories" behind. As tempting as it may appear to be to uphold the Great Man concept, who somehow possesses the right Juju, a much more promising definition for leadership exists. We must see that every great leader exists within a community and must be able to motivate others to work collaboratively together to accomplish great things. This is true leadership.

This definition implies a number of things:

* ✳ Leadership is a process, not a property of a person.
* ✳ The process involves a particular form of influence called motivating.
* ✳ Intrinsic and extrinsic incentives are not part of this definition.
* ✳ The consequence of the influence is collaboration in pursuit of a common goal.
* ✳ The "great things" are in the minds of both leader and followers.

Leadership, for Victor Vroom and Arthur Jago, is all about the relationships that one establishes with others.[8] Quite a bit of research over the years supports this notion. Many writers in the field believe that leaders can be divided into two groups: the first are task-motivated leaders who prize outcomes over process; the second are relationship-motivated leaders who cherished the collaborative process as the key element in achieving successful outcomes. Not surprisingly, research results often confirm that relationship-motivated leaders usually outperform task-motivated leaders.

Simply put, there is an interaction between person and environment which dictates what kind of leadership is required to achieve great things. Getting a good read on what is required in a particular setting or with a particular situation is both necessary and sufficient to achieve great results. Creating an effective team, delegating, sharing decision-making, enlarging jobs, placing your trust in people, and emphasizing that the customer must come first are typical influencing variables affecting competent leaders.

Self-absorbed narcissists don't do these things very well.

Collaboration is the key. Psychologist, Dr. Kate Ludeman, captures this quite well in her book, *The Worth Ethic*. "There is no leader without followers. We succeed together or not at all. This is the essential "W.E." of the Worth Ethic, the belief in your indelible self-worth and the fundamental and potential worth of others...We can affirm our employees' worth. What's required of us is a paradigm shift that allows each of us, managers and employees alike, to move from an adversarial to a collaborative position."[9]

Effective leaders collaborate. Effective collaborators lead.

Presidential Leadership and the Bubble

Presidential politics more often appears as raw entertainment than true leadership.

America's "dream ticket" has become a front-row seat to American Idol. Like many reality shows, we begin with relatively likeable people, then reduce them to irreducible fault lines, gloss over the real issues they once stood for, until each candidate becomes Machiavellian enough to devour the other in head-to-head, gut-splitting combat. Of course we witness all of this carnage for free – no pay per view needed – in the open broiler systems we call cable news, IM's, web mail, and other electronic message systems. Leadership qualities – suggesting creativity, intellect and vision – seem to be vestigial remains in these campaigns. Instead, marketing and advertisement budgets make or break these titanic struggles, knowing that a lot of folks just want to be entertained than think!

The 2008 Presidential campaign, in particular, offered Americans an unparalleled opportunity to witness transparent form over substance, medium over message, and negatives over positives – all in the name of narcissism. We read about Sarah Palin's hairdo and her red, high-heeled, 3-inch, peep-toe pumps marketed by a company by the name of Naughty Monkey. Not missing a greedy upstroke the company soon capitalized on the growing Palin zeitgeist by sending out pictures of the Republican VP nominee with the slogan "I vote for Naughty Monkey." Shoe sales jumped 50 percent and sold out in four sizes. Even Barack Obama received fashion advice from actor George Clooney according to London's *Daily Mail* newspaper.

We are enamored by the creation of pseudo image. The media knows we love bubbles!

Image created by media blitz and iconic hypes are all about bubbles. We started off positively enough in '08. We had Senator Barack Obama championing "hope and change;" Senator John McCain commandeering the "straight talk express;" Governor Sarah Palin corralling in all the "pit bulls with lipstick;" and then there's Senator Joe Biden capitalizing on his congressional tenure as the "seasoned legislator." A nice montage all in all. Who among us wouldn't like a hopeful, straight-talkin', gun-totin', lipstick-seasoned bull dog to lead our country? If we could just overlook Palin's supposed ban of library books – like Huckleberry Finn, Canterbury Tales, and Merriam-Webster's Ninth New Collegiate Dictionary – we'd be alright.

We love our American Idols.

Then Senator Obama and Governor Palin were rock stars who emerged from nowhere to become oases for all our deserted hopes and dreams. Energy, looks, pedigree, and chutzpah were all there. Greek coronation on the one hand, beauty queen on the other! Then, in milliseconds, we got to slice and dice over night.

We soon witnessed small bore, nasty diversionary tactics which derailed the "straight talk express" on one side of the aisle while upending the "chariots of fire" on the other. McCain's campaign soon falsely asserted that Obama supported "comprehensive sex ed" for kindergartners. Obama's campaign howled that "You can put lipstick on a pig; but it's still a pig." McCain then falsely retorted that Obama would raise taxes on the middleclass and was "conveniently vague" regarding both domestic and foreign policy. Not to be outdone, Obama asserted that McCain supported a "hundred year war" in Iraq.

Amidst all this hyperbole the real issues get lost, perhaps intentionally!

Negative caricaturing and campaigning attracts bloggers and cable news producers. This stuff is a cash cow for the news networks – and we love it! We are addicted to each candidate's imperfections as long as we are one step removed from it. We love to observe it – we just don't want to embrace it within ourselves or our loved ones.

Even the comedians had their fill:

Jon Stewart: After a quick meet-and-greet with King Abdullah, Obama was off to Israel, where he made a quick stop at the manger in Bethlehem where he was born.

Conan O'Brien: Oprah Winfrey is in the middle of a scandal today, because she is refusing to have Republican VP candidate Sarah Palin on her show. The friction started because Palin said if she were elected she'd be the most powerful woman in the country, and Oprah said, "The hell you will."

Jimmy Kimmel: Should we be nervous about a man who preaches against wasteful spending when his wife is wearing a $300,000 outfit at the Republican National Convention? If Cindy McCain were a plane, Sarah Palin would sell her on eBay.

There is no real, meaningful dialogue in Presidential politics – only sound bites meant to tantalize, sensationalize, and supersize differences into entertainment weekly blogs. Presidential politics is about life in a bubble. First you ride one, then you burst one, and then – if you survive – you live in one. Columnist George Will has captured this quite well:

> *The tech bubble was followed by the housing bubble, which has been topped by the Palin*
> *bubble. Bubbles will always be with us, because irrational exuberance always will be. Its*
> *symptom is the assumption that old limits have yielded to undreamt-of possibilities. The*
> *Dow will always rise, as will housing prices, and rapture about a running mate can be*
> *decisive in a presidential election.*[10]

The Sarah Palin bubble was a gem. First you hide her for two weeks – forbidding her to answer any questions from the media; then you squash the living spirit out of her by extinguishing all her natural spontaneity; then you hire scores of conservative advisors and marketing aces; then you sanctify her and motherhood; then you spring-load her with well-rehearsed sound bites which are repeated in 10-second, saccadic, machine-gun bursts; and then you release her to mild-mannered Charles Gibson for a practice round until he squirms in his chair because he can't take it any more. There, in two short weeks of silence, we witnessed Governor Palin being transformed from an obscure, rifle-hunting, personnel-firing, God-fearing beauty queen into a sword-swallowing, party-favoring, slogan-bearing member of the Republican Triumvirate.

Once you survive the highs and lows of the campaign you get to be president or vice president of the United States – you get to live life in a bubble surrounded by advisors, writers, and the party-faithful. This is where things can get dangerous. This is where people can get killed.

It is one thing to live life within the catacombs of advisers and marketing personnel; it is quite another to live life within the tender folds of the American underbelly.

This catacomb of advisers, marketing teams, and good ol' boys failed President George Walker Bush. So did we! It was our responsibility to be heard. How could Mr. Bush end up with an approval rating hovering around 30 percent and a disapproval rating somewhere around 1000 percent – a lame-duck perch, so rebuffed and solitary, he chose not to attend the 2008 Republican National Convention?

Solitary living did Mr. Bush in!

George Walker Bush believed in solitary living, often referring to this realm as his "bubble." There's very little, if any, true collaboration in a bubble world. In an interview with Bob Woodward in December of 2001, Bush insisted that "anybody who says they're an outside adviser of this administration on this particular matter is not telling the truth. First of all, in the initial phase of the war, I never left the compound. Nor did anybody come in the compound. I was… one guy in a bubble."[11] Two years after the Woodward interview, Pat Robertson tried to give this same President some advice about the coming invasion of Iraq. Robertson, who co-founded the Christian Coalition, supported Bush but told him to prepare the nation for the likelihood of casualties.

Bush's reply: "We're not going to have any casualties!"[12]

Self-absorbed leaders are too tunnel-visioned to see the wider panorama.

Let's catch our collective breath for a moment. President George Walker Bush was not the only one living in a bubble. We were as well. We went along for the ride, just as members of Congress did when they financially supported the Iraq invasion. Most of us were content to live in our own narcissistic bubbles – continuing to stay immersed in our worlds of pride, possessions, power and prestige. As one acquaintance put it, "Give me my beer, my remote, and my red Mustang convertible and I'm in seventh heaven!"

As many of us floated comfortably along on our billowing waves of abundance, President George Walker Bush capitalized on our national mourning by advocating a simple philosophy: In order to be for something, one must be against something else. In the President's words, "You are either for us, or you are against us." There is no dialogue here, only caveats and ultimatums. Where was the broader, more inclusive world view here? Where was the common good and collaborative spirit here? Somehow, we went along for the ride – for four years, then eight years! Why?

We endured silently because each of us was able to live comfortably in our own bubbles – until our children started dying on foreign turf, until our travel visas became more difficult to obtain, until our 401K's began to tank, and until a painful economic recession bit us in the ass. Even our ocean-bound, protected bubble called America – clearly blown to pieces on September 11th, 2001 – could not deny a painful reality: many of us have been personally jolted or economically decimated by the goings-on in Washington. Now and only now – when we are in pain – do we stand up and protest.

Many opportunities to be heard, to have a voice, exist during a lifetime, no matter the color of our robes. Whether we are president or emperor, governor or senator, father or mother, teacher or farmer – each of us must learn to collaborate for the sake of community, for the survival of all. If we choose instead to live life in a narcissistic bubble, each of us is at great risk of possessing an:

* ✳ Uncompromising self-absorption,
* ✳ Which alienates others,
* ✳ And compromises the greater good.

So What's Wrong with Us?

Like New Yorkers listening to Kitty Genovese cry out for help, we sit in silence.

In January of 2007, we were witness to a spectacle of cross examination in which former U.S. Ambassador to Iraq Paul Bremer squirmed in a hot seat specially designed with him in mind. Congressional oversight committee members wanted to know what he did with 363 TONS of newly printed, shrink-wrapped $100 bills he had carefully transported to Baghdad. That cool cache of bills equated to $12 billion in cold, hard American cash – the kind of money you and I work very hard to pay the government each year in the form of taxes. Bremer was doing OK with his deposition until they got to question of where did the money go?

Well, it seems that Mr. Bremer dolled out lots of cash to ministries of the Iraqi government to meet payrolls that were clearly fraudulent. In fact, an audit by US authorities revealed that the payrolls were padded up to 90 percent with "ghost employees" – folks who didn't really work there, or in some cases, didn't even exist. So, $12 BILLION dollars later, a lot of heads are rolling. How did our congressional leaders allow this to happen? Where were the "checks and balances" when we needed them?

And, how about Dr. Richard Carmona? He was our country's highest ranking doctor as Surgeon General until 2006. He told the House Committee on Oversight and Government Reform that the Whitehouse prohibited him from speaking about condom use because the administration believes in abstinence-only sex education. He was also advised not to bring up stem cell research. And to cap things off, he was denied permission to speak at the Special Olympics, of all places, because that was seen as helping a political opponent! We see in these scenarios that we as a people are being denied health information and representation that may promote our physical and emotional well being by a restrictive White House living in an ideological bubble.

To be denied health information is outrageous, but our silence is catastrophic.

What will it take for the American people, not to mention Congress, to have a gag reflex over such incompetent management and leadership? This should be hard to swallow for all of us, yet most of us don't care. We live in our own little bubbles, glued to *American Idol*, and intent on fulfilling our own "missing ten degrees." We have become numb to the nightly news which over time merely registers as a distant murmur as we rev up our $500 Weber barbecues for a quick porterhouse or two. As the evening news is interrupted with one commercial after another, pushing Cadillacs, Hummers, and plasma TVs our way, we continue to ignore the tracings of truth which emanate mutely over the airways. We ignore the thousands who lie dying abroad, we ignore the horrid credit histories of thousands who "qualified" for home mortgages, and we ignore an insulated and arrogant administration intent on saving face and presumptively saving a world from evil.

There is no sacrifice on our part as we spin kaleidoscopically in our own worlds.

Prior to President Obama's election, our presidential nominees were too afraid to ask us to sacrifice. We witnessed this on October 7th, 2008, during one of three presidential debates between Senator John McCain and Barack Obama. When asked by Tom Brokaw how Americans might be able to sacrifice during tough economic times, both punted – refusing to answer the question. Too much honesty risks too many votes. When politicians refuse to be a voice for sacrifice, when both political parties refuse to sacrifice on favored programs, we have the makings of a disaster.

Now, in these hard economic times, we have no choice. We must sacrifice.

Our own self-absorption often blinds us to the realities out there. *Boston Globe* columnist, Derrick Jackson, writes, "almost everything about our lifestyles, from our obesity epidemic to our homes, reeks of not giving one whit about being only 4 percent of the planet's population yet creating a quarter of the greenhouse gasses that contribute to global warming. Even though the size of the American family has shrunk over the last half-century, the size of the average American home has more than doubled, with a single home in the suburbs loaded with more technology than whole villages in the developing world…The last thing voters want to hear from a presidential candidate is that a more secure America means a less selfish America."[13]

We are the reflecting ponds that sustain self-absorbed leaders and mystical gurus!

We elect them, re-elect them, and pay to hear them. We love gurus! Why? The answer is clear: because they seduce us with their promises, invite us to join them in Camelot, and entrance us to believe that we can be like them – for an easy price. For the right amount of change we can hear trance channeler Kevin Ryerson teach us that Saints are a step beneath Ascending Masters, who in turn are just a notch below Angels and Archangels. Creation theologian Mathew Fox even tells us that angels zip along at the speed of light. For Marianne Williamson, "Most women are priestesses and healers…We are all of us sisters of a mysterious order." Where do we sign up? For those of us living in misery, searching endlessly for "a missing piece," who would turn down such lofty, easy invitations?

We don't challenge these folks because they mirror what we most want to hear.

"We're not going to die!" "We can attract all that we want just by thinking about it!" Our fears are arrested, not our lives. "The most powerful charismatics," writes Wendy Kaminer, "are those who simultaneously invite identification and idolatry. Then, if they are divine, so are we. Indeed, the measure of our psychic or spiritual superiority is usually our openness to the guru's teachings…The guru offers us the opportunity to become leaders of our culture by becoming followers of his teachings. Gurus often tell us exactly what we want to hear. Our fears are assuaged. There is no death. There is no mortality. Spiritual peace and enlightenment does not require a lifetime of discipline. It requires only that you suspend your critical judgment, attend their lectures and workshops, and buy their books and tapes."[14]

We like the easy way out, be it a tape, TV remote control, or prescription from our MD. We are consumed and blinded by what we see. Marketing experts know this very well. We forget about Michelle Obama's brilliance and pedigree and instead fixate on her Isabel Toledo ivory and black dress, her chartreuse Jason Wu gown, her black Michael Kors jacket, and her Azzedine Alara belt. Somehow, this cultural blitz seduces us and then blends with nature and nurture to create a narcissistic cocktail that momentarily has blurred our vision, altered our state, and impaired our judgments.

What will it take for our leaders, so reasonable in private, to help us see the light?

Postscript: The Secretary of the Future

Towards the end of his life, author Kurt Vonnegut wondered what it would be like for the President to establish a brand new Cabinet position, the Secretary of the Future: Someone with a vested interest in keeping the planet safe for our grandchildren and great-grandchildren. "It'll never happen," Vonnegut would say pessimistically. Vonnegut thought it was too late for us to fix things. After all, we've treated the Earth cruelly and now the planet's immune system is trying to get rid of us. Human beings, past and present, have trashed the joint. Mankind's greatest addictions have been alcohol and fossil fuels and our last great American heroes may well be our librarians.[15]

Vonnegut got it right! Our librarians are the guardians of the written word. Our finest leaders, our truest guides, have left behind a wonderland of wisdom from which we can draw. Vonnegut read the works of Martin Luther King, Abraham Lincoln, Mark Twain, and the Holy Scripture. Vonnegut got the human condition. And while life may have beaten the cheerful optimism out of him he continued to believe in kindness as an elixir. Thankfully, he never lived long enough to know that Sarah Palin may have wanted to trash Mark Twain. He would have been amused.

Vonnegut knew that our national security was better achieved through our treasure-chest of written works as well as our inherent need to share what we know. Vonnegut knew that our national security would never be achieved through the destruction of our planet – or each other. Vonnegut knew that national security depends upon the willingness of those who lead to listen; for those who listen to lead – not to mention read.

The sounds of silence are simply not an option in a world order where bubbles can insulate leaders from constituents, countries from neighbors, and planet earth from an infinite cosmos.

CHAPTER **8**

The Roots of Nacissism — Psychotherapy

Oh! The comfort, the inexpressible
Comfort of feeling safe with a person;
Having neither to weigh thoughts
Nor measure words,
But to pour them all out
Just as they are,
Chaff and grain together
Knowing that a fateful hand
Will take and sift them,
Keep what is worth keeping,
And then, with the breath of kindness,
Blow the rest away.[1]

Socrates said the unexamined life is not worth living. Many of my clients show me that the unexamined life is often desolate. I have spent the lion's share of six decades examining mine. I am a psychologist who awakens with my personal demons sleeping next to me. Usually they awaken before I do! No doubt I would have been mesmerized by my naval nonetheless, but I feel certain that I would have chosen another field had my family not been so disturbed. Marketing and photography have caught my attention over the years. As professions, they were not meant to be. There is something about a narcissistic, suicidal mother, a mute father, and a conflagration of scorching infernos which had flung me into deep psychic spaces – into the realm of the self-absorbed.

I was meant to discover the difference between destination and destiny.

My destination during my formative years was a five by eight, pale blue bedroom where my bastion wasn't fortified enough to withstand the sounds of the bloody onslaughts occurring down the hall. Once I left home, my destiny was to become a psychologist. I even stated so in my high school yearbook. At the tender age of 18, I knew that inexorable forces had been set in motion that would shape me for a lifetime. I would choose psychology as a way of under-standing my own misery.

There was a time, during my sophomore year of college, when I sought out counseling for the first time. Academic pressures, frustrations with dating, and some force deep within me echoed, "Larry, Larry, you have unfinished business to deal with!" The counseling center at Temple University was a free service, so I made an appointment one dreary day. My destiny that day was to be assigned a blind counselor who was a literalist when it came to Rogerian psychotherapy. Carl Rogers had proposed that "client-centered therapy" be best conducted paraphrasing in the client's own words what had been spoken. I remember our first session going something like this:

"I'm really scared shitless that I may be sabotaging any chances for intimacy before I even get to first base with a date." My theoretically pure, blind therapist then responded, "So, you're really scared shitless that you may be sabotaging any chances for intimacy before you even get on base."

I then said, "Yeah, that's right." Going on, I oozed, "Somehow I'm just not confident in approaching women right now."

"I hear that you're not confident in the way you approach women right now. Is that cor-rect?"

"You bet! You're really getting it!" I murmured with a sigh of faded love. This echo cham-ber continued for a fitful hour. I returned a second and final time to see this man, knowing that he could not see me or truly hear me. I felt alone in his presence, desperate for a con-nection, but finding none. What kind of narcissistic nightmare was this? A narcissistic part of me really did long for a mirrored reflection, but I did not need endless reverberations of my own heartaches. A therapist who was a vulnerable, responsive, and imperfect soul would have sufficed just fine. I remembered psychiatrist Carl Jung once saying that the meeting of two personalities is like the contact of two chemical substances; if there is any reaction, both are transformed forever.

Where was my chemical catalyst?

That day, when personal contrition met blind repetition, I knew what kind of therapist I would not be! I so dearly wanted to see through a glass darkly, to share my pain, and to feel the comfort of an emotional bond. I wanted to stare at my gnarly underbelly and, then, eventually, to find a path toward others – even love. This kind man may have helped others but I realized early in my studies that I would be far more empathic, directive, and dynamic in creating a needed spark with others.

There are times when I succeed quite well; other times when I don't.

At times I am an invited guest on an epic journey; at other times I am the guest house itself. I understand why wayward travelers might consider me a "friend" or a "guide." After all, hospice, hospital and hospitality derive from the same Greek word hospes, meaning guest. My presence often illuminates a path but never determines the destination. Being let into another person's psychic universe is a supreme honor and reifies the notion that a grief observed is indeed a grief endured.

As humans, it is our design as well as our quest to share our painful struggles with another.

Knowing What We Want: Psychotherapy's Universal Calling

A few years ago I was traveling to Dallas to give a presentation. Once seated, I turned to the woman sitting next to me and introduced myself, as is my custom. When I asked her if she was also going to Dallas for business she reluctantly emerged from her more preferred cocoon to answer reluctantly, "Yes, I am on my way to a conference to discuss the theoretical framework for studying contracts and enforcement in settings with nondurable trading opportunities. I am particularly interested in implementing state-contingency payoffs, modeling trade actions, and structured game-theory frameworks applied to research."

I would say it took her about three minutes to realize that I didn't have the foggiest idea what she was talking about and for me to realize that her IQ was infinitesimally higher than mine. The last thing I remember before we both slipped back into our respective bubbles was that she had a Ph.D. in economics and that she appeared to be from India. Just before landing in Dallas I was unable to contain myself and I burst forth one more time to ask if there was an abundance of psychologists or marriage therapists in India.

"No," she replied.

"Well, is the divorce rate rising in India today given Western influence?" I wondered.

"No, people stay in their relationships."

"Well, if there are few mental health professionals, what do spouses do when they have difficult problems to solve?" I persisted.

"THEY JUST WORK THEM OUT!" she curtly remarked.

"Oh," I murmured as burning tires met hardened runway. I could tell immediately she was relieved to hear the braking wheels grip concrete and know that an undulating jetway would soon provide a needed escape from me. Yet, her words lingered on for me.

THEY JUST WORK THEM OUT! I wondered about these five words for days. Do folks in India cope that differently than we do in the United States? Are they more self-reliant, more accepting of givens, than we are here in the States? Or was she simply being pragmatic: "We don't have the financial resources in India you do in the U.S. and our population as a whole cannot afford counseling and personal growth seminars. Our patterns of wealth are different and our resources are not as plentiful for mental health."

While each of these notions was plausible, I knew that something more basic bridged the gap between her Ph.D. in economics and my Ph.D. in psychology; between her home-land 2000 miles away and mine: the belief that each of us wrestles with a basic anxiety which emerges deeply from all our endeavors, conscious or unconscious, to cope with the harsh facts of life – givens which define our existence. While both religious prayer life and psychotherapy have grown out of this need to answer questions about our existence (see Chapter 20), one in particular stands out: "What do you want?" What could be more basic than asking 300 people this question in a "personal-growth" retreat? Noted psychiatrist, Irwin Yalom M.D., has ob-served the following during such experiences[2]:

> *Often the room rocks with emotion. Men and women – and these are by no means desper-ate or needy but successful, well-functioning, well-dressed people who glitter as they walk – are stirred to their depths. They call out to those who are forever lost – dead or absent parents, spouses, children, friends: "I want to see you again." "I want your love." "I want to know you're proud of me." "I want you to know I love you and how sorry I am I never told you." "I want you back – I am so lonely." "I want the childhood I never had." "I want to be healthy – to be young again. I want to be loved, to be respected; I want my life to mean something. I want to accomplish something. I want to matter, to be important, and to be remembered. So much longing... so much pain, so close to the surface."*

We all have such existential pain. It's always there, whirring continuously; just beneath the membrane we call life. It doesn't matter if one's home is in Asia, Europe, or South America; it matters not whether one is a Hindu, Christian, or Jew; it matters not whether one has abun-dant or scarce financial resources. All one need do is ask: What do you want?

Just beneath us, in the molten lava of our beings, lie the creative forces which are shaped and molded by psychotherapy.

I remember working with a woman over 30 years ago who had a very nasty migraine pattern which left her curled up in bed for days. Her family doctor had thought that peripheral skin temperature, a form of biofeedback, might be helpful. This required putting a sensor, called a thermister, on one of her fingers and recording the warmth or coolness of her extremities – i.e., her finger temperature as she tensed or relaxed. A peripheral skin temperature above 90 degrees reflected a warming vasodilation; above 95 degrees revealed deep relaxation.

All of our blood vessels are lined with smooth muscles, so the more relaxed these muscles, the more blood flows into the extremities and the warmer our hands become. The opposite is also true. Assuming that one is a vascular responder, the more tense one is, the more con-stricted the smooth muscles of the peripheral blood vessels, the less blood is available, and the cooler our hands become.

For Donna, my client, relaxation was quite elusive. She seemed unable to find that sweet place where rivers flow effortlessly, where one is at peace with the world. I knew from her life history that one of her stressors was a conflict with her husband over a decision to have a child. So I asked her, "What do you want?" She answered: a child. Understanding her deeper pain I then asked her to visualize a possible pregnancy, envision the joy of gestation over many months, and the exhilaration of giving birth. I asked her to picture the beaming smile of her husband as she warmly held her newborn on her chest and to tune into the sounds of her child's first beckoning.

As Donna cried, I watched her peripheral skin temperature soar from her usual frozen tundra of 78 or 80 degrees to a scorching 97 degrees! We both cried. That was the last biofeedback session for Donna. A relational truth was self-evident. We began marriage counseling the following week during which time her husband worked through his fears of financial pressures which had constricted his visions of a larger family. Once reassured that they would work together to make ends meet – that Donna would return to teaching at an appropriate time – Dave relaxed. Their daughter Kate is now 28 years old, and I smile to this day when I occasionally see them all together.

While physiological measurements may have illuminated a path, this story is much less about opening veins and much more about opening hearts and relationships. It began with the relationship I created with Donna and ended with the relationship Donna and Dave created with Kate. If their story were understood on only a superficial level, we would tout the benefits of biofeedback and relaxation training. Techniques!

But the truth of the matter is that I failed in teaching Donna relaxation training.

My techniques did not work. Deep diaphragmatic breathing failed. Autogenic training failed. Progressive muscle relaxation training failed. Quieting reflex failed. Self hypnosis failed. Clinical intuition worked. Asking her to visualize and share what she wanted most in life – a child – broke through a frozen icepack and revealed a hot spring. It was this loving acceptance of a hidden hot spring which made all the difference for both Donna and Dave. In this world of psychotherapy the unexpected often lies in wait for those willing to look. The three of us smiled as we realized that maternal instincts are pre-wired, migraine headaches often hard-wired, and husbands occasionally hard headed!

Within each of us lies a mystery, overflowing with angst and urgency, calling out to be held by someone called to listen.

Perhaps Donna's destiny would have been different if she were born and raised in India. Without the therapeutic advance of biofeedback, without the serendipitous finding of vaso-dilation, without an intuitive moment between therapist and client, would she still have had a child? Would she JUST WORK THINGS OUT in India as my new "friend" suggested during our flight? Psychotherapy has evolved because we need it. There is mystery, not only within each client and therapist, but in this chrysalis we call therapy as well. Irvin Yalom captures this quite well.[3]

Though the public may believe that therapists guide patients systematically and sure-handedly through predictable stages of therapy to a foreknown goal, such is rarely the case; instead [as my story reveals], therapists frequently wobble, improvise, and grope for direction. The powerful temptation to achieve certainty through embracing an ideological school and a tight therapeutic system is treacherous; such belief may block the uncertain and spontaneous encounter necessary for effective therapy.

So what could be wrong with therapy! How could narcissism lurk here?

* ❋ Consumerism has packaged psychotherapy as a panacea for life's heartaches.
* ❋ The idealization of happiness as an end state obfuscates a fuller vision of life.
* ❋ A sharpened focus on the "inner self" may lead to blindness regarding others.
* ❋ Mere existence poses harsh questions regarding life, death, and meaning which may preoccupy us for a lifetime – leading to self-absorption for some.

Happiness: Psychotherapy's Cross to Bare

Some years ago a friend of mine, probing deep into cyberspace, asked the web a question: What is the purpose of psychotherapy? He found a critique that went something like this:

Our culture seems to be saturated throughout with beliefs about the human condition, as well as society, which provide a rich nutrient on which the psychotherapy industry often feeds. Men and women are expected to be happy! Further, anxiety, depression, and struggle are in no way acceptable. And, when they do "surface," they are to be banished as quickly as possible from the psychological scene.

Have we been seduced by our very own culture? Have our entertainment and print media branded happiness as an end product? Are we entitled to happiness as well as spiritual whole-ness? Has the "achievement" of our full potential blinded us to the realities of everyday life? Have "greener pastures" and "keeping up with the Joneses" been trumped by a human poten-tial movement which cries out for Viagra highs! Is there an alluring mystique surrounding psy-chotherapy which invites a blind reverence toward healers, gurus, doctors, and shamans? Are mystical healers endowed with special powers as expert "technicians" who can alter human be-havior and alleviate human suffering? Is ultimate knowledge the province of psychotherapy?

Now that we have entered a new millennium we must wonder: Has the realm of curative therapies given us false hope that consciousness raising and psychotherapy can cure our many psychic aches and pains? Have consumers been seduced into quick and easy fixes – feel-good fixes – believing that self-help books, talk show experts, mountain-top gurus, and fee for ser-vice therapy can always assuage hurts and teach us how to make lemonade out of the many lemons life delivers to us.

Scott Peck began his now epic book, *The Road Less Traveled*, with these words: "Life is difficult."[4] He is right. We eagerly seek ways out of pain and suffering. There is no exit from life's hardness. Difficulty simply blends with life's sublimeness. As we have become mired in our own reverie, some of us have confused self care with self-absorption. Psychotherapy is often that time when we are able to lick our wounds, sound our depths, and explore our visions of a good life. This is self-care. There comes a point, somewhere, when self-care becomes self-absorption. At this point, our own mirrored reflections mesmerize us to such a degree that we are no longer available to those who need us and those who love us. Some of us have now become uncompromisingly unavailable.

The "self-love" movement, enmeshed in self-esteem building, can be blinding.

As many of us have become mired in ourselves we often talk about our mental health issues as if they are a new brand of sex. Some folks appear to be getting a serotonin high when talking about their recent visit to a "shrink." Even psychopharmacology has turned into a commonplace service as we overhear our friends talking about their medications – or the ones their kids are on. These days, it seems that almost everyone is either a patient or close to someone who is. The scent of therapy is in the air, the culture, and in everyone's medicine cabinet. People even introduce themselves with a pallet of personal "recovery" stories which literal strangers are expected to listen to! For many laypersons, psychotherapy is often about smoke and mirrors. For others, psychotherapy is about self-absorption – and that is the rub!

Psychotherapy *must* be a different kind of rub – a friction, a grinding against, which wears us down and truly bores into a core of debris long hidden from view.

Psychotherapy without this rub, without friction along the sides of the rut which hold us captive, may not create enough heat to promote change. There must be a tension of opposites. As mythologist Joseph Campbell once said, marriage has little to do with being happy; it has everything to do with being transformed – by the friction of rubbing up against one another.

Affirmation, without prostration, is often just evacuation.

All meaning in life comes from contrast: the bad complements the good. We must face our shadows, wrestle with our demons, feel pain, and be challenged by challenging partners and therapists. There are times when therapy is the gentle swell we need to be calmly at peace with ourselves. There are other times, however, when the proverbial 2 x 4 is needed to see the light. Both are possible when I, as therapist, have helped to create a trusting atmosphere which can support both ends. I am willing to be that safe harbor when clients are willing to wrestle with themselves from the inside out. Like Charmin ferrying people across the river Styx, I frequently guide each to more stable ground after Hades has had her fill.

> *There is a bog just behind me.*
> *I know it well – its contours and dimensions,*
> *Its broad expanses,*
> *And I trust I've plumbed its depths.*
> *It is always near me – even now I feel*
> *The wetness at my ankles*

And turn resolutely away.
For to acknowledge the bog
Is to be in the bog –
To feel again the waters rising,
The airlessness, the panic, the choking mud
And sense of coming death.
In these dark, confusing eddies
I have known you.
To examine this alluring, swirling debris
Is to acknowledge a kinship –
Our shared past of love and longing, loss and lust –
And to be one with, to be claimed by, the bog.
For just one moment, let me lie panting –
Still covered in quicksand as I cling to dry land –
Filling my lungs with painful air
And not think about the bog.

For this client, M.L., grief from a broken relationship held her captive in a "bog" and I, for perhaps just one moment in her life journey, offered her the dry land she needed. M.L.'s painful floodwaters eventually subsided. She found a path beyond her loss which led her to other relationships and other cherished goals in life. Her grief was the human price she paid for loving someone. Yet, like a flower turning toward the sun, she would never have had it any other way. Therapy, while painful, went well for M.L. Beyond the emotional lifts or gulfs, the insight bursts and the behavioral breakthroughs there was transformation. Therapy for M.L. helped release her from pathos, reaffirmed special qualities, and unearthed hidden strengths. Therapy helped M.L. move out of her stuck place within, toward more nurturing bonds with others.

Through self-care we find our way back to one another – our true destiny.

We struggle in life. Why shouldn't we expect to struggle in therapy? For that matter, why shouldn't we expect to struggle after therapy? Author Anne Lamott captures this quite well in her book: *Grace (Eventually): Thoughts on Faith*. In her humble, prostrating self-portrait, Lamott bemoans the fact that "I've had many years of recovery and therapy, years filled with intimate and devoted friendships, yet I struggle."[5]

Therapy does not fix our propensity to struggle. In fact, a dependence on therapy to lessen one's struggles can be addicting in its own right. Breaking the therapy habit is often an enlightening process in itself. In a wonderfully self-effacing article in *The Family Networker*, one of our most respected psychotherapy journals, Fred Wistow wrote a piece entitled "Confessions of a Lifelong Therapy Addict". At the age of 29, after years of three-time a week analysis, Fred finally found a psychologist on the Upper East Side in New York:

I went once a week to this psychologist who provided ballast as I split up with my wife.
What did I learn? The only memory that survives is one of self-assertion. One day, instead

of receiving sympathy or an analysis of whatever terrible problem I had just described, my therapist, as usual, gave me an anecdote, a typical instructional dose from her own life, as if every aspect of my life could be illuminated by some experience of hers. I blew up. Fuck that, I don't want to hear about you, I blurted out. I want to talk about me. That act of rebellion I took as the sign that I was ready once more to brave my self-inflicted slings and arrows without a therapist's shield.[6]

It also didn't hurt that Fred had begun to go out with an older woman who nurtured his abilities. For Fred, therapy had been either a life line or a life raft most of his life – until he found a life partner! Hundreds of hours and thousands of dollars later, Fred wondered what he had to show for all this investment. Stridently he proclaimed, "Perhaps there were insights, perhaps there were new techniques and "tricks" to help manage a crisis or two, and perhaps a tad bit less depression overall…but does therapy create permanent change or change the leopard's spots? Life seems to throw at us so many opportunities for our own particular collapse that permanent change looks like an illusion." Is permanent change even a realistic outcome of psychotherapy?

Perhaps it was enough for Fred to see himself – a therapy junkie. Perhaps because of those very maligned "anecdotal stories" from his therapist Fred got what Kierkegaard was telling us: "While life can only be understood from the past, life must be lived forward." Fred got into a cab on the Upper East Side and headed to the box office on 44th street to buy four tickets to a Broadway show – two for him and his love; two more for friends worth loving. The seductive eddies of "the room of doom" had gripped him long enough. Now it was time to affirm that his love of life was stronger than his fear of loss. He took action.

Perhaps therapy had done its job!

As Fred's story teaches, there is a tipping point in psychotherapy when self-care morphs into self-absorption. This can occur in three ways: [1] the individual therapist, as a substitute for intimacy, may become a source of dependency, rather than empowerment; [2] feel good personal growth may become more important than get-well therapy; and [3] too much focus is spent in Western cultures on the self "within" (the egocentric self) rather than the interpersonal self (the socio-centric self). Professor Maureen O'Hara, in her work on relational empathy, captures this tipping point quite well:

When conflicts exist at an intrapsychic level, and many of them do, focusing consciousness at this level is appropriate in that it may yield solutions to situations of concern. But not all psychological conflicts or difficulties exist at this level. Nor, for that matter do all resolutions. The individual psyche may not always be the relevant level for therapeutic attention. Some have even suggested that excessive focused attention by psychotherapists on these intra-psychic levels of awareness has led to the rampant narcissism of contemporary Western life and has contributed to the problems of twentieth century life rather than to their solution.[7]

Marilyn and Steve's Tipping Point

Marilyn and her individual therapist found the narcissistic tipping point. Marilyn and Steve had been married 15 years and had built a successful mortgage business together. Over the years Marilyn had tired of Steve's adult children as well as the emotional and financial support he occasionally offered them. During the prior two years, Marilyn had become active in a series of natural healing seminars, found an individual therapist within that network, and also discovered that the universe had synchronistically put her literally in the hands of a more-than-willing chiropractor who just delighted in being her "sidekick" socially and at the healing seminars. Steve obviously became concerned and was finally able to convince Marilyn to do some couples work with me. Six weeks into our therapy, Marilyn literally walked out of her house one Sunday morning (while her enabling mother was actually staying with them), hopped on a plane, and flew to Indianapolis with her chiropractor "friend" for one week. In a series of e-mails to Steve she shared her thoughts:

Steve: I have been made aware through different energy systems and awarenesses that I have been living in what I sense is a death state. I am working to change this and how I see myself on my path to greater awarenesses. Now that I am in Indianapolis, I am much more aware of my mind/body connection. A sense of calmness exists. Centered! My intent is to keep this stillness in me when I get back.… Yes, I can see how all appears about myself. I have lived a very long time thinking about everyone else and their feelings. I now know that if I take care of myself I can be a better person to those around me. I don't see this as a negative thing. My therapist understands and supports this personal growth.

Abandonment? I have certainly felt that hollow abyss or feeling soooooo many times in our marriage. I pushed it back, covered it up, and accepted it as it was, or what I deserved. It is a very cold and lonely place to be. I am working on myself to free my spirit from going to that cold, lonely, pain body again. I now experience a spiritual high. I hear the pretty brook in the back with the puffs of snow on the leafless trees.

Though I see that nothing will ever make sense to you or maybe to others and explanation words only tease the fingertips but don't attach themselves to form what the truth of knowingness was and is. I certainly have found center and my aim is to be there in all my "now" with everyone. This "escape" as you guys seem to understand it, was my begging for stillness answered. My intention of course is to keep this presence and feel no vices squeezing the life from my soul. With the support of my therapist and a few special soulmates, I know I will be in a better place for everyone else, but also for me. Does Bugen want to see me alone? I can just imagine what he thinks and said about me taking off so suddenly. Well, I don't know if he gets it or not!

Steve's reply: Marilyn, contrary to what you think, the only thing I don't understand is how you can justify running off with your "friend" after making a commitment in front of Bugen that you wouldn't even talk to him during our therapy. Your new religion appears to be all about self and has no laws except for "I can do anything I want to do. I am pure

potential, I am God....to take care of myself, be true to my self, satisfy my every desire, ful-
fill my every emotion, listen and look for what I need, immerse myself in the knowingness
that I can satisfy my every need — no matter how it affects any one else. It is OK to hurt
someone to get what you need.

While Marilyn was getting in touch with her "knowingness," she refused to look at the impulsive and compulsive patterns embedded in her family of origin, the addictive personalities
of her two brothers, the significance of an alcoholic mother who judged her as "not good
enough," and a period of seven grief-stricken years during which her mother dropped her "like
a hot potato." Certainly, there was a great deal of hurt, rejection, and abandonment lurking
beneath the surface for Marilyn. She had been rejected by her mother, just as Steve had been
rejected by her. She had found ways to hide her pain just as her mother had done. Needless
to say, Marilyn also refused to look at her marriage vows – you know, "through sickness and
health, good times and bad…."

Marilyn also refused to look at the *Six Gifts*, particularly "humility."

Instead, Marilyn stared at her bulging muscles and her lean physique in fitness center mirrors every day. Compulsive exercise, athletic competitions, and now idealized, romantic love
served the same purpose for her as alcohol and a medical career did for her mother. Marilyn
was a dry drunk. Her challenge was to embrace her grief as a daughter, her fears of abandonment, and a husband willing to explore the depths of her pain with her. Instead, Marilyn
spiraled into a world of personal entitlement supported by a therapist and lover more than
willing to go along for the ride.

Both Narcissus and Marilyn were blinded by their own reflections.

**The challenge for any therapist and client is to forge a collaboration in which a client
expands both inwardly and outwardly.**

This elasticity helps a client experience herself in a new way. Some would say that Marilyn did
indeed experience herself in a new way as a result of individual therapy. A more fundamental
question remained for me however. When does immersion in one's own prana – real life energy
– become self-intoxicating? Further, when does the support and nurturance provided by a therapist facilitate the sometimes painful work of expansion rather than being an end in itself?

Couple's therapy fell short for Marilyn and Steve. I was unable to contain them long
enough for any real work to begin. I was unable to be that catalyst for "acceptance," "forgiveness," and renewal that couples therapy must become. There were too many other forces at
work here. The quest for self-actualization, the allure of a soulmate, the sanctimonious celebration of personal growth, and an individual therapist whose sight was perhaps tunnel-visioned
all conspired to create a narcissistic cocktail in which any hope for this marriage dissolved.
While Marilyn and her individual therapist might say that she was expanding within herself –
finding her true beingness – she crossed an all too-familiar line. Marilyn just left. When does
self-expansion compromise lasting love?

There is a limit to expansion. On one side of the tipping point, the human condition is honored, relationships are renewed, and virtues lived out. In other words, WE JUST WORK THINGS OUT! On the other side a seething narcissism is set free, as was the case with Marilyn who mirrored an:

[1] uncompromising self-absorption, which
[2] alienates others, while
[3] compromising the ultimate good of all.

My work with Marilyn and Steve was frustrating in a number of ways. First, it is always difficult to compete with romantic love. Marilyn's enchantment with her new lover easily trumped her disenchantment with Steve. Second, termination of therapy was abrupt, with little opportunity to process endings – with me as therapist, or with Steve, as husband. Finally, there are times when rival therapies sabotage the collaborative renewal being worked on by a couple's therapist. I believe that this happened in their case. I take some solace from Irvin Yalom's wisdom.

In his extraordinary book, *Love's Executioner*, Yalom helps me understand why therapy fails with folks like Marilyn. He states, "I do not like to work with patients who are in [romantic] love. Perhaps it is because of envy – I, too, crave enchantment. Perhaps it is because love and psychotherapy are fundamentally incompatible. The good therapist fights darkness and seeks illumination, while romantic love is sustained by mystery and crumbles upon inspection. I hate to be love's executioner."[8]

Marriage is the ultimate litmus test. I once heard that, if one has not grown during the course of a marriage, it has been a dreadful disaster. Mere longevity is not worth celebrating if our souls have not been replenished. We hurt those we love the most because we want the most from those we love the most.

We harbor nasty, spiny thoughts, we shut off our emotional spigots, and we withdraw into silent, self-absorbed pools of pain. We turn outside our love bonds to get what we think we want when the truth is that we don't know what we really need. We give up turning toward each other to work through the imperfection of being "Not OK". We stop trying. This is our spiritual death. As we turn away from each other, we abandon the transformational power of love which creates communion by resurrecting solutions. And the solutions don't even need to be right – as long as we don't abandon the process of seeking them.

While individual and perhaps couples therapy often has the feel of friendship, even love, it is neither. A true loving relationship is mutual in self-disclosure and all forms of intimacy. A therapeutic bond is one way, not two way, and does not build layers of intimacy beyond the emotional level. Even emotional intimacy, in the form of self-disclosure, is pretty much one way. A therapist's vulnerable underbelly can only take away from the client focus which, after all, is their paid entitlement!

The feel of friendship, even love, is beneficial to therapy but it is based on the narcissistic notion that my therapist is totally here for me, giving me undivided attention.

Put another way, nothing in this world can separate my therapist from me and my feelings, my needs and my concerns; s/he focuses on nothing else but me. It is out of this primordial soup that an individual client's attachment hunger is soothed and his or her needs gratified. Somehow, couple's therapy changes all of this. Now, the fantasy of being the beloved, cherished exclusively in the eyes of another, can no longer be attained.

Instead, both partners now find a collaborator, a harmonizer, and a facilitator.

In Closing

If there is a central theme to this chapter it is one built around the eloquence of relationship being the sine qua non of most successful therapy. Indeed, our healthy relationships, both in therapy and out, are the simple abundance which makes life worth living. I have also attempted to demystify therapy as well as the mystique of therapists as miracle worker. There is a story of two monks that makes the point:

> Once upon a time two apprentice monks were discussing their respective masters while cleaning their Buddhist temple. The first novice, with great pride, tells his companion about numerous miracles that he has seen his famous master perform. "I have personally seen," the young novice says, "as my master has turned an entire village to the Buddha, has brought forth rain fall from the sky above, and has moved a mountain so that he and his supplicants could pass."
>
> The second novice, after listening calmly and patiently, then demonstrates his deeper understanding by responding. "My master also does many miraculous things. When hungry, he eats. When thirsty, he drinks. When tired, he sleeps."

In the early 1970's I once was enamored by the mesmerizing, miracle work of certain masters in the psychotherapy field – people like Gregory Bateson, Milton Erikson, and Virginia Satir. The work of each of these pioneers, along with many others, was offered up to me in the form of videotapes, plenary addresses, and personal workshops where I, and a throng of others, hoped one day to be like these masters. I have let go of these fantasies as well as these masters. Instead, like the second monk, I have become more content with the simple pleasures and rewards of my work: creating a caring relationship, fostering a safe environment, instilling hope, honoring personal strengths, encouraging forgiveness and renewal, and teaching that love of others must always balance love of self. Successful therapy always results in the betterment of relationships with oneself and others. For me, these essential and minimalist goals are the eating, drinking, and sleeping of the second monk.

CHAPTER 9

The Roots of Narcissism: Religion

Imagine there's no Heaven
It's easy if you try
No hell below us
Above us only sky
Imagine all the people
Living for today

Imagine there's no countries
It isn't hard to do
Nothing to kill or die for
And no religion too
Imagine all the people
Living life in peace

You may say that I'm a dreamer
But I'm not the only one
I hope someday you'll join us
And the world will be as one[1]
                    —John Lennon

And the world will be as one. Is that too much to hope for? It wasn't for John Lennon, the spiritual Godfather for the Beatles. Yet it was too much in my fraternity house in college, where there existed "brothers, pledges, and the riff-raff on the street." Is it too much to hope for a world where pride, prestige and power don't eclipse our community of humankind – our humanity for one another. It wasn't for one white man and one black man in the *Shawshank Redemption* where we heard these words: "Hope is a good thing; Maybe the best of all things. And a good thing never dies!" Hope wasn't too elusive for Neil Armstrong as he stepped forth upon the moon's cratered surface on July 20th, 1969. At that awe-inspiring moment, Armstrong glanced back at a glorious, majestic globe called Earth, and remarked, "That's one small step for man, one giant leap for mankind." For Neil Armstrong, there was, for a brief moment, a glimpse of oneness few of us get to behold.

Hope is about vision. Religion is about power. God is about love.

To be as one is the vision of monotheism – which underlies all of Christianity, Islam, and Judaism. Is it too much too hope that our religious faiths or our spiritual quests would lift each of us from our narcissistic islands and realign our drifting Tectonic plates into a harmonic worldly vision – to be as one? Well over three and a half billion people have monotheistic oneness as their spiritual foundation, claiming Abraham as their patriarch. Abram, or Abraham as he would be called, symbolized hospitality, peace, faith, obedience, and loving kindness. What would dear Abraham think of the goings on here on planet Narcissus today?

Lennon goes on to sing about a brotherhood of man not entrapped by possessions, greed, or hunger – a world in which people share with, not ravage one another.

Being brothers and sisters to one another is no longer merely a religious or spiritual hope: it is biological reality! The Reverend Martin Luther King was biologically correct when he repeated Jefferson's words on August 28, 1963 that "We hold these truths to be self-evident: that all men are created equal." We now know from the Human Genome Project that all men and women on planet Earth share 99.85 percent of their genes with one another. Out of 30,000 genes, only a tiny sliver of .15 percent differentiates an Aboriginal male in Australia from a Nordic female banker in Switzerland or a Muslim pilgrim in Mecca from the Pope in Rome. That's only 45 or so gene variants out of 30,000 that fashion our uniqueness from one another. We know that Israeli males and Arab males are brethren, genetically speaking, yet each wants to obliterate the other. Narcissistic nationalism runs rampant throughout the world.

Why aren't our religious lampposts illuminating a better path for us?

Are our religions the nurturing womb we had hoped for, or are they anachronistic, narcissistic towers of self-absorption? Are they the towers of power which lead General William Boykin to strut his peacock feathers as United States Undersecretary of State, and remark that "Our God is bigger than your God"?[2] While evangelical churchgoers applauded this bravado, one billion Muslims rose up from their "principalities of darkness" – as former President George Walker Bush once termed it – and voiced concern. Skipping over the obvious Freudian innuendo here, is this brand of deity supremacy the kind of solution we need following 9/11?

If we're not looking up to see whose God is "bigger," we always have the Reverend Jerry Falwell and company to point us downward – into hell and damnation. For the Reverend Falwell, it was "the pagans and the abortionists and the feminists and the gays and lesbians… who helped 9/11 to happen. I point my finger in their face!"[3] If I am a grieving mother of a gay son buried beneath the rubble in Manhattan, I don't find these words of religious zeal comforting.

The famous psychoanalyst, Carl Jung, once wrote[4]:

"Where love rules, there is no will to power; and where power predominates, there love is lacking."

Each one is a shadow of the other. Why does the world of love which John Lennon dreamed about need to be so distant from a world of global struggle where one religion battles another, while fanaticism dwarfs tolerance? This is clearly not the world that Jesus dreamt about when he spoke courageously to folks like you and me in his Sermon on the Mount:

> *Blessed are the poor in spirit,*
> *for theirs is the Kingdom of heaven.*
> *Blessed are those who mourn,*
> *for they will be comforted.*
> *Blessed are the meek,*
> *for they will inherit the earth.*[5]

The Reverend Bob Lively, from Austin, Texas, reminds us that Jesus challenged us to deny the [*self-absorbed*] self we have created, pick up our crucible – no matter how heavy we believe it to be – and [1] to turn the other cheek after we have been stricken, [2] to offer our coat to the one who has ripped off our shirt, [3] to break bread with the poor and needy, [4] to choose a more laid back meekness when our primal urge is to win and vanquish, and [5] to love so deeply that we can pray for – or forgive our enemies. The problem with religion for Bob Lively is that the "decision to follow Jesus is daunting; consequently there can be little wonder why most professed Christians would rather actually worship the form of their faith – that is the rites, rituals, creeds and doctrines – than actually do what Jesus did and risk surrendering the ego's insatiable questing after power for a stance of genuine humility that exudes mercy, compassion and the like."[6] We must relinquish our attachment to what Richard Rohr terms the siren call of pride, power and possessions in order to attach to one another.

Love, as imperfect as it may be, can be the answer. But, we must permit it to be.

On June 28th, 1970 my wife Claire, a Catholic, and I, a Jew, honored our imperfect love and betrothed one another with the assistance of a Unitarian minister, the Reverend Albert Q. Perry. We had not previously met Reverend Perry, nor did we ever see him again following that day. Yet, on that day, he did more for us than thousands of years of Christianity or Judaism could ever do: He married us! Neither a Catholic priest nor a Jewish rabbi would consecrate our union. Each religious kingdom rejected us, choosing instead to honor its own purity, rites, rituals, creeds, and doctrines. We sought union in the name of love and were denied. Without adopting anachronistic, religious doctrines written centuries ago, we were heathens, outliers, and rejects in the eyes of the Church.

If you think theocratic blessings are hard to find, you can imagine our plight in dealing also with the lack of parental blessings from my family. For my father, it was a matter of subtlety three weeks before our wedding: "Son, remember there are many fish in the sea!" For my mother, blatant, blinding narcissism prevailed. "Don't count on me to show up anyplace where I can see a cross within five miles." Ah, the sweet swell of surrender and sacrifice! We found a way out, a way in, and a path forward. While the spirit of religion left us high and dry we somehow were buoyed by the spirit of love.

The core question this chapter will address is the following: Given the ubiquitous presence of organized religion in the United States, why have we spiraled into a room of narcissistic doom and forsaken each other so painfully? Why are so many of us adrift within ourselves, detached from meaningful moorings, in a relational world? Has the Church become impotent in helping us? How can any religion save us from our own self-absorption if each religion is too absorbed by its own self-image? I offer three explanations for the problem with religion today:

1) **A narcissistic culture trumps the teachings of the Church.**
2) **A narcissistic Church trumps the will to love.**
3) **The written word of man trumps the felt presence of God.**

A Narcissistic Culture Trumps the Teachings of the Church

Americans are a remarkably religious people.

In order to understand the gravitas of this observation we must grasp the extent to which religious thought is deeply imprinted within our thinking. According to a 2003 Harris poll[7]:

* 90 percent of American adults believe in God
* 84 percent of American adults believe in survival of the soul after death
* 84 percent of American adults believe in miracles
* 82 percent of American adults believe in heaven
* 80 percent of American adults believe in the resurrection of Christ
* 77 percent of American adults believe in the Virgin birth
* 69 percent of American adults believe in Hell
* 68 percent of American adults believe in the Devil
* 51 percent of American adults believe in ghosts
* 11 percent of American adults believe in evolution

That is, only one of ten adults in the United States believes that humans evolved from other life forms without any involvement from God. Far more Americans believe in angels than in Charles Darwin. This Gallup poll in 2003 revealed that no less than 45 percent of Americans agreed that "God created human beings pretty much in their present form at one time within the last 10,000 years or so." The most startling aspect of these poll results is not so much that Americans by and large reject evolution, but that these results haven't changed much in over two decades. The creationist belief that God alone, and not evolution, produced human beings has never elicited less than 44 percent of agreement. The political implications of these findings are profound. It is now clear that the political schism in the United States has less to do with being male or female or even living in a Red State vs. a Blue one, but more between those who attend church regularly and those who don't!

Viewpoints are quite different in Europe: Europeans do not embrace God as we do in the United States. According to *National Geographic News*, in European countries such as Denmark, Sweden and France, more than 80 percent of adults surveyed stated that they accept evolution.

So, if religion predominates in the US, how do we lose sight of its teachings and each other? Father Ronald Rolheiser is a Roman Catholic priest and author of *The Shattered Lantern: Rediscovering a Felt Presence of God*. A central premise for Fr. Rolheiser is that "our struggle to experience God is not so much one of God's presence or absence as it is one of the presence or absence of God in our awareness. God is always present, but we are not always present to God."[8] Thus God would be as likely to be present with us in a bar as much as a church, synagogue, or mosque. It's just that we are more likely to be aware of God's presence in our houses of worship than a tavern.

John of the Cross once wrote that each of us may experience God as silent either because God is "obscure" or because we are "blind." "An object can be vague because it is too distant or because we have bad eyesight. Hence, God can withdraw his presence in order to purify our faith, i.e., John's obscurity, or we can have a weak experience of God because there is something wrong with us, i.e. John's blindness."[9] The former has been called a "dark night of the soul" while the latter is often considered a problem with contemplation or focus.

We are often too blind to notice the love in our personal lives as well. Our struggle to experience each other is one of awareness more than whether each of us exists or not. We are always present to one another if we are not too self-absorbed — too distracted by other things which blur awareness needed for vibrancy and aliveness in our connections to one another.

Narcissism blinds us to one another.

It is these distractions to which I now turn, particularly with the problem of focusing on one another. Our cultural dilemma, particularly in the United States, is that we are not contemplating what we need to be contemplating, and we desperately need a wakeup call.

At least the Europeans take a three-hour lunch to meet, greet, and eat each day.

For Fr. Rolheiser we are in contemplation when we humbly stand before reality, the world we know, and experience it without the limits created by [1] *narcissism* – our headaches and heartaches, [2] *pragmatism* – our daily tasks of living, and [3] *excessive restlessness* – our unending dreams for more and more. Is this "pride," "envy," and "gluttony" calling to us? We are there for one another if only we would only open our eyes and hearts.

In a culture where "me-ness" trumps "we-ness", contemplation gets distorted!

Marriage preparation classes are a wonderful offering by most dioceses throughout the United States – often a requirement by the Catholic and other churches. Fr. Rolheiser has found that many participants are in these classes reluctantly and resentfully. The resounding echo heard throughout the room is often one of "Why is the church concerned about my marriage?" "My marriage is nobody's business. This is my life, my love, my sex, my honeymoon, my future, and my concern."

These same individuals are likely to believe that my heartaches, my financial obligations, my devotional tasks, my life history wounds, my rent, my mortgage, my boat, my bank account are my issues and no one else's! In effect, I am drawing a circle around me. Everything within this circle is real to me. Everything outside the circle is not. Other people, society at large, and God's concerns are not real. Reality is what I control, what I can buy, and what I achieve. What's mine is mine – until I decide when to share it! This cultural, narcissistic ideology trumps the Church's theology.

Church membership does not inoculate us from Yuppie narcissism.

Our egos, our shibboleths, and our moral compass point exclusively inward in a wayward society. We are ruled by our quality of life, our pursuit of excellence, our upward mobility, our material comforts, and our winning at any emotional cost. Our centering prayer is focused on how beautiful our tanned bodies are, how beautiful our homes are, and how beautiful our children are! Our clear cultural ambition is to leave the pack behind on our way up our personal mountains. In short, we get too attached to our image and our stuff.

> *Around the end of the nineteenth century, a tourist from the United States visited the famous rabbi Hafez Hayyim. He was astonished to see the rabbi's home was just a simple room filled with books. The only furniture was a table and a bench.*
>
> *"Rabbi, where is your furniture?" asked the tourist.*
> *"Where is yours?" replied rabbi Hayyim.*
> *"Mine? But I'm only a visitor here."*
> *"So am I," said the rabbi.[10]*

Unbridled materialism and individualism run rampant throughout America and trump any sense of community as a virtue worth pursuing. Self-development becomes our salvation. For Fr. Rolheiser, everything – especially marriage, family, community, justice, church, morality, service to others, sacrifice – makes sense to us only if it enhances one's self. Our self-development needs to be pursued with the passion and asceticism that once was formerly reserved for religion.

We would rather watch *American Idol* than see our false idolatry.

Neil Postman describes this phenomenon in his book, *Amusing Ourselves to Death*, wherein he chronicles the 1983 commencement exercises at Yale University of all places. After a very reserved audience endured a number of Honorary degrees being bestowed upon such notables as Mother Teresa, the moment each had been waiting for finally arrived. When the name of the final recipient, Meryl Streep, was mentioned, the audience "unleashed a sonic boom of affection, enough to wake the New Haven dead!"[11] This is our culture.

In our culture, we would rather be a star than a servant or saint.

When we add "pragmatism" and "unbridled restlessness" to this mix the teachings of the Church really get lost. Pragmatism works against contemplation. We become mired in what we do. We bind our self-worth to what we do, becoming addicted to achievement. Paradise is indeed lost when our sense of wholeness is fed more by what we achieve than who we are. Prayer and contemplation get lost as non-utilitarian. They simply have no use in a society where "results" pay off. Contemplation and prayer are often considered a waste of time, accomplish nothing, and do not produce anything "concrete" in our lives. As we continue to be caught up in the doings of our cultural efficiency, we continue to be lost in truly "being" our imperfect selves.

When contemplation is lost, we give up an interiority worth knowing.

A Narcissistic Church Trumps the Will to Love

It is one thing for us human beings to prop ourselves up, become self-enamored, and be mesmerized by our own image. After all, this thread of narcissism is woven throughout our nature, nurture, and culture. It's quite another thing to have one of our healing institutions mimic us in its self-absorption rather than leading us forward to the Promised Land. Put quite simply, the church of all denominations has become as narcissistic as those it serves and, by being so, has minimized its transcendent gifts. The Church has muffed its mission by using power in three inappropriate ways:

1) To swell its ranks,
2) To bloat its golden pond, and
3) To cull its chosen few.

For centuries the Church has attempted to swell its ranks by including more and more. Just as we today attempt to enhance our image by buying more and more, the Church of old attempted to enhance its image by usurping more and more. In the words of author Scott Peck, "The absence of meaningful Christianity from institutionalized religion is hardly a recent problem. The history of the Church for the past 1600 years has innumerable instances of institutional blasphemy. The Church has marched off in crusades to murder Muslims in the name of Jesus. It is the Church of the Inquisition that killed and tortured in the name of Jesus. It is the Church of Rome that stood by during the Holocaust doing nothing in the name of Jesus."[12]

The Church has tried to be as inclusive as it could, not in the service of community but in the service of numbers; it has not welcomed the stranger so much out of love as out of greed. It is not out of a desire for community that it has refrained from asking members to stand up and be counted; it has been out of fear. It cannot argue that it has been undemanding of its members in the interest of community, because it has not had community in the first place. The plain reality is that by and large the Church has not been in the community game; it has been in the numbers game...Churches in the numbers game are wishy-washy social clubs, churches that lack community and the spirit of community, churches where the gospel is glossed over, churches where the members don't seem to take Christ seriously, churches that seem to stand for everything and hence stand for nothing.

And the numbers are not looking very pretty right now in spite of these efforts to swell ranks. While nine of ten Americans believe in God, only 50 percent of us claim affiliation with a religious group according to the *Christian Science Monitor*. American's formal ties to churches, synagogues, temples and mosques are in flux and continue to weaken. The over-all increase in religious affiliation did not keep pace with the rate of US population growth – i.e. 8.8 percent vs. 13.2 percent. The Church of Jesus Christ of Latter-day Saints grew most rapidly at a rate of 19.3 percent. The Latter-day Saints, with their greatest support in Utah and surrounding states, sends its young people out to recruit in the United States and abroad. Mainline Protestant memberships declined the most, with the Presbyterian Church dropping by almost 12 percent over the last decade. Some attribute this slide to internal controversies that developed after conservatives gained control of their denominations, particularly the Southern Baptist Convention.

How could the Church not be a beacon for inclusiveness and blessed acceptance of one another? How could the Church lose sight of its mission to create and preserve community? How has the Church failed so badly in resuscitating us from our own self-righteous peril – our own self-absorbed meanderings? How could Jesus get lost in the shuffle? Has the Church become too bloated by its own golden pond to survive?

We, the self-absorbed, need guiding messages which weave a dialogue of possibilities rather than rigid dogmas of exclusion. It is distressing enough when we display such intolerance as individuals; it is blasphemous when we see our religious bodies perpetuate it. Just listen to the headlines:

* *Vatican document asserts that other faiths are inferior – A Vatican declaration says that only faithful Catholics can attain full salvation from earthly sin; Other beliefs, including Protestant Christians, have defects that render them inferior.*

* *Lesbian minister is defrocked by United Methodist council – The decision by the highest court within the United Methodist Church found that she violated the denomination's ban on "self-avowed, practicing homosexual" clerics.*

* *IMAX theaters shun films for fear of offending religious sensibilities – A number of IMAX theaters, including some in science museums, are refusing to exhibit movies that mention the Big Bang Theory or the Earth's geology for fear of offending those who take the Bible literally.*

We are purging one another in the name of righteousness. These abuses of power are about extremism, intolerance, and self-annoitedness. The narcissistic belief that one is the Messiah has led to polygamy, genocide, and a sense of grandiose omnipotence. These struggles are not about God; they are about power. And the Church is not protecting us from our own God-given narcissism. For author Jon Krakauer, this fundamentalism means that we are killing one another in the name of God:

> There is a dark side to religious devotion that is too often ignored or denied. As a means of motivating people to be cruel or inhumane – as means of inciting evil, to borrow the vocabulary of the devout there may be no more potent force than religion…Men have been committing heinous acts in the name of God ever since mankind began believing in deities, and extremists exist within all religions…History has not lacked for Christians, Jews, Hindus, Sikhs, and even Buddhists who have been motivated by scripture to butcher innocents. Plenty of these religious extremists have been homegrown, corn-fed Americans. [Prologue][13]

In Chapter Two I mentioned that on November 13th, 2000, my journey in life became a much lonelier one. My friend Chuck died. The Reverend Charles Meyer was an Episcopal Priest whose life touched many thousands of people in Central Texas and around the United States. Jokingly, he had become known as the Stephen Spielberg of death and dying. To know Chuck meant that we had to know how reverence and irreverence were inextricably woven together in an unforgettable tapestry. Chuck loved God and wrote about God in each of his 13 books. God, for Chuck, was a personal God who accepts humor, imperfections, and ordinariness in each of us. God suffers with us, feels helpless with us, and shares with us our sense of being out of control. For Chuck, God breathes with us.

If reverence vs. irreverence defined Chuck's style, living vs. dying defined his message. Years before he died, I realized something very important to me: Chuck was not teaching us about dying at all. He was teaching us about living. How to live a good life! He showed us how to see one another, how to work as teams with one another, how to serve one another, and how to have fun with one another. No matter what cards a person had been dealt, he showed how important our choices were – how important it was to have a foundation of strength, value and courage and to continue to put one foot out of bed and onto the floor each morning.

Chuck rejected theology by slogan. He resented the platitudes and "one-liners" such as "Time will heal all wounds" or "You don't go until your number comes up!" Chuck believed in God but was having a midlife crisis regarding the Church in the years just before he died. He saw the Church grasping at straws, desperately pushing evangelism over true theism, thinking that swelling its ranks would improve its chances of survival. He saw the Church spending large amounts of money and time trying to proselytize and cajole people back into "an institution they left because it was irrelevant thirty years ago." For Chuck:

> *The Church is dying, crumbling from within. It is no longer doing its job as a channel for interaction with God, as a method of providing community, for teaching the message of reconciliation, healing, forgiveness, acceptance and new life. It has become the exact opposite of what was intended, an obfuscating impediment to our communication and community. The vessel has hardened into a stone stumbling block that is now crumbling to gravel.*[14]

Chuck was indeed irreverent. He believed that it is past time to let the dying church die, so that the long-term resurrection might begin. He believed that there were a number of things the self-absorbed Church must start doing now so that the reborn Church could go on serving the community and not it's own image.

First, he urged, let new community paradigms and models replace existing ones. We must question everything we do. We must see the ludicrousness of "large corporate worship" in structures – our bloated golden ponds – that are used only a few hours each week and cost millions upon millions of dollars to build – money better spent in the community. Why do we need multimillion-dollar structures which compete with the Reverend Jones down the block? If there were a moratorium on new churches, people wanting to serve just might have to meet in each other's homes or other public places. Imagine that!

Second, close your fancy churches down on Sunday mornings and do something really useful with your family. Concentrate on a genuine Sabbath, not just putting in your two hours. As we continue our journeys in this new millennium time is of a premium. Meet in small worship groups on Thursday evening and create meaningful rituals with your family on Sundays. And while we're at it, Chuck thought we ought to dump Sunday school – an otherwise subtle continuance of educational segregation.

Third, demand that more egalitarian structures emerge with the church community – beyond the clergy/laity dichotomy – which utilizes teams and team leaders. Try to establish solidarity of purpose without bricks, mortar, or organizational charts.

Fourth, for church membership, require a time commitment devoted to some cause in the community. Church is a social commitment not a social club. Commitment is not about a church building – a golden temple to worship. Instead it is about living one's belief out in the living community.

Fifth, examine church financial records to ensure that fair employment practices are being honored. Refuse to conduct business with vendors or suppliers who do not subscribe to non-exploitative or ethical guidelines.

Sixth, make your church communities truly inclusive. Get over homophobia, racism, sexism, and other manifestations of social bigotry that have no place in the Kingdom.

Seventh, pay taxes. One of the biggest free rides in the country is tax exemption for religious purposes. In the Reverend Meyer's opinion "The Dying Church" hides gross financial irresponsibility under the blanket of these exemptions, and therefore is not a full corporate player in the economic community. "If you can't raise enough money to make something work and pay your fair share of taxes, maybe God is telling you something."

Finally, if it ain't broke, break it! Experiment! Make mistakes! Think outside the box! Risk being: "Not OK!" It just might be "OK." In a world of personal computers, stop building more classrooms and put a few courses on line in a virtual classroom. What would a virtual church look like? Is that too much to hope for?

So far we have seen how the Church uses power to enhance its grandeur.

These manifestations of glory are not unusual or abnormal. The church is as interested in perpetuating itself, in all its glory, as is each mortal soul. Ironically, this is the nature of evolution, not divine revelation. The laws of natural selection apply to corporate structures, managed by imperfect human beings, just as doggedly as they do to individuals. What gets real messy is the level of violence these corporate entities are capable of manifesting in the name of divinity. This is where power abuses. This is where people get killed in the name of God, when it is really about greed and intolerance.

Pentecost, celebrated 50 days after Easter, is a festival commemorating the descent of the Holy Spirit upon Jesus' disciples, enabling them to speak the many different languages of all those who gathered to pray in Jerusalem. Pentecost is a celebration of diversity; the red altar hangings and red clothing symbolize the flames in which the Holy Spirit came to Earth in order to spread the Gospel in the many different languages represented in the community. In some churches, the festival of Pentecost is marked by different native apparel, different ethnic foods, and different ethnic games, art and music. In short, it is OK to be different.

For Emilee Dawn Whitehurst, President of the St. Edward's University Alumni, "Pentecost is but once a year, yet the sharing of traditions, food, and language should be encouraged and celebrated throughout the year. The spirit of Austin is a global community! God has given us resources that are plentiful, and we should share them with those around us."[15] In the name of diversity, let alone God, why can't we be one? Little Linda Jean understood this clearly in church one day:

> *A preacher put this question to a class of children: "If all the good people in the world were red and all the bad people were green, what color would you be?"*

> *Little Linda Jean thought mightily for a moment. Then her face brightened and she replied, "Reverend, I'd be streaky."*[16]

We are imperfect beings. We're all a bit streaky. We're all mixed. We're all mixed up. We're all finite in an infinite universe. Let's breathe in together and, as we exhale, let us embrace one another as perfectly imperfect – just the way it ought to be.

The Written Word of Man Trumps the Felt Presence of God.

Inerrancy, literalism and infallibility all seem to be kissing cousins of narcissism. There is a tipping point for narcissism within religious circles. At what point does my body, my house, my car, my golf, my wife morph into my church, my God, my promised land, and my salvation? At what point does having sex with my wife become my right? At what point does my written word trump yours? At what point does my Messiah trump yours? At what point does my "calling from God" trump yours?

At what point do we put down our arms, actually see one another, and embrace each other in love, rather than kill each other in the name of "our" God. Believing that God exists in our own image is narcissistic enough. But we even trump this! The single belief that we are the "chosen ones" grants us entitlement feelings, bordering on grandiosity, which reeks of self-importance and uniqueness above all others.

Being the "chosen ones" can be blinding – at least until we are able to see again.

> *When the bishop's ship stopped at a remote island for a day, he determined to use the time as profitably as possible. He strolled along the seashore and came across three fishermen mending their nets. In pidgin English they explained to him that centuries before they had been Christianized by missionaries. "We Christians!" they said, proudly pointing to one another. The bishop was impressed. Did they know the Lord's Prayer? They had never heard of it. The bishop was shocked.*
>
> *"What do you say, then, when you pray?"*
>
> *"We lift eyes to heaven. We pray, 'We are three, you are three, have mercy on us.'"*
>
> *The bishop was appalled at the primitive, the downright heretical nature of their prayer. So he spent the whole day teaching them the Lord's Prayer. The fishermen were poor learners, but they gave it all they had and before the bishop sailed away the next day he had the satisfaction of hearing them go through the whole formula without a fault.*
>
> *Months later, the bishop's ship happened to pass by those islands again, and the bishop, as he paced the deck saying his evening prayers, recalled with pleasure the three men on that distant island who were now able to pray, thanks to his patient efforts. While he was lost in that thought, he happened to look up and noticed a spot of light in the east. The light kept approaching the ship, and as the bishop gazed in wonder, he saw three figures walking on the water. The captain stopped the ship, and everyone leaned over the rails to see this sight.*
>
> *When they were within speaking distance, the bishop recognized his three friends, the fishermen. "Bishop," they said, "we so, so sorry. We forgot lovely prayer. We say, 'Our Father in heaven, holy be your name, your kingdom come....' then we forget. Please tell us prayer again."*
>
> *The bishop felt humbled, "Go back in your homes, my friends," he said, "and each time you pray say, "We are three, you are three, have mercy on us!""[17]*

The bishop's reliance on scripture was transformed by his human experience. He saw the light! We are witnessing a "letting go" process for the bishop as he felt the presence of God in these three men. Giving up what we know as Gospel, or what we think we know to be true, is no easy matter. Indeed, it is humbling. In the words of theologian, Marcus Borg, it may require *Reading the Bible Again for the First Time.*[18]

For Borg, conflict over how we see and read the Bible is far and away the single greatest issue polarizing Christians in North America today. For one group of Christians the Bible is the inerrant, literal, and infallible Word of God: "As a divine product, it is God's truth, and its divine origin is the basis of its authority." As some of us may have seen on car bumpers from time to time, "God said it. I believe it. That settles it."

For a second group of Christians, the Bible is seen as a human product – the assembled writings of two ancient and historical communities: one Hebrew, the other early Christian. What is represented in the Bible is the response of these two communities to their personal experience of God. "As a product of these two communities, the Bible tells us about how they saw things, not about how God sees things."

The former group of Christians is often referred to as fundamentalists, whose devout belief is summed up in one sentence: be a Christian now for the sake of salvation later. Well, in a pluralistic world, this means a lot of trouble for some other guys down the block. After all, when you look around, we tend to be a religious pluralism. In the words of Borg, "Does it make sense that the creator of the whole universe would be known in only one religious tradition, which (fortunately) just happens to be our own?"[19]

My God-way or the highway!

For Marcus Borg, the invention of the printing press in the 1400's contributed to how scripture was viewed at the time. Before the fifteenth century the Bible was cherished as a collection of separate manuscripts and was referred to in the plural as "scriptures" – meaning a collection of books or homilies. Once the Bible became a bound volume, and was mass produced by means of the printing press, it became easier to consider it as a single book with a single author – namely God! Furthermore, when each of these books was translated from either Hebrew or Greek, into other languages, the meaning and intent of certain passages was certainly lost in translation.

Because the Bible is a collection of separate manuscripts it is implausible that there must be internal consistency within it. The Bible is an inconsistent collection of imperfect stories about imperfect people in an uncertain time of history. We are being asked to think about, talk about, and reason our way through these moral tales of imperfect choices and a flawed human condition. In short, the biblical manuscripts invite each of us to learn how to be OK in a world filled with people who are not! When the word of God trumps our willingness to reason, we diminish the one gift from God which distinguishes us from all other species: our abstract ability to use logic.

The absolutes of a literal reading of the Bible create a thrombosis which blocks our heartfelt connection with one another.

One solution to a rigid, materialistic dying church in a post-modern world is to experience God spiritually in an everyday manner. While some might consider the distinction between religion and spirituality spurious, others see each one quite differently. The "spiritual" see rigidity when looking at "religion;" The "religious" see sloppiness when looking at "spirituality." Religion evokes images of boundaries, while spirituality's borders are often hard to define. The language of religion seems solid and pedantic, while the language of spirituality is more ephemeral and fluid. In a post-modern world where experience defines meaning, many people are more likely to acknowledge being spiritual rather than religious.

Spirituality, for many, is the experiential dimension of religion.

God is everywhere for the spiritually minded. God is present within us and around us. While we may not be aware, God is there, and here, and there again. Marcus Borg invites us to wake up, to be enlightened, and to be illuminated. Borg recognizes that we see God differently than our ancestors did centuries ago. He is not afraid to refer to this awakening of a new felt experience of God as mysticism. While recognizing that mysticism was practiced widely before the Protestant Reformation, Borg rejoices in its vibrant reawakening during the last 125 years. Mysticism is the experience of union, of connection with the sacred, with each other – with what is God. This could be our neighbor next door, our park around the corner, the crickets calling to us in the evening, or a sunset glistening across a scarlet sky well above our heads.

First and Foremost, We Are A Community

Once upon a time I had as a client "Father John" who had arrived in Austin with the hope that he would find a community which welcomed him. Instead he found within his Holy Order an atmosphere of ridicule, contempt, and isolation. His sessions with me were largely about healing and comfort, intended to lessen the pain of living within a religious community where the "Head Honcho" humiliated him about his weight, his lack of cleanliness, and his lack of eloquence in his homilies – which had long been a strong suit for Father John. Each evening, he and his fellow priests would meet, pray, eat, and then silently retreat to his own room. Few talked during the meal. Amidst these sounds of silence, Father John prayed for warmth, for heartfelt communion, an evening walk, and for a community of care. This never happened and Father John moved on, hope forsaken!

Few of us ever get the opportunity to experience monastic living. At first glance it is difficult to imagine that such a community would be anything less than intimate, communal, and emotionally grounding. Yet, celibate priests are human. Their imperfections reflect the deeper conflicts that lie within each of us and, like shifting fault lines, tremors are often felt above the surface. These destabilizing tremors were experienced as 8.8 Richter quakes for Father John. Sadly, there were no efforts within the parish community itself to reach out to one another – to find one's brother. Yet, from Fr. John's ashes a phoenix can arise.

There are grassroots efforts being made to create community.

Scott Peck illuminates this hope in *The Different Drum: Community Making and Peace*. The story concerns a monastery that had fallen upon hard times. It is entitled "The Rabbi's Gift":

Once there was a great religious order. As a result of waves of anti-monastic persecution in the seventeenth and eighteenth centuries, as well as the rise of secularism in the nineteenth, all its branch houses were lost. It became decimated to the extent that there were only five monks left in the decaying mother house: the abbot and four others, all quite elderly by now. By all due accounts, this was a dying order.

In the forests deep lived a rabbi whose hermitage lay very close to the monastery. While they seldom met, the monks had developed a keen sense of intuition as to when the rabbi retreated to his hermitage for personal prayer and renewal. Quietly, the monks would whisper repeatedly to one another, "The rabbi is in his hermitage. The rabbi is in his hermitage." As the senior abbot agonized over the immanent death of his order, it occurred to him that the rabbi just might be of sound counsel and be able to provide wisdom that might save the monastery from a certain death.

The senior abbot was graciously welcomed by the rabbi on this fine day. But when the abbot explained the nature of his visit, the humble rabbi could only commiserate with him – offering little in strategy or direction. "I know how it is!" exclaimed the rabbi. The people have lost their spirit, their religious zeal. Hardly anyone comes to synagogue anymore in my sacred community as well. This shared loss triggered a shared grief which brought tears to both the abbot and the rabbi. Once they grieved together they each read from their respective scriptures, both the Torah as well as the New Testament. They reflected about deep things but time had come for the abbot to leave and return to his monastery. "It is indeed special that we have met after all these years, Rabbi, but I feel that I have failed in my purpose in coming to see you. Is there not something which you can tell me which might illuminate a path to follow for me and my fellow parishioners? Is there no piece of unearthed wisdom you might offer me which might save my dying order?"

"No, I am sorry," the rabbi responded. "I have no advice to provide you which will save the day. Humbly, I can only simply suggest that the Messiah is one among you!" One among you!! What could that mean, wondered the seemingly desperate monk?

When the senior abbot returned to his monastery his fellow monks eagerly approached him wondering what wisdom the rabbi had imparted. "Well," the senior abbot muttered, "He really didn't impart the hidden gem we all had been waiting for! We merely wept together and read from the Torah and the New Testament. The only elusive thing he did say as I was about to leave was that "The Messiah is one of us and I don't know what he meant!" THE MESSIAH IS ONE OF US!

In the sparse days and weeks that followed each of the old monks wondered who among them might be the Messiah. Could there actually be significance to the rabbi's words. Which one of us could be the Messiah? If the rabbi meant anyone, he probably meant Father Abbot who has been our leader for more than a generation. On the other hand, Brother Thomas is a very holy man – a man of true light. Yet again, could the rabbi have meant Brother Elred! Brother Elred does get a bit cranky from time to time – a real thorn in people's sides - but he certainly has opened spiritual paths for many. Maybe the rabbi did mean Brother Elred. But surely not Brother Phillip! Phillip is so passive, a real nobody. But then, quite mysteriously, he seems to possess a gift for being there just when you need someone special to carry the burden of care and compassion. He just appears by your side when you least expect him. Maybe Brother Phillip is the Messiah.

So, as the days dwindled by, one after the other, each monk wondered about the unknown mystery that lay before them. As they contemplated and prayed, each began to treat each other with extraordinary respect on the off chance that one among them might actually be the Messiah. And, given the very, very remote chance that each monk himself might be the Messiah they began to treat themselves with more respect and kindness.

Because of its centric location to a local park, the monastery was occasionally visited by people having picnics and lunches on the plush green grass nearby. People would wander along the nature paths and occasionally visit the old dilapidated chapel to meditate. As they did so, without even being conscious of it, they sensed this aura of extraordinary respect and kindness which seemed to permeate the five aging monks as well as the entire monastery. There was something inviting, even compelling, about this unspoken atmosphere. People, without being asked to do so, kept coming back to the nature paths nearby, the picnic tables, and the monastery itself to play, to eat, and to pray. They began to bring their friends who in turn brought their friends. In time, the monks would join all these friends in walks back into town, into the shops, and into the marketplace itself.

And as it happened, some of the younger men became entranced with the wisdom and humility of the older monks and started to talk more and more with them. In time, one after another, each asked if he could join them. Then another! And another! And so it was, a monastery so immanently close to its demise was reawakened with a spirit that permeated the entire community and once again became a thriving order – a vibrant center of light and spiritual thought which transcended the entire realm. All of this was possible because of the Rabbi's gift.[20]

Religion is a creation by our species. It has been said that people go to church to find God but then find one other. This is the creation of community described in "The Rabbi's gift." It is also the community that the Reverend Chuck Meyer prayed for. People playing with their children, walking their dogs, skipping along nature trails, tolerating reconcilable differences like crankiness and passiveness – all found one another and became a thriving community. The glory of it all lay in the discovery that no one was the Messiah – but everyone could be! Each of us is anointed. We must remember that glory means the radiant presence of God in nature, in all life forms, and yes – in all our houses of worship. If we are truly to have a mystical moment, in theologian Marcus Borg's term, we must have an experience of connection, of union, with one another as if each of us were the sacred. Surely "we can live with one another in such a way that we reconcile our individual differences for the greater good of all." In the words of President Barack Obama, "It's a prayer worth praying and a conversation worth having!"[21]

There is a revolutionary change occurring in Christian consciousness these days. It is a titanic shift of heart and mind that has been a long time in coming according to Father Rohr: "Emerging Christianity is both a longing for and moving toward a following of Jesus that has much more to do with an actual daily lifestyle than with believing things…there is no Methodist or Catholic way of loving. There is no Orthodox or Presbyterian way of living a simple and non-violent life. There is no Lutheran or Evangelical way of showing mercy. There is no Baptist or Episcopalian way of visiting the imprisoned."[22]

Each of us needs to be seen as precious.

There was a better way for Father John who left Austin a beleaguered man. Where acceptance might have flourished there was contempt; where love might have bloomed there was disdain; and where community might have taken root there was isolation. Self-absorption at an individual level or a societal level blurs our presence with one another. Let us all join hands in celebrating Father Rohr's blessing for an emerging theology, or dare I say, spirituality:

1) Jesus is a model for living than an object of worship.
2) Affirming peoples' potential is more important than reminding them of their brokenness.
3) The work of reconciliation should be valued over the primacy of judgments.
4) Gracious behavior is more important than right belief.
5) Inviting questions to be valued more than supplying answers.
6) Encouraging the personal search is more important than group uniformity.
7) Meeting actual needs is more important than maintaining institutions.
8) Peacemaking is more important than power.
9) We should care more about love and less about sex.
10) Life in this world is more important than the afterlife.

LOVE'S SANCTUARY

Intimacy is our best antidote for narcissism. Yet, I am afraid of it at times! Perhaps you are as well. In this section I will first explore how the concepts of intimacy and attachment are woven together. I will explore the secrets of healthy attachment as well as the burden of unhealthy attachment – knowing full well that the scars of life's earliest traumas often leave a lasting imprint. Narcissists are often byproducts of poor attachment and thus become poor attachment figures themselves. This can be changed during our adulthood years, if we are open to it. The "Nine Adult Intimacy Styles," in the last chapter of this section, can help create healthy relationships regardless of our childhoods.

When the concept of attachment is understood it is easier to see how love metamorphosis's right before our eyes. Before we can truly understand the "paradox of love" – that after we fall in love we must fall out of it in order to experience a truly loving, committed relationship – we must understand the meaning of this complicated and misused word: love. What is this mysterious process of falling in love? Of breaking up? Of experiencing a broken heart? Of building a successful marriage? This section of the book describes in detail the three phases of love: romance, disenchantment, and mature love.

This section of the book highlights that [1] the need for attachment endures throughout our entire lives, [2] attachment is our best antidote for narcissism, and [3] mature, lasting love is vastly different from a more chemically-driven romantic love. The last chapter in this section, Chapter 14, is experiential – inviting each of you to honestly explore "Nine Adult Intimacy Styles" in such a way that you will know your preferences, your strong suits, and your weak suits. With this knowledge you will be better prepared to lift yourselves out of self-absorption in order to *actively* transform stagnating relationships into the vibrant tributaries they were meant to be.

CHAPTER 10

Our Need for Attachment

The very first impressions we receive as living beings must be sensations of intimate body contact, as we float snugly inside the protective wall of the maternal uterus. The major input to the developing nervous system at this stage therefore takes the form of varying sensations of touch, pressure and movement. The entire skin surface of the unborn child is bathed in the warm uterine liquid of the mother. As the child grows and its swelling body presses harder against the mother's tissues, the soft embrace of the enveloping bag of the womb becomes gradually stronger, hugging tighter with each passing week. In addition, throughout this period the growing baby is subjected to the varying pressure of the rhythmic breathing of the maternal lungs, and to a gentle, regular swaying motion whenever the mother walks.[1]

Intimacy is our best antidote for narcissism.

Yet, we fear it! While intimacy, with its focus on another, remains our greatest ally in our struggle with narcissism, our fear of intimacy drives us apart, away from each other and deep into ourselves where we are swallowed up by lofty self-image, loneliness, and a prevailing sense of inadequacy. We often feel abandoned, adrift, and struggling with one another instead of mutually connected and safe. We dream of personal power, possessions, and prestige more than love. Yet there is something profound, something primeval and archetypal about intimacy.

We gestated in a womb of intimacy – an amniotic sea of comfort. The profound comfort we experience from physical presence has its unspoken origins in the womb itself as ethnologist Desmond Morris so beautifully describes above. We don't live in such close, intimate quarters without becoming imprinted to its sweet music and gentle, swaying motions. We become used to it, unconsciously yearning for more of it throughout the remainder of our days. Satisfying this need for intimacy is relatively easy for some during the first months of childhood: being tightly swaddled, suckling a breast while listening to mother's heart beat, and feeling the gentle pat for that necessary burp are all early ways of experiencing intimacy. What can be more comforting than to be rocked and swayed as one is attempting to release a bubble of distress. Each gentle rock and sway yields yet another layer of healthy attachment.

"Bubbles of distress" of infancy, however, can morph into bubbles of self-doubt, conflict, and inadequacy of adulthood. These burdens need to be released as well. For those of us who have experienced shattered intimacy with maladaptive, dysfunctional, and disturbed parents it is downright scary to let others know about our pain. Instead of sharing our private fears, our unmet needs, our weakest links, even our prurient fantasies – our true selves – with one another, we run and hide from a deeper bond which can buoy us for a lifetime. The fear of being judged as not OK, of being rejected, drives us underground where our egos think it's safe. The fear of rejection is the twenty-first century's cross to bear since it weighs so heavily on us today.

This was certainly the case for a client named Jim:

Somebody please tell me what it is I am so afraid of!

I am often overwhelmed with feelings that have been with me since my earliest recall. It begins in the pit of my stomach as a mild burning, and then spreads to my chest as tightness. I am often overcome with the urge to cry but my eyes deny me, and no tears flow. My thoughts get jumbled and I seem flooded by a sea of anxiety and sadness.

As a kid I was besieged with ample amounts of acne and scruffy hair. My self-confidence was low and my social skills were few. I lived on an isolated farm far from easy access to friends and neighbors. By the time I was old enough to be interested in girls, it seemed hopeless that any girl would be interested in me. Over time, I turned inward – becoming very reflective and introspective. I became self-conscious around other people and tended to avoid rather than seek out interactions with others.

Growing up my isolation led me to idealizing things I could not (or would not) participate in. I was not popular, cool, "in", but wanted to be. I longed for that which I did not have and I longed to be something I was not. I sometimes lived out much of my social life entirely in my head. I cheated myself out of much.

I've run from my own life for oh, so many years. Hurt and isolation were never dealt with. The debt I owe my past must somehow equate with the pain I experience now. I am so afraid, but what am I so afraid of?

Jim was married to a wonderfully attentive, nurturing woman for 23 years at the time he sought me out for counseling. A successful business and two delightful children were not enough abundance to offset decades of self-doubt, anomie, and emotional withdrawal. As we immersed ourselves into his pattern of self-absorption we learned that Jim negated most everything good around him, not to mention within him. Jim was afraid of abject rejection – a virtual mudslide of unworthiness. Self-rejection gripped him in a suffocating way, which in part explained the tightness in his chest as well as his shallow breathing. In time, Jim did affirm the love in his life, but not until he accepted himself as "the Beloved" in Henri Nouwen's words.

For theologian Nouwen, "There is a voice, the voice of love, that speaks from above and from within that whispers softly or declares loudly: "You are my Beloved, on you my favor rests."[2] Theologically, Nouwen is quoting Mark 1:10-11, "You are my Son, the Beloved; my favor rests on you." This, for Nouwen, is what it means to be blessed.

For me, the words, "I am the beloved," are not a religious offering; this sentiment is a personal invocation – a personal calling – to fundamentally accept myself. This is a very intimate act! How can we hear the voice calling our name in such a way that the words reverberate warmly throughout our entire being? This is often quite difficult when our worlds have been filled with misery, abuse, and neglect. If all we heard growing up is "You're not smart enough," "You're not achieving enough," "You're ugly," "You're not thin enough," or "You're worthless, a nobody," how can we believe we are good enough? Under such harsh conditions, how can we believe that we are beloved – that we are OK – even though our love partners, our children, and our friends are whispering this sweet music daily in our ears?

If we truly believe we are worthless, not good enough, not perfect enough, not special enough, not valued enough, not successful enough, we will live out our days trying to validate ourselves to prove we are OK! This trap of endless striving, mindless doing, and mirrored self-absorption is the narcissistic "room of doom" I described in Chapter Three. It is our greatest trap in life. As we compulsively seek more beauty, popularity, success, or power we run but cannot hide from the self-judgment which lurks within us. There is indeed a seductive quality to fame, fortune, and fluff. They seem to be attractive solutions to a soul which has grown weary with self-doubts and loneliness.

Self-rejection and arrogance are two ends of the same self-absorbed continuum.

Both poles reflect a lack of acceptance of who we really are. While the depressed soul berates himself in repetitive self-lashings, the arrogant one is desperately putting herself on a pedestal to avoid being who she really is! Arrogance is simply another way of dealing with worthlessness feelings. Underneath our arrogance lies much self-doubt, just as there is much pride hidden beneath our self-rejection. Self-rejection is frequently seen simply as the neurotic expression of an insecure person. For Henri Nouwen, self-rejection may be the greatest enemy of our spiritual life because it contradicts the ever-present, sacred voice that calls us the Beloved.

Whether we are inflated or deflated, self-absorption removes us from love. Attachment to others remains superficial and calculated rather than authentic and deep. I experienced my comeuppance early, thankfully, when I was courting my wife Claire in 1969. Our commitment to courtship ignited quickly. Since I was living in Philadelphia, Claire and I rather wisely chose Manhattan, where she lived, as our weekly, weekend rendezvous point. When I arrived the first weekend after meeting her, I was well aware that she had been dating three other guys at the time. She greeted me warmly and enthusiastically proclaimed the weekend as a romantic dream come true.

"Not so fast!" I muttered. "How do I know you really wanted to see me this weekend and not one of your other boyfriends?"

"Larry, I've been counting the days until you arrived. How can you say that?"

My cynicism escalated quickly, and I actually accused her of seeing others during the week, not truly wanting me there in New York for the full weekend and tacitly hoping the weekend would pass by in a flash. Claire was reduced to tears as we talked, walked, and fought amidst the brownstones of Manhattan where other lovers were surely having a better day. Claire's tears evoked great sadness and guilt in me for blasting her with such anger, doubting her true desires, and absolutely gutting a Friday night in the Big Apple. We talked things through, I apologized, and we resurrected a spectacular Saturday and Sunday until the New Jersey Turnpike beckoned me back to Philadelphia where I taught 4th grade at that time.

The following weekend I returned to New York City where Claire greeted me warmly and enthusiastically – once again proclaiming the weekend as a romantic dream come true. Great restaurants, museums, and Central Park awaited our most playful and joyful forays.

"Not so fast!" I persevered. "How do I know you really wanted to see me this weekend and not one of your other cronies?"

"Larry, how can you say that? I've been counting the days until you arrived." Once again, my cynicism escalated, I accused her of seeing others during the week, not truly wanting me there in New York. and tacitly hoping the weekend would pass by in a flash. Once again, Claire was reduced to tears; I felt great pangs of sadness, guilt and loss. I apologized – once again shamefully shedding my own tears as well. We resurrected a spectacular Saturday and Sunday until the New Jersey Turnpike beckoned me once again.

I'm humbled to admit that Claire and I are still uncertain how many weekends this harrowing ritual was obsessively, compulsively, and painfully repeated. Our best guess is four, maybe five times! This Friday night tumult clearly was not about Claire. It was about my deep-rooted insecurities, feelings of inadequacy, and sense of unworthiness borne of years of emotional traumas, emotional dislocations, and a pervasive fear of rejection. I was not emotionally secure! At that point in my life – age 23 – my longest love relationship had probably been only two or three days – max!

The beauty of this story is not that Claire somehow endured my outrageous behavior, forgave me, and managed to preserve hope in the eye of a very insecure, neurotic storm cell. The real beauty, which I did not realize until many years later, was that unwittingly, I had presented to Claire the worst of me at the very beginning – parts of me that were clearly not OK. This is highly unusual behavior for two people in courtship who generally present their best qualities as a first impression. I broke all the rules of engagement. She had experienced my anger, my wretched insecurities from my beleaguered past, my jealousy, and my lack of groundedness. While there were certainly a few positives to serve as kindling within our crucible of romance, the last thing she needed was to be predictably indicted each and every Friday night for five weeks.

Yet, Claire endured in the spirit of love.

When Claire cried, I did as well. When she forgave me, I was cleansed. When I revealed my wounded self to her, she found a place for all of me in our relationship – the good, the bad, and the ugly. My wounds became our wounds that we worked through together. These early experiences of "humility," "forgiveness," "acceptance," and "compassion" are a few of the *Six Gifts* I describe in the last section of this book.

When she cried, I knew I was not a random array of atoms, insignificantly passing by her Manhattan brownstone. Her tears somehow meant that I really mattered, which somehow satisfied my needy, hungry narcissism. Her emotional investment in me somehow reassured the insecure me.

Her greatest *Gift* of all, however, was not the "acceptance" of my apologies – i.e., that she "forgave" me. Her tears, her words of endearment, and her total embrace of me meant far more, something that I realized many years later. I knew that if Claire could accept me at my worst, I could trust that she truly would love me at my best. I no longer had to hide my thoughts, feelings, needs, and desires in a self-absorbed reverie which boggled my mind. I could drop my defenses. With this reassurance I was able to begin building a secure base in my life for the first time – with another person.

I was learning that intimacy is not simply a feeling; it is a process, a living architecture that is constantly in the works.

My weary, solitary travail of finding security on my own had finally ended.

In this cauldron of emotions, I was able to understand what attachment to a love object (LO) really meant. For the first time in my life, I was beginning to experience what it meant to be vulnerable – to be real without fear. Like my client Jim, I was learning what real intimacy was about. Being vulnerable while rising up from the ashes of solitude, deprecating self-doubts, and abhorrent self-esteem gave me hope. I stopped struggling and began to accept intimacy into my life.

A concept of "secure attachment" was beginning to get kicked up in buttermilk!

Once upon a time two frogs fell into a large pail of buttermilk. Frantically the frogs climbed on each other, splashed furiously, and did whatever they could to stay afloat. As they grew weary and even more fearful of drowning, they thrashed about more desperately. Finally, approaching exhaustion, the frogs ceased struggling and prepared for the worst. Only then did they realize what their terrified minds never saw: All their seemingly futile and frustrating struggles had started turning the buttermilk into butter. Their random efforts were creating a platform on which they could float.

The frogs saw new purpose to their struggles and renewed their efforts with determination and collaboration. They kicked with less angst and paddled with greater ease. Eventually their efforts allowed them to rise above the milk. What once threatened their very existence became a resource for survival.[3]

Secure Attachment

Who would think that *adult love* and *parent/infant love* are similar? While adult love is certainly more "mature" than the love between an infant and its mother, I would like to suggest that a common thread ties the two together. This thread is called *attachment*.

It has been my painful observation that narcissists are byproducts of poor attachment and thus become poor attachment figures themselves.

Our relationships with narcissists often become a ludicrous journey of one-sided love. What can go so wrong? Much of our understanding of attachment comes from the work of John Bowlby whose volumes titled *Attachment*[4] have impacted two generations of theorists and clinicians since 1969, the year I met Claire.

Bowlby was a keen observer of how infants reacted when they were separated from their primary caregiver (usually the mother) for various lengths of time. Separation, after all, was not in the interest of the infant from a survival point of view. In evolutionary terms, proximity to a nurturing, protective caregiver increases the infant's chances for survival from predators, harsh environments, and unforeseen dangers. In addition to survival benefits (sounds like social security benefits to me), an infant's proximity to its mother was a good meal ticket as well as a comfort benefit when emotionally upset.

This latter benefit – when emotionally upset – is known as "emotional regulation." Its absence is known as "emotional dysregulation" or, more commonly today, "affect dysregulation." Affect dysregulation is an internal emotional storm. It is a byproduct of psychological trauma and "presets" our bodies for flooding with stress hormones like cortisol and adrenalin when threatened. A traumatized child believes, and therefore "knows," that bad things do happen to good people and without warning. Dysregulation is the painful pool that remains after repeated chronic shocks – sonic booms of parental neglect and abuse.

Because the infant's very survival depends on proximity to a secure caregiver, evolution has selected a few behaviors for infants that increase the likelihood of being securely protected, fed, or comforted. They include crying, smiling, cooing, clinging, looking, reaching, or movement toward the mother. All of these, collectively, are considered "attachment behaviors" that are intended to achieve a certain goal – close proximity to the mother, father, or caregiver – needs I missed out on growing up!

In my case, I demonstrated most of these during those first few Fridays in Manhattan when I began my courtship of Claire. My unstated purpose was not only to seek proximity but a secure base with her that would quiet the storm of insecurities flooding me on the inside – archaic residues from my childhood. Clearly, our need for attachment does not end with pubescence. It gestates within us for a lifetime.

Bowlby was not available to observe me on those streets in New York in 1969 (thankfully), but was able to notice what happens to infants who are separated from their mothers. Predictably, a number of reactions unfold. First, an infant will protest. This is typically a crying out or an active search for the mother, as well as an active protest to the soothing efforts from others. The second reaction will be despair which marks the predictable feelings of sadness and helplessness resulting from the infant's inability to find his or her secure base. Finally, there may be a detachment which marks an active avoidance of the mother when she does return. Remarkably, Bowlby also found the first two reactions in most other primates (e.g., chimps, monkeys) as well.

Something truly wonderful happens when mothers, fathers, or other caregivers predictably respond to attachment behaviors of infants. The infant appears healthy, alert, and confident and then begins to explore his or her environment with a real sense of curiosity and equanimity. Over time this leads to a sense of mastery and efficacy – a real belief that one's efforts can actually bring fulfillment. Exploration also allows for the creation of new relationships in the child's world, a benefit in regards to social development for years to come. All of this is possible only if the mother, or caregiver, becomes a "secure base".

When children are embedded in a loving bond, one that is predictable and nurturing, they play happily, sing and coo happily, smile happily, share toys and teddy bears happily, and discover hidden treasures happily. Everything from insects to lint on the floor becomes part of an inviting and dynamic universe that is safe to explore. Our worlds come alive with possibility and promise. Relationships become the warm nests they were intended to be. Attachment, under the banner of attentive love, becomes the basis for joy, confidence, and a pervasive sense of security which can last a lifetime.

The process of romantic love, between two adults, is remarkably similar to the secure attachment process just described with infants and their parents. If you doubt this, just think back to your early courtship days and remember that when you truly felt embedded in a loving bond – one that was predictable and nurturing – you played happily, sang and "cooed" happily, and perhaps even shared a few toys and hidden treasures – happily. There is a mutual desire for exclusivity, kissing, hugging, caressing, and ear-to-ear smiling in both scenarios. Both processes are biologically wired, hormonally driven, and well-evolved by the powerful tides of evolutionary forces.

Here's the bottom line: When an attachment object is present and responsive, both infants and romantic lovers feel secure enough to be [1] separate for periods of time, [2] able to explore on their own, and to [3] interact with others in a secure way. As we have seen, adult love is often the arena in which we heal childhood loss.

Insecure Attachment

So what happens to us when our connections go south?

In a test of John Bowlby's thinking, Dr. Mary Ainsworth conducted a series of famous studies. She found that a mother's sensitivity and capacity to respond to an infant's needs and signals are critical during the first 12 months of life. So critical, in fact, that a child grows up secure or insecure depending on these very interactions. Dr. Ainsworth found that there were three types of attachment possible for the infant depending upon a mother's availability and responsiveness. The three styles are referred to as secure, anxious/ambivalent, and avoidant.[5] More recently, experts in the field have added a fourth style of attachment called disorganized attachment.[6]

1) **Secure** – These infants have had repeated experiences with a mother who was consistently available, responsive, and care-taking during the first year of life. Even when the mother was out of sight, these secure infants believed she was accessible to them. As a result these infants explored their world with more confidence.

2) **Anxious/Ambivalent** – These infants cry more than securely attached infants and seem to demonstrate separation anxiety when mother is not present. These infants act as if they know their mothers will not be available and grieve accordingly in anticipation of their mother's departure – with intense distress.

3) **Avoidant** – These infants are more likely to have had rejecting mothers who rebuff their infants physically when they need to be held or they desire close bodily contact. These mothers are often more angry and irritable when compared to mothers of securely attached infants. This pattern results in infants who appear to be grief-stricken or in a guarded state after a period of separation from their mother.

4) **Disorganized** – These infants appear to have significant difficulty with both social relationships and their own emotional regulation. The infants are flooded by an internal storm of fear and terror that is so profound that they must dissociate in order to cope. These infants are at risk of developing a life-long pattern of Post Traumatic Stress Disorder if they are exposed to trauma later on in their lives.

Insecure attachments, the last three mentioned above, leave emotional scars.

In fact, many of these infants – particularly the disorganized ones – experience what might be called a "biological paradox." The parent who "should" be available for physical soothing and comfort is the same parent who is the very source of alarm. Numerous studies demonstrate that without proper interventions or changes in family functioning, these insecurely attached youngsters form attachment patterns in infancy that persist throughout childhood.

Even at the age of two, insecurely attached children appear to lack self-confidence, self-reliance, or enthusiasm in solving problems. By the time these kids are four or five years old, they are often the "problem kids" noted by teachers. They relate poorly to peers and seem to possess very little resiliency, that resource that allows us to bounce back from life's adversities. And at age six, these same children appear to have a pall about them which conveys hopelessness in the face of anticipated separations from attachment figures in their lives.

The negative impact of "insecure attachment" is not easily reversed.

After living through a disastrous experience with an absentee parent(s), you would think that insecurely attached children would find a "substitute attachment figure" if their primary bond has been fractured by an impaired mother, father, or other caretaker. But it's just not that easy as Robert Karen points out in an article in *Atlantic Monthly*:

The insecurely attached youngster often has difficulty finding an alternate attachment figure because the strategies he has adopted for getting along in the world tend to alienate him from the very people who might otherwise be able to help. The behavior of the insecurely attached child – whether aggressive or cloying, all puffed up or easily deflated – often try the patience of peers and adults alike. It elicits reactions that repeatedly reconfirm the child's distorted view of the world. People will never love me, they treat me like an irritation, and they don't trust me, and so on.[7]

As if this weren't enough, a visual MRI picture of these kids can get even bleaker, revealing shocking evidence of parental neglect and chronic shock. The brain development of severely neglected and abused children shows significant damage on Magnetic Resonance Images. According to Dr. Daniel Siegel[8] these include 1) smaller overall brain size, 2) damaged corpus callosum which connects the right and left hemispheres, 3) impaired growth of the regulating GABA fibers to the hypothalamic nuclei, and 4) elevated levels of cortisol, a stress hormone, which is toxic to growing neurons in younger children and adolescents. GABA, an amino acid, helps induce relaxation and sleep, inhibiting fearful excitation in the brain once it occurs.

There is a wake up-call here!

The key to reversing negative, narcissistic patterns, whether physiological or psychological, is to understand what Siegel has called a "coherent adult narrative." An adult with a coherent life story has made sense of his own childhood experience and knows how his past influences his present – particularly as a parent. An unresolved narrative represents an insecurely attached adult's inner dialogue about the horrors of manipulative people, the inevitability of abandonment, and how unlovable I really am!

These inner dialogues become the springboard for adult self-absorption:

* ❋ Securely attached narratives are built around a belief that other people are essentially well-intentioned and good-hearted.
* ❋ Anxiously/ambivalently attached narratives are built around the notion that one is inadequate, misunderstood, and chronically underappreciated.
* ❋ Avoidant attached narratives are built around the notion that other people are cold and rejecting.
* ❋ Disorganized attached narratives are built around the idea that the world is a pretty scary, chaotic, and an unpredictable place to live.

These coherent adult narratives explain far more accurately than the early childhood experiences themselves why we act and react the way we do in our adulthood relationships. I refer to negative adult narratives as themes; Chapter 12, Disenchantment, is devoted to these narratives because they color every love relationship we're ever in.

As we will see, it's not what happens to us that counts, but how we look at it!

To heal our childhood wounds we must be able to enter into and experience a healthy secure attachment as an adult. The process by which an insecure person becomes increasingly more secure and confident requires three things: first, a healthy attachment process in adult-hood called romantic love; second, a realistic understanding that separation and disenchant-ment (i.e.. temporary loss) with a love partner is normal; and third, that reconnection and renewal is possible as long as we breathe life back into our relationships using any of nine different "Adult Intimacy Styles."

> *Twenty-first century lovers still have not learned that romantic love blooms from a bed of narcissism and a chemical high and was never intended to be the basis for long-lasting love, which I term mature covenant love.*

True attachment leads to long-term bonds which stand the test of time and the multitude of disruptions which occur along the way. The wrong chemical mix creates disaster in our relationships, and we are destined to crash and burn. Let's take a moment to understand what works and what doesn't work in our brains.

Oxytocin vs. Cortisol: An Epic Struggle

What do a lactating mother, an orgasmic husband, and a hug have in common?

A strange question, you might be thinking! Yet, the answer has far-reaching implications. Each of these experiences has oxytocin in common – a neuropeptide in the brain which creates a sense of well-being. Oxytocin has been called a "bonding" hormone by some or a "cuddling" hormone by others. The number of oxytocin receptors in the expectant mother's brain multi-plies dramatically near the end of her pregnancy. This makes the new mother highly responsive to the presence of oxytocin. These receptors increase in the part of her brain that promotes maternal behaviors.

When the release of oxytocin ignites receptor sites in the brain, we feel more attached to whoever is associated with its release – an example of classical conditioning. A center in our brain says "I feel good!" and "I want more of this – please!" This is true for the breast-feeding mother, a beaming husband in afterglow, as well as a weak-kneed wife following a gentle mas-sage and hug.

I love oxytocin and oxytocin helps me love!

Other activities that produce oxytocin are meditation, yoga, exercise, caring for a pet, belonging to a support group, prayer, and so forth. While these activities increase our levels of oxytocin, nothing rivals its crucial importance in love relationships. The "secure attachment" benefits that accrue from being in a love relationship are so significant that Dr. Dean Ornish points out that love and intimacy may be such powerful determinants of health and well-being that if they were mass-produced in pill form, doctors who failed to properly prescribe them for unhealthy patients would be guilty of malpractice.[9]

Oh, if only we could create this health benefit by swallowing a pill. Yes, it has been tried. Unfortunately, oxytocin does not cross the "blood/brain barrier" successfully. The only way we get it is by producing it naturally in the brain once our relationships become more intimate.

The couples I meet in therapy have often obliterated most of what remains from healthy courtships. They are avoiding each other and have depleted oxytocin levels to mere traces of what they once were. Now, in the midst of a war zone, we emit a stress hormone called cortisol which the adrenal cortex is more than happy to spit out in anger to prepare us for "fight" or "flight" – both of which are common in distressed couples. A sudden threat triggers the fight-or-flight response associated with adrenaline. Adrenaline steps up heart rate, increases respiration, activates muscles, and promotes hyper-alertness. Longer-term stress (from a few hours, days, or weeks) increases a different stress hormone: cortisol. Cortisol, too, makes us hyper-vigilant, but its evolutionary functions are quite different than the temporary jolt of adrenaline designed to propel us out of danger. Adrenaline is for a sprint, cortisol is for a marathon.

When we live in conflicted relationships – filled tension, apprehension, walking on egg shells, and countless arguments that are never resolved we sleep poorly, eat poorly, act irritably, concentrate poorly, and feel helpless and hopeless. We turn toward our partners not with a sense of trust, comfort, and centered peace but rather with resentment and anger, releasing even more corticosteroids – like cortisol. We feel miserable. Oxytocin equates with love; cortisol equates with fear.

We fall in love with oxytocin and fall out of love with cortisol.

Apart from its functions of inducing emotional bonding, labor, and lactation, oxytocin counters the bad effects of cortisol. Fear hampers intimacy. Oxytocin promotes it. Before we explore the ways to counter the effects of chronic cortisol, Marnia Robinson reminds us how oxytocin promotes better health:[10]

Let's remember, being touched anywhere on the human body increases oxytocin!

Fear - Cortisol	Love - Oxytocin
Aggression	Anti-stress hormone
Arousal, anxiety, feeling stressed-out	Feeling calm and connected, increased curiosity
Activates addictions	Lessens cravings and addictions
Suppresses libido	Increased sexual receptivity
Associated with depression	Positive feelings
Can be toxic to brain cells	Facilitates learning
Breaks down muscles, bones, and joints	Repairs, heals, and restores
Depresses immune system	Faster wound healing
Increases pain	Diminishes sense of pain
Clogs arteries, promotes heart disease and high blood pressure	Lowers blood pressure, protects against heart disease

Conflicted couples not only have less attachment, they compromise their health!

As you can see from the chart above, most of the negative effects of continued stress on the body and mind are clearly related to elevated levels of cortisol. These include chronic anxiety and depression, emotional over-reaction, negativity, weight gain, heart disease, high blood pressure, and weakened immunity. Oxytocin, by countering cortisol, ameliorates many of these conditions.

Here's the key: in women who do not have a history of "secure attachment" – presently, or in the past – cortisol blocks the oxytocin receptor sites. This finding by Rebecca Turner, Ph.D. is extraordinary: it means that even when "insecurely attached" women are receiving hugs, cuddling, and experiencing orgasms with partners, they may not have a secure feeling of well-being because they live in fear – fear of abandonment, conflict or loss. Paradoxically, the brains in these women have learned not to trust "feel good" experiences and literally block the availability of receptor sites.

The opposite is true: a close, regular relationship influences the responsiveness of oxytocin. Women whose oxytocin levels rise in response to massage and hugs are usually in a positive relationship, have a history of positive bonding, report having little difficulty setting appropriate boundaries, and tolerate being alone. More to the point, women who were currently involved in a healthy, committed relationship experienced greater oxytocin increases in response to positive emotions than single women.[11]

Adult courtship is a birth process – which has the promise of oxytocin release.

Courtship potentially allows us an opportunity to experience many of the tender, intimate feelings that 66 percent of securely attached individuals cherished during their childhoods. Because the release of oxytocin can be classically conditioned, once we repeatedly have sex with the same partner, just seeing that partner will release more oxytocin, making you want to be with that person all the more – and you bond!

Such feelings are created by two people who are engaged in a mutually agreed upon dance which is intended to select "me" over all other potential partners. While the psychological underpinnings of courtship will be covered in the next chapter on romantic love, this section highlights the distinctive behaviors which have evolved for Homo sapiens to create attachment with one another. Desmond Morris believes that there are twelve distinct behavior patterns of courtship, all of which entail a progressive unfolding from lesser intimacy to greater intimacy.[12]

> 1) *Eye to body*. In that fraction of a second when we first set our eyes upon one another, we begin to "size" each other up. Shape, height, animation, and other attributes all begin to contribute to the selection process.
>
> 2) *Eye to eye*. While we first connect with others, they are also connecting with us. Our eyes must eventually meet. In this moment, we may either look away in embarrassment or we may smile, thus removing the first barrier to intimacy.
>
> 3) *Voice to voice*. In the beginning, our conversations are somewhat trivial as we attempt to break the ice. This small talk, e.g. interests, hobbies – by keeping the conversation superficial – allows for a polite exit if more substantial signals do not materialize.
>
> 4) *Hand to hand*. Beginning with a handshake or an effort to help, we may touch

hands for just a few seconds. Later, within the context of a growing relationship, these hand-to-hand touches may become undisguised intimacy, as in more sustained hand-holding or arm-holding.

5) *Arm to shoulder*. Now, for the first time, two bodies may come into contact. In this uncommitted posture, two partners look ahead rather than at each other. An air of ambiguity exists here, somewhere between friendship and romance.

6) *Arm to waist*. This posture more romantically conveys intimacy, since friends are unlikely to walk together in this fashion. Each lover's hand is now closer to the beloved's genital region as well.

7) *Mouth to mouth*. When kissing is combined with a full frontal embrace, a significant commitment toward intimacy has been achieved. Both partners have acknowledged a willingness to accept the other and may begin to experience sexual arousal.

8) *Hand to head*. As an extension of passionate kissing, two lovers may begin to caress each other's hair, neck, and face. Their embrace now becomes more entranced and more prolonged as each finds comfort in the other. Since we rarely touch heads in our culture, this is a true sign of emotional commitment.

9) *Hand to body*. One partner's hands may now begin to explore the other's body in an escalating display of emotional and sexual arousal. Lovers may now squeeze, fondle, and stroke one another's genitals or breasts.

10) *Mouth to breast*. At this point, two lovers have become so aroused that privacy is necessary in order to be intimate with one another. If for no other reason than to obey the law, two lovers must now seclude themselves.

11) *Hand to genitals*. As manual and oral exploration of the body continues, the genitals are eventually stimulated. Gentle actions eventually give way to rhythmic rubbing and inserting that stimulate pelvic thrusts.

12) *Genitals to genitals*. The full stage of copulation is reached with orgasm. Each stage, leading to this one, has served to further tighten the bond of emotional and sexual commitment. This final consummation, with the possibility of fertilization, permits a renewal of this cycle in later generations.

During early romantic love, we are sometimes led to believe that we are "special" only when intimacy develops beyond "hand to hand," "arm to waist," or "mouth to mouth" (steps one through eight). To be truly "special" during early love, many lovers believe they must experience sexual intimacy – "hand to body," "mouth to breast," "hand to genitals," and "genitals to genitals" (steps nine through twelve).

For a narcissist, sexual intimacy may only represent a conquest, a cold and heartless mark etched in one's belt. When this intense level of sexual sharing bypasses the earlier attachment steps, the courtship process may often appear real when it is, in fact, an illusion. The innocent love bird caught up in the magic assumes, "Though you may be hugging, touching, or even kissing other people, I know that you are not having intercourse with anyone else at this time.

Therefore, I must be special to you. You must care about me if you are making love only with me." Sexual intercourse thus becomes the keystone of reciprocal attachment for many. Is this real commitment, or real intimacy, that is building "secure attachment"? What better under-pinnings for disaster!

Later on, when the magic of romantic love – infatuation – gives way to the bitterness of disenchantment, or detachment, you and your partner make a tragic discovery: the only basis for "secure attachment" now appears to have been sexual passion, that natural and allur-ing dance whose siren song still beckons. The potent swell of arousal, the gush of hormones, may still sweep you away on Saturday night. But on Sunday morning you awaken to vacuous sounds of silence. For the narcissist, this aloneness is a disaster.

Only pools of cortisol remain.

The real tragedy for many men is that encasement within a vaginal wall is the only way they will permit themselves to retain the intimate comfort of their lost womb. These men are conditioned to believe that penile engorgement is the only permissible standard for fullness in a relationship.

Turning Toward, Turning Against, and Turning Away

Psychoanalyst Karen Horney reminds us over and over that we have three choices in our re-lationships: [1] we can move toward one another; [2] we can move against one another, as in conflict; or [3] we can move away from one another, as in withdrawal.[13] Clearly the first of these behavior patterns promotes attachment far more than the others.

As we look ahead to the remaining chapters in *Love's Sanctuary*, the third section of this book, keep in mind the importance of turning toward others. My office is strewn with the disheartened, burned-out souls of so many who stagnate in the "Room of Doom." Each is truly self-absorbed. Their lives are filled with long-harbored resentments which have cascaded into stormy conflicts and arid withdrawal from those who matter most – love partners and children.

The tragedy continues.

Often, because of the demands of our lives, we have little time to invest in all *Nine Intimacy Styles* available to us. We may be working long hours, away on repeated business trips, up with the kids till 10 pm doing homework, or just too preoccupied during the day to think of calling one another. This constant pattern erodes a feeling of closeness in many relationships. As a result, we may begin to turn away, turn against, or turn off from partners who seem too distant to really care. At this point, the embers of intimacy that remain are never enough to hold us together. We need more.

Love is our best antidote for narcissism, yet it remains a mystery to many. For love to serve its greater purpose of transformation it must be given enough time to form, deform, and then reform once again. This takes time. This is why the true intimacy of mature, covenant love is a marathon – often taking a lifetime to unfurl its heralded stars and stripes.

The chapters ahead are intended to answer your questions about love, about its evolution over time, and its core ingredients. While love is often viewed as sweet nectar from the Gods, I would suggest instead a more earthly view of love – as sustenance which nurtures life daily. We can't live without it. Four questions will be answered in the pages ahead. [1] What is romantic love and why does it become a vapor trail over time? [2] What is disenchantment and why must it be a necessary phase in our most intimate journeys? [3] What is mature, covenant love and how does it provide a lifelong womb for safety and security? [4] What are your preferences, or styles for intimacy, and how might these expand over time? Let's now explore romantic love more fully.

CHAPTER **11**

Romantic Love

Romantic love is the single greatest energy system in the Western psyche. In our culture it has supplanted religion as the arena in which men and women seek meaning, transcendence, wholeness, and ecstasy.[1]

Most relationships are thrust into being by one great narcissistic force or another.

In more traditional Eastern societies, these forces are often religious, economic, or political in nature. Marriages are often arranged by self-serving parents or ruling families. The perpetuation of one's blood lines, societal structures, spiritual beliefs, or financial holdings determines who will marry whom. The bride and groom in such cases may not even meet one another until the wedding day. In other societies, marriage can be a different kind of strategic game. For instance, emigration from certain countries might depend on marriage to a "citizen" of another country. People in such situations often desperately advertise in the classifieds for a "suitable" bride or groom. Love is irrelevant.

Religious structures also influence who marries whom, both in the East and in the West. Despite the growing number of intermarriages, a Christian is still encouraged to marry a Christian, and the same is true with a Jew, a Muslim, or a Hindu. If God is to bless the marriage, or even be a part of it, then certain sacraments or covenants must be adhered to. We take vows or commit ourselves to sacred promises which are to last until death does part us or, in the case of the Mormon marriage, for eternity.

To many people in Western societies, such meddling by outside forces – secular or religious – is practically blasphemous. We indignantly believe that there is only one great ruler, one majestic force that can or should unify two disparate souls: romantic love. Only love can elevate us from our lonely, desolate state to one of joyful majesty. Only love can provide the glue to hold us together. Only love can justify committing our bodies, our property, our lives to another person. But only recently in human history have we been so daring to combine love, sex, and marriage in one institution. Most prior civilizations knew better!

In his wonderful book *We*, Robert Johnson reminds us that our Western culture has been replaying the myth of romantic love since it was first introduced in our literature during the Middle Ages. In his retelling of this romantic tale about two lovers, Tristan and Iseult, we learn that:

> *Romantic love doesn't just mean loving someone; it means being "in love." This is a psychological phenomenon that is very specific. When we are "in love" we believe we have found the ultimate meaning of life, revealed in another human being. We feel we are finally completed, that we have found the missing parts of ourselves. Life suddenly seems to have wholeness, a super-human intensity that lifts us high above the ordinary plain of existence. For us, these are the sure signs of "true love." The psychological package includes an unconscious demand that our lover or spouse always provide us with this feeling of ecstasy and intensity.*[2]

Romantic love is a narcissist's dream come true!

Romantic love becomes the magic elixir for our "missing ten degrees." Our beloved will fill any void that exists. We are perhaps the only culture to have marketed romance as a mass phenomenon. Romance is a media event. Our society bombards us with images that glorify romance. Our favorite movie idols teach us how to seduce and be seduced in one torrid scene after another. Then, as if this were not enough, weekly tabloids fuel our fantasies further by revealing the "real life" affairs of these same actors and actresses. TV soap operas and commercials subtly or blatantly remind us that something very mysterious and fulfilling is just around the corner, if only we project the right image, wear the right clothes, and use the right deodorant.

Some people experience romantic love as a flood of powerful emotions: burning excitement, exquisite yearning, and profound joy. For others, the experience is more cerebral: constantly whirring thoughts about their lover, memory reruns of special moments, elaborate plans for the future. And for some, romantic love is experienced as both gushing emotions and spinning thoughts. Regardless of whether romantic love is experienced more as feelings or as thoughts, it is marked by eight characteristics:

1) Intense passion
2) Ecstatic loss of judgment
3) Obsessive focus on the beloved
4) Desire for exclusivity

5) Self-centered preoccupation with oneself

6) Selective focus on positive qualities

7) Exaggeration of real or imagined qualities

8) Secret codes, private meanings, special language

These physical and psychological characteristics are destined to shatter as the foundation for love. They must shatter because they are built upon a fluid base of emotions, feelings which by their very nature are vacillating and momentary. Romantic love is fueled by a chemical high which has a life-expectancy of less than three years. It is not until later on, during the wisdom of mature covenant love, that we can be assured of a long-lasting love. While a foundation of trust may be laid during romantic love, romantic love is not to be trusted.

Romantic love often appears bizarre by mental health standards – a blend of mania, dementia and obsession that separates one from friends, family, even reason. Out of character behaviors such as compulsive phone calling, yelling from rooftops, and talking nonstop throughout the night can almost rival the behaviors of a psychotic. Now, we have research findings which even suggest that the "drive" for romantic love is literally intoxicating. Functional MRI technology now reveals that an area of the brain called the caudate nucleus is activated during romantic love. This area is dense with cells that produce dopamine, an amino acid that circulates actively when we are craving or desiring something like food, water, or drugs. Falling in love thus triggers a passion-related region of the brain which is clearly related to longing, desire, and addiction.

Physical addiction begets obsessive predilection.

The obsessive illusions of romantic love must shatter as well. The attitudes that accompany them are too brittle, too absolute, and too extreme to serve as the foundation for a love that can endure the bumps of everyday living. Two reciprocal sets of needs seem to underlie all love relationships: (1) self needs versus other needs and (2) need for novelty versus need for familiarity:

	NOVEL	FAMILIAR
SELF NEEDS	Romantic Love	
OTHER NEEDS		Mature Love

Romantic love, by its very nature, is a narcissistic, self-absorbed experience.

Romantic love is characterized by self-oriented needs that require the stimulation of novelty. In our heightened physical and emotional state, we clamor for more and more supercharged experiences to perpetuate the high we call "romance." Candlelight dinners, passionate love in the morning and sentimental mementos of places where we spent time together develop into a pattern of intensity that we expect to sustain over time. Although romance itself can certainly endure, this level of idealized intensity is destined to wane. If our appetite for intensity is stronger than our sense of satisfaction in our current relationship, then pursuit of novelty can become addicting as we flit from one "new" relationship to another.

Eventually, if we are to experience the fulfillment we yearn for, we must come to appreciate the "paradox of love" – the paradox that after we fall in love we must fall out of it in order to experience a truly loving, committed relationship. We must learn that something better – mature, covenant love – can augment and enrich the fading intensity of romantic love. We must learn to cherish the needs of others within a life structure which is familiar to us. Here we find the security, predictability, and rootedness that we need to be truly and sustainably happy. This chapter, as well as the next two, explores the process of evolution in loving relationships. But to understand the process of reaching mature love, we must understand the eight characteristics of romantic love.

Romantic Love

Romantic love is characterized by intense passion. Courtship is driven by powerful hormones that are felt as intense emotional and physical passion. And lovers become even more passionate to overcome any obstacles (real or imaginary) that threaten to prevent union with their beloved. Sex! It exhilarates our moods and excites our imaginations. Richard Burton, upon meeting Elizabeth Taylor by a swimming pool, effused: "She is the most astounding, self-contained, pulchritudinous, remote, inaccessible woman I have ever seen. Her breasts were apocalyptic. They would topple empires down before they were withered."[3]

The word passion originally meant "to suffer." Lovers suffer because there are obstacles to overcome. Physical separation due to school or military service, religious or cultural differences, and parental objections may create immense barriers to romantic fulfillment, yet lovers will strive passionately to overcome these barriers. Even other men or women – the competition – can present obstacles; yet passionate lovers can be quite creative in establishing a special status above the rest.

There are times when the competition can actually be the husband or wife of the beloved. This was certainly the case in the Middle Ages when knights would charm a lady by doing a great feat and troubadours would travel from castle to castle to entertain and woo these women. It was this extramarital passion that was defined as love. In fact, it was not until the Middle Ages that the phrase "courtly love" came in vogue. Perhaps the most symbolic obstacle of the time was the chastity belt, which the lord of the castle hopelessly believed would deter penetration by a passionate lover. Today's version of this chastity belt is, of course, the wedding band.

These passionate women of the Middle Ages would actually gather in small groups to discuss their extramarital affairs, since sex outside marriage was fashionable. Their groups, called Courts of Love, defined the then current norms and traditions of "loving." Under the leadership of the Countess of Champagne, in May 1174, one group of women created a code of love. Their list of 31 principles included these five tenets [4]:

 * Marriage is no good excuse against loving.
 * Whoever cannot conceal a thing cannot love.

✳ Love that is known publicly rarely lasts.

✳ An easy conquest renders love despised, a difficult one makes it desired.

✳ The true lover is haunted by the co-lover's image unceasingly.

These passionate lovers had to overcome the rather unique obstacles of their time. As do we. Dual career marriages, changing gender roles, and evening soccer leagues may all sabotage our desire to be "unceasingly haunted" by a co-lover's image. Certainly, waiting for the kids to go to bed hardly encourages spontaneous passion. Perhaps the first principle listed above should read "Kids are no good excuse against loving"! Yet it is these very obstacles that make us wonder "Where did all our passion go?" Waiting for the reappearance of those rare delicious moments is hardly the basis of a solid relationship. Spent passion usually gets washed away in the laundry the next day.

Is nature duping us?

Courtship may be a biological lure that allows us to perpetuate ourselves as a species. Once we copulate, nature's aims have been fulfilled. Erotic love, driven by powerful hormones within the body, is nature's gift to enjoy, but we must be careful not to marry for this gift alone. When our initial attraction for a person's height, legs, or breasts diminishes in intensity – when the novelty wears off – our relationship may disintegrate if nothing more holds it together. We need all nine intimacies described in Chapter 14. Erotic feelings, when they are most important to us, may seem to be absolutely vital to our relationships, but they never will be sufficient for continued loving. In fact, for some couples erotic feelings are actually unimportant, perhaps even unnecessary.

Romantic love is characterized by ecstatic loss of judgment. Ecstasy, from the Greek ekstasis, originally meant "deranged"! In many ways, lovers are actually "out of their minds" when they fall in love, blinded by a montage of compelling images and sensations. Early love is powerfully fueled by the smell, the taste, the sight, the touch, and the sound of one's lover. Our responses are beyond reason and self-control. We may not know what we are doing, or we may be in such a stupor that we are unable to make sound judgments. Blinded by ecstatic desire, we may repeatedly choose lovers who are unable to make a living, who abuse us physically, who fear commitment, or who cling to Mommy or old friends. Not only are our responses beyond reason, but we may be driven by unreasonable motivations as well. Our ecstatic love may be based on unconscious needs for dependency, approval, or safety. Perhaps we have a desperate urgency to cling or bond which shows our inability to be alone or self-sufficient. Or we may be unable to stand feeling bored or restless.

These powerful, primal urges blur the distinctions between reason and emotion, thought and feeling, mind and body. These distinctions, however, actually are artificial. Both reason and emotion envelop one another as they dance together throughout a love relationship; though emotion may take the lead in the early going, the presence of reason determines how long the dance will last.

Romantic love is characterized by obsessive focus on the beloved. Often lovers are distracted from their normal thoughts and activities by constantly intruding thoughts about their romantic partner. We become preoccupied with every aspect of our lover's personality, history, current life, and so forth. Our capacity to concentrate on important tasks may be impaired by constant romantic daydreams. The more complex the task, the worse this condition can be. Some of us become so distracted by thoughts of our lovers that even our most basic cognitive functions seem to be on vacation. We can handle only the most routine, rote tasks – mindless chores that require no thinking, planning, or decision-making. In other words, we can handle the grocery shopping, but somebody else has to prepare the list.

Our thoughts are preoccupied with what might be called "rendezvous work." Rendezvous work can be a full-time job. Schedules must be juxtaposed, excuses found, and rationales provided. We devote tremendous amounts of thought and energy to figuring out when, where, and how we might meet with our beloved – either by design or by chance – and we often exhibit great creativity and cunning in pulling off our romantic plans.

Obsessed with our beloved, we may consciously make risky choices that previously would have seemed unthinkable. Meeting for an early morning rendezvous may seem a higher priority than attending an executive planning session. Giving a special expensive gift may seem a better choice than replacing the bald tires on our car. Going away together for the weekend may seem much more important than attending our child's awards banquet.

Obsessive preoccupation with our beloved i.e., self-absorption, is often exhilarating, but can also be an energy drain. Sleep patterns are often disrupted, appetites suppressed, and normal routines disturbed. But none of this seems to matter at the time. All we want is to submerge ourselves in the depths of our beloved.

Romantic love is characterized by a desire for exclusivity. Romantic lovers feel a need to merge with their beloved, a need to lose their separate, individual identities and "become one." The presence of other people in our lover's life – other romantic contenders, best friends, even children from a prior marriage – interferes with this experience of union. Our hunger for exclusivity can be understood in light of our deep need to feel completed in some sense.

In union with another we hope to find a missing part of ourselves desperately needed to fulfill our human experience.

Exclusive love is exhilarating, as if we are somehow lifted above the average plane of life. We soar to new heights. This transcendence beyond normal, ordinary life drives us to seek such fulfillment in love. Is it any wonder that we would so cherish time spent alone with our beloved? Can there be any doubt that such a meaningful union – such exclusivity – is likened quite often to a religious experience?

Through romantic love, the banality of our lives is somehow transformed into something exciting, even mystical. Our mundane world is somehow "linked" once again to a

blissful world which usually belongs only to the Gods.

Herein lies a bitter truth: what we have been taught to seek in others, by way of romantic love, cannot be found there. The exclusivity we cherish is supposed to provide us with a bottomless vessel, an ever-flowing source of emotional and spiritual sustenance to nourish us all our lives. This is a narcissistic fantasy. The lover we seek this exclusive bond with is not a real person but instead a projection of our most basic needs. Whether the need is nurturance, attention, affection, assertiveness, or playful sexuality, we see in the other the hope of getting what is sorely missing within ourselves: "Heal me, fill me, and quiet the storm within me!" These things are impossible because enduring love requires that we find unity and wholeness more in the transformation of ourselves than in the projected fantasies that we create about one another. Robert Johnson goes on to say:

> When a man's projections on a woman unexpectedly evaporate, he will often announce that he is "disenchanted" with her; he is disappointed that she is a human being rather than the embodiment of his fantasy. He acts as though she has done something wrong. If he would open his eyes, he would see that the breaking of the spell opens a golden opportunity to discover the real person who is there...This is mature love. It is equally the chance to discover the unknown parts of himself that he has been projecting on her and trying to live through her.[5]

Romantic love is characterized by preoccupation with oneself. The fact is that we receive far more than we give during romantic love. This phenomenon is rooted in the similarities between romantic love relationships and parent-child relationships. Most of us came into this world with an attentive parent-figure who attempted to meet our burgeoning narcissistic needs. We had to trust that our needs would be met in order to progress in a normal psychological manner. We cried and someone fed us or held us. We walked and someone applauded our every step. We stumbled and someone caught us. The more our needs were met, the more we believed that the entire universe was in harmony with us. We were somehow complete because of this oneness with our parents. Youthful narcissism is like this and it is quite normal for this phase of our unfolding life.

But we outgrow this narcissism, don't we? I'm not sure we do.

We bring this self-absorbed preoccupation with ourselves with us throughout life. Many of our courting behaviors that appear to be loving are really selfish. During candlelight dinners we glow with warmth from all the "loving" attention we get. Passionate lovemaking reminds us of how desirous we are to others. The more special we feel in these moments, the more our basic needs appear to be met, the more we want to love. According to psychiatrist Don Jackson, even the distress and misery that romantic lovers typically suffer when separated is caused by "selfishness of the most egocentric type."[6]

Unfortunately, this self-centered sense of fulfillment is sure to fade once work routines, children, and other life-style changes complicate daily schedules. If our selfish preoccupation requires megadoses of undivided attention, we are in for a rude awakening. The average American couple probably spends less than fifteen minutes together per week gazing into each others' eyes. Furthermore, most of us have never taken enough time to truly know what our basic needs actually are.

An ideal partner can complement our ego ideal. (We all have an unconscious desire to improve ourselves by choosing the right partner. In this way, we feel more complete.) But in this search for an ideal, are we finding romantic or mature love? Erich Fromm, in his book, *The Art of Loving*, points out:

> *Infantile love follows the principle "I love because I am loved." Mature love follows the principle "I am loved because I love." Immature love says "I love you because I need you." Mature love says "I need you because I love you."* [7]

We may become so preoccupied with all that we are getting that we love only because we are loved or give only because we receive.

Romantic love is characterized by a selective focus on positive qualities. If you were asked, in the heat of your passion, what attracted you to your lover, you might point out that she or he was disciplined, bright, perceptive, spirited, silly, creative, energetic, gentle, confident, and certainly sexy. If you were then asked what negative qualities you find in your lover, this second list of adjectives would certainly be most sparse compared to the former list. This is the nature of romantic love. From millions of potential partners in the United States alone, we choose one person. Then from thousands of adjectives and adverbs we choose less than ten (usually less than five) to describe this one person out of millions.

Certain positive qualities have actually been found to be more culturally embedded, perhaps more significant than others. "Warm" versus" cold" is one such dimension. Most of us put warmth right at the top of our positive quality list. Research shows that we are attracted to people who exude warmth, perhaps as a reflection of our incessant quest to find warm acceptance, a safe harbor, and secure attachment.

Romance serves to focus our attention on positive qualities while blurring our vision regarding more negative qualities. We only get part of the picture. But there's more. The bad news is that the positive qualities that initially attract two lovers are seldom sufficient, or even apropos, to meet the long-term needs of mature love. Disenchanted clients tell me so each day.

Romantic love is characterized by idealized exaggeration of real or imagined qualities. What we see in our lover is not what we get. Like two used car salespersons, each of us is presenting our very best features. Notice my exterior finish, my flashy undercoating, my acceleration and pickup. What we don't see are bent wheels, grinding gears, and leaky bottoms!

The two key words here are idealized and imagined. In our hunger to find what we are looking for, we do more than just notice positive qualities. We sanctify these qualities. We exaggerate their presence and their importance. Physical attraction may prompt us to idolize her golden hair, his rounded chin, her svelte slimness and firmness, or his towering height. All positive qualities, in the beginning, will appear more pronounced than they really are.

Romance is also based on imputed qualities that we wish our partners had. If we want to be taken care of, we will somehow find some measure of caring in our lover. The observation that he feeds his dog once a day may be enough for us to assume that he will nurture our needs as well. Only later do we begin to notice that his dog has fleas and tangled fur. Only later do we discover that our nurturing lover refuses to talk to his alcoholic father, believes his controlling mother is a bitch, and prays that his Ivy League brother will be crushed by fourteen cars at the Port Jefferson branch of the Long Island Railroad. And this is the guy we believe will care for us!

Therapist Muriel James makes a further distinction: "Being in love with a person is quite different from being in love with love. The romance in loving a person involves recognizing and treating that person as someone special and wonderful – but not someone adored or idealized. Romance is for real; romanticism is not."[8]

Romantic love is characterized by secret codes, private meanings, and special language.
As lovers we sustain our fantasies about our beloved – and the special relationship we share – by communicating with each other in a personal, exclusive language, especially when we are in the company of others.

The intensity of romantic love is marked by very personalized communications. We use the blandest of words – words like "peanut," "treasure," or "dewdrop" – to connote very special meanings. We refer to body parts, a sexual act, or a sexual setting by a secret code. This allows us to build fantasies about one another while in the company of others. The clandestine nature of these communications is deceptive and adds to the intensity of the relationship.

Virtually all of the senses might, in some way, be part of a secret code. A certain glance or wink, a certain dress or shirt, a certain aromatic meal, or a certain way of touching or massaging may send a message. During our courting days, we spend much time and money creating interludes where our senses can be titillated. An evening out may build in intensity as we dress for one another, perfume for one another, and begin to touch one another. Usually the dessert for such a romantic evening will be the richness of sexual passion.

Though many codes will die away during the course of a love relationship, mature lovers will delight in finding new ways to enchant and to entreat. This is not the case with romantic lovers, who never grow beyond their original codes.

Many of these characteristics of romantic love can be found in love letters. One of my clients shared this past lover's note with me. It captures the illusory power of romantic love quite well.

Dear Sandy,

I am delighted that you came by the other day - twice! Nothing like doubling your pleasure, doubling your fun! I only wish that we could discard all that intrudes in our lives so that we could totally immerse ourselves in one another. [Exclusivity]

When I saw you at the door the other morning, I don't think it was chance or irony which explains how just before you arrived you were firmly set in a dream which often comes to me. [Obsessive focus - not to mention divine intervention]

It is strange how events occur which change our lives. Some are for the better, some for the worse. And some keep you right where you are, making you wonder if this is really what I envisioned. I am not sure what you have in mind or have up your sleeve (or elsewhere- ha!) but I think you know the consequences that could result from our "special encounters" [Secret codes, private meanings], *but I want you to know that I am always here for you - no matter what - whenever you need me day or night. This will ALWAYS be true!* [Ecstatic loss of judgment]

When I saw you the other morning I was quite stunned! I couldn't believe that you were there - radiating that incredible essence of yours. Then we talked for a while and you let me kiss you - one of those long "special" kisses with those very "special" lips. Well I felt too good to be true - and many great memories started to flow ...oh!! What a morning! [Selective focus on positive qualities]

I often think about making love to you again and again. When we do, these are surely some of the sweetest and most erotic times in my life [intense passion]. *Why is it that even though we're not together, people I meet cannot compare to you? Feelings I get just cannot be compared in any way. It's going to be very hard, maybe impossible, for me to find some- one that can fit those shoes that I keep by my bed for that someone "special" (guess who) whenever she comes by.* [Idealized exaggeration of real or imagined qualities]

Well, I shall try again to go back to sleep. Since I can't have you next to me now, I'll do the next best thing; I'll dream about you – perhaps a nice wet one! I LOVE you very, very much.

—*Sam*

Sam's love note to Sandy is not unusual. All the components of romantic love are evident in just these few words. Sam is experiencing the real thing – he is truly in love. He is in romantic love. He has found not only the right woman but the right experience. If he insists on pre- serving Sandy and this profound romantic experience as they are, he will go down in the very flames that have ignited his current passion. He will crash and burn unless he understands much more about loving relationships.

Romance: Its Promise

Romantic love, as a magic potion, has been with us for many centuries. Its wondrous status as "the greatest force in the Western psyche" reflects its high performance ratings by consumers over the years. As we know from supply and demand economics, products and services that perform poorly are not wanted, resulting in less demand and value for those commodities. This is hardly the case with romantic love.

Romantic love has been "selling and trading" quite well in most national and international exchanges.

Its market "highs" are noteworthy, and its market shares are growing at a rapid pace. Consumers are obviously very interested in its upward cycle of growth and are willing to invest huge sums of capital and personal reserves in its behalf. Remarkably, romantic love seems to be the one investment people take "stock" in where it is not necessary to buy "low." Buying in when "high" seems to bring greater dividends to the average consumer, at least for a while! Even though people "crash" and burn daily in the marketplace of love, investors are as persistent as ever in betting it all on a blue chip winner!

TV talk shows make this point daily. Once, while tuned in to a television talk show I actually heard one member of the audience disdainfully put down one of the guests who clearly was not as intoxicated by love's magic as she had been: "How can you talk of financial security, family background, and career goals as important qualities to look for in another? What we need are more sparks, more flames, and more dreams to live by. That other stuff really doesn't matter. In fact, it's boring!"

Romance does have its place so long as we do not attempt to bottle it – to preserve it over time. This is precisely what we attempt to do in romantic love. We idealize our most intense experience of "falling in love." We project our most cherished images of perfection onto the beloved. We turn a wonderfully human experience into a divine one. We attempt to transform a delightful human being into a revered king or queen. We rigidly encapsulate a breathtaking, but fleeting, experience of romance by creating molds that must eventually fracture or break.

We place one another on narcissistic pedestals from which we must fall.

Romance is that sometimes intense, often tender, experience when two souls taste the wonders of oneness, when for the briefest of moments we transcend our lonely status as individuals and instead find ourselves immersed in another. Romantic lovers worry and fret that this experience will dissipate – for them a sure sign that "love" has ended. It is the notion that one should be able to drink the everlasting love potion for all time which underlies the absurdity of romantic love. Such a notion implies both insatiability and a belief in a perpetual flame that never goes out. Such abundance is certainly implied in our rituals of faith (such as Chanukah candles), but is, at best, a divine notion that only destines us mortals to despair when the light flickers out.

Mature lovers know better. In fact, the irony is that mature lovers know more about romance than romantic lovers do. Mature lovers know that romance has its seasons – its springtime passion and its wintertime repose. They know that romance waxes and wanes as do most natural things of beauty. Romantic lovers, in contrast, begin to pack their belongings when winter clouds start rolling in. But no amount of shoring up can prevent this intrusion. No wall, no moat, can hold off the inevitable – that disenchanting interlude when the intensity of romantic love fades and renewal has yet to commence.

Mature lovers know how to maintain romance as a power pellet in a loving relationship. Mature lovers know how to tap into romance as a fluid source of energy that sustains a relationship over time. Each of the eight characteristics of romantic love, just described, can be transformed into this special promise of renewal:

Intense passion can become genuine intimacy where we truly risk being known. We learn to reveal our true nakedness which we entrust to another's tender touch. We learn what turns each other on and take great delight in doing so. We learn that passion can be driven by an other-directedness that enjoys seeing the other so satisfied. Erotic intensity may also be transformed into a deep, abiding pleasure in the other's company and presence. We finally learn how to care about another by demonstrating effective communication, warm, loving affection, and reflective intuition.

Ecstatic loss of judgment can become a generosity of judgment in which we accept those of each other's flaws that aren't destructive to the relationship. This tenderness and tolerance of one another, in the face of obvious shortcomings, promotes the creation of a safe, loving environment where we can lose our self-consciousness as well as our harsh judgments of self and others. By providing a safe, secure harbor for our beloved, we offer a fertile setting where mutual growth can occur.

Obsessive focus on the beloved can become thoughtful reminders of love which convey our caring. Flowers, cards, surprise notes on the bathroom mirror are all ongoing ways to demonstrate our feelings which, in turn, trigger romance in our relationships. Mature lovers learn to create endearing moments when specialness is celebrated, instead of clinging to an illusion that specialness should be unflagging.

Desire for exclusivity can become the special night out, the lunchtime date, or the planned weekend for two (no kids allowed) that allow us time to renew our focus on each other as well as the "we-ness" we have come to share. In daily life, our time together is eroded by children, work demands, or other independent activities. Mature couples, within the context of these "interruptions," learn to stoke their romance on a more time-limited basis. When we learn to accept the complexity of our lives beyond one another, we are well positioned to enjoy the quality of our exclusive time together – even when the quantity of time is limited.

Preoccupation with oneself can become our intrepid dedication to attending to the demands and needs of the relationship while maintaining our own independence. We are solitary beings by nature and must accept this in order to be fully mature. Sometimes we try to shield ourselves from this truth by possessing one another in our quest for oneness. We must remember that we are born alone, we die alone, and we must live a portion of our lives alone – separate even from those we feel most close to. Mature lovers, knowing this, come to embrace each other with more devotion and romance as each cherishes the miracle of sharing that which can be shared by two separate individuals.

Selective focus on positive qualities can become the framework for healthy confrontation. By recognizing the many good qualities in our partners, we are actually freer to point out those that trouble us. Confrontation is an invitation to look at oneself honestly. This process is always easier when we know that our positive qualities have not been forgotten by our partner who confronts. Now, instead of idealizing the beloved or his or her qualities, we learn to prize the commitment we have made to a life together. By reassuring one another that our focus is on a lifelong journey, more than on personal qualities frozen in time, we are each free to find romantic renewal over the seasons of our relationship.

Exaggeration of real or imagined qualities can become the dreams and life-planning of the future. Loving couples know how to dream real dreams. They know how to envision their first home, their first child, a special trip, or retirement down the road. Romance is largely a state of mind. If we can unintentionally exaggerate the imputed qualities of a beloved during romantic love, we can surely create intentional visions of the future during mature love. These visions may change, but mature lovers seldom fret, for the meaning in creating a dream, more than the dream itself, marks true love.

Secret codes, private meanings, and special language can become the memories, words, and phrases which make our relationship unique. Romance continues over time when we discover new nicknames and special touches for one another. Love relationships that endure do not need to lose their reliance on symbols to convey meaning. If anything, we expand our common base of facial expressions, favorite TV shows, and rituals to signal feelings and thoughts to one another. There are signals for dinner, lovemaking, and for "it's time to go home."

If romance can truly be refueled and renewed in this fashion, why do so many loving couples crash and burn, often ending up in a therapist's office? Why do so many people find themselves wounded and bedraggled and wondering what went wrong? How could something so wonderful suddenly be gone? In these painful times, we actually grieve the loss of an experience much more than the loss of a person.

In romantic love, we narcissistically believe that we are entitled to a romantic experience that will mysteriously endure on its own. We shouldn't have to do anything ourselves to sustain this bliss.

What a deal! We do nothing, yet expect our partner, or nature, to do it all. This is a narcissist's dream come true. Then, when we slam into the wall of disenchantment, we end up blaming the other person for somehow taking away the experience. In these somber moments we learn that disenchantment, a necessary passage in all love relationships, must be understood. Let's go there now.

CHAPTER 12

Disenchantment

It is emotional distance – not conflict – which determines whether a relationship flourishes or flounders.

As I approach my 40th year of marriage, I can remember a glowing November day in 1969 when I met a gorgeous young blonde and fell madly in love. You have already heard about this gorgeous young blonde as well as my first five weeks of courtship. Claire was beautiful and bright. She worked in Manhattan and lived in Greenwich Village, a lifestyle that seemed utterly exotic and glamorous to me. Once I owned up to my personal wounds, our romance bloomed in the rarefied atmosphere of The City, charming restaurants in the Village, Broadway shows, the Staten Island Ferry, the Sunday *New York Times*. Our cherished moments together were all the more precious to us since we couldn't be together all the time. I would obsessively struggle through my week in Philadelphia, yearning for Friday afternoon when I would hop in my blue Pontiac Firebird which somehow eked out nine miles to the gallon on the New Jersey turnpike.

Nine months later, we went on our honeymoon – three weeks in beautiful Nova Scotia. Like many young newlyweds we were on a tight budget, so we decided to cut expenses by staying in motels only part of the time; the rest of the time we would camp out. Being an outdoorsy guy, I thought our ideal itinerary would alternate six nights camping with one night in a cheap motel. Claire, on the other hand, thought that one night in a tent was really roughing it and six nights in a Holiday Inn were necessary to recuperate from the ordeal. In the end, of course, we compromised: for every three nights spent camping out, we would spend one night in a motel.

If I'd been paying attention, I would have realized that Claire and camping didn't mix. But it wasn't until we were spending our first night together under the stars that I discovered that my beautiful bride would not make love in a tent! Sex in a tent made Claire paranoid. She believed that wild animals (raccoons and owls were particularly likely candidates) were spying on us. The underbrush was full of little beady-eyed voyeurs chuckling and drooling over our nakedness, so further compromises had to be made. Very quickly Claire and I fell into a pattern of making love every fourth night.

Toward the end of our second week, I found an incredibly beautiful campsite overlooking the Atlantic Ocean – dramatic coastal cliffs, roaring waves below us, a refreshing saltwater breeze, lush pines hovering close to the ground, and a thicket of greenery separating our campsite from the others. A more romantic place could not be found. Surely Claire would respond to the glory of this private paradise, this Garden of Eden made just for us. As I pitched our tent, I began to fantasize about the extraordinary sensual experiences we would share in this exhilarating setting. This was to be the backdrop for our ultimate union, our most profound expression of passion and commitment, the place where Claire and I would burn our intense love into the side of an entire continent enveloped by the eternal sea.

I had to wait for the dark of night. (By this time I knew that daytime lovemaking was not even a remote possibility.) As the sun began to sink behind the mountains, I romantically suggested to Claire that we should retire early that night. But she quickly deflated my expectations. "Larry! What if someone needs a match for their Coleman stove? Can you imagine how embarrassed I would be for the rest of my life?"

"But Claire, we would hear them approaching and have plenty of time to pretend that we are looking for snails in our sleeping bags," I pleaded.

"My God! If we can hear them approaching our tent, that means they can hear us making love! I knew the animals could see us, but now everyone on the North American continent will get a peep show! Forget it, Larry. I can't believe you would put me through such misery. Let's wait until we get to the Holiday Inn next week."

That evening I tried every strategy I could think of to dispel Claire's fears. I stood 30, 40, then 50 feet away from our tent and moaned in an ecstatic voice, asking Claire if she could hear me. I went inside the tent and conducted unusual shadow experiments, designed to demonstrate that two passionately undulating bodies would not create silhouettes on the tent walls in the moonlight. I even suggested that we could make love without moving! None of my strategies worked. The omnipresent guilt of a Catholic upbringing had won over my passionate vision of union.

That night I crawled miserably out of our tent and sat alone in the moonlight. Feeling in total harmony with nature (if not with my fellow man), I imagined all the animals around us uniting spontaneously and freely, responding fully to the rhythms of life. I longed to live in the same natural way and bleakly concluded that I would never have the chance with Claire as my wife. Gazing down at the ocean glistening below, I numbly thought back to those exciting moments when I first met that young, gorgeous blonde now sleeping so peacefully nearby. I struggled with her fall from grace. How could this wondrous woman, this shining free spirit living in Greenwich Village, not like to make love in tents?

Though I wondered how I could possibly endure this ordeal much longer, I felt grateful that we were scheduled to be at a motel in only three more days. I knew that fresh linens, closed drapes, and concrete walls would make all the difference to Claire. In Nova Scotia, where endless sea met rugged coastline under the shimmering moon, I began learning my first important lesson in love:

Love must end before it can truly begin.

This chapter is intended to reveal the inevitable shift that takes place once romantic love has had its day. I, like so many others, needed to discover that what I was holding onto was [1] a state of grandiosity that was as far from reality as Hoboken, New Jersey, is from paradise, [2] a sense of entitlement that my needs would always be honored over Claire's, [3] a preoccupation with the fantasy, the magic, and an altered state called "romantic love," and [4] an overidealized image of Claire that deprived her of the empathy and understanding she needed as a real person with real needs of her own.

Disenchantment thrusts us out of paradise. We mourn accordingly.

This is our challenge. When disenchantment grips us we must choose to float perilously in a bleak "room of doom" or find the courage to cast ourselves out into the main stream of renewal – like spawning salmon – where vibrancy and aliveness await us. The room of doom is our place of self-centeredness, self-absorption, and entitlement. Our attachments seem severed. Disenchantment is a separation from a prior state of bliss. Our choices abound. We only get three billion heartbeats in a lifetime. Let's use them well.

Disenchantment invites us to be "OK" with that which is "Not!" Disenchantment invites us to not only see our partners more realistically, but to see ourselves more honestly. Romantic love, while glorious is so many ways, is a distorted house of mirrors.

Change is constant....Life is cyclical....To everything there is a season. Nothing stays the same, yet there is a natural human tendency to cling to anything which is known, be it blissful or painful. When we learn to let go of things as they are and anticipate the inevitable changes that will occur, we are infinitely freer to live each moment more fully.

The starkness of winter gives way to the colorful blooms of spring. Menopause signals the inevitable "change of season" that women are destined to experience. Our days follow the inevitable pulse of circadian rhythms and lunar tides. Tadpoles become frogs and caterpillars transform into magnificent butterflies. And how awesome to consider the powerful forces that exert evolutionary changes upon the planet itself – not to mention our species! Who can doubt that nature – that life itself – has its cycles?

We can't hold on to spring, menstruation, childhood, or lunar tides for very long, nor can we preserve the idyllic wonders of romantic love. Love also must follow rhythms, experience cycles, change seasons. The romantic forces which attract and bond two lovers inevitably must encounter resistance, the painful experience that I call disenchantment. Our illusions must shatter.

For many of us, disenchantment is a narcissistic impasse. Our relationships, once a source of such delight and hope, end in confusion, hurt, and anger. We hold our partners accountable for our misery, believing we are entitled to more attention, more sex, or more freedom – usually self-absorbed distortions. But disenchantment need not signal the end of a loving relationship. In fact, it can be the catalyst that transforms the ephemeral pleasures of romance into the deep fulfillment of a well-grounded, enduring, committed love. In truth, romantic love must end before mature covenant love can begin. There are four inescapable reasons why romantic love cannot go on indefinitely:

* The tarnishing effect
* The eye-opening effect
* The distraction effect
* The existential effect

The Tarnishing Effect

The tarnishing effect demonstrates how our thoughts are distorted by the powerful force of our emotions. The singularity of our hearts during romantic love actually creates duality in our minds, a polarization of our perceptions and beliefs that secretly sets the disenchantment process in motion even when we are just falling in love. Our beloved is not just a sensitive man – he is the most sensitive man we have ever known! She is not simply hard-working – she is the most industrious woman we have ever met! We somehow find the best, the most, the fastest, the smartest, or the funniest person around.

These extremes arise from our deep longing for wholeness and perfection. They are the unconscious projections – illusions – of our most important unmet needs, the sum total of our unfinished life experiences. At a profound, visceral level, we expect our beloved to complete all the incompleteness of our lives. To do so, he or she must be cast in idyllic terms – extreme terms – which convince us that we are making the right choice.

Illusions are destined to waver and fade, to become tarnished, as we experience the true complexity of another human being.

It is ironic that during the process of disenchantment we come to believe that our most prized "other" is actually the absolute opposite of who or what we previously believed. We swing on the pendulum of extremes from the idyllic to the blasphemous. That same most responsible person is now the most irresponsible S.O.B. we have ever known! That most attentive lover is now the most inattentive, aloof iceberg we have ever met! In truth, both extremes are illusions. In the former case, the bliss and rapture of romantic love create an overly positive perspective. In the latter case, the hurt and anger of disenchantment create an overly negative perspective. With mature covenant love we learn to be OK with a more moderate view rather than a projected fantasy about one another.

The Eye-Opening Effect

As love matures, we not only realize more about our real partners, but we also learn more about our real needs. It is inevitable that we eventually realize the following:

* Our partners possess certain obnoxious qualities or traits that we were not aware of in the dawn of our relationships.
* Our partners lack certain constructive qualities or traits that we need for an enduring love bond.

Somehow these qualities – or the lack of them – either weren't noticed or didn't seem important during romantic love. We discover these things only after the first flush of romance has passed. Truly an eye-opening experience!

Has this ever happened to you: You are sitting in a movie theater, deeply engrossed in a suspenseful and dramatic scene. Suddenly, your stomach gurgles, first quietly, and then with the gusto of a Hawaiian volcano. You start fantasizing about roast beef or cheesecake and lose track of the movie's plot. What you experience during the next ten minutes is a vacillating shift in attention. One moment the movie actors are figure (that is, they are your focal point) while your hunger pangs are ground (meaning in the background of your awareness). The next moment, figure and ground reverse in your attention. This process continues, of course, until you get up and buy yourself a jumbo bag of popcorn.

This shifting perceptual focus from figure to ground occurs with all our senses as well as our higher levels of cortical functioning. What we perceive or believe always occurs within the context of other perceptions or beliefs. We hear our child's cry, even though many other people are talking, or pick out the melody of a violin over the rest of the orchestra. We notice our friend's beautiful turquoise rug and miss the lovely back-yard view through the plateglass window. We see the disfiguring scar on a new acquaintance's cheek but only notice his smile when we have become friends.

Lovers do this all the time. What we notice about one another during early love is dramatically different from what we focus on during disenchantment – or even mature love, for that matter: our attention is drawn by sparkling eyes during romantic love, dirty laundry during disenchantment, and tender forgiveness during covenant love. Each phase of love is a truly wondrous discovery, an eye-opening experience, which welcomes the curious traveler who is patient enough to make the journey.

The Distraction Effect

Like morning dew, the exclusivity of early love is destined to evaporate before our eyes. The business of life dramatically interferes with the quality time we once enjoyed as a romantic couple. In our drive to build homes, families, and careers, we end up driving ourselves apart. Our human relationships are being pushed and pounded by technological advances, accelerated lifestyles and what has colloquially been termed the "rat race." Since 1971, leisure time has shrunk by 37 percent and the average workweek has jumped from 41 to 47 hours. As *Time* magazine notes:

If all this continues, time could end up being to the '90s what money was to the 80s. In fact, for the callow yuppies of Wall Street, with their abundant salaries and meager freedom, leisure time is the one thing they find hard to buy. Their lives are so busy that merely to give someone the time of day seems an act of charity. They order gourmet takeout because microwave dinners have become just too much trouble. Canary sales are up (low-maintenance pets); Beaujolais nouveau is booming (a wine one needn't wait for). "I gave up pressure for Lent," says a theater director in Manhattan. If only it were that easy.[1]

My clients Tim and Ann provide a perfect example of this phenomenon. Only their financial success makes them untypical of the couples I see. Tim is a twenty-eight-year-old entrepreneur who started one clothing store that soon mushroomed to three. Ann, a top executive in the cable industry, earns a hearty six-figure salary and receives bonuses of as much as $40,000 at a pop. They drive fast cars, take lavish trips, and have more bank accounts than most people have friends. Yet, as a couple, they are miserable.

"I never see her!" grumbles Tim as he considers the fact that Ann travels around the United States 12 to 15 days a month. But Ann retorts, "If Tim would stop spawning clothing stores as if they were million dollar fisheries, maybe we could get something going. We never have time for love, and I doubt if he finds me attractive any more."

Inevitably, the counseling process reveals a couple who have forsaken the "nine styles of intimacy" for a lifestyle that pushes and presses and demands entirely too much of them. Intimacy becomes a scheduled event, rather than a naturally occurring experience. We plan our sexual encounters, evenings out with friends, and yearly vacations to fit into a blurry-eyed blitz of ballet recitals, summer camps, and professional commitments that never seem to end.

The way out for some is to sell the home, give up the careers, grab the kids, and head for Colorado – without jobs in hand – as one couple I know are doing. This is too daring for most of us, who must be content with carving out time for Sunday brunch and private evening walks. We must constantly dam back the distractions that dilute our values and drown out intimacy.

Very few elements of mature love can be expressed if we are limited, by our own hellish lifestyles, to milliseconds of interaction with one another.

The Existential Effect

Ultimately, all of us must come to realize that we are alone and mortal. At its best, marriage is a safe harbor within which we can attempt to reconcile life's most painful incongruities. However, the inevitable realization of our individual human dilemma may estrange us from one another as we search for the meaning of our separate lives.

In the beginning, we enter our love bonds with the infinite hope that all our dreams will be met in an exclusive arena created by God himself. We see marriage as an opportunity to reconcile all of the crucial dichotomies of our lives: man versus woman, mind versus body, good versus evil, autonomy versus dependence, thinking versus feeling, love versus hate, controlling versus controlled, and included versus excluded. Where else can we risk being known to such degree?

Where else can we find ourselves, discover who we are? Where else can we allow our thoughts, feelings, and actions to run their full course, through the seasons and cycles of our lives?

Yet we are destined to realize that no person, regardless of his or her special powers and gifts, can complete what will never be completed within us. When we cannot synthesize or reconcile the emotionally charged dichotomies of our lives, we become entangled in our own knots. When ambiguity cannot be reduced to certainty, we withdraw our commitments from one another, believing that our sense of neglect and abandon leaves no other option. Wanting it all, we desperately fear a profound psychological and spiritual death. That unspoken and unconscious yearning for wholeness or completeness that pervades our psyche is now revealed for what it is – a pipedream, a tunnel-vision, an illusion. Thinking we have been duped, we blame each other and believe the perfect union must be elsewhere. Instead of working on the integration of cherished hopes and shattered dreams, we seem recklessly programmed to throw them away and start all over again, someplace else with someone else.

No matter whom we turn to, however, we cannot stop attempting to reconcile opposites. There is an inherent quest for order, purpose, and predictability in our lives. Our salvation as individuals, as well as a species, depends on our capacity to balance meaning with confusion, harmony with disharmony, love with hate, aloneness with togetherness, and life with death.

There are no simple solutions for life's dichotomies.

Marriage, I believe, is our most sacred haven – a special place in which we create a union to reconcile life's extremes. There is no clear path. We must each be pathfinders. We must each be willing to transcend our solitary uniqueness in order to find a place of balance and reconciliation in our coupled lives. We must each be willing to give in order to receive, to receive in order to give, to hate in order to love, to love in order to hate, and so on. And if our disenchantment leads us to turn away from each other, we miss the chance to find what Sheldon Kopp describes as life's "amalgam of compromises," which is the very best any of us could possibly hope for. (2) The search will be hard work. For a start, we must begin to see things for what they are: We must rip off our blinders, hold up our mirrors, and take a long, honest look at the hurt, anger, and resentment that underlie our disenchantment.

A Case in Point: The Nine Signs of Disenchantment

What does disenchantment look like? What are the telltale signs of a couple in distress? A number of such signs can best be explained by telling you about one such couple: Gail and Don.

I still remember Gail's first visit. She appeared for her appointment wearing a crisp white blouse and ankle-length plaid skirt. She seemed eager to tell her tale. "Don and I have been married for about three years, Dr. Bugen, and I am depressed as hell. I don't know why I am so depressed, and I don't know why I am in this damn marriage."

Gail told me that in the beginning she was attracted to Don's upward mobility. His architectural firm was booming. He seemed stable, secure, and devoted to his career. Surely he would be devoted to her as well. And, in sharp contrast to her first husband, Don was very attentive.

As I got to know more about them, I learned that in the spring of their relationship Don saw Gail as bright, articulate, and vivacious. Always agreeable, she was eager to please. She seemed able to charm anyone she met. These traits made her a highly successful salesperson. A clever entrepreneur by day; a wanton sex goddess by night! Don figured he had it made.

Within two years of tying the knot, Gail came to see Don as an undependable con artist. He was slick and silver-tongued with others but strangely distant from her. The more she protested his avoidance, the more he seemed to withdraw. He insisted that his long hours away from home were necessary in order to sustain his success as an architect. This physical and emotional vacuum only reinforced Gail's long-standing belief that she was excluded, shut out of others' lives. This belief had taken root during her first marriage to a physician, who had also created a work schedule that gave him little time at home.

For his part, Don grew to see Gail as a runaway freight train. She was constantly nagging him about too little time together, too little money, too many possessions, too many drugs, and too many friends. She was as demanding as his father had been many years before, when he ran away from home at age 16. He had learned very early on that he couldn't please anyone. Escape away from people would be the answer: escape into drugs, escape into sailing, and escape into work.

At that first session, Gail brought along an audiocassette tape: "I knew I would have difficulty telling you about Don and me, so I talked Don into letting me tape one of our Sunday bitch sessions. I think this is typical of what happens to us, and I'd like you to listen to it."

That evening I settled comfortably into a lounge chair with tape recorder in hand and once again found evidence of the deep disenchantment so common in troubled relationships:

1. A specific triggering event. Disenchantment begins when one partner doesn't fulfill the other's expectations, causing frustration and disappointment. Every love relationship, no matter how compatible the partners are, encounters countless situations that may trigger frustration or disappointment.

"Don, I found a glass in the car which reeked of alcohol," Gail said in the first part of their taped Sunday bout. "Drinking and driving is one of the worst things you can do … YOU don't think that there is anything wrong with it. Drinking and driving is a part of your life… You had parents who abused the stuff and you abuse the stuff yourself … You didn't learn that drinking and driving is bad. If anything, your parents encouraged drinking."

"Uh-huh. I agree," Don responded.

Finding Don's glass in the car triggered Gail's disappointment. Disappointment is a thought, while frustration is a feeling. Both may characterize our response to a disenchantment-triggering event.

For instance, how do you feel when you prepare a wonderful meal and your spouse is three hours late? How do you feel when he or she forgets your birthday, an anniversary, or Valentine's Day? Do you ever get frustrated when your amorous advances are rebuffed? And let's not forget the weekend porcupine who sticks his face in the TV during a football game when you need some help with an employment crisis.

2. Reciprocity. Disenchantment is mutual. Both partners experience it, although one may experience it before the other does. In fact, disenchantment in one partner can trigger disenchantment in the other.

"I'm not going to be on your case all the time about drinking," Gail tried to back off. "But it's just that I feel differently about drinking than you do."

Don reacted: "Gail, I feel the same about people bitching and swearing at me. See, my parents discouraged that. But in your house it was 'damn' this or 'damn' that."

"Bullshit!" Gail snapped. "I don't like bitching or swearing!"

"One other thing," Don returned. "Every one of you would go into the room and slam the door. To you, that's normal! I was just drunk!"

Gail hears her disappointment; Don hears his own. Neither truly understands the other's plea for help. Instead, they are caught in an enmeshed web of hurt, which becomes more entangled over time.

When patterns of frustration and disappointment reoccur in love relationships, it is likely that both partners are keeping score. If couples are to untangle their reciprocal patterns of disenchantment, each partner must own up to three assumptions: First, if I have been disenchanted for some time, it is likely that my partner has been as well. Second, if my partner is partly responsible for not meeting my needs, it then follows that I am partly responsible for not meeting his or her needs. Third, it is absolutely necessary to recognize unmet needs in a relationship in order to sustain the well-being of the bond.

3. Underlying themes. Ninety percent of the hurt and anger that disenchanted lovers experience mirror deeper resentments or "themes" in the relationship which have little or nothing to do with the immediate situation. Together, we might refer to hurt, anger, and resentment as the "disenchantment triad."

Hurt and anger are the "big gun" emotional byproducts which result after repeated frustrations and disappointments have occurred and noticeable behavior patterns have emerged. However, resentment is not a feeling, as many believe. Anger and hurt are feelings, but resentment, like disappointment, is a thought. We commonly say, "I feel resentment about such and such." But think about that for a second. Our resentments are actually well-memorized storage centers.

Gail: "Well, you get mad, too! You've ruined many an evening when you just walked out of a room after having one drink and hearing my protest, particularly when you ask me to drive so you can drink some more!"

Don: "I'm the one who came back into the room ten minutes ago and told you I just thought about me and my drinking and realized how destructive it was. I'm admitting it! I'm the one who brought it up! I'm the one who said, 'Hell, I just saw this lousy pattern which branded these two people ... The pain, the anguish, the distance in this house, instead of dealing with it.' I'm aware of this! That's why I brought it up!"

Gail: "So you want to control your drinking?"

Don: "Hell yes, I want to control my drinking."

Gail: "Are you recognizing that you have a drinking problem?"

Don: "Oh God, Gail, YES! But do you see you have a problem with arguing?"

Gail: "NO!" she shouts back.

Resentments mean not giving in.

Men are often very good at remembering their resentments but very poor at identifying their feelings. Although Don recognizes the anguish and pain of their relationship, it is more common for men, when they do identify a feeling, to express it as anger. Very rarely will a man admit that he feels hurt because of something his lover did or didn't do. This is quite significant, since hurt underlies all anger. Until both men and women can identify and discuss their painful hurts, lovers are likely to remain stuck with their angry barbs.

Resentments, like dead skin, must be exfoliated on a regular basis!

Once you have stored up enough anger, you can play the "I remember" game. "I remember when you ripped the upholstery with your hunting knife." "I remember when you left me sitting in a hotel bar for four hours." "I remember when you went fishing for two weeks during my ninth month of pregnancy."

People often tell me that they have the right to express anger when they feel it. This is a ridiculous notion, since anger only shocks, devalues, and alienates the other person.

If we would be more assertive in expressing our frustrations and disappointments earlier, the intense build-up of anger might be avoided. Fortunately, when we finally allow ourselves to become vulnerable by sharing our hurts, something remarkable happens – anger melts away.

4. Negative cycles of behavior. Disenchanted lovers often engage in self-defeating cycles that feed off one another. Coming home late leads to loss of sexual desire, which leads to coming home late, and so on.

"Do you realize," Don pointed out, "that these two things feed each other? The more we argue, the more I drink, the more we argue."

These negative cycles are all fueled by the disenchantment triad of resentment, anger, and hurt. Each cycle is a modern day corollary of biblical metaphors: an eye for an eye, a tooth for a tooth. Such cycles may have represented justice in our biblical past, but hardly heal our present-day heartaches and despair. Instead of working toward harmony, lovers will often begin to play the tit-for-tat game. From other couples I have worked with I've heard: "If you don't pick up the kids, I won't make dinner." "If you don't stop smoking, I won't stop drinking." "If you continue to work overtime, I'll make a showing at every happy hour I can find." "If you choose to sleep rather than make love, I will find another lover."

5. Caricaturization. When caught up in a negative cycle, disenchanted lovers polarize their attitudes toward each other, deliberately distorting their mental images of each other. All human beings strive to make sense of their personal experience and their success in doing so largely depends upon the language structures they adopt. Each of us labels our experiences, in a positive or negative direction, along a continuum. Each continuum is best understood as a polarity. Note how Gail's experience of Don has polarized:

Gail screamed at Don: "I think you misinterpret me a lot. You never really talk to me."

"Oh, this should be good," Don bellowed.

"It's that ... that ... I mean it's like ... well, not arguments. You just always misinterpret. When I am on the phone, you always know why. You are always drunk when you talk to me. You never remember what we talk about," Gail said. Don never really talks. He always misinterprets. He never remembers. To break the disenchantment cycle, we must shatter our polarized views of one another, and rediscover that gray is OK. This is an important distinction for Dr. Martin Seligman who believes that we should "globalize" the good things and "localize" the bad things in his book *Authentic Happiness*.[3]

6. Scientific research. Like mad scientists, disenchanted lovers look for any data that support their negative beliefs about each other. It is never enough to merely label our lovers in negative terms. We must be able to support this belief with new data. Each of us, on a daily basis, is conducting countless experiments just like scientists, well-trained in the scientific method. Each experiment attempts to support a hypothesis or theory:

Theory 1: My lover does not like my body.
Theory 2: My wife cares more about the kids and her job than about me.
Theory 3: My husband is an alcoholic.
Theory 4: My wife is insensitive.
Theory 5: My husband only appreciates me after we make love.

Each of these theories requires close observation over time. Theory 1, for instance, was recently put forth by one of my clients, who first informed her husband of this belief during a counseling session. (This hidden-theory technique is quite handy, since our partner, without feed-back, can continue to unwittingly support our biases without knowing what he or she is doing.) This client was able to provide voluminous data. She told her husband how far away he slept, how often he had initiated love-making during the prior month, when he had touched her breasts, and actual dates and times that he "stopped reading the newspaper to notice those Hollywood hussies on TV," instead of her.

"Aren't you the wonderful party animal!" Gail asserts.

"What are you talking about?" Don wonders.

"Don, you know damn well that you have been putting moves on any of my friends who would be stupid enough to listen to your garbage. I've actually watched you pour drinks for Mary and Stephanie and then, for an added nightcap, give each of them a hug."

"Gail, if I had your fantasy mind, I'd become a movie producer. What a bunch of crap."

Note the evidence that Gail has compiled to support her case that Don is flirting with her girlfriends. Her theory helps us understand her plight more clearly. Don has been avoiding her, turning instead to his booze. Gail is not feeling very special to Don, and her jealousy regarding other women reflects her hurt and distrust.

Beware that your observations may be too selective, so that you see only what you want – or fear – to see.

7. Personal indictments. Disenchanted lovers often attack one another with "You are ..." statements rather than admit their own needs. Every therapist knows how difficult it is for clients to say "I feel ...," "I need ...," "I want ...," or "I am...." We feel so vulnerable when we reference ourselves by saying "I." How different it could be! Instead of preparing for war, we might instead prepare for clarity and understanding. We might say, "Bill, try to hear me out. I need more affection from you. I want to feel you hug me when I come home. I feel frustrated when you don't ...." Instead, anger and resentment build to a crescendo that obliterates good communication. Lovers go on the attack:

* We negatively label our partners: "You're a cold son-of-a-bitch!"
* We ignore feelings.
* We show boredom when he or she is talking to us.
* We do not give eye contact.
* We change the topic.
* We use incomplete sentences.
* We give irrelevant responses.
* We show inappropriate affect (like laughing).
* We make frequent judgments.
* We point our finger, fold our arms, sit rigidly, lean away, and stare away.
* We say, "I didn't hear a word you said!"

Without a clear understanding of Gail's need for reassurance about his matchmaking, Don simply packages the feelings that he sees in her and labels them as anger.

"Don't you understand," Gail pleaded, "I know you won't, but don't you understand what you are doing? You don't even know what you are doing!"

"Do you know what I'm doing?" Don responded.

"I don't think so." "I don't know what you are doing," she returned.

"I don't even think you know how this came about. I think that it's just your anger ...." he replied.

8. Mistaking symptoms for real problems. Excessive drinking, eating, spending, sleeping, and arguing aren't the real problems in a disenchanted relationship. They simply mask the real issues. We escape into activities like these in order to somehow numb ourselves to an unbearable pain - the pain of unmet needs.

Escape patterns usually emerge after we have created "themes" about our lovers. These themes express the polarized and negative generalities we use to caricature our loved ones. Familiar themes I have heard include: "She doesn't care!" "He is totally irresponsible!" "He lacks ambition!" "She smothers me with demands or complaints!" Rather than work through these themes, which are always lying in wait, people go shop-ping, get drunk, watch too much TV, read excessively, make chocolate cakes, or go to sleep!

For Gail and Don, the alcohol and the arguing mask underlying pain that they dance around rather than examine with clarity. Their themes are "Gail, you control too much of my life!" and "Don, you are neither responsible nor loving as my husband!"

9. Mutually exclusive blame. Disenchanted lovers blame each other for screwing up the relationship, rather than recognizing that both are responsible for mending it. Blaming, like anger and resentment, only separates lovers from one another. Blaming our partners, if that is our style, entitles us to be part of the problem rather than the solution. Until we are willing to accept our role in making things worse, we will never accept our role in making things better.

Lovers continue to grow over time, not because they lack their share of problems, but because they mutually resolve their share of problems.

Gail made the first move by lowering her voice and letting her real feelings come to the surface: "I don't have a sense of myself anymore. I don't really have a sense of me and that's real scary, and I don't ... I don't feel real secure."

And Don, instead of taking advantage of his opportunity to move in on Gail's vulnerability, tenderly acknowledged her fear and his own responsibility. "Why don't we do this, Gail? Why don't we plot a course? That will give us a sense of security so we'll know where we are going."

The Four Phases of Disenchantment

At the dawn of the 20th Century, a gifted German artist named Paula Becker married a well-known painter named Otto Modersohn. Before her parents granted her permission to marry, they insisted that she attend two laborious months of cooking school in Berlin so that she would be properly suited for her new role as wife. In a translated version of her personal letters and journals, we are invited to view what the *New York Times* Book Review described as "the tragic essence of Paula Modersohn-Becker's great dilemma: How to live her life both as a woman and as a serious artist."

> *Marriage takes away the illusion that had sustained a belief in the possibility of a kindred soul. In marriage one feels doubly misunderstood. For one's whole life up to marriage had been devoted to finding another understanding being. And is it perhaps not better without this illusion, better to be eye to eye with one great and lonely truth? I am writing this in my housekeeping book ...sitting in my kitchen, cooking a roast of veal.[4]*

Each of us, like Modersohn-Becker, learns something about "a great and lonely truth" during the course of our love relationships: We are inevitably and predictably disappointed in our search to find a soul mate, someone who will always understand us, someone who completes us. As one client recently wrote:

> *We shared our souls, we shared your bed.*
> *I held your hand, you cradled my head.*
> *You touched my heart, you touched my soul.*
> *You changed my life, my dreams, my goals.*
> *Love is blindness, but I could see,*
> *One man, my passion, I wanted for me.*
> *Oh love, I was addicted to you.*
> *And now I don't know what to do.*

The process of discovering this truth begins from day one of our relationship and follows a predictable pattern over time. But the process is not a dead end. As we follow disenchantment through its phases, we can gain insight into our own experience and learn how to overcome the deep confusion or pain that appears to be an emotional impasse.

All disenchantments involve thoughts, feelings, and behaviors. Once the glow of romantic love has faded, these thoughts, feelings, and behaviors pass through three sequential phases. During the first phase, *REALITY SHOCK*, we begin to experience countless situations that disappoint us or frustrate us. Birthdays or anniversaries are forgotten. Our partner shows up late for a date or shrugs off a sexual advance.

During the second phase, called *THE MOODY BLACK AND BLUES*, these frustrating situations repeat themselves so often that they become patterns in our relationships. We experience intense reactions of resentment, anger, and hurt. Then we perpetuate our misery by polarizing our beliefs about our partners and indicting them with negative, resentment-based "themes." "You are a slob," we think. "You are too sensitive." "You are irresponsible." "You never support my goals." "You always put me down."

We experience phase three, *BURNOUT*, when we cannot take the emotional pain any longer. At this point, we are disinterested and apathetic toward our partners. We may feel deeply weary or numb, as if we are just going through the motions. We may be clinically depressed as well.

Though the phases are sequential, we more often than not cycle in and out of them on a schedule all our own. It is possible to stay stuck in one of the last two phases, but never both at the same time. We either choose to stay in pain – the moody black and blues – or get out of pain through burnout. Beginning with the magic and romance of the honeymoon, the disenchantment cycle triggers our thoughts, feelings, and behaviors like this:

	THOUGHTS	*FEELINGS*	*BEHAVIORS*
THE HONEYMOON	Expectation	Excitement	Move Toward
REALITY SHOCK	Disappointment	Frustration	Move Against
THE MOODY BLACK AND BLUES	Resentment	Anger/Hurt	Move Against
BURNOUT	Disinterest	Apathy	Move Away

The model is eloquently simple, yet it seems to describe the experience of all the couples to whom I have introduced it. Let me say at this point that it is crucial to distinguish among thoughts, feelings, and behaviors. People process their experiences and construe their worlds in very different ways. Some of us are more stoical, more intellectual, or more cognitively oriented than others. Consequently we express our disenchantment as disappointment, resentment, or disinterest. We don't lay claim to intense emotional feelings. We may even completely deny being pissed off when our partner smashes the car up for the third time this year!

On the other hand, some of us are much more emotional in our experience of disenchantment. We moan, bitch, or cry whenever we feel we have been wronged. Our style is more feeling oriented. Letting out our frustration or our anger is no problem for us at all!

Others of us deny being hurt, angry, or resentful about a thing. We may not display emotional upset, and we may deny having disturbing thoughts – but our actions give us away! I know of one husband who, after 12 years of marriage, wanted to spend every weekend riding his Harley Davidson (and not spend time with his wife), and yet he consistently denied his disappointment (thoughts) or frustration (feeling), insisting that he was committed to the relationship. Each of us has our own pathway thru disenchantment.

The self-absorption of disenchantment must evolve into something more mature so that our relationships survive.

This takes wisdom and courage. We must paddle hard as a couple. We must learn that both romantic love and disenchantment are different facets of self-absorption. The former idealizes while the latter bastardizes. We are blind in both phases – seeing only through distorted lenses. Yet, there is hope if we are willing to be "humble" and to "forgive." If we forge ahead with optimism, built upon the *Six Gifts* presented in the last section of this book, we will eventually discover a more mature, covenant love to which we now turn.

CHAPTER **13**

Mature Love

Two roads diverged in a wood, and I –
I took the one less traveled by,
And that has made all the difference.
—Robert Frost

Commitment is nonnegotiable.

Everything in a loving relationship is up for grabs except for that special pact that each of you will not abandon the other. Such a pact or covenant is easily threatened by the consuming outrage, quiet desperation, or detached numbness of disenchantment. For many of us, commitment is like a winning hand, a full house or royal flush that we play close to the vest on the condition that our partners give us what we want. But this puts the cart before the horse. It is perfectly normal to expect our partners to change, but commitment must precede expectation. We must extend to our imperfect partners the reassurance that, although we may have painful grievances about our relationships, we are going to stay in order to work them out. Since many of us are secretly afraid that we are not worthy enough to be loved, it is most comforting to know that we won't be abandoned as soon as disenchantment begins to take its toll on our relationships.

A loving commitment to another person is the best antidote for narcissism.

In most relationships, the signs of broken commitments inevitably surface. I am not thinking of the more dramatic events, like affairs or trial separations. Usually commitment dies more slowly than this – not with a bang but a whimper. Our commitment dies in those daily moments when we meet our partners with bland indifference, passive resistance, or more open rebellion. In each of these quietly decisive moments, we make the choice not to commit. We say to ourselves:

"Why should I come home right after work?"

"I know she is worried about driving in the snow, but I sure as hell won't go out of my way for her!"

"She puts her career and the kids before me, so why should I respond to her lovemaking?"

I am amazed at how perceptive, vigilant, and imaginative spouses can be in detecting broken commitments, even when an objective accounting by a Big Eight firm wouldn't justify the claim. Examples are often subtle: we leave the kitchen light on, we stop attending church, and we only call home once on a two-day conference trip. Less subtle examples include the maintenance of a separate checking or savings account or staying late at Happy Hour with co-workers every Friday.

One female client, who had been rip-roaring mad for the preceding three years, could isolate the event when her husband actually "abandoned" her. She remembered her shock at discovering her pregnancy with twins, a feeling that mushroomed into fear and anger when her husband advocated keeping the pregnancy viable. Such a decision not only had implications for her physical health but would lock her into a domestic role for many years. She had wanted an abortion, but his advocacy and eagerness in behalf of the two unborn fetuses won out. To her it was obvious that this meant that he was choosing the welfare of two strangers over her own. Given the risk factors associated with multiple births and her career aspirations, his insistence was an outrage which could not be forgiven.

For my client, this "clear abandonment" on her husband's part easily justified her own withdrawal from him – a response which perpetuated the inevitable downward cycle of disenchantment. The "road less traveled" in this instance, as with most disenchantment, is to transcend our immediate, intense reaction in order to find a more balanced, fair-minded response. This point seems reasonable enough ... unless we feel so wronged that we cannot shift our attention from the evil wrongdoer or the knot of resentments that harden our hearts and stiffen our necks. Our self-absorption rules us. We insist on blaming our partners for all our pain and thereby missing an opportunity to look beyond – to look inward – to find something better. This chapter is about finding "something better" and is tied together by three premises:

Premise 1: Mature committed love begins when romance has palled and we find ourselves glaring daggers into each other's eyes.

Premise 2: The capacity for mature, committed love is well established within our families by the time we reach 18.

Premise 3: Mature, covenant love – once it is understood – becomes the real foundation for lasting love.

A commitment to renew love is our most profound opportunity for real growth.

Let me comment briefly on each of these premises. First, I do not believe that a mature commitment can exist at the time of the marriage ceremony. The wedding vows we agree to – "for better or for worse, in sickness and in health, for richer or for poorer, till death do us part" – are blanket commitments based on illusions and blind faith. We can't possibly know about mature commitment until we experience the "worse," the "sickness," and the "poorer." On our wedding day, we actually are committing ourselves to the state of our love at that time. Marriage is a commitment to an already known and shared time and space; covenant love is a commitment to the kind of bridge building that can arch into the unknown and span both time and space.

Second, I believe that the psychological maturity needed for committed love results from the capacities that people bring to their relationships. Unfortunately, many of us are stuck in a developmental dead-end, cornered by our biological impulses, our reflexive biases, and our fragmented experience of life. When we marry, most of us have not developed the characteristics of maturity. More significantly, we are incapable of mature love because of wounds we experienced in our families of origin. Most of us don't know how to love because we never learned how to love. We never saw mature love between our parents and never experienced it as children within our families. Our own parents didn't know how to love, and so were unable to teach us.

Third, the wounds of childhood can be healed within a committed relationship! This is a profound notion: by committing ourselves to our partners when romantic love has faded, we actually can develop a mature wholeness. If we don't commit fully to a long-term relationship we cannot comprehend or value mature, covenant love. Thus, when we commit, we nurture our own spiritual healing as well as the healing of our relationships. Let's see what a healthy, long-term relationship looks like.

The Characteristics of Mature, Covenant Love

The capacity to love can be learned if we are willing to move through the immediate pain of disenchantment and evolve beyond romantic longings. Mature, committed love begins when we shift emphasis from meeting "me-centered" romantic needs to meeting "we-centered" relationship needs.

Narcissistic preoccupation must give way to a more dynamic, living architecture created with another person.

Rather than continuing to seek out the novelty, excitement, and self-gratification that characterize romance, we must also focus on equally important needs for familiarity, trust, and mutual fulfillment. Novelty, excitement, and self-gratification need not be sacrificed to the "ho-hum" of a long-term relationship – "ho-hum" is evidence of disenchantment, not covenant love. Lovers in a mature, committed relationship simply shift their emphasis to create an exciting balance between passion and affiliation, between attachment and interdependence.

For a loving relationship to endure, it must embody the following characteristics of covenant love:

    ✻ A mutual balance of met needs
    ✻ Other-directedness
    ✻ Realistic values and expectations
    ✻ Tolerance
    ✻ Yearning to be known
    ✻ Freedom to express all emotions
    ✻ Separate identities, AND
    ✻ Transcendence of two separate selves into one identity

Let's take a loser look at each of these characteristics:

A mutual balance of met needs: Both partners have needs of equal importance; both understand and accept those needs; and both are willing to meet those needs as often as possible. Loving couples find ways to meet each other's needs in an equitable fashion. Equitable does not mean equal: it means fair. One partner may have compromised more than the other – not because he or she is an inferior in the relationship, but because a fair resolution required compromise. Loving couples find equitable ways to share affection ("Can I have a massage tonight?"), vacation planning ("Since we went to Mexico last year, I'd like to go to Colorado this year!"), exercise schedules ("If you jog on Tuesdays and Thursdays, I can do aerobic dance on Mondays and Wednesdays"), household tasks ("Would you do the dishes tonight since I'm so tired?"), financial obligations ("I can put an extra $50 a month into savings; can you handle an extra $50 out of your salary, too?"), childrearing ("If you take the kids in the a.m., I'll be able to get them in the p.m., okay?"), and spiritual pathways ("I know you don't like organized religion, but it means a lot for you to go to Sunday services with me"). Each couple works out its own formula for sharing.

Other-directedness: Each partner experiences meaning or pleasure from the other partner's fulfilling his or her own needs – and actively helps him or her to fulfill those needs. Other-directedness implies celebration: we are pleased, touched, and even ecstatic that our partners seem so happy. Perhaps she received a promotion, a raise, or an award of some kind. Perhaps he competed in his first 5K run as she stood in the cold drizzle and watched it all. Perhaps she lost ten pounds or kicked some other habit. Or perhaps he is having a playful moment with the children or the cat. The bottom line is the same – you have the capacity to smile, clap your hands, and celebrate the moment.

Often we must stretch ourselves in order for our partners to meet their needs. If your partner is on a diet, you make the considerate decision to not buy gallons of Blue Bell ice cream for the freezer. Or you realize that your partner will need an extra pair of sweatpants on race day and drive the ten miles to deliver them. Or your wife is frolicking with your daughter and you grab the video camera in order to capture the moment for all to share later.

In each of these moments, you are giving your partner the gift of empathy. You deeply understand the significance of his or her moment of self-expression or accomplishment, and you even serve as a power booster to propel him or her further. Relationships endure because partners delight in each other's delight!

Realistic values and expectations: Both partners jettison stereotypes about men and women, husbands and wives, love and marriage. They make their assumptions explicit to each other and avoid extreme points of view. Why would a nurse who understands the demands of medicine marry a physician and then bitterly complain that he or she is never home for dinner by 6:00 p.m.? Call schedules, emergency office visits, and hospital rounds obliterate the best-laid plans of any physician to be home on time. Yet resentment often breeds in this familiar scenario in which cold soup, bedraggled children, and sarcastic remarks all are thrown at the unwitting doctor as he or she enters the house – late again!

Realistic expectations are flexible, not rigid, and flexibility requires a moderate point of view. After years of doing therapy, I am convinced that there is absolutely no place for absolutes in marriage. Fixed mindsets about men, women, and marriage can only lead to conflict. Real men do eat quiche, do cry real tears when emotionally moved, and do even need to be cuddled. Real women do like standing on their own two feet, do relish being physically challenged, and do take pride in their careers outside the home. Rigidly insisting that the children be put to bed by 9:00, that your wife make love every night, or that your husband visit your mother with you every Sunday afternoon will inevitably result in disenchantment.

Although needs may be reasonable, expectations often are not. Mature couples put more stock in the process of getting their needs met than in investing in a single expected outcome.

Tolerance: Mature loving partners do not expect to find perfection in each other. Instead, they accept each other's attitudes, beliefs, and actions. They discuss problems on a situational level, rather than on the level of personal indictment. They learn to forgive. During romantic love, we often think that we have found it all – everything we need to fill our own void. Then we discover the flaws, the incompleteness, and the very real differences that naturally distinguish one person from another. It is at this point that our capacity for acceptance, forgiveness, and true appreciation is revealed.

Surely our tolerance is tested weekly, if not daily. One partner likes to make love as the sun rises, while the other prefers the stillness of moonlight. One partner is meticulously clean, while the other can step over unpacked suitcases and dirty socks for weeks at a time. One partner likes two cats and a dog, while the other resents the intrusion of a goldfish. Beyond these natural "compatibility" differences, there are other situations in which things simply go wrong. Your wife tells an embarrassing joke at a neighbor's party or forgets to pick up your suit at the cleaners before you must fly out on a business trip. Your husband arrives a half-hour late for your son's soccer game or has a headache one night and rebuffs your seductive overtures.

You have a choice in these situations. You can trigger the long-lasting themes of disenchantment ("You're so incredibly thoughtless" "You're such a boring sexual partner"). Or you can treat the behavior as situational ("I wish you had thought about my position before you told that story about me" "I really wanted you to see this game with me, and I feel frustrated that you missed it"). With mature tolerance, we do not indict the person, no matter how much we may deplore the situation.

In thinking about mature, self-actualized persons, psychologist Abraham Maslow once said, "One does not complain about water because it is wet, nor about rocks because they are hard. ... As the child looks out upon the world with wide, uncritical and innocent eyes, simply noting and observing what is the case, without either arguing the matter or demanding that it be otherwise, so does the self-actualizing person look upon human nature both in himself and in others."[2] This mature capacity for tolerance and acceptance can short-circuit our resentments and allow us to work through problems, not get stuck in them as if we were spiraling in a "room of doom."

Each of us screws up because we are imperfect. Each of us must be forgiven.

Forgiveness is more an act than a sentiment.

Although we often experience feelings of warmth or compassion when we forgive, forgiveness is really more a demonstration of commitment, an act of will. When we choose to forgive and accept, we actually set ourselves free from the triad of resentment, anger, and hurt that underlie so many negative cycles of behavior. In fact, the refusal to forgive buries us, as well as our loved ones, in a storehouse of unforgotten memories of hurt or bitterness – self-absorption. As mature lovers, we must learn how to accept and forgive, because the real victims of resentment are those who carry it.

Yearning to be known: Both partners value the safe harbor of their relationship, the place where they can put aside their societal masks and truly be themselves. Mature relationships nurture this process of becoming fully known. In order for love relationships to sustain their vitality, they must be based on trust and openness. Both partners must believe that each can express his or her feelings, beliefs, and actions with relative impunity. We must have a sense of being in a protected place in which we can let down our guard and open up.

For many of us, this kind of trust is not easy. One of my clients recently accounted for his quietness with this observation: "If I wasn't being teased by my friends for being too fat, I was humiliated by my parents for the twitch in my eye or the cowlick in my hair." Silence became the best policy in all relationships for this man – until he met Jan. Suddenly, this sensitive man was thrust into a different world where a special woman invited him to look deep within himself and then open up, to disclose to her all that he was. In time, he learned to trust.

Mature love offers us the wondrous gift of a safe harbor – a haven where we can truly be ourselves, fully open, and natural. To lose this capacity for openness – to hide behind our personas – is to sentence ourselves to a lifetime of silence. We must learn to heal ourselves by becoming more introspective, more trusting of our partners, and more open with our thoughts and feelings. This responsibility is ours alone, not our partners. In the familiar words of an anonymous writer:

> *Don't be fooled by me,*
> *Don't be fooled by the mask I wear.*
> *For I wear a mask,*
> *I wear a thousand masks,*
> *Masks that I'm afraid to take off,*
> *And none of them are me.*
> *Pretending is an art that is second nature to me!*

Soren Kierkegaard, the Danish philosopher, believed that our most common despair was in not choosing to, or not being willing to, be ourselves and that the deepest despair is in choosing to be other than ourselves.[3] The will to be as we truly are is a deep responsibility that can be achieved in a healthy love relationship. What is required is a mature capacity to put aside masks, which we often mistakenly think are a part of our real selves, and find instead a new freedom to think and feel and be.

Freedom to express all emotions: Both partners encourage each other to express all their feelings, including sadness, remorse, anger, and embarrassment. And each is open about expressing these feelings. Psychiatrist Fritz Perls has said, "In any plant, any animal, ripening and maturing are identical. No natural animal and no plant exists that will prevent its own growing. So the question is how do we prevent ourselves from maturing? What prevents us from ripening?"[4]

In my opinion, not expressing feelings stunts emotional and psychological growth. Perls (like other Gestalt therapists) believes that "awareness" by and of itself can be curative. But, awareness of what? In large part, he is talking about awareness of our emotions, our feelings. Both awareness of feelings and the expression of feelings are utterly natural. Maturation depends on such expression. As infants, we would not get nourished if we had no tears. As adults, we would not be assertive if we had no frustration, nor would we be sexually satisfied if we had no desire. Maturity depends upon our willingness to listen to the natural wisdom of the organism – of ourselves – without interfering or interrupting this process.

Some couples express their emotions very well. Partners allow themselves to cry when there is loss, to be scared when out of control, to be embarrassed when personally humiliated, to be frustrated or angry when promises are broken, to be joyful on a sunny day, to be excited before a trip, or to be sexually excited when the senses are aroused. How very wise of Perls to remind us to lose our minds and come to our senses!

Mature love is seriously impaired by a loss of spontaneity. Observe any healthy family and you will see normal people responding emotionally and naturally throughout the day. They will express frustration when they can't find something, fear about a presentation the next day, anger about an insulting remark, affection when greeting each other, laughter when being teased, and so forth. All of this emotion is natural. If you are wounded in this dimension, you can learn to heal yourself within your loving relationship simply by learning to express your emotions more spontaneously.

Separate identities: Maturely loving partners recognize that each has a unique set of personality traits, skills, and aspirations. They give each other freedom to explore their separate interests and friends without judgment or undue restriction. Mature love offers us our most profound opportunity for regaining wholeness, not because our partners will fill all of our emptiness, but because we can use the embrace of a loving relationship to nurture ourselves toward greater maturation and ripening. An eagle or hawk, when taken airborne by a warm summer breeze, does not claim the breeze as its own. In a similar manner, lovers who are carried airborne by their own magical experience of love, must not claim their partner as their own. We must allow ourselves to be inspired, comforted, and renewed without trying to possess and control the source of our sustenance. In the words of Kahlil Gibran:[5]

> *Let there be spaces in your togetherness,*
> *And let the winds of the heavens dance between you.*
> *Love one another but make not a bond of love:*
> *Let it rather be a moving sea between the shores of your souls.*

In his book, *The Road Less Traveled*, M. Scott Peck defines dependency as "the inability to experience wholeness or to function adequately without the certainty that one is being actively cared for by another."[6] When we are so concerned with our own nurture, we cannot possibly encourage our partners to nurture themselves. Instead of smothering or restricting one another, mature lovers learn to encourage each other to pursue their unique paths. Encouragement both validates and facilitates our partner's yearning for growth.

Mature lovers help each other find opportunities for growth. I have seen this done in so many ways: by urging one another to take courses at a local college or university, giving photography or art lessons as a gift at Christmas, or encouraging one another to develop new friendships with colleagues at work. Recognizing that your partner has a unique identity that must have its own space to bloom is intrinsic to mature love.

Transcendence of two separate selves into one identity: Both partners in healthy relationships enjoy celebrating their "we-ness" through time spent together in shared activities, creating a shared identity. And with this shared identity comes a joint sense of worth, a shared feeling of esteem as a couple which goes beyond individual self-esteem.

The marital whole is much greater than the sum of its parts. A love relationship endures because both partners have learned to conceive of their bond as serving a higher purpose than the gratification of individual needs. Mature love is an abstraction built upon principles, values, shared beliefs, and common goals. Couples who have matured to this point want to grow old together because they have learned to take pride in a life they have built together.

Couples who love maturely have learned to gauge their happiness by more than the transient satisfactions of well-prepared meals, clean rooms, sexy nightgowns, and balanced checkbooks. Instead, happiness becomes a pride in, or perhaps a celebration of, the less tangible accomplishment of being superb dancers, gracious hosts, loving parents or grandparents, sage mentors, or well-seasoned voyagers of life. Mature lovers transcend petty conflicts between themselves as individuals by focusing on more meaningful qualities they share as a couple.

Mature love brings with it the promise of abundance, a realization that our lives are fuller, more connected, more expanded, and more empowered than ever before. We have a clear sense that life, by virtue of this connection, has become more substantial, that it has evolved into something different that would have been impossible had we not connected with another. Through this celebration of connection we learn to take pride in the "we" that we have become. For a love relationship to mature, both partners must experience a deep feeling, a tacit belief, that there is something quite special about them which would never have happened had each not contributed to its creation.

Wisdom

These eight characteristics underlie wisdom, maturity, and commitment in loving relationships. Each may seem reasonable enough – perhaps even too obvious to put much stock into! Yet every couple who struggles with the impasse of disenchantment seems to have "incapacity" in one or more of these characteristics. During such an impasse, each partner will insist on blaming the other for repeated failures to perform as a loving husband or wife should. In time, I am usually able to convince each partner to look inward, to scrutinize his/her own capacity to love or to commit.

At this point, each partner inevitably recognizes wounds from childhood – those telltale experiences that leave us incapable of fully relating, fully loving, or fully committing. These wounds, from earlier decades, impair our capacity to demonstrate the characteristics of mature love.

Each of us now confronts a bitter truth: Our current unhappiness with love has more to do with our own incapacity than it does with our partner.

As we face this uncomfortable reality, we must be kind to ourselves, remembering that this incapacity is not our fault. Like our parents, we are only capable of relating as we have been taught to relate. Our partners face the same uncomfortable reality – and for the same reason. We must be tolerant of ourselves ... and of them.

Charles Hampden-Turner, in summarizing the work of Erich Fromm, says that we human beings are "freaks of the universe. We are part nature and subject to her laws, yet we also transcend nature through culture, language and symbolism. We are set apart from each other, as Adam and Eve realized in their nakedness, yet we yearn for the harmony from which we are cast out. We plan and try to empower ourselves, yet we were thrown accidentally into this world and will be pulled inexorably out of it. We have vast potentials, yet in the course of our short span on earth, we can hope to realize but a fraction of our endowments. Reason is then our blessing and our curse, enabling us to solve the more superficial issues, until we reach the impasse beyond."[7]

Confronted with contradictions of this magnitude, we often tend to claim or affirm one end of the spectrum while negating the other. That is, in our need to reason our way through dilemmas, we often force a choice between two extremes when an integration or reconciliation of the two is more appropriate.

What better dilemma to try to reconcile than that of love? We are each faced with the contradictions of novelty and familiarity, of romantic sparks and meaningful covenants, of nascent yearnings and numbing impasses. In our need for finitude, we may repeatedly choose novelty over familiarity, or romance over covenance, or new beginnings over impasse resolution, but what do we really learn about ourselves, as well as life itself, by doing so? The mature personality, the mature lover, instead chooses to reconcile contradiction and impasse. If our capacity to reason underlies our freakish status in the universe, then we must use this capacity to transcend the difficult contradictions of our lives.

The resolution of contradiction within marriage is no easy matter, as author Adolph Guggenbuhl-Craig and many others have pointed out. We must learn to reconcile our needs for happiness and well-being, on the one hand, with our equally strong need for salvation, which entails the antithesis of happiness: suffering! Guggenbuhl-Craig states: "every path to salvation leads through hell. Happiness in the sense that is presented to married couples today belongs to well-being, not to salvation. Marriage above all is a sotereological institution, and this is why it is filled with highs and lows; it consists of sacrifices, joys and suffering."[8]

He goes on to say that "marriage is not comfortable and harmonious; rather it is a place of individuation where a person rubs up against himself and against his partner, bumps up against him in love and rejection, and in this fashion learns to know himself, the world, good and evil, the heights and the depths."

We thus can learn from our suffering, from our disenchantments in love.

Renewal can reconcile.

Recently I described the contents of this chapter to an old family friend whom I hadn't seen in years. In discussing our early family wounds, my friend told me that her own upbringing had been abominable. She experienced both poverty and neglect. There never seemed to be enough clothing, food, or attention for eight children, particularly after her father died at a young age. Yet she sat before me with her Ph.D. in hand. And she was not alone – many of her brothers and sisters possessed graduate degrees as well.

I also was aware that her marriage had had difficulties. During her doctoral course of study, she and her husband lived in separate states for part of the time so that she could complete her coursework. This almost split up their family, with the inevitable likelihood that their children would be split in different directions. Theirs was a dual-career marriage which almost didn't survive. Yet they did survive and seemed to flourish beyond their early dreams. She mused kindly over her years of suffering and pain as she thought how far they had come. I watched her smile and breathe deeply as she spoke lovingly of her husband, children, and career.

Yet I was puzzled. How could she bring so many elements of mature love to her marriage when she had been so obviously wounded in her birth family? Now, years later, she was so clearly equitable, empathetic, flexible, accepting, open, emotional, independent, and transcendent. By comparison, her parents had been oriented in exactly the opposite direction on these dimensions. This presented no quandary to my friend. She remembered a day when she was 12 years old, a day she was helping her mother bus tables in a local restaurant. Watching the dinner guests holding hands, laughing, and appearing to be content with their lives, she made a vow to be among them one day. This was not an emotional moment. It always seemed matter-of-fact to her as she recalled her vow: "I simply made a decision that my life would be significantly different from what I had experienced so far. My pattern of relationships, as well as my quality of life, would be vastly different from the misery I had known." And so it was!

Consider this for a moment. My friend could not have made her vow had she not first experienced the hardships and turmoil that marked her early family life. From the depths of her pain, she was able to recognize and envision something better, a life worth having for herself. She used her knowledge, as painful as it was, as a backdrop for a new audition. This is also true of love.

Mature love can begin only when we have come to know our partners as they truly are – imperfections and all – not as we had imagined them. Only at this point in a relationship can we begin to like and care for them as human beings. Only at this point can we demonstrate our own capacity for love. Erich Fromm has described this capacity as "productivity" – meaning the creative synthesis of our most human powers in a way that fosters an active expression, or pouring out, from within us. It is this active pouring out that has led writers like M. Scott Peck to suggest that love is as love does. Love is willful, love is a demonstration, and love is a decision, a choice based on knowledge and experience about another person. Love cannot mature otherwise.

Mature love is that process by which we learn to integrate the differences, rather than try to eliminate them.

Romantic love is characterized by a need to suspend our partners in a timeless prison so that our projected images of them as gods and goddesses can endure. In contrast, mature love allows for the natural evolution of two disparate souls to occur in a mutually satisfying manner. In closing, let's summarize mature, covenant love:

MATURE, COVENANT LOVE

✳ **A mutual balance of met needs.** Both partners have needs of equal importance, they both understand and accept these needs, and they both are willing to meet these needs as often as possible.

✳ **Other-directedness.** Each partner experiences meaning and pleasure from the other partner fulfilling his or her own needs – and actively helps him or her to fulfill those needs.

✳ **Realistic values and expectations.** Both partners jettison stereotypes about men and women, husbands and wives, love and marriage. They make their assumptions explicit to each other and avoid extreme points of view.

✳ **Tolerance.** Mature loving partners do not expect to find perfection in each other. Instead, they accept each other's attitudes, beliefs, and actions. They discuss problems on the situational level rather than on the level of personal indictment.

✳ **Yearning to be known.** Both partners value a safe harbor in their relationship, the place where they can put aside their societal masks and truly be themselves. Mature relationships nurture this process of becoming fully known.

✳ **Freedom to express all emotions.** Both partners encourage each other to express all their feelings, including sadness, remorse, anger, and hurt. And each is open about expressing these feelings.

✳ **Separate identities.** The partners recognize that each has a unique set of personality traits, skills, and aspirations. They give each other freedom to explore their separate interests and friends without judgment or undue restriction.

✳ **Transcendence of two separate selves into one identity.** Both partners in healthy relationships enjoy celebrating their "we-ness" through time spent together in shared activities, creating a shared identity. And with this shared identity comes a joint sense of worth, a shared feeling of self-esteem as a couple that goes beyond individual self-esteem.

CHAPTER 14

Self-Assessment

Sunday mornings have always been special for us – all of them! It is the one day of the week we force ourselves to sleep in or at least stay in bed longer than we normally do. Our friends know NOT to call before noon. We would be in bed with whatever number of cats we had through the years. Cuddle each other, maybe make love, no, usually make love and cuddle some more. As we cuddle we usually bring up issues that might be troubling us and take the time we need to sort them through. Then one or both of us would make coffee. For years we had coffee and Kahlua, newspaper, and nice music. Dressed in our robes, we were in a warm and fuzzy glow. Serving each other coffee, reading interesting articles to each other from the paper, toes wiggling to the music, leaning over to kiss or touch softly with a warm smile and "sweet eyes." After we read the paper we usually cook a great Sunday breakfast or perhaps brunch – if it's late enough. Oh man….if we didn't have those Sunday mornings our weeks would not start refreshed. After noon, the phone usually starts ringing off the wall, but we're ready for anything since the coffee has kicked in by then and we have already recharged our tanks.

This is "secure attachment" for one of my clients, Rachel, who is snuggling within her protective wall. Instead of a maternal uterus, however, we find her wrapped in the arms of her husband on a very splendid Sunday morning where the two of them are restoring a shared vibrancy which will nourish them for a full week – until they repeat this ritual again. Do you notice the various ways this couple celebrates intimacy?

Maintaining attachment with one or more of nine intimacies promotes long term survival for couples.

Adults have an advantage compared to young children in regards to attachment: we have nine different ways of securing attachment not possible for infants. These attachment styles are life support for mature, covenant love. A sumptuous smorgasbord actually exists from which we can energize, revitalize, and breathe new life into our relationships.

Attachment is a biological need that must be honored throughout our lifetimes. A committed love bond is the essence of human relationship. This togetherness must be alive; it must be dynamic; and it must be fed. This "living architecture" requires that we roll up our sleeves and do the necessary work each day to maintain it. Passivity is not an option here – we are building a life together.

We are not merely giving ourselves to another in love; we are actively surrendering into something greater. This something greater requires that we actively create a secure, warm haven for one another; that we actively give 100 percent, not 50-50; and that we actively commit to all nine intimacies which follow. Remember that each of the following intimacies is a source of energy that empowers us to move "toward" one another with a renewed vigor.

The Bugen Adult Intimacy Scale (Copyright: 2010)

Directions: Allow yourself a time to unwind. Get comfortable and relax. Try to visualize the totality of your relationship with your partner. As you think about each of the questions below keep the following in mind when responding: **1** means **Never True**; **2** means **Rarely True**; **3** means **Occasionally True**; **4** means **Usually True**; and **5** means **Always True**.

1. *Emotional Intimacy* – We eventually must trust someone enough to reveal ourselves from the inside out. Emotional intimacy occurs when we put our personas – our masks – aside and begin to let a significant other know our deepest feelings, our most troubling thoughts, and our heaviest baggage. Mutual emotional intimacy is the sine qua non of a healthy bond that connotes the highest level of comfort, trust and communication between two people:

   a) We let each other know about any emotional baggage from the past.   1 2 3 4 5

   b) We let each other know about any current feelings and thoughts.   1 2 3 4 5

   c) We let each other know about any unmet concerns/needs.   1 2 3 4 5

   d) We let each other know about any unmet dreams.   1 2 3 4 5

   e) Overall, I am satisfied with the level of emotional intimacy in our relationship.   1 2 3 4 5

                                                                              TOTAL_____

2. *Intellectual Intimacy* – We are blessed with a cerebral cortex which allows us to share thoughts, to find a deep meaning in Winnie the Pooh, and to marvel at the creative genius of Rembrandt or Michael Angelo Buonarotti. Whether we find ourselves discussing the plot of a delightful movie or the benevolent efforts of a foreign dignitary, we deepen a bond when we turn toward one another for discussion's sake:

   a) We are comfortable presenting opinions on different topics.   1 2 3 4 5

   b) We enjoy discussing themes of different books or movies.   1 2 3 4 5

   c) We believe each other's ideas are worthwhile.   1 2 3 4 5

   d) We are able to stimulate new ways of looking at things with one another.   1 2 3 4 5

   e) Overall, I am satisfied with the level of intellectual stimulation in our relationship.   1 2 3 4 5

                                                                              TOTAL_____

3. *Recreational Intimacy* – You can only have fun helping other people have fun if you're having fun doing it. Or, as John F. Kennedy might have said, "Ask not what fun does for you, but what you do for fun!" Every couple must make time for pleasure where the only purpose of the pleasure is to have it. When I refer to recreational intimacy I mean the solitary courtship time a couple takes WITHOUT anyone else present to renew its charge, i.e. no children, no friends, and no neighbors. Being a couple means being a nucleus where a proton bonds with a neutron on a regular basis. This creates energy:

a) We enjoy dinners, movies, or concerts together.	1	2	3	4	5
b) We enjoy walking or exercising together.	1	2	3	4	5
c) We have our special ways of de-stressing.	1	2	3	4	5
d) We enjoy planning weekend or vacation.	1	2	3	4	5
e) Overall, I am satisfied with the level of recreational intimacy in our relationship.	1	2	3	4	5

TOTAL_____

4. *Social Intimacy* – When fun and pleasure include others, it is social intimacy. One indication of a couple "in trouble" is the lack of couple friends in their life. Somehow, when we begin to spiral away from each other we often resist celebrating life with others as well. Social intimacy reflects the network of people in our lives who mirror our own joy in being together:

a) We enjoy entertaining others in our home, e.g. at the holidays.	1	2	3	4	5
b) We enjoy going out with others for dinner, sports or a show.	1	2	3	4	5
c) We have our fair share of friends who know us and our family quite well.	1	2	3	4	5
d) We enjoy planning fun events and get-a-ways with family or friends.	1	2	3	4	5
e) Overall, I am satisfied with the level of social intimacy in our relationship.	1	2	3	4	5

TOTAL_____

5. *Creative Intimacy* – Creative intimacy is the celebration of what we have created as a couple that would never have seen the light of day without our union. This might include children but also includes the design and architecture of a home or pond in the backyard. At the heart of it, creative intimacy is the catalyst for something wonderful to spring forth.

a) We celebrate the presence of our children in our lives.	1	2	3	4	5
b) We have enjoyed redecorating a room, or more, in our home.	1	2	3	4	5
c) We enjoy taking pictures or creating family albums where some of our favorites memories are treasured.	1	2	3	4	5

d) We work together as a team in some capacity that make a   1   2   3   4   5
   difference in our community.

e) Overall, I am satisfied with the level of creative intimacy in   1   2   3   4   5
   our bond.

TOTAL_____

6) *Spiritual Intimacy* – When we bear witness to the splendor of the universe it is a time
   to be humbled by a greater force. Whether we call this force God or Mother Nature is
   insignificant. Spiritual intimacy is the reverence for something far greater than ourselves
   which invites humility and awe. While a morning prayer might serve this purpose for
   some, an evening sunset might suffice for others. When couples share in this way, there
   is often a sense of transcendence or a soulful merger where timelessness exists but for
   a moment:

a) We usually take time for prayer sometime during the day.   1   2   3   4   5

b) We sometimes take a moment to sit outside on our patio   1   2   3   4   5
   deck and look at the stars or hear nature.

c) There are times when we read a poem or some prose to one   1   2   3   4   5
   another that has special meaning to us.

d) We find it gratifying to attend religious services together or   1   2   3   4   5
   with our family.

e) Overall, I am satisfied with the level of spritual intimacy in   1   2   3   4   5
   our bond.

TOTAL_____

7) *Task Intimacy* – It has been estimated that one third of married life is directed to the
   pragmatics of "doing" life chores, maintaining a household, or fulfilling responsibilities to
   and for others. Many of these tasks are usually "adopted" by one partner vs. the other, just
   out of preference. So while one person's throne exists in the kitchen, the other partner's
   province might lie outdoors amidst the palms and junipers. Any task is an opportunity
   for connection if a couple is open to it. The shared delight in preparing your home for
   entertainment has as much "attachment" value as any other form of intimacy:

a) We share in food shopping, food preparation, and cleanup.   1   2   3   4   5

b) We cooperate in keeping our home clean and orderly.   1   2   3   4   5

c) We share in the care of our children or other needed   1   2   3   4   5
   priorities in our lives.

d) We delegate to one another as needed.   1   2   3   4   5

e) Overall, I am satisfied with the level of task   1   2   3   4   5
   intimacy in our bond.

TOTAL_____

8) *Problem-solving Intimacy* – Problems exist in every relationship. There is no escape. Each of the six major quality of life domains may challenge us to find strategies: Love, Work, Leisure, Health, Finances, and even Spirituality. I have referred to these six domains as the "pillars of happiness" elsewhere. They often require creative solutions. When problems exist within a relationship itself, a couple must develop confidence that solutions are possible. We must know that we can reconcile, repair, and renew once a rupture has occurred. A couple lacking confidence it its ability to achieve a peace accord will avoid discussing problems from the outset. This stonewalling is tragic and prevents renewal from occurring:

a) We clearly identify what our problems actually are.   1   2   3   4   5
b) We understand each other's point of view.   1   2   3   4   5
c) We create strategies or options that might help us solve   1   2   3   4   5
   problems.
d) We stay calm when we are dicussing a problem.   1   2   3   4   5
e) Overall, I am satisfied with the level of problem solving   1   2   3   4   5
   intimacy in our relationship.

                                                    TOTAL_____

9) *Sexual Intimacy* – We are sexual creatures. The mutual seduction and physical arousal of one another is considered sexual intimacy. For most people, arousal results in orgasm. For many, however, sexual intimacy is more about a seductive dance, mutually choreographed, which causes one partner to desire the other. While desire may wane once the state of romantic love ends, creative lovers find creative ways to stimulate each other for decades to come. Stendhal eloquently stated: "Love is like a fever that comes and goes independently of the will:"

a) We stimulate sexual desire or arousal in one another.   1   2   3   4   5
b) We are able to talk about sex.   1   2   3   4   5
c) We have grown sexually over the years as we have learned   1   2   3   4   5
   about each other's needs.
d) We bring each other to orgasm.   1   2   3   4   5
e) Overall, I am satisfied with the level of sexual intimacy in 1   2   3   4   5
   our relationship.

                                                    TOTAL_____

Do you see how intimacy is a "living architecture?" It is a work in progress. A healthy relationship is soulful. It is alive and vibrant. The nine styles of intimacy just described are pathways to this aliveness. Without them, our relationships become necrotic and begin to atrophy. While I do not have comparative norms for this scale, I believe the following would be a modest interpretation. If your Total Score in each of the nine intimacies is 20 or above, count your blessings, and keep on keeping on! If your Total Score is 10 or below, you are hurting as a couple and need to refuel.

When you think about each style of intimacy, remember that each is a symbolic, symbiotic umbilical cord which feeds both nurturer and nurtured concurrently. We must awaken and actively share life with one another. We have an obligation to inspire, to breathe life into a relationship. To be a soul mate means not just to share one's life with another but to enliven it along the way. Thomas Moore has captured this quite well:

> *Marriage may look like an arrangement of persons, but at a deeper level it is a profound stirring of the souls….Something deeply mysterious and profound, like an animal lying at the very heart of relationship, far within its marrow, keeps a marriage moving, changing, and shifting! This is what the Romans called the genius, others called the daimon, and still others the angel – an influential yet hidden presence that is impervious to our explanations and rationalizations….In getting married, we lay ourselves open to the influence of the genius, not just to hold the marriage together but to make something out of it.1*

Discussing the following questions with your partner will help you understand your intimacy scores:

A. Which categories of intimacy are above 20 points for me? For my partner?

B. Which categories of intimacy are below 10 points for me? For my partner?

C. Which categories of intimacy did both my partner and I agree were high?

D. Which categories of intimacy did both my partner and I agree were low?

E. Which category of intimacy am I most afraid to explore? Why?

F. Which category of intimacy do I believe we should address first? Why?

G. Which of the following distractions interfere the most in my efforts to be intimate:
   (1) Am I too distracted by time spent with other friends?
   (2) Am I too distracted by time spent with other family members?
   (3) Am I too distracted by time spent at work outside the home?
   (4) Am I too distracted by time spent at work inside the home?
   (5) Am I too distracted by time spent alone, pampering myself?
   (6) Am I too distracted by time spent buying things for myself?
   (7) Am I too distracted by time spent buying things for others?
   (8) Am I too distracted by time spent pursuing my own pleasures?

(9) Am I too distracted by time spent being too depressed or resentful?

(10) Am I too distracted by time spent pursuing my personal good at the expense of the greater good.

The title of this book is ***Stuck on Me: Missing You***. Do you see how being self-absorbed, being stuck on yourself, interferes with intimacy? Consider for a moment how each of the above distractions is a turning away from one another. Now, consider what it would take to rebalance each of the above actions so that you may share more fully with another.

H. I am willing to do the following three things immediately to lessen the distractions in my relational life:

   1)

   2)

   3)

I. You may have noticed something holds you back from being more intimate – like fear. Tell your partner which of the following fears holds you captive:

   (1) Fear of being known
   (2) Fear of abandonment/loss
   (3) Fear of rejection/hurt/pain
   (4) Fear of inadequacy
   (5) Fear of loss of self

Each of us has a preferred way to be intimate. What is good for the goose may not be good for the gander. This is quite normal. Having different preferences for intimacy is not a problem. Not knowing each other's preferences is the problem. So, for the sake of clarity, let's explore what your preferences may actually be.

A Couple's Sharing Inventory

Part A:

You will find a number of statements below which describe ways that couples prefer to spend time together. Partners have different preferences in what they value in the way of shared experiences with one another. Please rate the importance of each of the following to you by circling a number from 10 to 100.

	NOT PREFER					STRONGLY PREFER				
____Enjoying recreational fun and play	10	20	30	40	50	60	70	80	90	100
____Discussing important ideas regarding life or current events	10	20	30	40	50	60	70	80	90	100
____Sharing deeper thoughts and feelings about oneself or another	10	20	30	40	50	60	70	80	90	100
____Socializing with friends or family	10	20	30	40	50	60	70	80	90	100
____Being soulful or spiritual	10	20	30	40	50	60	70	80	90	100
____Creating something new or special	10	20	30	40	50	60	70	80	90	100
____Completing a project or task together	10	20	30	40	50	60	70	80	90	100
____Facing one of life's challenges successfully	10	20	30	40	50	60	70	80	90	100
____Being aroused sexually	10	20	30	40	50	60	70	80	90	100
____Planning ahead financially	10	20	30	40	50	60	70	80	90	100

PART B

Now that you have rated each of the above nine intimacies independently, would you please place them in order of importance to you by placing the number 1 on the blank line in front of the most essential kind of sharing you would prefer in an ideal relationship. The number 2 would be placed in front of the second most important to you and so forth.

J. Compare your highest three priorities for intimacy with those of your partner. How do they compare?

K. Looking at your partner's highest priority what three things are you willing to do to meet his or her needs immediately?

L. Have you experienced higher levels of intimacy with prior partners? Which intimacies in particular?

M. What factors in your current relationship have influenced this change?

N. Sometimes it is a lack of knowledge, lack of ability, lack of experience, or a lack of interest which blocks the flow of intimacy. Which of these apply to you?

At the heart of intimacy lies a need for affirmation. When we actively "turn toward" others we are validating them. We are affirming one another. This need to be special underlies all healthy relationships. In the words of author John Bradshaw we are not merely "human doings," we are "human beings." Each of us longs to be cherished for who we are, not merely for what we do.

How often have you just wanted someone to say:

You are a good person.
You are a wonderful parent, spouse, employee, mentor, or friend.
You are loved.
You are kind and giving.
You make a difference in my life.
You mean the world to me.

At the core of intimacy lies the universal, existential hope that our journeys have been meaningful – that we have meant something to someone... that we are worthwhile.

I conclude this chapter with a final exercise which illuminates this need to be special, to be valued, and to be worthwhile. When you are finished with the exercise take a moment to carefully consider the questions that follow.

"Being Valued" Questionnaire

Directions: This is an exercise that asks you to consider (1) how you are "valued" by your partner and (2) how you "value" your partner. In other words, how "special" are you to one another? By value, I mean ANYTHING POSITIVE that the two of you **do** for each other, **give** to each other, **provide** for each other, **share** with each other, are for each other.

Please take a moment to think about THE PAST 24 HOURS. In column one, write one thing you can truly say you appreciated, or valued, about your partner. In column two, write one thing that you believe your partner appreciated, or valued, about you. ALSO, please indicate the INTIMACY STYLE with the brackets [   ].

When you have completed the exercise compare responses with your partner.

What I Valued About My Partner	**What My Partner Valued About Me**
[ ] Sunday	[ ] Sunday
[ ] Monday	[ ] Monday
[ ] Tuesday	[ ] Tuesday
[ ] Wednesday	[ ] Wednesday
[ ] Thursday	[ ] Thursday
[ ] Friday	[ ] Friday
[ ] Saturday	[ ] Saturday

Intimacy Styles: **E** = Emotional, **I** = Intellectual, **R** = Recreational, **S** = Social, **C** = Creative, **T** = Task, **PS** = Problem Solving, **Sp** = Spiritual, and **Sex** = Sexual.

O. In what ways are my partner and I out of balance? Do I value him/her more than I am valued in return – or vice versa?

P. Have I been too self-absorbed – too negative – to notice any positives about my partner? (Surely there must be some inherent good in your partner!)

Q. Have I been too self-absorbed – too negative – to appreciate positives that my partner sees in me?

R. Has my definition of intimacy been much too narrow to appreciate the greater good that exists between us?

For many of us, the word intimacy has taken on only sexual connotations. You now know that it means far more than that. It connotes all the different dimensions of our lives – the physical, emotional, mental, and spiritual – and can be expressed in the nine different ways I have described. By now you better appreciate that intimacy really means a total life sharing.

Our capacity to love can be learned if we are willing to evolve beyond romantic longings. With mature, covenant love we begin to shift emphasis from meeting "me-centered" romantic needs to meeting "we-centered" relationship needs.

Narcissistic preoccupation must give way to a more dynamic, living architecture created with another person.

There are six foundational pillars upon which a lasting love rests: *Humility, Forgiveness, Acceptance, Compassion, Vision, and Sacrifice*. For love to be sustained, for intimacy to flourish, we must be willing to nourish each other with these *Six Gifts*. Let us now turn to these precious gifts.

THE SIX GIFTS:
ANTIDOTES TO NARCISSIM

	Past	**Present**	**Future**
Self	*Humility*	*Acceptance*	*Sacrifice*
Other	*Forgiveness*	*Compassion*	*Vision*

Emergence from self-absorption depends upon our capacity to honor *Six Gifts* during our lifetime. Each serves as kindling which permits the Nine Intimacies to burn. Without these gifts couples are merely living on parallel tracks – just going through the motions of life together. Each gift is unique, yet all six are woven together in a rich tapestry. Each represents a higher virtue that fulfills our unique destiny as human beings. Two of the gifts – *humility* and *forgiveness* – release us from the past. With humility, we release ourselves from pride. With forgiveness, we release others from the death grip of resentment. In both cases – humility and forgiveness – the past no longer reigns supreme.

Two other gifts – *acceptance* and *compassion* – allow us to live more fully in the present, embracing life with an open heart. With acceptance, we release ourselves from perfectionism and the "tyranny of the should's." With compassion, we widen our care circle beyond ourselves so that we may embrace others in their epic journeys.

The final two gifts – *sacrifice* and *vision* – allow us to live our lives looking forward instead of backward. With sacrifice, we purge the trivial from our lives and commit to what truly matters. With vision, we take time to wonder about the real meaning of our lives by peering inward and optimistically beyond.

Humility, acceptance, and *sacrifice* each reflect changes occurring within the SELF. With each of these three gifts we turn inward, finding tattered parts of ourselves that need mending. *Forgiveness, compassion*, and *vision* each reflect changes between our selves and OTHERS. With each of these latter three gifts we turn outward to bless the loving connections we have with one another – with life itself.

The six gifts require us to make tough choices each day. Will I choose *humility* over pride? Will I choose *forgiveness* over resentment? Will I choose *acceptance* over judgment? Will I choose *compassion* over indifference? Will I choose *sacrifice* over self-indulgence? Will I choose *vision* over habituation? The problem with all of these virtues is that they require us to act against impulses defined by our very nature. This is especially difficult for many who simply prefer to do what comes naturally!

Note to Couples

The following chapters provide a closer look at the Six Gifts. After many years of doing couples' therapy I have noticed that the gifts seem to work in tandem with one another. For instance, Humility is often paired with Forgiveness. We often hurt those we love the most. When we do we must be humble enough to embrace our imperfection so that forgiveness might be offered. Being vulnerable is the gateway for intimacy in all love relationships. It is this merging of flawed nakedness with the outstretched arms of a forgiving heart that allows us to move on in our journeys.

Acceptance and Compassion are often paired as well. Acceptance in a long term relationship requires complete openness and an understanding that a partner may be the very source of one's pain. We use compassion to confront the inevitable disenchantment that appears. We don't just recognize imperfection and resign ourselves to it; we embrace what is broken with an open heart and give these gifts daily as conflicts arise.

Finally, Vision is not likely to be fulfilled without Sacrifice. We must actively trade up for "something" more valuable than the present moment when we choose to sacrifice. Choices abound but life teaches us what to value. Often it is a personal goal relating to one's name, fame or personal gain. Greater wisdom – and happiness – requires that we value relational goals in addition to personal goals. It is within this crucible of love – with your partner, your family and your community – that a meaningful life is defined. Sacrifice occurs when we "make" time for all that we value.

Embedded within each of the following six chapters you will find brief notes written by partners from three marriages. The chapters on humility and forgiveness each present letters written by spouses from the same relationship. The letters in the acceptance and compassion chapters are written by a second couple. Finally, the last two chapters on sacrifice and vision are written by yet a third couple. My hope is that you see how these Gifts are woven into colorful tapestries that complement one other.

CHAPTER 15

The Gift of Humility

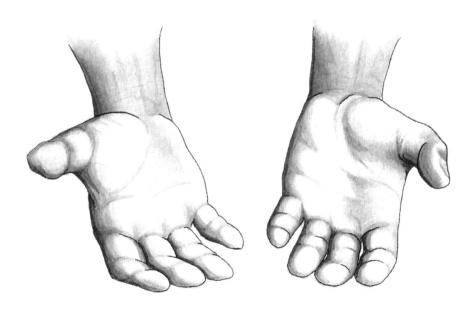

A church realized the importance of humility, so it formed a committee to find the most humble person in the church. Many names were submitted and numerous candidates evaluated. Finally, the committee came to a unanimous decision. They selected a quiet little man who always lived in the background and had never taken any credit for things he had done. They awarded him the "Most Humble" button for his faithful service. However, the next day they had to take it away from him because he pinned it on.[1]

In a "Me First" or "I'm Number One" kind of society, being "Most Humble" would seem to have value – that is, up to the time you're proud of it! This is known as the humility paradox: Will humble people acknowledge their humility? Prophets and philosophers have wrestled with this paradox for ages. Even a passage from the *Tao Te Ching* speaks to this dilemma: "To know when one does not know is best. To think one knows when one does not know is a dire disease." And an old Sufi saying goes, "A saint is a saint unless he knows that he is one."

The word "humility" comes from the Latin root – humus – meaning dirt. When we are humble, we are grounded. We look at life from the ground up. We are comfortable with our humanness, our imperfection, and our human be-ing – *being in* the middle! While it may be sinful to be prideful, there is no sin in ordinariness – the essential acceptance that being human is often good enough. Humility, as earthiness, is well-captured by Ernest Kurtz and Katherine Ketcham in their wonderful book, *The Spirituality of Imperfection*:

> *Humility signifies, simply, the acceptance of being human, the acceptance of one's human being. It is the embrace of the both-and-ness, both saint and sinner, both beast and angel, that constitutes our very be-ing as human. Beginning with the acceptance that being human – being mixed (and therefore sometimes mixed-up) – is good enough, humility involves learning how to live with and take joy in that reality…After all, humor is the juxtaposition of incongruities.[2]*

Not long ago I learned once again that pride, rather than idleness, is the devil's workshop and one must eat a bit of humble pie occasionally to get grounded. These are not easy lessons, but if we are to laugh at ourselves and smile at Ernest Becker's vivid depiction of "man as a god who shits," we must not take ourselves too seriously. On August 19th, 2006, I competed in the Sixth Annual "Deep Eddy Mile Swim" event in Austin, Texas. I had just turned 60 years old, just been diagnosed with prostate cancer, and my robotic surgical procedure was scheduled one month hence. This was a very traumatic, emotional time for me. I knew this would be my last swim before I would, hopefully, become a cancer survivor. A numbing cocktail of fear and apprehension swirled within me like an eddy between Scylla and Charybdis. Knowing that a catheter would be my only release for some time following surgery, I wanted to cherish the feeling of being healthy while swimming with spirit and vigor.

I did so. I won the 60 and older mile event, breaking the old record by over two minutes. Along with fellow swimmers, I was surprised by the consistency with which I metered each 100-yard interval – one after another – hitting one minute 27 seconds for each 100 yards as if I were a Swiss time piece. I had not only slithered effortlessly through the refreshing 72-degree water at Deep Eddy, I had also put cancer out of mind for a half hour or so.

What I didn't anticipate was the pride I experienced afterwards in the thought that I was the fastest miler over age 60 in Austin, Texas. I often was inspired by this self-reverie throughout the year. I often had thoughts about defending my title the following year. One person I did not notice after my victory was the man who came in second in my 60-64 age group – a fellow I had beaten by 30 seconds. I was too busy basking in my own limelight to notice him.

For a moment in time, nothing mattered more than my attainment of a lofty goal. Since this man was inconspicuous to me, I didn't know his name or his reasons for being there. All I knew from the heat sheets was that he, like me, had just turned 60. I wondered if he as well was motivated by thoughts of mortality – of running out of time.

Fast forward one year to August 25th, 2007, where we find ourselves again at the newly remodeled Deep Eddy Pool at the Seventh Annual Mile event. I am about to defend my glorious, impregnable, imperious title! It's approximately 11:30 am on a Saturday morning, and I'm sitting in the shade trying to shield myself from the piercing rays of the sun which seemed to sap my strength from above. In the midst of a revivalist pep talk I am giving myself about a nagging lethargy which has gripped me for three days, I begin to fear that I don't have the needed petrol for the day. I wanted to assume that this sluggishness was allergy related and fleetingly wondered if some nasty Greek tragedy was in the process of being played out. Just the day before I could barely stand up – but stand up to what!

At 11:40 am, my event was called.

As I peered across the pool deck, I noticed a man clearly over 60 squeezing into a Superman outfit. "What in God's name is he putting on?" I wondered. Could it be Nike's Swim Hydra suit or perhaps Speedo's EZ-Pro racing suit? The world's fastest swimmers wear both because they use high density microfibers, chlorine-resistant elastane nylon threads, water-repellent coatings, and vertical seams to reduce drag! For $220 to $340 these suits can be yours. I knew I was in deep ca ca when I noticed the vertical seams!

Then, as he pulled his slick, skin-tight racing suit over his hips and upward where he slowly squished his well-muscled biceps and triceps through the tiny tight orifices left for arms, I remembered why he looked familiar: he'd come in 30 seconds after me the year before. Once adorned in this silky, golden-looking fleece, he surreptitiously peered over at me with a certain look – a look which somehow conveyed, "I've seen you before and you are about to die in my wake." I had only seen one other swimmer take senior master's events so seriously as to don such an accoutrement. I proudly sucked in my gut and slowly meandered over to the far side of the pool where it was customary to gather before the start of the race.

As we took our lane assignments, one fellow I recognized from the year before stepped up to the lane on my right. As I looked left, I saw the silken form of Superman slowly creep into view. I extended my hand to both competitors, wishing each a "Good race!" Only one of these two men graciously made eye contact in receiving my hand.

Moments later, drama building, we each heard the call: "Swimmers are you ready? Take your mark!" Then, the horn! We were off. As I began the first of 53 lengths of the pool, I wondered if it was too late to get myself some of those vertical threads. After all, Superman did look more godlike – like Nike – than I did in my racing briefs, attire our daughter Jessica once told me she would ban and make illegal for any man over 30!

When I realized that Superman was swimming exactly at my side, matching my flip turns perfectly, lap after lap, I decided to "take him out" early. I sped up. By the end of one quarter mile – i.e., 13 lengths, I had a five-yard lead. Then, my body caught up to my mind and said, "You're a haughty fool, and you're going to pay dearly for this!"

I was done. I was cooked. I was puppy chow.

I could not press on at that pace. Within two lengths of the pool, Superman had caught me and was "speedo-ing" by me. I released myself from the bondage of supremacy and found ordinariness in my stroke pattern. "Easy does it," I reminded myself. "Regain your form and breathe." I humbly instructed myself, "Finish well, or well enough!" There would be no title brought home on this day.

Superman beat me by 45 seconds – a sound victory!

A friend, who was timing for me, suggested that I may have gone out too fast. I knew better. It wasn't that I went out too fast. More truthfully, I started out too high – as in high and mighty. Yes, allergies may have played a part in this Greek tragedy. At the heart of it, however, I needed an attitude adjustment more than a speed adjustment.

Once the race was completed I swam out to the center of my lane where Superman had swum to cool down from his winning swim. I wanted to give him a high-five, congratulate him on his swim, and bond with him a bit. Clearly, he had been thinking about this event for a full year since I had trimmed his sails the year before. As I looked at him, trying to find his eyes – his soul – he averted my glance, fleetingly accepted my high-five and made his way back to poolside where his friend muttered, "You rule! You are "Super" – man! You kick ass." There would be no schmoosing with this gladiator on this day. There would be no friendship kindled, no warmth exchanged, no comradery created.

Superman may have won the swimming race, but he like me lost a human race. Superman seemed to lack namaste, a Hindu word for greeting which means to pay homage to the inner light as the thinking mind bows to the wisdom of the heart. I wondered if I had pridefully lacked this same namaste the year before. There is sacredness in all things. Namaste's roots in Sanskrit are very poignant for those of us living in the West. "Namas" means to bow in reverence as we do in yoga to close our practice. In reverence, we are humbly saluting one another in silence. "Te" means "to you." The word literally means "I bow to you." Namaste is the preferred way to greet one another in Indian culture. The two hands are pressed together close to the heart with one's head gently bowed. By greeting in this manner, each person is being honored and celebrated. While namaste appears to be a social gesture, it is in fact a spiritual experience. The gesture lessens our sense of ego, self-absorption, and self-centeredness. The bowing of heads in the East, when greeting, is a humble act compared to the thrusting of hands forward in the West which can often signify arrogance.

The deeper meaning of the hands held in union signifies the oneness which binds us all together, the integration of spirit and matter, as well as the self meeting the self. It is this latter meaning – self meeting self – where insights relating to one's humility lie. Many Hindus in fact believe that the right hand represents our higher or more divine nature, while the left hand represents our lower, worldlier nature.

On August 25th, 2007, I was not only reaching out to my "brother", I was reaching in to myself. The humble part of me was meeting the arrogant, prideful part of me. While the chemistry in this union is often corrosive, on that day I found peace. The worldly part of me wanted to win again in the name of pride and ego. The spiritual part of me knew that eventually there would be a life lesson learned from losing – coming in second! So called "winning" often just separates us from one another.

How many of us take one step forward in a competitive race, only to lose ground in the human race?

Surely we can all do better honoring the divine in one another, if only for a moment. A handshake, a bow, a high-five, a smile, or a soulful meeting of the eyes can acknowledge our humanity as well as our shared experience as heroic warriors who gleefully embrace the thrill of victory or painfully resist the hollow emptiness of loss. Ironically, either can be enriching.

Packing away my racing briefs for 2007 I knew that swallowing one's pride seldom leads to indigestion. I treasured the lessons learned from Superman and knew that he too would find his comeuppance the following year at the Eighth Annual Deep Eddy Mile. Others, more endeavoring and talented, would turn 60 in time to devour both of us in the pure spring water of Deep Eddy pool.

While the prideful part of me treasures the knowledge that my record time stood for one more year, the humble part of me smiles – knowing that only a fool would hold onto pride, power, or prestige as a meaningful life marker. I now know that namaste can help me heal my wounds from competition. *[Nevertheless, I wonder whether I should head to the sporting goods store tomorrow for some new elastane, ultra fine, and vertically seamed nylon threads!]*

Our Dark Night of the Soul

Taking on pride, the mother load of all narcissistic toxins, is not easy. Learning to be humble is not for the faint hearted, but I begin this last section of the book with humility because I believe it is the most important gift. It is a gift which conveys a core connectedness to one another. "I'll tell you about my emptiness, my pain, if you tell me about yours." It is a gift which knocks us off our mountain peaks and gently lifts us from our deepest valleys. Humility is a *Gift* that we learn after humiliating ourselves enough times.

For a variety of biological and cultural reasons we men seem particularly in need of "humility training." My counseling sessions with couples often reveals this need amidst the maelstrom of emotion and torment. This was true for Patsy and Victor who were attempting to renew their relationship following the discovery of Victor's affair. After months of heart-wrenching work to heal from his indiscretions Victor was able to summon a letter of humility for Patsy:

Patsy, my life-long Sweetheart: Through our pain it is has become belatedly and tangibly clear to me: I've neglected, damaged, and misled – but hopefully not lost – the best and most important part of my life: you and our love. I wonder daily, and will probably ponder for the rest of my life, how I could have risked your heart and your presence in my life. I am humbly sorrowed by both my failure to honor you as well as by the distress I have created for you and the kids. Compromising the happiness of those I love the most is not what I lovingly offered to you in our wedding vows years ago. I pledge to unceasingly work on individual behaviors and habits, on insight and deeper understanding, and hopefully on transformation. Going forward, I hope to do my share in creating something we can both respect and cherish.

Humility is something that I probably don't fully understand yet. Early on, as a young man, I was taught – even encouraged – to be the tallest and fastest, and to strive, push, shout, and get what I want in battle. A boy hears and believes that a man must sow, harvest, compete, and be fleet-footed. A man's high status in the pecking order, in the tribe, and in the pack is our learned destiny. The future is a calling, not a quest; it's the place where one is pulled, not merely attained. Then, after this early brainwashing, the stretching and hormones of young man-dome set in: the perfect jump shot, the perfect head fake on the field, the better biting joke, the most clever prank, the best looking date – and yes, the best sexual adventure – all elevate a guy to a slightly higher, louder, and splashier rung on the status ladder of life among peers.

Then life happens! Realism calls. The other guy gets the better grades and the girl! I begin to know failure. I fall. Seeing there are other fleeter fish in the sea makes me gasp. Being told by my boss that it's time to move on makes me gasp. Seeing our savings dip because of my underemployment makes me gasp. Understanding your sleepless nights makes me gasp.

Humility helps focus on the present, the better stuff, which makes life whole. And humility makes a man see that it's all about the village, the tribe, and what's best for the family, not the sole soldier. Looking back on my life I now know that I was never running alone as the young buck – I was enabled by elders, matriarchs and many others. Humility has helped me heal from the isolation of an insatiable ego by opening my heart instead. It is my eternal hope that perhaps our mate-ness can transcend my male-ness: Love Victor.

Victor was able to capture some goals of a *humility* letter:

* Acknowledge that you have "fallen" short in some way and apologize.
* Acknowledge that you have created pain and misery in the life of another.
* Affirm that you have learned a profound lesson(s) from this "fall."
* State your intention to stand upright once again.
* Affirm the value of love, as well as your love-mate, in your life.

True humility neither exaggerates nor minimizes: it merely accepts what is. Humility is the face of acceptance of one "self" and all others. Humility overcomes pride. Humility is a *Gift* which can be learned involuntarily through hardship – as we have seen with Victor – or more volitionally as a chosen way of life. As an involuntary happenstance, humility is often a prominent feature of a "dark night of the soul."

Before exploring this experience further let's first take a moment to understand the differences between humility and arrogance. Psychologist Wade Rowatt, from Baylor University, helps us see the two from an observing ego's point of view.[3] In the case of humility, our ego is healthy enough to embrace both imperfection and incompleteness in life. With arrogance, we avoid, deny, and run from human frailty.

I find myself on both sides of the lists. Where are you?

Humility	Arrogance
1) Open to new and contradictory ideas	1) Conceited, egotistical, condescending
2) Eager to learn from others	2) Overly competitive with others
3) Acknowledging one's mistakes	3) Denies faults
4) Accurate sense of one's true abilities	4) Overestimates abilities/accomplishments
5) Accepts failure with pragmatism	5) Attempts to hide failures
6) Asks for advice	6) Know-it-all
7) Has a genuine desire to serve others	7) Self-serving
8) Respects others	8) Disrespectful of others
9) Shares honors and recognition	9) Takes more credit that s/he deserves
10) Accepts success with simplicity	10) Brags about successes
11) Repels adulation	11) Narcissistic, seeks praise
12) Shuns public adulation	12) Attempts to be the center of attention
13) Doesn't blame others	13) Blames others for mistakes/failures
14) De-emphasizes "self"	14) Over-concern with "self-image"/vanity
15) Down-to-earth	15) High-and-mighty

Arrogant people often have rude, involuntary awakenings.

A "dark night of the soul" is a term used to describe a specific phase in a person's spiritual life, when something far greater than a Deep Eddy Mile is at stake! Theologically, it is a time when we feel like God has walked away. We feel alone – profoundly empty. It is generally associated with a crisis of faith in the Roman Catholic tradition. It is used as a metaphor to describe the experience of loneliness and desolation that can occur during spiritual growth. The phrase "dark night of the soul" is taken from the writings of the Spanish poet and Roman Catholic mystic Saint John of the Cross, a Carmelite priest in the 16th century. *Dark Night of the Soul* is the name of both a poem, and a commentary on that poem, and is among the Carmelite priest's most famous writings. They tell of mystic development and the stages this man went through on his quest for holiness.

Humility, during a dark night, is a somber reminder of our helplessness. We are not in control. Being out of control means we suffer. No matter how smart, determined, or virtuous we may be there is a time when we are at the mercy of greater forces than those we design. We fall. Who among us has not known of such times? A troubled relationship may have ended unexpectedly, an aspiring career may be upended without due cause, a loved one may suddenly die without warning, one's finances may take a tumble, or one's faith in mankind may be shaken by a September 11th calamity! Or, as is my experience, a relatively healthy body is diagnosed with cancer.

Unexpected, appalling life events humble us. We find ourselves prostrated.

A time of chaos may become that dark night where no mooring, no grounding, and no safe harbor exists. We suffer. We cannot make it through such times alone. We must find a relationship, a warm heart, or a vision of hope to guide us through. Still, there are times when no one on earth can make the inevitable horror of our lives go away. We must face it; indeed, we must bury our face in it. We can run but not hide from the pain, the misery, and then the inevitable transformation that comes from it.

No one who lives a life of interiority can escape this humbling human hell.

Alcoholics Anonymous considers humility to be the backbone of recovery. Without it, no alcoholic will be able to stay sober for very long. Most alcoholics in recovery have been bludgeoned enough by life experiences to know humiliation. There are those who awaken with their arms around a toilet bowl following a night of drunken debauchery. The bottom of the world has fallen out and one must pick up the phone to call – to call someone, anyone! Every alcoholic, indeed every human being, must learn that life cannot be lived exclusively by our own individual efforts and achievements.

Egos must be punctured. Only then can humility, like a lotus blossom, surface.

In couple's counseling I often observe egoistic individuals who have developed a false belief that they must be absolutely independent beings, or selves. "I must make something of myself. I must do well. I must win. My worth depends on it!" During a dark night of the soul, we mourn this loss of self-reliance and glorification of our "selves." We suffer. Through a painful process we begin to understand that reconnection to our true ordinary self, as well as to one another, is not a singular event. Reconnecting to ourselves, each other, and God is a life experience. It is ongoing. Any false sense of self, known as a pseudo ego, must be burned up in the hellacious fires of reality.

A realization then occurs that service to self, others, and God are virtually the same because love connects us all.

Love is the message of Susan and Don Cox who created The Christi Center in Austin, Texas, along with their son, Sean. On October 26, 1985, a hit-and-run, drunken driver killed their 23-year-old daughter, Christi, a spirited and beautiful young woman attending the University of Texas in Austin. Susan, Don, and Sean were thrust into their own death spiral, their own dark night of the soul, their own living hell.

Knowing that other grievers, like themselves, needed affordable services and many loving hearts to guide them in their journey, Susan and Don steadfastly created a center that is clearly a national model of community service – designed with grievers in mind. Most of the meetings and programs take place in a renovated house, turned into a warm and nurturing home. Comfy furniture, porch swings, a children's art studio, and many other caring souls welcome weary travelers needing a safe haven to heal. Grievers are welcome to drop in anytime – a God-send for those lost and needing to find a way home.

Yes, there are times when a dark night meets the bright light of hope.

For Susan, Don, and many of us, dark nights are of course undeserved and unbelievable horrors. There are other times, for unknown reasons, that a dark night of the soul experience presents itself. There are many life lessons each of us is here to learn. Perhaps your dark night has arisen to salvage the remainder of your life when living has become bloated with disharmonious habits and you are no longer living consciously or virtuously. Or, perhaps your dark night is an offering by your spirit to meet the challenge of purification and renewal before the end of your life. Whatever the reason, within such a conversion process, a person must muster every ounce of conscious energy needed to accept this deeply painful transformation of ego energy back into meaning, purpose, and service. After all, they are one and the same.

A "dark night" is the humbling experience that unites each of us in our pain.

It is interesting that A.A. never uses the word "sin" in their healing or recovery groups. Instead, A.A. talks of "defects of character" or "shortcomings." Clearly there is recognition that the word sin has become a word of religion, of absolutes. Shortcomings, on the other hand, is a concept that captures the whole of humanity, a notion built upon the idea that each of us is imperfect and is flawed.

We are "Not OK", but that is "OK" in A.A. We all "fall short!" We all are humbled.

The very awareness of "falling short" implies two related realities. First, we are trying, and second, we need to try again. There is no failure here, for spirituality, as the ancients reminded over and over again, involves a continual falling down and getting back up again. That is why humility – the knowledge of our own imperfections – is so important, and that is why spirituality goes on and on and on, a never-ending adventure of coming to know ourselves, seeing ourselves clearly, learning to be at home with ourselves. The great need is for balance – when we are down, we need to get up and when we are up, we need to remember that we have been, and certainly will be again, "down." [4]

Humility is the acceptance of our own imperfections and incompleteness.

Kenosis

When we empty ourselves of pride, all that remains is humility.

There is a well-known Zen story reported by Senzaki, called *A Cup of Tea*, which captures well the role of humility in our everyday lives. When a university professor approaches a Japanese master to inquire about Zen, he is served tea. The master pours the professor's cup full...and then keeps pouring. As the professor watches his cup overflow he is unable to restrain himself after a few moments. "Zen Master, it is overfull. No more will go in!" implores the professor.

"Like this cup," replies the Master, "you are full of your own opinions and speculations. How can I show you Zen unless you first empty your cup?"

Some of us are so full of ourselves there is no room for others or personal growth.

Often it is pride that fills us up. We dash through our living rooms, drift through life, inflating ourselves with thoughts about how beautiful our homes are, how accomplished our children are, how bountiful our 401(k)'s are, and how youthful our appearances are. Some of us may even be self-absorbed with how fast our swim times are!

Pride is always about image – a projected portrait of our "selves."

Kenosis asks only that we empty ourselves of pride and the trappings of ego that we think bring us happiness! Yet we resist emptying ourselves of pride, power, and prestige. We get too attached to our material possessions, our achievements, and our notoriety. We seem to resist the deeper truths of life and are often afraid to embrace our brokenness. Many of us seem afraid to look at the empty space that remains after we clear out the ego trappings of our lives. To be vulnerable somehow means we've failed!

Humility is the process of looking at the emptiness – the missing ten degrees – that remains once we remove the glory and glitter from our lives. In the West we fight against doing so as psychiatrist Mark Epstein point out in his book, *Going to Pieces Without Falling Apart*:

> *In Western theories, the hope is always that emptiness can be healed, that if the character is developed or the trauma resolved that the background feelings will diminish. If we can make the ego stronger, the expectation is that emptiness will go away. In Buddhism, the approach is reversed. Focus on the emptiness, the dissatisfaction, and the feelings of imperfection, and the character will get stronger. Learn how to tolerate nothing and your mind will be at rest…Emptiness is vast and astonishing, the Buddhist approach insists; it does not have to be toxic. When we grasp the emptiness of our false selves, we are touching a little bit of truth. If we relax into that truth, we can discover ourselves in a new way.[5]*

One of the more important truths – and certainly a cornerstone of the First Noble Truth of Buddhism – is that our lives are layered by incompleteness and impermanence. This is known as dukkha (Viparinama). Anything that is not permanent is destined to change, and may be considered dukkha. Since nothing is permanent suffering is inevitable. Even happiness is dukkha, because it is not permanent. Great success fades with the passing of time, friends come and go, children lose their innocence, and the bubble of marital bliss bursts. We suffer. Dukkha is that suffering.

We can run but can't hide from dukkha.

Humility requires the deepest kind of honesty. We open our eyes, we see who we and the world truly are, and then accept it all. Such lucidity is often painful, but this discomfort is borne not out of arrogance and self-righteousness, but of compassion. Humility teaches us to embrace the mysterious brokenness that lives within each of us with the spirit of an open-armed cross of God.

Looking at emptiness, brokenness, or the "missing ten degrees" may seem to be a waste of time in our hurried life styles of the 21st Century. Meditation is often difficult. But much is happening in what appears to be a timeless abyss of emptiness. It is the nature of our universe that transformation is constantly astir – be it the universe within or without. As a 2010 *National Geographic Magazine* on Chile pointed out, "No place on the planet is fully at rest. Only time – unimaginable stretches of time that conceal from human eyes the dynamic natural forces shaping the Earth – creates the illusion of stasis. But sometimes, if you're lucky, you come upon a place where time seems compressed, where you can feel in your bones how kinetic even geology really is."[6]

We must wonder what remains when we remove the scaffolding of our egos.

Recently, a new client was referred to me for depression. Within 10 minutes I learned that he had graduated summa cum laude from a prestigious university, spoke three languages, traveled extensively throughout South America and Europe, and was good looking enough to have his fill of many women he might choose. As I unraveled the early threads of his life, I somehow expected a boastful climax to occur, something of the order, "I'm pretty damn special, and I'm not appreciated as I should be!"

Instead, he identified himself as a depressive and expected me to fall into the predictable pro forma as a therapist: "Let's reframe your heartache and focus on some positive thoughts here!" But something warned me, "Caveat emptor." He had already fired three psychologists, had been resolutely noncompliant regarding any antidepressant medication, and thought self-help books were garbage.

Paradoxically, I agreed with him and jumped on board his depression – suggesting that it might not be a bad idea to spend this period of his life spiraling in a room of doom. I encouraged him to be calm, to look at his situation without judging it, and to spelunker within the mystery of darkness. He became interested in my lack of orthodoxy, and we soon began to explore what it meant to be the root system of a tree – destined to rot and decay in the Earth, versus the branches of the tree – yearning upward with unlimited potential.

This client, Gary, willingly relinquished his hold on a morose depression. This is kenosis. Gary emptied himself of the image which had attracted so much attention within his family and care-giving community. In time he found a "zestful" side of himself that he liked – and was now ready to find love! In Gary's case, unlike the glory or prideful vanity, it was self-loathing or debasement which had to be voluntarily regurgitated. Thus, narcissism can appear not only as glory but as disdain or self-reproach as well.

When we willingly surrender one part of ourselves, life changes!

We must remember that every facet of who we are has a shadow side. This is the nature of dualities which govern our thinking and the memory system of the brain. Our cognitive processes are comprised of polar opposites like [1] warm vs. cold, [2] selfish vs. selfless, [3] honest vs. deceitful, [4] insightful vs. shallow, or [5] proud vs. humble. Just because we claim one end of the continuum over the other doesn't negate the existence of the other pole. Projecting an image of myself as warm, selfless, honest, insightful, and humble doesn't eclipse those times when I feel or actually demonstrate being cold, selfish, deceitful, shallow, or prideful. Remember, we are both/and!

Often, it is love which replaces that which is surrendered. Humility is the honest, heart-rending, gut-spitting, mind-numbing assault we wage upon the bedrock of our very being. Even Mother Teresa was possessed by this inner storm.

For me, the silence and the emptiness is so great, that I look and do not see, listen and do not hear – the tongue moves but does not speak... Such deep longing for God – and ...no zeal. The

saving of Souls holds no attraction – Heaven means nothing… What do I labor for? If there be
not God – there can be no Soul – if there is no Soul then Jesus – you also are not true…I am told
God loves me and yet the reality of darkness and coldness and emptiness is so great nothing touch-
es my soul. Did I make a mistake in surrendering blindly to the Call of the Sacred Heart?[7]

Mother Teresa's journal reveals that a dark night's emptying is often silent.

The origin of the word kenosis actually derives from Philippians 2, a passage in the *New Testament* that acknowledges that Jesus is both God and man, simultaneously both divine and human. Jesus is the self-emptied God. Kenosis reveals Jesus emptying himself of the Divine so that he can be in relationship to the world. While Jesus possessed the very nature of God within himself as the divine, he took on the form and the nature of a servant. Jesus is thus seen as one person with two natures – just like us! It is the relationship of dual natures that becomes important.

We must reconcile both ends of every aspect of who we are – not just one!

As marriage partners know, tension always exists when two seemingly irresolvable polarities come together. It is one thing for God to voluntarily choose to limit Himself in becoming human, but quite another to reconcile how we as "average" humans can honor both the divine and our most human natures at once – all in one lifetime. This is a paradox that has challenged the most insightful thinkers of our time such as Soren Kierkegaard who believed that this tension of opposites is our core human paradox:

> *The Tree of Knowledge symbolized that man is a union of opposites. He is self-conscious within a physical body, the only animal capable of reflecting on his condition. Transcendent over nature like the branches of a tree, he is yet rooted in the earth, destined to return thence. Man's fall into self-consciousness brings him fear and trembling…The contradiction and anxiety are so intense that human beings overemphasize the either/or of living, and either commit themselves to the transcendent, the imaginative and the ideal, listening to the promise of the serpent…or they become obsessed with the finite, the corporeal and the real.*[8]

Kenosis embraces the whole of who we are as human beings. All dualities perpetrated by the ego are being dissolved, disintegrated, and reintegrated during this most painful emptying process. In a sense kenosis is not an actual loss of anything! When we abandon the projected images we have created to enhance ourselves we find acceptance. Out of this lonely struggle deep within us begins to flow the wisdom of living purely for virtue's sake, free of our pretentious self, our ego's distortion that everything you do must be rewarded. Eventually, our fears subside, feelings of alienation subside, and a fear of rejection by the world subsides.

We are no longer between two worlds but start to come home.

Managing two worlds within ourselves is our life work as Socrates has described in a piece entitled, Steer the Chariot of Your Soul. Socrates, a renowned storyteller among the Athenians, depicts our lifelong struggle for emotional and spiritual harmony though a powerful image: a charioteer challenged to control two mighty steeds – a universal duality: "Of the nature of the soul, let me speak briefly, and in a metaphor: a pair of winged horses and a charioteer," he says in *The Republic*.

One of the horses is noble, and the other is ignoble, and driving them is immensely difficult.

The right-hand horse is upright and cleanly made – he is a lover of honor and modesty and temperance; he needs no touch of the whip, but is guided by word only.

The other is a crooked lumbering animal; he is insolent and proud, shag-eared and deaf, hardly yielding to whip and spur.

This vicious steed goes heavily, weighing down the charioteer to the earth because he has not been thoroughly trained: this is the hour of agony and extremest conflict for the soul.

The charioteer must drag the bit out of the teeth of the wild steed, force his legs to the ground, and punish him sorely. When this has happened several times, and the horse has ceased from his wanton way, he is tamed and humbled, and follows the will of the charioteer.[9]

We, too, must become adept at the task of the charioteer in his great metaphor. Each of us must learn to balance the hunger of our unrelenting, self-absorbed, prideful endeavors on the hand with the upright, modest temperance of humility on the other. Unrestrained, the former can lead to an uncompromising narcissism that can bring us to grief despite rational intelligence. These forces, when understood and managed (not merely ignored or stifled), can become the wellspring for motivation and passion in life. Sit quietly, and consider the following as you cultivate your humility.[10]

* I realize that there are times I am not humble.
* I make mistakes and go beyond my limits.
* I accept success with grace.
* I avoid boasting about accomplishments.
* I avoid taking too much responsibility for success.
* I attempt to be well-grounded, approachable, and down-to-earth.
* When timid, I maintain assertiveness.
* I give my best effort even on seemingly small or menial tasks.
* I acknowledge strengths in others.
* I avoid blaming others.
* I ask for advice when needed.
* I am open to others' ideas.
* I give credit where credit is due.
* I share honors and recognition with collaborators.
* I engage in community service.
* I appreciate the beauty in each person and of the natural world.

CHAPTER 16

The Gift of Forgiveness

Rabbi Elimeleck of Lizensk was asked by a disciple how one should pray for forgiveness. He told him to observe the behavior of a certain innkeeper before Yom Kippur. The disciple took lodging at the inn and observed the proprietor for several days, but could see nothing relevant to his quest. Then, on the night before Yom Kippur, he saw the innkeeper open two large ledgers. From the first book he read off a list of all the sins he had committed throughout the

past year. When he was finished, he opened the second book and proceeded to recite all the
bad things that had occurred to him during the past year. When he had finished reading both
books, he lifted his eyes to heaven, and said, "Dear G-d, it is true I have sinned against You.
But You have done many distressful things to me too. "However, we are now beginning a new
year. Let us wipe the slate clean. I will forgive You, and You forgive me. "[1]

While this forgiveness story of Rabbi Elimeleck appears to be one of arrogance – assuming he is on the same level with God – it more genuinely reflects the sometimes humorous dialogue with God that many Jews treasure. Yom Kippur, more than any other Jewish holiday, invites Jews to forgive themselves, one another, and even God. With humility, we release ourselves from pride. With forgiveness, we release others from the death grip of resentment. In both cases – humility and forgiveness – the past no longer reigns supreme. With the former, we relinquish an inflated view of ourselves. With the latter, we relinquish a deflated view of another. By doing so, we are now free to live more fully in the present.

Over the years I have noticed a resentment paradox. At first glance, resentment is about someone else's shortcomings and faults. Somehow, an imperfect other has failed us, neglected us, hurt us, or angered us. They are "Not OK!" We then choose to hold this "other" captive so that we may regale our woundedness as scar tissue worn thin by repeated lashings. The Greek Titan, Prometheus, was chained to a mountain and tortured by Zeus for giving fire to mankind. Like Zeus, we chain others to their imperfections so that we are free of our own. Pause for moment, however, and look at yourself!

Resentment, more accurately, is self-absorption.

Resentments are the obsessive whirlpools of thoughts which circulate in our heads like eddies in the room of doom. We are stuck revisiting our hurts, recalling broken agreements, and re-gurgitating old injuries. Round and round we go, experiencing and re-experiencing the pain of being wronged. Often, we disdainfully rip the scab off healing wounds in order to stay stuck in the swirling array of human frailties that lie before us.

We get mesmerized by our self-absorbed reflection in the pond: "self-as-victim."

Resentments can become a lethal arsenal of anger, hatred, and disdain that ignites instantly whenever a problem arises between partners, family members, friends, and colleagues. Anger – and the resentment that underlies it – blocks the flow of caring, inhibits resolution of problems, denies the possibility of mature love, and can damage physical health and well-being. It is also impossible to recognize the fullness of our own lives when we are angry and resentful toward others. In AA, *The Big Book* is on target when it asserts that "Resentment is the 'number one' offender. From resentment stems all forms of spiritual disease!"[2]

Taking on resentment is no easy task. Who among us has not carried the boulder of resentment after we have been hurt, deceived, or abandoned in some way? This was understandably true for Patsy from the previous chapter. As you recall, her unfaithful husband Victor had deceived her – leaving Patsy awash in a sea of despair. Once Victor was able to express the *Gift* of humility, Patsy was slowly able to offer the *Gift* of forgiveness in her letter below:

Forgiveness is much more than a single, spontaneous act that takes place in a moment. It is a series of minute, incremental choices. The choice to hold a hand when crossing one's arms in anger would be easier. The choice to hold one's tongue when lashing out would be more deeply satisfying. The choice to kiss when thinking of all the places the other's lips have been. Those are the "easier" choices, often within reach. Where the going gets rough is as follows: The choice to feel compassion for human failings versus pointing fingers at evildoing. The choice to imagine fully trusting again: both trusting you and trusting my own intuition. The choice to forgive myself for being naïve, for not being strong enough to take bolder action earlier. The choice to forgive you for deceiving yourself regarding your lack of ethics or responsible behavior.

Each choice, small or large, is like a raindrop. At first the rain barely wets the pavement, and the sun might dry it out. But if enough drops fall, eventually a small pool will form. Slowly, slowly, forgiveness will accumulate. There will be periods of drought, of doubt. But with nurture, someday forgiveness can be complete.

"Someday" seems very far from today, but I know I must carry on even in the valley of the shadow of doubt. That's where I am now. There is a mountain of hurt. Maybe I'm too busy counting the rocks. But I'm so bruised – I've been flung down a landslide of rocks, I physically ache. Someday I hope I can wake up and notice that the mountain is off in the distance. I think there will always be a view of the mountains for me. But hopefully in the foreground there will be a garden that you and I have labored hard for and then nurtured together.

Patsy fought hard to reconcile two images of Victor: one as her college sweetheart, a second as a monster who was able to break her heart. Her "forgiveness" letter reveals her struggle to forgive. She does not begin her letter with his name; nor does she end her letter with her name in love. Still seeing herself as a victim she had great difficulty believing, let alone affirming, many of the elements of *forgiveness.*

* Believing the transgressor has taken responsibility for the pain created.
* Believing the transgressor feels genuine remorse/regret over his/her actions.
* Believing the transgressor has learned from his/her mistakes – the fall.
* Believing the transgressor will be mindful of his/her actions from this day forward – pausing to consider the impact of all behaviors on others.
* Believing the transgressor gave the gift of time needed to heal and rebuild trust.
* Believing that one is truly special again.
* Affirming one's willingness to leave the past behind so that a renewed love might take root.

Over time Patsy began to see herself much less as a victim and much more as a soulful traveler on a heroic journey. She learned to trust once again with Victor's help. For each of us, the vision of our self-as-victim is the antithesis of spirituality for authors Ernest Kurtz and Katherine Ketchum: "Spirituality begins with the recognition of our own imperfection. Focusing on the past faults and failings of others blinds us to the reality of our own present defects and shortcomings….The anger that metamorphoses into resentment isolates us, creating the illusion that the world has stopped in its tracks and has come to focus entirely upon our hurts, *our* desires, *our* victimhood. In resentment there is no chance of release but only imprisonment in a painful past and the gradual stifling of all serenity, indeed, of all humanity." (3)

Patsy struggled with forgiveness because Victor struggled with humility. There was a time in therapy – too painfully long for Patsy – when Victor vigorously defended himself, believing that deeper problems embedded in their marriage would somehow justify his infidelity and chronic acting out. This "self-justification" or rationalization on his part made forgiveness next to impossible. Oftentimes, the transgressor believes his/her actions were justified because of unresolved disenchantment embedded within the relationship. Forgiveness from the hurt partner, Patsy, cannot occur until the transgressor, Victor, becomes vulnerable. Once Victor was able (1) to look inward to see his own imperfections, (2) to look outward to see the pain he had created, and (3) to loudly proclaim his love for Patsy once again was she able to forgive and move on.

Resentments, as you might have already gleaned, are not feelings – yet another paradox! While the word resentment derives from the French "re + sentire" meaning literally to feel again, resentments are not feelings. They are memories! We are blessed with a cerebral cortex that allows us to recall memories of all the situations which have occurred that have formed the themes we believe to be true of other people's character. Actually some folks have an uncanny ability to recall incredible detail from their past memories – as if they are accessing a computer file:

❋ On October 12th you said you would go to Lubbock with me to visit my brother and then blew me off at the last minute.
❋ On Christmas Day, 2002, you promised you would spend the entire day with your family and instead hit golf balls for 30 minutes.
❋ On February 14th, Valentine's Day 1943, you fell asleep as we were making love!

And then it happens again. They hurt us again! We experience a gush of feelings. Our muscles tense, our pupils dilate, our blood vessels constrict. We spew out an angry litany of charges against them that makes a cross examination by F. Lee Bailey or Johnny Cochran pale in comparison. Of course, the recipient doesn't know what to respond to, since they are being deluged with indictments against them that date back to the signing of the Magna Carta. In our anger, we are frankly aggressive as we verbally – and perhaps physically – strike out against our "enemies."

Barbara and Ken were such a couple. I had been working with them for over six months. During this period we wrestled with the dark demons that had propelled them into counseling initially as we explored their families of origin, which influenced so much of their interactions as a couple. I thought that things were going well when I asked both of them how their week had gone.

Ken believed they had had a spectacular week. "I found myself adoring Barbara publicly and privately. We were able to attend an extraordinary Billy Joel fundraising event and, if I do say so myself, I marveled at how beautiful Barbara looked that night. She was the most gorgeous woman there by far. Our nights have been toasty, and the hot tub filled with warmth and tender hugs."

Barbara's story was completely different. "I've been depressed as hell!" Barbara chimed in. "How could you not even notice my mood? Furthermore, how could you lie to me again?"

"Well, you've obviously hidden it well! What on earth could have upset you this week?" bemoaned Ken.

"It's just more of the same old crap regarding trust. You talked to your ex-wife without telling me ahead of time. You had agreed to tell me whenever you were going to talk to her. And as far as our table at the Billy Joel concert, it wasn't anything close to what I expected. You had really built up the idea that we would be at table two or three – perhaps close enough to see him dribble his food before he performed. We were so far away from him that I even felt self-conscious sneaking close with my point and shoot camera. To be honest, I felt like a second class citizen there!"

"Well, Barbara, if you felt that let down about being at the gala – even though we had special international entertainers at our table – there must be something going on here that I'm missing. As for my ex-wife, she had a relationship with my mother who is dying from cancer, and all I did was email her about the situation so that she could contact her – if she wanted too! What blows my mind is that I literally told you about it 10 minutes after I sent it. What am I missing here? Doesn't my ex have the right to know that her ex-mother-in-law is dying? For heaven's sake, what am I missing here?"

Six Critical Tasks

Ken was mystified, not about himself, but about Barbara.

He had not missed an earlier focus on him in therapy which revealed an excessive sexual hunger – some would say an addiction. He was not a resistant client. He honestly owned up to a sexual freedom, a "passion to respond to life", which had eroded trust in two previous marriages. Forces deep within him had cultivated a sexual appetite much greater than one person could handle. A gift of gab, a charismatic charm, and a compromising belief that he could have any woman released a sexual frenzy which lasted decades. He had pulled Barbara, his third wife, into countless sexual adventures with him. While he focused on sensual seductions, sexual arousal, and other aberrant adventures, Ken somehow missed Barbara's history of sexual and emotional abuse. While he was busy trying to keep sex on a physical level, he failed to realize that it inevitably stirred up a plethora of emotions.

In many ways Ken knew he was in rebellion. No circle of love would contain him. He had long escaped from a cascade of expectations that were put upon him in his youth. "Be an example." "Be everything to everyone." "Be a gifted artist and writer." "Be a community and religious leader." "Be an Eagle Scout." "Be on a pedestal!" BE SELF-ABSORBED!! In her song, *Building a Mystery*, Sarah McLachlin sings "Be a beautiful fucked up man; you're setting up your Razor wire shrine." Rebellion from all constraints became his raison d'etre.[4]

Eventually, this mixture of trauma, tears, and titillation would blend into a frothy sea of pain that Bacchus himself wouldn't be able to swallow. Bacchanalia, or Roman orgies, were infamous celebrations that also got out of hand because of their alcohol-induced sexual extremes. They were introduced in Rome around 200 BCE to honor the Greek god Dionysus. Ironically, after only 14 years, they were forbidden by the Roman senate in 186 BCE. Paraphrasing Clint Eastwood, "Every man must know his limitations."

Being pulled into one tryst after another was demeaning enough for Barbara. But the shit didn't hit the fan until she discovered that Ken had had two flings outside their own tacit agreements and commitment to one another. This was the last straw for her. With an endless stream of tears, each one overflowing from years of being discounted and abandoned, she threatened to leave Ken if he didn't commit to therapy.

Ken eventually became part of the solution once he understood his part in the problem. He labored hard to win back the trust he had shattered over the preceding years. He and Barbara read and reread Dr. Janis Abrahms Spring's wonderful book, *How Can I Forgive You?*[5] He committed to all six critical tasks for earning forgiveness:

Critical Task One: Look at your mistaken assumptions about forgiveness and try to understand how these assumptions block your efforts to earn it. *[Ken had lived so much of his life believing he was a king he feared appearing to be weak if he admitted any wrongdoing. What he discovered was that he didn't relinquish any power by acknowledging that he was "Not OK," but rather gave Barbara back the power he had taken from her over the years.]*

Critical Task Two: Bear witness to the hurt and pain you have created. *[Ken preferred to be a celebrant of life, usually choosing harmony over conflict, hyperbole over facts. Barbara's periodic rages overwhelmed him to a point where he preferred her numbness and muffled pain over her stormy cloudbursts. They had little of the problem-solving intimacy that I described in Chapter Ten. Eventually he learned that a couple cannot move "on" until they move "in." He discovered that no one can let go of pain without feeling it and sharing it.]*

Critical Task Three: Apologize genuinely. *[Ken needed to meet three criteria for apologies described by Dr. Spring: first, take responsibility for his actions; second, care deeply about the pain he created; and third, declare his intention never to repeat the transgression. As Ken took responsibility for each and every improper act he committed, he realized that he himself was not inherently evil – only his actions were. By sharing all of himself within the circle of Barbara's embrace, he was free to be more of the imperfect, inconsistent, and "Not OK" fellow Barbara truly loved.]*

Critical Task Four: Commit to a deeper understanding of your behavior and r e - veal the inglorious truth about yourself to the person you have hurt. *[Ken needed to take himself off the pedestal of being a messiah, a prophet, a king, and a Romeo. His misguided rationale that he was "merely responding to the energy in the universe" needed to be exchanged for a more accurate belief that he, and the inflated bubble in lived within, were creating negative energy in the universe with every discarded soul. He could be both "damaged goods" and "enlightened spirit" concurrently. Both/and are possible.]*

Critical Task Five: Work to earn trust back. *[Ken committed to both low- and high-cost trust-building behaviors, outlined in much of the work of Abrahms Spring. These behaviors are best viewed as visible acts of atonement which remind the hurt partner that you are serious about your vow never to repeat the transgression. For Ken, they included changing his cell phone number, deleting all data storage of names, addresses, and phone numbers relating to his coterie of playmates and agreeing to let Barbara know whenever he heard from anyone reminiscent of their shared inglorious past.]*

Critical Task Six: Forgive yourself for hurting another person. *[Ken embraced the notion of being "perfectly imperfect." Having done his work on forgiveness, he knew that Barbara was Not OK, he was Not OK, yet both of them were OK! In his words, "I just want to say thanks to my teachers, to my preachers, and even to the streakers, who, despite the short time given, have driven me again, just a little closer to all that I am and am not!"]*

Ken, as a poet, offered the following piece to Barbara as part of his work to earn her trust back as well as find the integrity and self-acceptance he longed for in his own life. The piece is en-titled, "To My Barbara Again:"

My work on me must
Through you
Be done, on earth as it was
In Heaven done,
Your vessel perfect chosen, shattered,
Pieces stolen, broken, scattered and thrown to the floor.

Rock, Paper, and Scissors

There is a layered reality in life.

On the surface everything seems so clear to us. Beneath the obvious lurks deeper truths which must be understood. This is certainly true of anger. I have often said to people that 90 percent of anger has nothing to do with the precipitating event which triggered it. If this is even remotely accurate, where does 90 percent of anger come from?

Resentments! More pain comes from inside rather than outside our heads.

There was no doubt that Ken provided many good reasons for Barbara to be angry, fearful, and sad. But the resentments were Barbara's to carry. Resentments for her were the fuel and the electrical charge within the storm cloud which generate the burst of energy she felt as anger. Resentments, like clouds themselves, become her capacitors for positive and negative ions to clash and usher forth the lightning bolts of disdain and disenchantment.

Most people only see the anger expressed. They don't see what lies beneath the anger, and that is usually fear and sadness. This was certainly true of Barbara as will be shown a bit further on in this chapter. First, we must understand how these three emotions are layered upon one another. Kurtz and Ketcham suggest that *anger, fear,* and *sadness* are connected to one another in a closed circle paradigm very similar to a favorite childhood game, "rock-paper-scissors."

> *In the absence of resentment, anger, fear and sadness tend to heal each other. Anger can act like a scissors, cutting through fear – the fear that like an enveloping shroud wraps itself around and threatens to smother the rock that is sadness. But that very sadness, which rises from the realization of our own transience and the ultimate futility of our human efforts to control, is the only tool we have to blunt anger....Anger and sadness butt against each other, steel against stone. But just as scissors "take" paper, and rock "takes" scissors, sadness will finally take anger – if we let the sadness through. For sadness, shared, can heal.... Denying fear and scorning the sadness that is shared, resentment refuses the possibility of going through and beyond anger into forgiveness....The danger of anger...lies not in anger itself, but in resentment, the clinging to and prolonged attachment to anger. Resentment is the refusal, out of fear, to cross the bridge of sadness and let ourselves back into the impermanent world of relationship. Anger as resentment refuses relationship, slashing at everything and everyone that comes close. But our pain can be healed only by some kind of closeness, some kind of connection with others. Sadness opens us to the need for unity and community.[6]*

With anger we act; with fear we hide; and with sadness we interact.

My goal with Ken was to help him let go of his pedestal of pride while my goal with Barbara was to help her release her resentments so that she might then forgive. I knew that excavating down to the sadness for both of them would be the key. This is where their true intimacy would be experienced – an inner world set free with their tears.

There is an oceanic difference between seeking forgiveness from another and offering up an apology. There is a universal requirement for forgiveness: contrition. To be contrite, Ken learned one must be grieving and penitent regarding shortcomings and imperfections. Furthermore, one must share this grief openly and directly with the person(s) who has been impacted. When we ask for forgiveness we are opening up a dialogue with those who have been hurt the most. We transact. True forgiveness always involves a dialogue, and it is within this dialogue that healing occurs. Imperfection abounds and intimacy awaits those who find it:

Ring the bells that still can ring.
Forget your perfect offering.
There is a crack in everything.
That's how the light gets in.[7]

The key for Barbara was to get below her anger, and go inward, where her fears and sadness resided. Like Leonard Cohen, in the above verse from *Anthem*, Barbara needed to forget her "perfect offerings" – finding instead the hollow that remains. Barbara's conscious self-absorption was wrapped around her fear of abandonment. Whenever Ken seemed too attendant to others, too devoted to his clients, or too doting with any warm-hearted friend – male or female – she ricocheted away from him as if he were a hardened criminal. Admittedly, she knew that this intentional distancing sank her deeper into the room of doom where she had dwelled 15 years before when she was severely depressed.

This dark haven was actually a kind of safe place – a chamber of self-loathing she knew all too well from childhood. Growing up, Barbara's mother was abusive, both physically and emotionally. She was beaten often with a hairbrush, pinched until she bled, and told she would be thrown out of the house where the police would be waiting for her. She described her mother as a prescription junkie, controlling, volatile, and just plain mean. Barbara was repeatedly told she was not good enough as one chore after another was heaped upon her. There seemed to be no escape for Barbara, whose spirit was shattered by an unrelenting onslaught of criticisms.

Amidst the ashen trauma of her childhood was yet a deeper pain which Barbara needed to face: the absence of her father. There was no paternal phalanx protecting her from a delirious mother. Her father was aloof, egotistical, and MIA. When he was available, he further stripped her of her dignity by calling her a "slut" or a "fat horse." He once pushed her out of the way so that he could see the TV better! No comfort station, no warmth, nor solace would be found with this man. She truly was on her own, neither seen nor wanted as a being in her own right. Barbara found her sadness as she told her story. She softened. Ken held her and cried with her as she unraveled the painful odyssey. And, there was more misery lurking in the underbelly of her dreary past. Not until she shared her guilt about an abortion 12 years before was Barbara able to wrap her arms around her own self-doubts, her own imperfect journey, and her own need for self-acceptance and forgiveness.

Ken knew that Barbara hated to be angry while she still clung to anger – almost as if it defined her. It was this self-image which needed to shatter even as she clung to it. Understanding dualities, Ken knew that a dark side called to Barbara. But he also knew that "Barbara is for real, inside, a wonderfully sensitive, kind, warm, trusting, loving human being…extremely intelligent and talented…wanting more than anything to dance and sing and be free of all that she is not." It was this image of Barbara that awakened his muse:

...Something hard said long ago
Pushed down deep that sparkling soul,
Sweet innocence was lost,
A little girl's dance, the final cost.

...Something sad done long ago,
Sank her spirit, oh God, so low,
Stopped that precious voice's song,
What can be done to right the wrong?

...That something dark from yesterday,
Through LOVE is blown away!
Forever now, that something's gone,
The little girl has found her song!

Would you look now!
God, can this Woman dance?!
Can this Woman sing?!
This Woman now plays
In strength, in power, every day!

Ken found the inherent good in Barbara. The inherent good exists in everything and reflects the worth and value that is inborn. No achievement is needed to demonstrate its presence. Inherent good is our birthright and no one can take it away. For Barbara it was her sparkling soul, her sweet innocence, her strength and power.

Renewal [Re-New-All]
At the core of resentment lies sadness.
At the core of forgiveness lies empathy.

Sadness is layered beneath both fear and anger. Most people block any attempt to feel this deep layer of pain because peering deep into our sadness is like opening an empty box at Christmas. It hurts. It hurts a lot. Something precious is missing. There is a "missing ten degrees." We can't experience the fullness of the 350 degrees of the circle; we are distracted by the missing ten degrees.

For some of us the missing ten degrees is the love we never received, the financial security we never possessed, or the children we were never able to conceive. For others, the missing ten degrees is the career success we were never able to attain, the stature above others we were unable to claim, or the home we were unable to obtain. These are serious, vacuous gaps which may preoccupy the forlorned for years and years. Yet, amidst desperate groping and angry protesting, the missing piece may actually be the sadness which lurks far below.

In this sadness there is visceral recognition that our time is limited on Earth.

Everything we see and know is transient, including our "selves." We hunger for a full life without the full reflection of what we truly need. As George Carlin reminds us, "We spend more but have less. We buy more but enjoy less. We have bigger houses and smaller families; more conveniences, but less time. We've been all the way to the moon and back, but have trouble crossing the street to meet a new neighbor."[8] We get lost! Each of us gets lost with time running out. And as we try to find our way home, we often find that sadness is the key to getting home safely in the time we have left. Sadness is the best compass we will ever have for finding our way home. Often what we discover is surprising.

The only thing of value that we take with us is what we leave behind.

And what we leave behind are the relationships we have had on earth. Yes, there is a sadness that these relationships must end one day. Yes, there is a sadness that love must end, often before it really began. Yes, there is sadness that even the fullest vessel of love was unable to fill a thirsty void within. And yes, there is sadness in looking at the cratered landscape which marks each and every one of our lives.

But what are we so afraid of? Father Henri Nouwen reminds us again:

God, I am so afraid to open my clenched fists;
Who will I be when I have nothing else to hold onto?
Who will I be when I stand before you with empty hands?
Help me to gradually open my hands and discover that I am not what I
*   own, but what you want to give me;*
And what you want to give me is love, unconditional, everlasting love.
And what am I holding in my clenched fists?
I don't know where you're leading me.
I don't know what the next day, week, or year will look like.
But as I try to keep my hands open, I trust that you will put your hand in
*   mine and bring me home.*[9]

Now, try reading this using a loved one's name instead of the name of God. Try to think of a loved one who has hurt you or wounded you. What do you notice when you do this? At first glance you will notice that the clenched fists often represent your anger, fueled by your resentments. A deeper probe, however, will reveal that it is fear which you cling to – the fear of not knowing if you're loved, the fear of rejection, or the fear of being abandoned in an infinite cosmic space where you truly are alone. For some, there is even the dark fear of never believing that one is truly welcomed in human existence. These are very real fears!

But what are we really holding in our clenched fists?

Perhaps it is our deep primal need to be the Beloved! Our balled up, tense, constricted, clenched fists symbolize our protest about not being blessed. We become too self-absorbed to see beyond ourselves. We refuse to see other possibilities, other perspectives, other feelings, and other people. Our clenched fists represent the whirling debris of our inner lives. The room of doom is the same stuck place symbolized by clenched fists. We spiral deeper and deeper into our anger or our fears. There seems to be no way out. But there is, if we choose to keep our hands open.

Relationships are the way out – just as they were the way in.

Each of us, deep down, wants to be seen as blessed, as special, as loved unconditionally. If you recall from Chapter Ten, Henri Nouwen believes that the voice calling us the Beloved is the voice of our first love – a love that existed before we came in touch with a mother or a father. For Henri Nouwen this voice is the voice of God calling to us, telling us unconditionally, that we are valued, cherished, and loved. Isn't this what we all want: truly to be OK in the eyes of another?

The need to be cherished is the deepest spiritual calling that exists within a love relationship.

Each of us enters into a love relationship with this unconscious hope that the ultimate communion will occur on earth. For many, communion is a holy word, representing our connection with God, with Christ. For me, communion embraces our search for connection with all that is holy – be it nature, people, or life itself. Let us remember that the word communion literally means "union with." Union is our salve for loneliness, isolation, and fear. Con means with, connected to, or bonded to.

This is our human calling: to be bonded to other people.

We want to be loved – bonded – fully, completely, and unconditionally with an "other." In the words of John Donne, "No man is an island." Yet these relationships are destined to fail us for two reasons: first, because they are human relationships and therefore imperfect; second, every human relationship is built upon a foundation that is conditional, rather than unconditional.

Isn't it true for Ken and Barbara, for you and me, that each person we love the most also hurts us the most? Isn't it true that our friends, our lovers, our colleagues, or our loved ones create our deepest pain? Isn't it true that enemies and strangers, both near and far, are not the persons who are likely to hurt us the most? We respond only to those we have let inside our circle of love. It is these significant others who are positioned to honor communion or break our hearts. More accurately, it is these significant others who are destined to break our hearts because they love us humanly – imperfectly and inadequately. This was true for Ken and Barbara, and it is true for you and me. While I would like my wife Claire to love me perfectly, she can only do so imperfectly, as can I!

So what do we do with all of this? We take a giant step for humanity.

It is the greatest step a human being can take. It is the step of forgiveness. Forgiveness is the name of love practiced among people who love poorly. The hard truth is that all of us love poorly. We do not even know what we are doing when we hurt others. We need to forgive

and be forgiven every day, every hour — unceasingly. That is the great work of love among
the fellowship of the weak that is the human family. The voice that calls us the Beloved is
the voice of freedom because it sets us free to love without wanting anything in return.[10]

At the core of forgiveness lies empathy. Our capacity for empathy reflects our ability to gently lift ourselves out of our own self-absorption long enough to really understand the feelings of another human being. Therapists would say that this capacity to understand is intended to grasp the experience of someone else from their personal frame of reference: in other words, we try to put ourselves in their shoes.

Each of us loves poorly and conditionally, and most of us do not suffer fools gladly.

Empathy allows us to let go of our self-absorbed reverie of self-as-victim and recognize that imperfection drives human behavior and all human behavior is destined to be imperfect. People in glass houses should not throw stones. Let he who is without sin cast the first stone. While the teachings of Jesus can guide us here, we need only to look inside our pain to recognize that we have been forgiven many times by others — often not knowing until years later.

This is the key. If others have forgiven us because we were worthy enough in spite of our misdeeds or imperfections, should we not be able to extend the same to others? This is empathy. This is our capacity as human beings to re-new-all! We have a responsibility to do so in our most cherished relationships — which means we have the ability-to-respond. Kurtz and Ketcham help us again here:

> *How can we expect anyone else to be perfect if we ourselves are imperfect? Within that*
> *understanding comes the profound realization that we have been forgiven for our own*
> *imperfections. And then there follows, in time, a second and equally profound internal*
> *transformation; we understand that we have already forgiven others....We are forgiven*
> *only if we are open to forgiving, but we are able to forgive only in being forgiven — we get*
> *only by giving, and we give only by getting.*[11]

Ken and Barbara found their way back to each other. Understanding her own imperfection allowed Barbara to give Ken a gift which brought tears to his eyes. Being an artist, she was able to draw a woman kissing a man's forehead. Just behind them, piercing the sacred space between, beamed a radiant light which symbolized their own transformation as individuals as well as a couple. In return, Ken wrote one final poem:

Forgiveness

"For to Give." To give up. To give in.
To "Forge" with the "Given."
The dancing light with us all,
Driven,
Shimmers out all shadow,
Takes us by our hands
And pirouettes us cleanly cut from dark and weighty fears,
Steering us to freedoms reaches,
Searing us with music, the singing of the spheres.
And here,
Forgiveness,
The Goddess of the Given,
Frees us all, every wrong thing!
And soaring above and beyond it all,
We find the song of peace.
"For to Give." To give up. To give in,
We "Forge" with the "Given."
Barbara, you are my forgiving light within.

CHAPTER **17**

The Gift of Acceptance

We live in an insane state, between two opposing realities – one ideal, the other real. Our true madness is that we reject our real self and choose instead to embrace an ideal self. We accept what's unreal and unattainable, while rejecting what's real and readily available.
– Larry Bugen, counseling note

Acceptance requires the willing and total embrace of one's life.

Accepting one's life is not easy if we just mirror society's incessant cry to crave more, be more, and believe we deserve more. Acceptance requires a journey inward to the humble center of our beings where we courageously face our fear of "not being enough." We are enough and must let go of some perfect ideal. To go on such a journey, we must [1] **let go** – of magic! We must let go of the belief that we can control or "attract" whatever we want, whenever we want it. We must let go of finding *The Secret*:

> *The earth turns on its orbit for You. The oceans ebb and flow for You. The birds sing for You. The sun rises and it sets for You. The stars come out for You. Every beautiful thing you see, every wondrous thing you experience, is all there for You. Take a look around. None of it can exist, without You. No matter who you thought you were, now you know the Truth of Who You Really Are. You are the master of the Universe. You are the heir to the kingdom. You are the perfection of Life. If you want something, just imagine it – it's yours! And now you know The Secret.*

It's one thing to change a negative attitude; it's quite another to change reality.

We are not the master of the Universe. If you believe that the stars come out just for you, keep reading! I do believe that if people take responsibility for their intentions and their actions they are more likely to achieve their goals – with a lot of help from unintended sources. Success in life takes shared sacrifice and hard work. Sustaining love relationships takes hard work. Even personal transformation requires hard work, not to mention necessary pain and suffering. The real "secret" to life is knowing that anything worth holding onto requires blood, sweat and tears. Unfortunately, narcissistic people usually expect the world to simply come to them.

Surely if we materialistic people could live more simply others might be more able to simply live.

Accepting one's life is not easy. To do so, we must [2] **go with the flow** – often holding onto the debris which floats along with us! We must be able to embrace the good people and good things in life that we take for granted each and every day. We must also be able to embrace the bland, the bad, and unfortunate things we face as well. There are times when we don't get what we deserve; but, there are other times, we get far more than we deserve! Open your tightened fists to both. Life is not a shopping mall where we select what we want and freely exit down the escalator. Songwriter Don Henley captures this spirit of receiving quite well in his exquisite lyrics of acceptance, *For My Wedding*:

> *To want what I have,*
> *To take what I'm given, with grace;*
> *For this I pray,*
> *On my wedding day.[2]*

The bliss of wedding days innocently shelters us from the storms that lie ahead. This was true for two of my clients, Will and Grace, who struggled to rekindle the spark in their relationship after the discovery of a painful breach in fidelity on Will's part. For many months, desolate from her pain and shattered dreams, Grace wondered whether her marriage could be saved. In this chapter Grace sheds light on her *Gift* of "acceptance," offered to Will once enough tearful, healing work had been completed. The following chapter, on the *Gift* of "compassion," will present Will's parallel letter to Grace:

> *Another anniversary…this one marks a very different year for us. One I am very sure neither of us ever expected to endure. And yet, endure we did. Nurturing, working, hoping, crying, fighting, learning, growing, changing, and even loving! It's been quite a ride. Oh, that this "cup" could have passed us by and we could have learned our lessons in another way. But it did not and I have come to accept that. I think of how often Rosemarie, our friend, has said, "It is what it is." Such true words! For so long I saw you, me and our marriage in a very different way. I thought we were somehow exempt from the drama and hurt we saw in others. But now I can accept that these imperfections exist very much in our marriage. And that acceptance is good. It's much more real. I have thought about this writing since Tuesday – wondering exactly what to say. Wondering if acceptance is the same as resignation? I think not!*

> *Acceptance of what we have been through and continue to work through is active, unlike resignation. Although we have both "accepted" the responsibility for the problems in our marriage, I feel sure that the finger-pointing still lies within each of us. So much has been put on the table for us both to digest and learn from. To accept these revelations is the thing that will help us moving forward.*

> *I know it is hard for you to understand or accept that I need you to have a different wedding ring. But it is symbolic to me of a new marriage. What I **won't** allow myself to accept is the marriage we had. By accepting what we have learned and keeping true to what a real marriage partnership can be, we can have the love we both want in our marriage. As we look ahead – the memories will be tough – yet I appreciate how willing you are to listen, to understand, to hold, and to cherish all that we may be.*

The capacity to embrace one's source of pain is one of humankind's greatest triumphs.

Grace was able to express many of the core elements of *acceptance* in her letter:

 ✳ Affirm that life is best lived *not* being governed by "I deserve" beliefs.
 ✳ Affirm that there is "good," "bad," and "ugly" in all relationships.
 ✳ Be able to distinguish active "acceptance" from passive "resignation."
 ✳ Cultivate the wisdom that imperfection and heartbreak reveal deeper truths.

* Express gratitude for something real, something solid, within the relationship.

* Commit to living forward in what can be – letting go of what should have been.

Accepting one's life is not easy. To do so, we must [3] **see the light** – to discover what truly matters most in our lives! We continue to be blinded by the missing 10 degrees – what's missing in our lives! That's all we see. In our circle of living, the fullness of 350 degrees is often overshadowed by a lurking omnipresent arc of yearning. Regrettably we try to fill this emptiness with instant gratification, Gucci handbags and stints on *Dancing with the Stars*. We become intoxicated by the lifestyle of celebrities, instead of treasuring the life we've been given. The siren's call becomes our beck and call. Stop! Look! Listen! Again, Don Henley guides us in *Learn to Be Still*.

> *Learn to be still*
> *We are like sheep without a shepherd*
> *We don't know how to be alone*
> *So we wander 'round this desert*
> *And wind up following the wrong gods home…*
>
> *Now the flowers in your garden*
> *They don't smell so sweet*
> *Maybe you've forgotten*
> *The heaven lying at your feet.³*

Accepting one's life is not easy. To do so, we must [4] **express gratitude** – to emphatically affirm the life we have been given. Letting go, going with the flow, and seeing the light reflect the quiet stirrings of a soul. In contrast, being grateful, calls forth the need to make a palpable offering of thanks. Be it to a Higher Power or the living spirit within your loving bonds, we must pause long enough to demonstrate gratitude for what we have been given. We must say it, write it, show it, and offer it in ways that reveals to others that we are grateful – silence is not an option here!

"If the only prayer you say in your entire life is 'Thank you!' it will be enough."⁴ These prophetic words of Meister Eckhardt triumph our freedom over narcissism. Gratitude reflects a shift from negatives to positives, from self to other. Gratitude is an attitude we can freely choose in order to create a better life for ourselves and others. Don Henley also opens our heart to gratitude in *My Thanksgiving*:

> *For every moment of joy,*
> *Every hour of fear,*
> *For every winding road that brought me here,*
> *For every breath,*
> *For every day of living,*
> *This is my Thanksgiving!*
> *For everyone who helped me start.*

> *And for everything that broke my heart.*
> *For every breath, for every day of living,*
> *This is my Thanksgiving.*[5]

Each inhalation, each breath we take, can awaken us to acceptance. Often, we hold our breath as we get caught in either the "trance of belittlement" or the "trance of entitlement". The former reflects our prior failures/rejections and catapults us into the room of doom where we spit venom amidst the debris of our past. The "trance of entitlement" projects us into a future fantasy that prevents us from living more fully in the present.

We know we are free when we experience gratitude for everything we have in our lives NOW – ALL OF IT – the good, the bad, and the ugly. Why can't we love our lives – what we have been given, what we look like, and what we have created – just the way it is? We somehow get seduced. Nature, nurture and culture conspire to blur our vision. The story of Midas captures addiction to a material world painfully well.

As you recall, a King named Midas pleased the God of wine, Dionysus, by taking care of one of his loyal followers. Dionysus wanted to thank Midas by granting him one wish. Without missing a beat, the greedy Midas asked that everything he touched be turned to gold. Filled with rapture, Midas quickly turned tree branches and stones into gold just by touching them. Believing that he would soon become the richest man in the world he ordered the finest wines and most sumptuous meal be delivered to an elegant feast – all in his narcissistic honor. Well, you know the rest of the story:

> *As soon as he lifted a goblet of very fine wine to his lips, it turned to gold and became impossible to drink. And when he broke a piece of bread to satisfy his growing hunger pangs, it too turned to gold. Slowly, he began to see the foolishness of his desires. There would be no way he could satisfy his basic survival needs. He would die. And everywhere he went, and everything he touched, quickly turned to solid gold bullion which he could not use to satisfy his genuine needs. If he sold the gold, his destiny was the same. Anything he received in return would also be turned to gold.*
>
> *He began to hate his riches, and he sank into a sullen despair. He soon fell to his knees and prayed for Dionysus to have pity on him and withdraw the original wish. And the God took pity upon him and instructed him to humbly and slowly walk down to the river Paktalos where he was directed to dip his head into the flowing water. Thus the power that created the gold was washed from Midas's head and he returned to a more learned state of being. From that day on, King Midas detested gold, jewels, and material wealth, choosing instead to live his life in a simple way – a more humble way - where he wandered about the Kingdom with the Queen and their children, listening to the birds, looking at his gardens, smelling the flowers and giving thanks for his "newly" found freedom.*[6]

"Acceptance" is a third Gift that counters narcissism. Unlike the gifts of "humility" and "forgiveness" which focus on the past, acceptance is a gift of presence – of living in the present.

Let's take a closer look at the four conditions for acceptance.

Letting Go

> *After years of searching, the seeker was told to go to a cave, in which he would find a well. "Ask the well what is Truth," he was advised, "and the well will reveal it to you." Having found the well, the seeker asked that most fundamental question. And from the depths came the answer, "Go to the village crossroad: there you shall find what you are seeking."*
>
> *Full of hope and anticipation, the man ran to the crossroad, to find only three rather uninteresting shops. One shop was selling pieces of metal, another sold wood, and thin wires were for sale in the third. Nothing there seemed to have much to do with the revelation of Truth.*
>
> *Disappointed, the seeker returned to the well to demand an explanation, but he was told only, "You will understand in the future." When the man protested, all he got in return were echoes of his own shouts. Indignant for having been made a fool of – or so he thought at the time – the seeker continued his wanderings in search of Truth. As years went by, the memory of his experience at the well gradually faded until one night the sound of sitar music caught his attention. It was a wonderful music, and it was played with great mastery and inspiration.*
>
> *Profoundly moved, the truthseeker felt drawn toward the player. He looked at the fingers dancing over the strings. He became aware of the sitar itself. And then suddenly he exploded in a cry of joyous recognition: the sitar itself was made out of wires and pieces of metal and wood just like those he had once seen in the three stores and had thought to be without any particular significance.*
>
> *At last he understood the message of the well. We have already been given everything we need: our task is to assemble and use it in the appropriate way. Nothing is meaningful as long as we perceive only separate fragments. But as soon as the fragments come together, a new entity emerges whose nature we could not have foreseen by considering the fragments alone.*[7]

This fable, as told by Piero Ferrucci, invites us to embrace all of who we are. Each fragment defines us more fully. Every fragment contributes to a greater whole. [1] We have already been given everything we need. [2] Our task is to assemble and use them in appropriate ways. First we must see the pieces of metal, wood, and thin wire of our lives. Both weaknesses and strengths make us who we are. Both disabilities and abilities make us who we are. Both failures and successes make us who we are. Both losses and blessings make us who we are. Both illness and wellness make us who we are. Both love and its loss make us who we are. Togetherness and separateness make us who we are. Both poverty and wealth make us who we are. Both adequacy and inadequacy make us who we are. As Merle Haggard croons, in the twilight of his life, "I'm just a seeker, I'm just a sinner, and I am what I am."[8]

We don't see what parts we do have because we're obsessed with getting perfect replacement parts from Macy's, Sharper Image, Tiffany's, and our plastic surgeons – even if we can't afford it! We are way too busy trying to supplant what we have been given! Columnist Leonard

Pitts gets it: "Face it, we – by which I mean people of the human persuasion – are control freaks. Particularly here in the United States of Plastic Surgery, where it sometimes seems as if everything we do is an effort to shrink space, reshape reality, impose our will. We inject saline in breasts and collagen in lips, peel skin, suction fat, clone sheep, blast mountains, computerize, accessorize, euthanize, theorize, invent, invert, improve, create and destroy in a never-ending flurry of attempts to remake the world to our liking. That's the source of human greatness. It's also evidence of human folly. Ultimately, control is illusion!"[9]

Being discovered terrifies us – so we control the universe so that few get to know us deeply. We hide. We hide behind our plastic surgeries, our beautiful homes, our hurried children, and our slim fast diets. We desperately want to look good enough because, deep down, we fear we're not. The truth of the matter is that all of us are "not good enough" – at times! Some days we're not the best parents, spouses, golfers, executives, motorists or therapists. Some days we hurt those we love the most. Certainly we need to be embraced on these messy, imperfect days. "Not being good enough" perhaps 20 percent of the time, however, is so much better than living with the fear of not being good enough 100 percent of the time. Let's humbly reveal it and deal with it.

We hide from the *fear* of not being good enough more than our imperfections themselves.

So we become obsessed with ideal images of ourselves, of others, of life – and won't let go. But, let go of what? The Emperor's clothes! What are we clinging to? What do we need to let go of so we might see the metal, wires, and wood of our lives? For starters, let's begin with Sunday night football or *Dancing with the Stars*! You may think I'm kidding, but we ought to accept one night of the week as family night when we just enjoy each other as we really are. *Dancing with the Stars* ought to bite the dust because too many of us are fantasizing about some ideal, svelte, handsome/gorgeous partner who dances flawlessly to the most exotic music we know. And the chances of finding this perfect partner are ZILCH! So, give it up, let it go. Let's get on with the show.

More seriously, here's a list of ten things we might let go of:

* an inflated image of ourselves
* a deflated image of ourselves
* an inflated image of others
* a deflated image of others
* flamboyant materialism
* histrionic emotionality
* mind-numbing intellectualizing
* pious religiosity
* too much work
* too many makeovers

Even when we have what we want we want less of what we have.

Just yesterday I heard from a young, ambitious couple. They were building a lifestyle without first building a relationship. I asked each to tell me what stressed them the most about their lives. He said a 75-hour work week, and she said "The kids, the $110,000 pool construction, his 75-hour work week, and the dirt that our three pedigreed dogs track into the house each day, as a result of the $110,000 mess in the backyard!" Even with the kids in mother's-day-out five mornings a week, this young woman seemed miserable. Tragically, each of them was missing the forest for the trees. Needing the money to support a lifestyle he didn't agree with this husband worked excruciating hours. Needing the love she didn't have, this wife yearned for a lifestyle she didn't really want. Like King Midas, everything of real value for this couple was turning to gold, and ironically each of them was yearning for less.

Each of them needed to surrender something material, something extrinsic.

Each of them needed to take a purifying dip in the river, as King Midas did, in order to cleanse themselves of false images and "perfect" material gods. Each needed immersion into the inner world of the spirit, of feelings, of love to see that real happiness is found from within, not from without. Seng-t'san reminds us of this:

> *Pursue not the outer entanglements,*
> *Dwell not in the inner void;*
> *Be serene in the oneness of things,*
> *And dualism vanishes by itself.* [10]

Sometime in life we learn that we must willingly let go of the life we have so carefully planned in order to accept the life waiting for us. This calls for surrender – a willing relinquishment of control. We must find the inherent good in all things. It is enough to accept the thin wires, pieces of metal, and wood, if we let go. For one country western songwriter, the message is pretty clear: "Work as if you don't need the money. Love as if nobody has hurt you. Dance as if no one is watching you. Sing as if no one is listening to you. And live as if this is paradise on Earth." [11]

We must not let the past ensnare us nor let the future beguile us.

Going With The Flow

Mary had the gift of perspective. She passionately embraced her life as it was:

> *Tonight, I stood with a friend on a hill overlooking a lake. I watched the gentle current of the water and gazed at the sea of stars above us. I put my arms out and ran alongside the edge. I smiled into the wind. Continuing to lose my vision, I felt free…Tonight I defied the gravity of my life. I spent five minutes simply admiring the beauty of something, never once feeling the need to question how many times I will be able to do the same in the future.*

For this young woman, a diagnosis of juvenile macular degeneration meant that she was slowly going blind. Soon the gentle current of the water and the sea of stars above would become cherished memories. Each day, over the course of many years, she would have to contend with the telltale signs that the cells in her eyes were dying because of her Stargardt's disease. There would be difficulty in identifying soccer chums running the field, discerning expressions of joy or pain on the faces of those she loved or detecting whether friend or foe approached. Yes, there was fear, but courage and wonder as well. In the midst of a darkening world, Mary would need to defy the "gravity" of her life in order to value more essential human experiences.

And she did.

Giving of herself freely, as she had many summers before, Mary spent her last summer before college at Camp Ranier. One evening amidst the quiet canopy of eight sleeping teens, Mary detected the sounds of one saddened soul "sobbing urgently into the soft material of the nightgown bunched at her knees." As their eyes met in the silence of the night, a connection was made. Mary's inevitable loss of sight merged with the pain of a young girl grieving the recent death of her father. As the evening moon glow engulfed them both, Mary realized that loss not only dims, but also illuminates:

> We talked on that small, wooden bunk for what seemed like an eternity. She told me about her sadness and I told her about mine. Upon the mention of her father, she began crying again, and I told her that if she kept it up, I was going to start crying too...Then we decided that the dark dungeons of loss weren't so horrible when we lit them with our torches of memory. We agreed that we can't really lose anything that we allow to live in our hearts. We talked about our day and tried to remember each time we'd laughed. She fell asleep listening to embarrassing and funny things I'd done as a camper at her age. I then tiptoed back to my bunk, and stretched out in a half-hearted attempt to fall asleep.
>
> I had realized that one of Ranier's greatest lessons is how to live with loss. I cannot imagine the depth of sadness I would have felt if I had lost my father at the age of eight. Yet, Jaclyn probably had more fun at camp than any of my other campers because of her great attitude and her will to move on. I hadn't realized, until I was back at a place that made me so happy, how sad I had been before.
>
> So that night, as I listened to the crickets and felt the wind against my face, I made a vow to myself: to laugh, play, and live more, and to remember, when I look at the sky, to fill my imagination with stars.

Very little more needs to be said after reading Mary's story. Mary clearly embraces the agony and ecstasy of life, both necessary ingredients for acceptance – for going with the flow. She lives in the present, connecting with others. With vision loss in her future, Mary reminds us of Helen Keller, who once remarked: "I have never believed that my limitations were in any sense punishments or accidents. If I had held such a view, I would never have exerted the strength to overcome them. I thank God for my handicaps, for through them, I have found myself, my work, and my God."[12]

Loving relationships rekindle hope when despair lingers in the shadows.

I learned from Mary and Helen Keller that going with the flow means that:

* ✳ Life's currents are powerful; at times, we only rudder at best.
* ✳ The surface won't tell you what the deep water knows.
* ✳ Fateful design shapes the "current" course of our flow.
* ✳ Flow varies: going fast or slow.
* ✳ The flow etches out a presence in the world around.
* ✳ All flows into something greater, something safe and something sound.
* ✳ The left side cannot get there before the right side may.
* ✳ Mother Nature has her way, regardless of our say.

Seeing The Light

Old age often teaches us to see more clearly.

> *On his birthday, an old guy visits his physician for his annual exam. The guy says to his doctor, "I feel great but I have these weird spiritual experiences."*
>
> *The doctor says, "What do you mean?"*
>
> *The old guy says, "When I get up in the middle of the night to use the bathroom, I open the door and God turns the light on for me. When I'm finished, I shut the door and God turns the light off for me."*
>
> *The doctor says, "I've seen this before in guys your age. You're not connecting with God …you're peeing in the fridge!" (Source Unknown).*

Thankfully, most of us do not need to wait for advancing years to see the light more clearly. I'll always remember an experience 15 years ago when I went to Bar Harbor, Maine to attend a photography workshop. Fall colors were beckoning and I couldn't resist the idea of capturing hillsides covered with sugar maples bursting with yellow, red, and orange leaves. The weather "cooperated" beautifully the entire week, allowing all of the workshop participants countless opportunities to revel in nature's annual fest.

I remember something quite special about that trip. When my dear friend Gene and I first met our instructor he commented on the beautiful weather being forecast, but then proceeded to tell us a story about the *prior* week – when he had led a group of intrepid warriors before us. It had rained not one day, not two, not three, but the entire seven days. These rain-soaked, soggy participants had to deal with an unending fall downpour which initially had dampened their spirits considerably.

But, as radio commentator Paul Harvey used to say, "There's more to the story – page 2." Faced with challenging weather conditions, this group had to first grieve their lost opportunities to shoot sweeping landscapes. They couldn't even see the hillsides through the mist and rain, let alone photograph them. Each of them had to let go of the many pre-visualized scenes which they had painted in their *imaginations* before they ever set foot in Acadia National Park. As the storyline of this prior week unfolded, I could hear emotion in our instructor's voice as he read aloud some of the letters left behind by folks who were supposed to be in mourning over missed opportunities, not to mention depleted bank accounts getting to Maine.

Faced with challenges they didn't expect these photo enthusiasts learned to see the light differently. Instead of panoramic hillside scenes, they began to see droplets of water beading on richly-hued, golden leaves. Instead of blue skies framing endless canopies of maple trees, they learned to see individual leaves floating in eddies which abundantly swirled along countless ponds and streams. Quite unexpectedly, each person on this trip was learning about macro photography – seeing close up!

It gets even better. Because of the constant drizzle, each participant had to be concerned about protecting his or her camera equipment in the rain. *Solution*: the entire group went shopping for umbrellas and patiently took turns shooting incredible photos while crouching on hands and knees. Above them, providing shelter from the storm, stood devoted partners who would soon need this same assistance later on. For seven days, these folks formed a caring community of helping hands within which a shared spirit lit up the landscape. Each person might have chosen to brood or bitch over what was missing in their lives – their missing 10 degrees – but instead each chose to embrace what they were given. Each person, bar none, left a note for our instructor stating that they had captured the best photographs of their lives. Each individual needed to transcend their "arc of yearning" to see *the heaven lying at their feet*. Appropriately enough, our instructor's eyes watered up.

Each participant had learned to *see the light* differently.

As each one of us skims the surface of life, just above the abyss of death, we have choices. For just a moment, we can choose humility, the serenity of forgiveness, a listening ear or the springtime bloom of a smile. We can choose hope over despair. Like Plato, we can choose kindness, knowing that everyone is fighting a great battle. Each choice is a leap of faith, a great force, which links us to one other. It is the same force – of awe – perhaps divine, which drove our ancestors to choose light over darkness in all its forms, design, and mystery.

Nicholas Evans says in *The Horse Whisperer*, "But what he chose to do instead was to go to the brink and look beyond. And he saw what was there and chose to accept it….Sometimes what seems like surrender isn't surrender at all. It's about what is going on in our hearts. About seeing clearly the way life is and accepting it and being true to it, whatever the pain, because the pain of not being true to it is far, far greater."[14] The deeper question in our lives is less about death and more about how we're living – how we embrace the fullness of each unfurled day. How we might embrace those we love.

Death is only one way of dying; living partially, living fearfully, is our more common, daily collusion with death.[15]

Sometimes we don't have to go to the brink to see the *heaven lying at our feet*! Sometimes, as we have just seen in Maine, we have occasion to discover it by doing…nothing: just being with someone or something you like. Imagine there is the sun, the rain, the light, the trees, the birds, and the sensory delight of life all around us. My friend and poet, Robert Ayres, helps us open our eyes ever more in order to see life's splendor in a poem, appropriately entitled, *Downpour.*

> *Had you come with me this morning, walking*
> *first the pecan bottoms along the creek,*
> *then the ridge upstream from where it bends, the sky*
> *scrubbed clean by last night's unpredictable storm,*
> *as though someone had suddenly pitched a bucket of water*
> *through the open window – each web glistening so,*
> *the sodden pasture visibly relieved –*
> *you would have seen the turkey hen, disheveled,*
> *sopping wet, cautiously threading her young brood*
> *through patches of blue stem, blooming broom weed*
> *and drenched in sunlight, the painted bunting perched*
> *on the upended cedar stump, little rainbow,*
> *bright promise from a distant land. Could he*
> *taunt or tease your dark-hiding heart to sing?*[16]

Expressing Gratitude

Children are taught to say it, and NFL players drop to their knees to show it. Every religion has rites and ceremonies to thank God and every disciple has rituals which honor his/her religion. Gratitude is the only positive sentiment we have in the United States that has a national holiday named after it, *Thanksgiving.*

Gratitude is an attitude, fueled by positive emotion, that compels us to perform an act of thanksgiving.

Yet we know little about gratitude in the social sciences. There has been relatively little study of it until the late 1990's when Martin Seligman spearheaded a national movement toward "positive psychology." Now we are beginning to discover that gratitude is linked to happiness, pride, hope, and a fresh appreciation of life. Gratitude has been rated among the top five personal strengths in over 40 countries around the world. Not surprisingly, the lack of gratitude has been found to be a major characteristic of clinically diagnosed, narcissistic personalities.

With self-absorption, we forget how to appreciate or say "Thank you!"

Drs. Martin Seligman and Robert Emmons are responsible for much of the work on "authentic happiness" in general, and gratitude in particular.[17] As a result of their research we now know that [1] the practice of gratitude can increase happiness levels by approximately 25 percent; [2] that this increase will last a full six months or longer by writing in a "gratitude journal" for only a few hours over the course of three weeks; and [3] the cultivation of gratitude benefits our overall health – in particular, better quality sleep. There are also positive activation changes in the frontal lobes of our brain!

I'm all for developing an attitude of gratitude. A recommended way to do it is to write something that you feel grateful for four times a week, for three weeks. That's it! The research shows this is enough to create the desired effects. If such a miniscule amount of effort produces such significant gains in our happiness, why don't we do it? Sadly, the answer for most of us is that we choose self-absorption, resentment, and anger over celebration and appreciation. Emmons also believes that, "Others simply don't want to feel obligated to the person who helped them, and never come to realize the boost in energy, enthusiasm, and social benefits that come from a more grateful, connected life."

Many of us are hung up around the pain that one person has created in our lives and ignore all the other people who bless our lives. We walk around stewing in our own juices often missing the abundant fruit on the vine. Once again, the "missing ten degrees" trumps the 350 degrees of fullness.

To counter this tendency, Seligman and Emmons suggest the following exercise. Write a "gratitude letter" to a person in your life who has exerted a positive influence on you, BUT whom you have not properly or fully thanked. Once you complete your letter, you are encouraged to arrange a meeting with that person and read your letter aloud – face to face! As I stated at the beginning of this chapter, silence is not an option here. We must say it, write it, show it, and offer it in ways that reveal to others that we are grateful. This is exactly what Grace did in her "acceptance' letter to Will earlier in this chapter.

Oh, yes. Then there's Merritt Myers who got lost in a parched, Big Bend canyon for a few days in 2010. With no exit possible most folks would have died. Sucking the juice out of prickly pear cacti kept him alive until Park Rangers were able to find him. Cherishing solitude, Merritt had often hiked alone. This sojourn changed him forever. Hours after being rescued from his ordeal – his dark night of the soul – Merritt gratefully proclaimed: "I never expected to see my wife again. That affected my perspective on needing to retreat to nature. People, and love from people, come from God as well!"

Simple, humble appreciation often grabs you by surprise. After exercising at my very exclusive country club one day – the YMCA – I was greeted by another fellow, aged 78, in the locker room:

"How are you, Larry?" Maurice asked.

"Great", I responded.

"How are you, Maurice?" I returned.

"GRATEFUL", Maurice answered back. Five minutes later, Otis greeted me.

"How are you, Larry?" Otis wondered.

"Great," I retorted.

"How are you, Otis?" I inquired.

"I AM BLESSED, Larry, thanks!"

As I walked out of the YMCA, I wondered who was actually talking to me that day. While I'm using some ridiculous rating scale from "poor" to "great" to assess my day, these guys are simply mindful of the gift of life itself.

I paused, and took a deep breath.

Oh, if we could truly accept life as perfectly imperfect – just the way it is! How different our lives would be if we were at peace with each and every day. A wise friend, Marlee Porter, captures this beautifully in his poem, *After Word*:

I am at peace
for once, it seems,
and even the trees agree.

I see now
each and every day
can be everything to me.

To take each day
unbidden,
virgin linen,
and then to paint
the rhyme,
the rhyme and the wonder
of
just
another
day!

It is everything.

CHAPTER 18

The Gift of Compassion

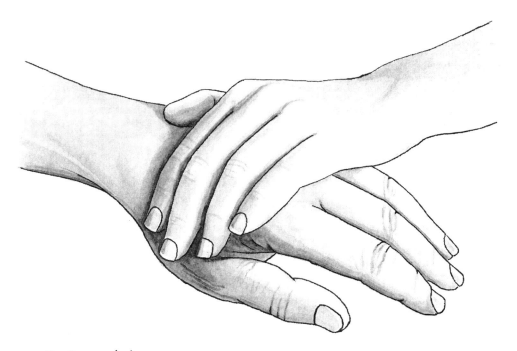

Can I see another's woe,
And not be in sorrow too?
Can I see another's grief,
And not seek of kind relief?...

Can a mother sit and hear
An infant groan an infant fear?
No, no! never can it be!
Never, never can it be![1]

Widening our circle of compassion beyond our selves defines a life well lived.

Forgiveness frees others from their imprisonment while compassion embraces them in their suffering. Each embrace widens our care circle and connects us more and more with humanity. We human beings would like to claim the gift of compassion as uniquely ours but we cannot do so. Russian primatologist, Nadia Kohts, made this clear in the beginning of the 20th century when she raised a young chimpanzee in her home. Occasionally, her primate progeny would escape to the rooftop of their home where she would attempt to cajole the chimp down with food bribes, which rarely worked. So one day she tried an experiment. Instead of putting out an offering of tempting morsels, she sat herself down within view of the chimp and began crying. Surprisingly, without much ado, the chimp quickly climbed down from the roof and attempted to comfort her. "He runs around me as if looking for the offender…He tenderly takes my chin in his palm…as if trying to understand what is happening."[2]

As if Kohts' story is not enough to stretch our understanding of compassion, we need only to remember the tale of Binta Jua, the gorilla who calmly rescued a 3 year-old boy in 1998 who had accidentally fallen into her enclosure at the Brookfield Zoo in Chicago, Illinois. Without missing a beat, the 8-year-old western, lowland gorilla gently rocked the unconscious boy forward and backward as if she were rehearsing a ritual passed down through the ages. She then carried the boy to a door where human trainers eagerly awaited the handoff. Her own 17-month-old baby, Koola, held on tightly throughout the entire incident.

A gorilla with soul – is it possible? What was Binta Jua thinking or feeling as she comforted the helpless boy? What force within her was ignited by the sight of a fallen angel? Are these stories of other primates any less convincing than our own? Surely each of us, dazed by a fall, has needed rescue by outstretched arms from a loving universe.

It is frightening to fall, to be in a free fall, not knowing when we will hit bottom, let alone find our way out. Being out of control, in pain, desperate, yearning for it all to end is agonizing. Surely someone will come forth – with their outstretched arms – to halt our spiral downward. Surely someone will lift us up and then gently rock us forward and backward until the pain begins to subside. Whether it is divorce, illness, or impending death, something we once knew has slipped away, leaving us chilled by its absence. Not surprisingly, the more patients feel a compassionate connection to their doctors the longer they live with their disease.

In a similar accord, the more spouses feel a compassionate connection to their partners the longer they live in their marriages. This was certainly true with Will and Grace from the previous chapter. The *Gift* of "acceptance" from Grace would not have been possible without the outstretched arms of "compassion" from Will. Let's take a few moments to look at this precious *Gift* that Will provided:

Dear Grace: Happy Anniversary. My sincere prayer and hope is that you find a place in your heart on this day for happiness. I regret deeply the emotional, mental and physical pain I have caused in your life through my mistakes, bad judgments, inappropriate decisions, and violation of the covenant we share. I appreciate very much your willingness this past year to be open to the healing that I think has taken place as a result of our work together, the Grace of God, the support of our family and the help and guidance of competent professionals. I want you to know that I understand – as best I can – the pain I have caused you and the terrible trauma it has brought to you and our lives. I have tried the best I can to listen to you over the past year and to hear what you are saying. This process alone has shown me that I have not done that over many years and that your voice was not always being heard. I do get that and I hope that the changes I have made – and continue to make – are evident to you through my actions. This is real change. I feel it inside and, more importantly, I welcome it.

I am grateful for all the many years we have spent together and am disappointed in myself for putting that at such serious risk. We have been through so much together and I know now that I should have come to you rather than falling for the temptations of sin. I do love you very much, as I always have, and I still want to grow old with you, enjoy life with you, and enjoy the richness of the many blessings in our lives together. But before any of that can happen on a consistent, ongoing basis, I understand that the healing process must take place. I want to ease the pain that I have created in your life. The best I can do is to demonstratively love you day by day and try to earn back your respect, your trust, your admiration and your love.

Know that there is nothing more important to me that to do just that. I ask for your continued help and support by letting me know when I am failing – and also when my actions are communicating my feelings of deep love that I have for you. I know in my heart that it is still possible for us to heal from this crisis I have placed us in. And it is my daily prayer that we do succeed and emerge from this period of time with a stronger, more satisfying and joyful marriage. That is what I want and I believe that it is what you want as well. Thank you so much for your hard work and continued commitment that has brought us this far.

I love you very much, Will.

Crises are kindling for the soul – allowing human frailty to set compassion on fire.

In his *compassion* letter Will was able to:

✻ Express a deep empathic understanding of the pathos Grace had endured.
✻ Express appreciation for Grace's openness/willingness to grow from her pain.
✻ Express his intention to ease Grace's pain in all possible ways.
✻ Express his intention to be "in tune" with Grace's inner thoughts and feelings.
✻ Express his patience with whatever time it might take to heal.

✻ Express his desire for feedback, knowing he was a wayward arrow off course.

✻ Express an unwavering belief in a more joyful and loving connection.

Compassion is what Mother Teresa considered "love in action." While we cannot say whether love existed in the first two primate examples above, it is clear that some wondrous force compelled both the chimp in Nadia Kohts' home and Binta Jua to move forward in an apparent attempt to comfort. It is this "moving forward with the intent to comfort" that distinguishes compassion from empathy. The *Miriam Webster Dictionary* defines compassion as the sympathetic consciousness of other's distress together with a desire to alleviate it. The compassionate person, or chimp, "bears with" or "suffers with" the other who is in distress. There is both a knowing and a desire to reduce the distress. Compassion requires "doing" something to help another, and is an antidote for disengaged self-absorption. We rise up, out of our self-absorbed reveries. We notice, then respond to, the needs of another.

The *Miriam Webster Dictionary* defines empathy as the capacity to understand, be aware of, be sensitive to, and vicariously experience the feelings, thoughts, and experiences of another. The empathic person "feels into" the feelings of another, as if these feelings were his own. It is a deep appreciation of another's situation from his or her perspective. To walk in another's shoes, to put oneself in another's place, or to imagine what another is going through – as if it were our own experience – is empathy. Of course, we can never really know what another is truly feeling – even with functional magnetic resonance imaging (fMRI). Empathy is our best, soulful attempt to see, "to feel into" another person's suffering. Then we are open to receiving and holding the other's experience without reservation or judgment.

Empathy is passive "knowing" while compassion is active "doing."

Relationships go bankrupt, belly-up, without empathy and compassion. Both compassion and empathy are essential human qualities that allow one to feel, understand, and respond to the suffering of others. Both qualities empower individuals to enter into and maintain relationships of caring. Our capacity to care may well be the fundamental virtue of the human condition. Every society on Planet Earth attempts to treat the sick, the dying, and the bereaved with compassionate care. This is a universal human response – even when we have created the suffering itself!

Plato reminds us: *Be kind, for everyone you meet is fighting a great battle.*

Dynamic compassion, or ahimsa in Hinduism, is known as the god-like quality within a person. It is an open-hearted active response of respect, service, and care for those in need. It was an essential piece to Gandhi's nonviolent liberation movement. Compassion is also a pivotal element within Buddhism. The Buddha manifested absolute compassion for all creation. Buddhist compassion, or karuna, is seen as the appropriate human response to understanding the interdependence and mutual welfare of all beings. In the Judeo-Christian tradition, compassion is a manifestation of God's love and mercy. Compassion reflects the eternal and divine God's value of interacting "with" and cherishing "all" living things. In each of these spiritual traditions, directly addressing the suffering of others through compassionate care is a religious obligation.

Our very survival depends on a shared humanity built upon compassion.

Compassion encompasses empathy, but is more. Compassionate action is a willingness to go beyond self-interest and give of oneself for the good of another. In this regard it is similar to altruism: to let go of one's own needs to attend to the needs of another. By doing so, we meet one of our own deepest needs – the need to be a part of a larger shared humanity.

With compassion we expand; with narcissism we contract.

Compassion is a chosen pathway from oneself to another that allows love to flow. It is the heating up of chicken soup. It is the changing of an abrasive diaper. It is the sitting with a friend going through chemo. It is reassuring a spouse when a child has become unmoored from everything he was ever taught. It is a Herculean shoulder to lean on for a saddened child not making varsity soccer. It is driving a bereaved spouse to a support group once her mother dies from cancer. It is bathing a humiliated father who just lost bladder control. It is emptying a husband's catheter bag in the anesthetized days following prostate surgery. It is sitting with another in silence when there is nothing more to say.

Devotional love is obligation without duty, while obligation is duty without love.

Compassion is both emotional and devotional love. I often make a distinction between the two when talking with clients: emotional love is a relationship of "being," while devotional love is a relationship of "doing." True emotional and devotional love are expressed without obligation. We do so because we love doing so! Emotional love reflects depth. We go deep into the being of another to understand their heartache, sorrow and longing. We enter their very private world of inner thoughts and feelings in order to accompany them on their life journey. We feel some of Will's compassion as he reaches out to Grace in his letter.

Devotional love, in contrast, reflects actions taken to love another. Many men prefer to show their love through devotional acts of love rather than in "in depth" conversations with a significant other. Often this is a source of conflict in a relationship. One partner wants to be known deeply while the other is busy demonstrating his love while cooking in the kitchen, keeping a well-manicured lawn in front of the house, and laboring with colleagues 50 hours per week to bring home a pay check. For my father, who seldom spoke, devotional love sprang forth whenever he saved a parking space by putting chairs in it for me, right in front of his haberdashery, whenever he knew I was coming home from college. Whenever I see two metal folding chairs, I fondly remember that this was his way of demonstrating love for me.

When life strips away all pretenses and renders us fully human, we need compassion. Fragility defines our humanness. Only when we fall, and powerlessness reigns supreme, are we open to the "care, concern, and solicitude" that Erick Fromm described so well.[3]

The good news is that we get to practice compassion daily. There needn't be a crisis of falling into a gorilla's den to elicit a compassionate response. It is noteworthy that we associate compassion with unfortunate life events. We also need compassion in happy times, when good things have happened to us. If compassion truly implies a sharing of life's passions, why would we not extend it during positive life experiences as well?

In fact, might compassion actually predict positive life experiences? Psychologist Dacher Keltner, from UC Berkeley, thinks so! He has studied smiles in high school yearbooks and has found that women with "warmer smiles" reported more contentment 30 years later! These women were more accomplished regarding their personal goals, less anxious on a daily basis, and were happier in their marriages.[4]

There are physical changes in the body when we truly are compassionate. In the primate world tender warmth is signaled by head tilts, open-handed gestures, and warm smiles. These simple, one-second bursts of behavior are enough to correlate with feeling love, desiring to get married, and cherishing a long-term life together.

Because flaws are universal, compassion must be as well.

Compassion is much more attainable when our kinship to others is based on the humble embrace of known flaws and imperfections. I'm not OK, you're not Ok, but that's OK. By contrast, pride only separates us from one another. The Dalai Lama has said, "If you want others to be happy, practice compassion; if you want to be happy, practice compassion."

A wonderfully wise Zen prayer captures this belief quite well:

> *Caught in the self-centered dream, only suffering;*
> *holding to self-centered thoughts, exactly the dream.*
> *Each moment, life as it is, the only teacher,*
> *being just this moment, compassion's way.*[5]

Compassionate Concern and Compassionate Care

Recently, I stepped down from serving on Hospice Austin's board of directors after 27 years. I was a founding board member and tears welled up as I said my last goodbyes and recalled the forces long ago that helped shape my interest in compassionate end-of-life care. I flashed back to 1971 and sitting alone in a cold, unpretentious waiting room in Easton Area Hospital in Pennsylvania. I recall staring mindlessly at a simple, stark clock on one wall of the waiting room. It was 3:00 am and I was alone and disconsolate. My father lay comatose from a brain tumor at one end of the hallway while my mother clung to life support at the other end, hours after she had ingested too many sleeping pills. I had long since ushered Claire out the entrance of the hospital in order for her to get some much-needed sleep.

No finger in a dike could help me that night. What struck me was not just the overwhelming sadness inside me but the profound silence all around. No one seemed to notice my existence. In a flurry of orchestrated movements, nurses, attendants, and other hospital personnel skittered about without so much as a glance in my direction. I was alone in a world I didn't understand as a 25-year-old.

Without understanding it I was discovering the proverbial "conspiracy of silence."

In the darkness of those bleak moments, I knew that more compassionate concern and care were needed for those who teetered on the rough edges of despair. Little did I know that in the subsequent years I would have an opportunity to teach a course titled "Death and Dying" at the University of Texas and then become a part of the hospice movement as it sowed its seeds in Austin, Texas, and sprouted into an organization much more humane and comprehensive than I could ever have dreamed.

I was to learn that compassionate care for dying people and those who loved them – indeed all people – involves taking care of the whole person – body, mind, spirit, heart, and soul. This compassionate care, or palliative care as it would later be called, was intended to help improve the quality of life for each person who is swirling in despair. Suffering can be ameliorated by a strong sense of connection. And suffering cannot be denied for very long, even though we try to do so!

Ernest Becker, in his book *The Denial of Death*, has declared that the human being is the only animal who must face each day with the knowledge that he or she will eventually die. The heaviness of this diurnal plight leaves us with only one alternative – denial! Becker asserts that we must deny death in order to cope with life.[6]

I suspect that much of what I have called narcissistic self-absorption in this book is really about the denial of death.

Assuredly, our mortality bubbles just under the radar each and every day. Rather than accept our limitations of time and longevity, we live in distorted cocoons where we weave fairytales about life. The purpose of this book is to help each of us face the death of shattered illusions more lovingly – each and every day. By doing so, we can face life with an open heart.

The "doing" of compassion is quite evident in hospice care. Hospice urges medical staff and patients to talk openly about the physical and emotional changes that occur as death approaches. Knowing what to expect allows patients and their loved ones to appreciate and make the most of the remaining time they have together. Even small tasks such as feeding, bathing, or reading letters to a patient offer opportunities for conversation. Toward the end, hospice volunteers run errands, write greeting cards, and assist with household chores. Family caregivers are thus able to get needed rest. Patients die surrounded by people that care about them, rather than alone in a cold hospital room.

Oh, how I wish it could have been different for me in that darkened hallway where hushed voices went about their chores without asking me to reminisce, share fond memories of happier days, hold my hand, or speak softly to my heart! I wondered about both my mother's and father's physical needs but was too afraid to ask and I wondered if they were pain free but again was too afraid to ask.

Since that lonely vigil in 1971, I have seen compassionate care at work many times. I eventually found the support I needed to cope with grief through family, friends, support groups and – strangely enough – from each client I attempted to help with their grief. Compassionate souls on their own grief journeys welcomed me into their circles. Within every caring circle that embraced me, I learned that while our loved ones may go away – through death or divorce – our capacity to love stays with us forever.

It is always a special privilege to witness the torchlight of compassion, empathy, and forgiveness being exchanged between two ex-spouses. In heartfelt letters, the divorced parents of one of my clients reflected these qualities beautifully as Anthony reached out to help Sylvia, recently diagnosed with cancer. What began as an insurance matter quickly morphed into issues that really mattered:

Sylvia, I will have the application for radiation benefits sent directly to me and I will take time to fill them out and get them to you with instructions on what must go with it. Basically we will need a doctor's statement concerning your diagnosis, the operation report, the laboratory (path) findings, and your doctor's treatment assessment. If you can obtain all your medical records I'll include those as well. We have some strange legislation, but be assured that I will keep pushing for congress on increase limits, but the GAO has issued a report that the funding for the problem is inadequate.

We will get through this. I pray for you constantly and have shed many tears of love and concern – which have never really stopped…like my heart keeps on beating…so those feelings of love and concern continue on. I do honor the here and now and have let go of the past except for the joyous history between us and the pride we will always have in one another and in our precious children. I am very sorry for the pain I caused you because of my stubborn pride and very stupid mistakes, for which I paid dearly in the most sorrowful ways. But, I have recovered and am a better man now because of the lessons taught and learned through my atonement. Thanks for being a strength to me and our children over the years….and still.

Please know that we will always love you and will be there for you, as you have always been for me, for us, and for each of our children. You are, indeed, an angel of the Lord.

In response to Anthony, Sylvia writes:

I can't thank you enough for the incredible letter written to me. I cried buckets of tears as my soul continued the cleansing and healing that has been so long in coming, in its completeness. I'm so grateful you shared our letter with our children. Thank you so much for doing so!

I've not called for the packet from the Radiation Exposure Compensation Program. Would you please just go ahead and take care of that for me? I'd so appreciate it. The person I spoke with was Elliot. He is working for the National Cancer Benefit Center. We are so much more comfortable having you take over for us. We appreciate it so very much. May God bless you as you work with us on this. I do feel stronger this evening, largely because of your gift of compassion.

Thank you so very much Anthony.

Why does it take the tolling of the bells to bring us to a shared fellowship with one another? Why do we need a personal crisis to awaken our capacity to "be there" for one another? Surely, as we look around, we see others in despair. Surely, we see brokenness in the darkened waiting rooms of life – each and every day. What are we waiting for? Acceptance and compassion are inextricably woven together! Tilden Edwards echoes this in *Living in the Presence*:

> *Humility is the deepest kind of honesty. It involves clear-eyed awareness and acceptance of the way we and the world are. Such awareness can be painful, but it is the pain of compassion, not of demanding and deceptive self-righteousness. It is a recognition of the mysterious brokenness of the world that God meets with an open-armed cross rather than an army.*[7]

The Wellsprings for Compassion

For extreme narcissists the *Six Gifts* of love may be the steepest of all mountains to climb. Compassion, for some, is the most difficult. The *Six Gifts* are nutrients – moral building blocks like DNA – which sustain the life of our relationships. We know that compassion is one of the more important nutrients. Our moral judgment beckons us to do the right thing. For Marc Hauser, professor of psychology at Harvard University and author of *Moral Minds*, "moral judgment" is pretty consistent from person to person. "Moral behavior, however," he says, "is scattered all over the place." We know what to do; we just don't do it very consistently. Forces within us are often at war with one another.

> *If the entire human species were a single individual, that person would long ago have been declared mad. The insanity would not lie in the anger and darkness of the human mind. And it certainly wouldn't lie in the transcendent goodness of that mind – one so sublime; we fold it into a larger "soul." The madness would lie instead in the fact that both of these qualities, the savage and the splendid, can exist in one creature, one person, often in one instant.*
>
> *We're a species that is capable of almost dumbfounding kindness. We nurse one another, romance one another, weep for one another. Ever since science taught us how, we willingly tear the very organs from our bodies and give them to one another. And at the same time, we slaughter one another. The past 15 years of human history are the temporal equivalent of those subatomic particles that are created in accelerators and vanish in the trillionth of a second, but in that fleeting instant, we've visited untold horrors on ourselves. In Mogadishu, Rwanda, Chechnya, Darfur, Beslan, Baghdad, Pakistan, London, Madrid, Lebanon, Israel, New York City, Abu Ghraib, Oklahoma City and an Amish schoolhouse in Pennsylvania – all of the crimes committed by the highest, wisest, most principled species the planet has produced. That we're also the lowest, cruelest, most blood-drenched species is our shame – and our paradox.*[8]

There is a moral war going on every day in our lives – in our minds.

The *Six Gifts* require that we make tough choices each day. Will I choose *humility* over pride? Will I choose *forgiveness* over resentment? Will I choose *acceptance* over blind ambition? Will I choose *compassion* over indifference? Will I choose *sacrifice* over self-indulgence? Will I choose *vision* over habituation?

Compassionate choices abound each day. Do we help a child sick in bed or let our spouse put a compress on her head. Do we visit a dear friend in a hospital room or watch a football game one Sunday afternoon? Do we pick up chicken soup for an ailing spouse or stop at a local pub like a wayward louse? Do we assist a stranded driver or actually speed up by her? Such dilemmas never end.

Scientists, with the help of brain scans, now know that making compassionate decisions creates conflict in two or more different parts of our brains. In the classic experiment, a runaway trolley is barreling down the tracks at warp speed toward five workmen who happen to be standing in the wrong place. They cannot be warned in time. As fate would have it, you are standing by the switch which controls the direction of the train as it bullets straight ahead toward the unsuspecting men. If you pull the switch, which would divert the train onto a side rail, one man is standing there who undoubtedly would be killed. Would you kill one man in order to compassionately save five? Suppose the isolated man was on a bridge, standing next to you. Would you push him onto the tracks in order to save the five other men – assuming he's large enough to stop the train? If you are a Caucasian American, would you be more likely to push him onto the tracks if he were Asian in appearance? While many people might divert the train away from the five unsuspecting men, 85 percent of us would NOT push the innocent man onto the tracks – even though we understood that five men were about to be hurled into Kingdom Come. What is really going on in our heads when we make these decisions?

These decisions literally light up different parts of the brain depending on how complicated the dilemma appears to be! Using a switch to divert the train away from five individuals, killing only one, activates the *dorsolateral prefrontal cortex*. This is an anterior part of the brain where "cool, utilitarian decisions" are made. When our moral dilemma gets much more complicated, as when we become more complicit in pushing a man to his death, the *medial frontal cortex* lights up instead. This area of the anterior brain is fueled much more by emotion and social thinking – important elements in both empathy and compassion. And, of course, if we were in danger of being killed by an oncoming train, the *amygdala* would be activated, signaling acute fear. We actually know what's going on in the brain while compassion is experienced.

Imagine a study in which spouses or unmarried partners were subjected to mild pain, perhaps charged electrodes. They were warned just before administration of the painful stimulus and their brains lit up in a characteristic way while they were being monitored by an fMRI (functional magnetic resonance imaging). Imagine as well that you were asked to watch your love partner as he or she experienced the dreaded electrodes. Experimenters watching you would see that your brain would light up along with your partner's: "What hurts you is obviously hurting me in the same way." Voila! Empathy to say the least! If you then ripped the electrodes from your partner's finger tips in a heroic effort, we would certainly consider this a "compassionate act"! In fact, the experimenters probably would have known that a chivalrous act was in your sights just by monitoring your amygdala, that wondrous almond-shaped mass of gray matter that serves as a legitimate gatekeeper for strong emotional responses.

So where was the amygdala, the dorsolateral prefrontal cortex, and the medial frontal cortex in Mogadishu, Rwanda, Chechnya, Darfur, Beslan, Baghdad, Pakistan, London, Madrid, Lebanon, Israel, New York City, and Abu Ghraib? How could these judgment centers for morality get so congested that heinous crimes were committed instead of acts of mercy?

One key to this absence of compassion is the concept of reciprocal altruism, a theory built around the Darwinian notion of in-group versus out-group survival. In the fields of sociobiology or evolutionary psychology, the basic assumption is that Homo sapiens behave in ways which increase the odds of "our tribe" getting to the next generation. In order for this tribal narcissism to succeed, we "know" that we should do everything possible to help members of our own tribe succeed in order to further our own chances as well. In other words, helping our family, friends, and community survive into the next generation, increases the odds of our surviving as well.

Or, "what goes round, comes round." This is called "reciprocal altruism" by Robert Trivers, who explains how repeated altruistic behaviors like compassion can occur between the same individuals over time. In 1971, Trivers listed five types of human behavior that he considered altruistic: [1] caring for sick, disabled, or otherwise incompetent individuals, [2] sharing knowledge, [3] sharing food, [4] sharing implements, and [5] helping in times of danger.[9]

Sharing food is a wonderful example of this principle. If we share our food now – in times of abundance – we may get a little less, but it may be a pretty good investment. Later on, when we don't have enough food, our prior altruism just might pay off: our fellow in-groupers will now take care of us. Similarly, when we compassionately take care of the sick, disabled, and walking wounded, we unconsciously hope that in our time of need this same care, concern, and solicitude will be returned in spades.

Reciprocal altruists are taking something of a risk – since the rewards come later. They are relying on the good will (and good memory) of the recipient to return the favor when they get the chance. Compassion, as a form of social reciprocity, is built upon the notion that "If I feel your pain, you feel mine later on!"

It turns out that "acts of kindness" spread surprisingly easily. In a 1010 study, researchers from the University of California, San Diego and Harvard provide the first laboratory evidence that cooperative behavior is contagious and may actually spread from person to person. In effect, when people benefit from acts of kindness they "pay it forward" by helping others who were not initially involved to begin with. This cascade of cooperation, e.g. compassionate behavior, literally influences dozens more in a social network.[10]

Reciprocal altruism may explain why helping others may benefit us, but it doesn't explain the care of spouses, infants, and children. In these "kinship" relationships there are acts of love which are never expected to be reciprocated. Parenting, for this reason, is considered to be non-reciprocal altruism. In every species that cares for their young, parents deliver care that they never expect to be returned. Indeed, human beings provide one of the longest care-giving patterns among all creatures on earth. So, what motivates us do so if it is not about reciprocity? And why, as I recently heard, would a self-absorbed parent refuse to see his child in a hospital room over four days of acute care?

Ultimately, "giving" compassion may not be about kinship group survival at all. If evolutionary psychologists are correct, the fundamental unit of evolution being "guaranteed" is not the organism but the individual gene. What other explanations do we have to explain why one

related ethnic group literally murders another? Evolutionary psychologists believe we may even
be more intentional, even cruel, in our efforts to survive the more genetically related a person is
to us – because our genes are programmed to do so! Some may say that this level of narcissistic
reductionism trivializes acts of kindness, but surely we need some help to explain the outrageous acts of destruction we see among tribal groups – whether Nazis, Branch Dravidians, or
any other radical, fundamentalist in-group on the planet. In such instances we're culturally
killing ourselves off in a frantic effort to genetically survive!

The *Six Gifts* allow us to talk to our genes more reasonably.

We need to reassure our genetic code that there is a higher code, a more evolved code, which
will assure survival. Our most treasured, loving bonds require this higher code to survive.
The spiraling divorce rate is troubling for the obvious reasons, not the least of which is the
destruction being wrought upon our gene pool, our kinship pool, and our community pool.
I close out this chapter with a seven-fold process for enriching our capacity to be compassionate. It is my hope that compassion, along with the other five gifts, will make a difference to our partners, our children, and our neighbors – domestically, internationally, and
cosmically.

A Seven-Step Guide for Cultivating Compassion

If you want to develop your capacity for compassion, listen to *zenhabits.net*. Why develop compassion in your life? Well, there are scientific studies that suggest there are physical benefits to practicing compassion — people who practice it produce 100 percent more DHEA, which is a hormone
that counteracts the aging process, and 23 percent less cortisol — the "stress hormone."

But there are other emotional and spiritual benefits as well. The main benefit is that it
helps you to be happier, and helps others around you to be happier. If we agree that it is a
common aim of each of us to strive to be happy, then compassion is one of the main tools for
achieving that happiness. It is therefore of utmost importance that we cultivate compassion in
our lives and practice compassion every day. There are seven different practices that you can
try out and perhaps incorporate into your everyday life:

1. **Morning ritual**. *Greet each morning with a ritual. Try this one, suggested by the Dalai
   Lama: "Today I am fortunate to have woken up. I am alive. I have a precious human life.
   I am not going to waste it. I am going to use all my energies to develop myself, to expand
   my heart out to others, to achieve enlightenment for the benefit of all beings. I am going to
   have kind thoughts towards others. I am not going to get angry or think badly about others.
   I am going to benefit others as much as I can." Then, when you've done this, try one of the
   practices below.*

2. **Empathy Practice.** *The first step in cultivating compassion is to develop empathy for your
   fellow human beings. Many of us believe that we have empathy, and on some level nearly*

all of us do. But many times we are centered on ourselves and we let our sense of empathy get rusty. Try this practice: imagine that a loved one is suffering. Something terrible has happened to him or her. Now try to imagine the pain they are going through. Imagine the suffering in as much detail as possible. After doing this practice for a couple of weeks, you should try moving on to imagining the suffering of others you know, not just those who are close to you.

3. **Commonalities practice.** *Instead of recognizing the differences between yourself and others, try to recognize what you have in common. At the root of it all, we are all human beings. We need food and shelter and love. We crave attention and recognition and affection and, above all, happiness. Reflect on these commonalities you have with every other human being and ignore the differences. Here is a five-step exercise to try when you meet friends and strangers. Do it discreetly and try to do all the steps with the same person. With your attention geared to the other person, tell yourself:*

Step 1: "Just like me, this person is seeking happiness in his/her life."
Step 2: "Just like me, this person is trying to avoid suffering in his/her life."
Step 3: "Just like me, this person knows sadness, loneliness, and despair."
Step 4: "Just like me, this person is seeking to fill his/her needs."
Step 5: "Just like me, this person is learning about life."

4. **Relief of suffering practice.** *Once you can empathize with another person, and understand his humanity and suffering, the next step is to want that person to be free from suffering. This is the heart of compassion — actually the definition of it. Try this exercise: imagine the suffering of a human being you've met recently. Now imagine that you are the one going through that suffering. Reflect on how much you would like that suffering to end. Reflect on how happy you would be if another human being desired your suffering to end and acted upon it. Open your heart to that human being and, if you feel even a little that you'd want their suffering to end, reflect on that feeling. That's the feeling that you want to develop. With constant practice, that feeling can be grown and nurtured.*

5. **Act of kindness practice.** *Now that you've gotten good at the 4th practice, take the exercise a step further. Imagine again the suffering of someone you know or met recently. Imagine again that you are that person and are going through that suffering. Now imagine that another human being would like your suffering to end — perhaps your mother or another loved one. What would you like for that person to do to end your suffering? Now reverse roles: you are the person who desires for the other person's suffering to end. Imagine that you do something to help ease the suffering or end it completely. Once you get good at this stage, practice doing something small each day to help end the suffering of others, even in a tiny way. Even a smile, or a kind word, or doing an errand or chore, or just talking about a problem with another person. Practice doing something kind to help ease the suffering of*

others. When you are good at this, find a way to make it a daily practice and eventually a throughout-the-day practice.

6. **Those who mistreat us practice.** *The final stage in these compassion practices is to not only want to ease the suffering of those we love and meet but even those who mistreat us. When we encounter someone who mistreats us, instead of acting in anger, withdraw. Later, when you are calm and more detached, reflect on that person who mistreated you. Try to imagine the background of that person. Try to imagine what that person was taught as a child. Try to imagine the day or week that person was going through and what kind of bad things had happened to that person. Try to imagine the mood and state of mind that person was in — the suffering that person must have been going through to mistreat you that way. Understand that their action was not about you but about what they were going through. Now think some more about the suffering of that person, and see if you can imagine trying to stop the suffering of that person. And then reflect that if you mistreated someone and they acted with kindness and compassion toward you, whether that would make you less likely to mistreat that person the next time and more likely to be kind to that person. Once you have mastered this practice of reflection, try acting with compassion and understanding the next time a person mistreats you. Do it in little doses until you are good at it.*

7. **Evening routine.** *Take a few minutes before you go to bed to reflect upon your day. Think about the people you met and talked to and how you treated each other. Think about your goal that you stated this morning, to act with compassion towards others. How well did you do? What could you do better? What did you learn from your experiences today? And if you have time, try one of the above practices and exercises.*[11]

These compassionate practices from *zenhabit.net* can be done anywhere, any time – at work, at home, on the road, while traveling, while at a store, while at the home of a friend or family member. By sandwiching your day with a morning and evening ritual, you can frame your day. As the Dalai Lama teaches us, "My message is the practice of compassion, love, and kindness. These things are very useful in our daily life, and also for the whole of human society these practices can be very important. This, above all, with bring happiness to your life and to those around you."

The key to making compassion a part of your life is to practice it every day!

CHAPTER **19**

The Gift of Sacrifice

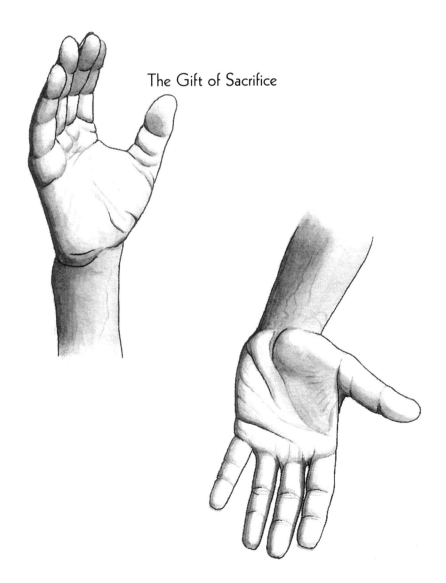

Look into my eyes - you will see
What you mean to me
Search your heart - search your soul
And when you find me there you'll search no more
Don't tell me it's not worth tryin' for
You can't tell me it's not worth dyin' for
You know it's true
Everything I do - I do it for you

Bryan Adams goes on to sing, "Take me as I am – take my life, I would give it all – I would sacrifice!"[1] Do you remember cherishing these thoughts on your wedding day? Do you remember these thoughts on your child's birthday? Then, as the years unfold, we opine over personal losses, blaming our partners – even our children – for unceasingly failing us. We feel put upon, believing with each disappointment that the quid pro quo of life has forsaken us. Our giving spirit may take a leave of absence. As we splash about in this sea of "misgivings" we often forget the very thoughts which beckoned us in the beginning – "Take me as I am – take my life, I would give it all – I would sacrifice!"

Most of us, by statistical accounts, are much too selfish to sacrifice for lasting love. The seven-year itch has now become the five-year itch according to new research from the Max Planck Institute in Germany which found that couples are at their greatest risk of divorcing just before their fifth anniversary! In a culture seduced by the magic of instant gratification, mere contentedness is no longer enough in marriage.

Sadly, mere contentedness requires too much sacrifice.

We want more! We think we deserve more! And we look for more!

It appears that young couples today are less willing to view early marital experiences as challenges and less likely to make the necessary compromises and sacrifices along the way. If you make it ten years, you're in better shape though and more likely to stay together for the long haul.

Yet, there are some couples who don't even make it to the altar. Pourquoi?

A thrice-divorced client, age 52, sought me out for individual counseling this past year. In the first session she described her new relationship with a widowed man who didn't seem to be very fair: 1) he refused to discuss his past or his prior marriage; 2) he had a rule that neither of them could be alone with "single" friends; 3) he insisted that he had the "right" to smoke; 4) he refused to stop smoking in the car and house, even though my client developed asthma from his second hand smoke, 5) he insisted on sex every day, between the hours of 5-7 pm, because that is when his G-spot required some lovin' in order to heal an enlarged prostate; 6) he insisted that dinner be served at 9:30 pm promptly, 7) he insisted that their wedding be in February, in Jamaica, where he knew it would be possible to buy marijuana on the beach without any problem; 8) he protested her traveling to Florida to see an aunt who was dying from cancer; 9) he refused to go to Florida with her to see this aunt who was dying from cancer. To cap it off, 10) he refused couples counseling.

My client was confused as to whether she should marry him in February. In her words, this man's life was "consumed with having sex, getting a buzz on, his G-spot massaged, and killing me with his smoking." She wanted to know what her options were. As I held a symbolic mirror up to her face, I empathically asked her to imagine the following options. First, she might offer yet another heartfelt plea for them to seek out counseling from a mutually agreed upon "helper" – be it a therapist, clergyman, or shaman. Second, she might "dress up" in her finest attire and then, with her dignity in tow, solemnly walk out the front door with her heels clicking to the beat of *Glory, Glory, Halleluiah!* Third, she might slip on a sleek pair of New Balance running shoes and dart out the front door as if her house were on fire! Already knowing that this narcissist didn't see her as "worth tryin' for" – worth sacrificing for – she chose door number three.

An unwillingness to sacrifice often extends downward to children as well. Just last week a couple shared their recent heartache with me. Sadly for the bride, her parents were ensnarled in a bitter divorce in Chicago at the very same time she was celebrating her betrothal. Each parent wanted this heartbroken bride, as well as her sister, to choose sides. Her father had made a simple request: "Testify against your mother, both in deposition and in court, and I'll contribute to your wedding! If not, you're on your own!"

Where is the proverbial 2x4 when you need it the most? In the examples above, the narcissistic "boyfriend" and "father" were certainly not emotionally dialed into the needs of loved ones, nor were they willing to sacrifice in the name of love. Each client was left to suck in unwanted nicotine toxins or to walk down an aisle alone without a father by her side. Reasonably indeed, each felt burned.

Getting To the Heart of the Matter

The boyfriend and father just described are immersed in a blinding narcissism that often reduces relationships to ashen ruins: "I *love* money!" I *love* my reflected image!" "I *love* being right!" These three thoughts topple the most upright of relationships. Sacrifice requires that we find proper measure with all three. We must share our money, we must forsake being right for being understood, and Narcissus must share the surface of a reflection pool. There are certain truths about sacrifice which help maintain healthy bonds:

* ✳ **Sacrifice means putting something else before oneself.** Each day is another opportunity to meet someone else's needs besides our own. Like any muscle in the body, our minds need to be conditioned to [1] pause, [2] wonder, and then [3] please a friend, colleague, or loved one so they can have a good day.

* ✳ **Sacrifice means giving up something we hold dear.** The things we give up must have value to us now or in the future. Be it time at work or time on *Facebook*, what is put aside reflects an object of love that has absorbed us or seduced us. These sacrifices may be more abstract, as in fame; or more concrete, as in playing golf. Sacrifice of abstract things – like pride, power and prestige – are worth far more than concrete sacrifice – like a new car or TV. Sacrifice means giving up what we love now for something we

might love even more later.

* **Sacrifice means devotion without measure.** Devotional love is obligation without duty while obligation is duty without love. We give because the act of giving is reward enough. We don't keep score and we don't put a higher premium on what we have given over what we have received.

* **Sacrifice means we see everything we do as time. All we really have is time.** Our lives are spent making choices about time. One of the essential truths regarding equality is that each person on earth is given the same gift of allotted time to spend each and every day. Our eulogies reflect the choices that we have made!

* **Sacrifice means we give up the need to be right, to be righteous, or self-righteous.** When ever I have an opportunity to officiate in a wedding ceremony I make one point over and over again: the most important thing we offer up as sacrifice in a marriage is the need to be "right." There is a time in every marriage when we must choose: Do I want to be "right" or do I want to be "happy?"

* **Sacrifice means that we see everything of value as "shared value" – not belonging to us.** Nothing of true value belongs to us. It is shared among us. All sacrifices lead to healthier relationships, healthier families, healthier communities, and a healthier planet. The love we take is equal to the love we make. As one good deed begets another, love begets love. We all prosper.

The most important things we possess in our lives are the things we leave behind.

The most important possessions in our lives are the relationships we leave behind when we die. These precious bonds require never-ending choices. I know it doesn't seem this way as we scurry about on autopilot each day. Yet, as we scoot out the front door to one commitment or another, we leave behind a world of other choices: playing with the dog, doing the laundry, calling cousin Vinnie in New Jersey who just had surgery, or taking time to read Emily Dickinson. In actuality, we are making decisions constantly, and each of these decisions is based on a hierarchy of values which serve as the bedrock for our lives.

Sometimes we learn *what* to sacrifice as we see in Sean's letter to his wife Elise:

Elise my love: I see clearly now that I have been adrift. I have drifted away from you and slid into a pattern of indulging myself with simple pleasures and distant dreams. Somehow the Siren call of golf, Lake Travis, and music has charmed me. I have become distracted. Somehow I thought that I deserved all these pleasures because I was working so hard to climb the ladder at IBM – for us. To be honest, I am selfish, and want what I want, when I want it, and I can't stand having to wait on someone else or bending my own wishes to accommodate someone else's "time" table. Things are now more clearly in focus. While trying to honor my parent's past legacy at IBM I somehow lost contact with present reality – the people who matter most to me. There is nothing I want to invest in more than "time" with you and the kids. You guys are my present and my future. Now, when I think of the weekend calendar, I realize there must be room for not only my name, but your name, Josie's name, and Rob's name.

I now realize that it wasn't all that time at IBM, or even on the golf course, that I needed to sacrifice. It was my need for "control," my belief in self-destiny. Somehow I had convinced myself that my happiness was solely dependent upon my own efforts to succeed, to be seen as successful, and to succeed in honoring the family tradition at IBM. I became Odysseus on a lonely journey. I now realize that If I did, I was afraid that I would be abandoned by you – leaving me stranded at sea. Ironically, it was this very abandonment that I experienced with my father who seemed never there for me. Thank you, my sweet Elise, for sparing me from a Titanic calamity. Thank you for helping me get back on course.

Love Sean

Sean captured many of the elements of *sacrifice* in his letter to Elise:

* ✳ Humbly accept that vision became blurred and a drift inward occurred.
* ✳ Acknowledge that anything of value requires making wise choices of the heart.
* ✳ Affirm that relationships are the most important thing in life.
* ✳ Declare an intention to invest "time" in those relationships that truly matter.
* ✳ Acknowledge what you are willing to forsake for the sake of these bonds.
* ✳ Acknowledge that sharing a love-life dictates the sharing of time as well.

Many choices in life are really approach/approach conflicts: that is, we have two or more equally desirable options and we must choose one of them. We literally want to approach, or choose, both options. You are invited to a Christmas pops concert with business colleagues the same evening your sister is scheduled to come into town – tough choice for some; not for others. Which deeply embedded value helps guide you with this choice? Which one will you sacrifice for the sake of a greater good?

If all sacrifice is about choice, all choice is about time.

We only get 24 hours, 1,440 minutes, and 86,400 seconds a day. All of our choices take place within these parameters. Most of our time is spent in the pursuit of abundance – the accumulation of money, possessions, and the ten-thousand things of life. From lampshades to bank accounts, we chase the sacred dollar bill in the hope that we might find value in what it buys. We spend countless hours making money, spending money, and paying back the money we spent.

My friend, Deacon Dick Orton, likes to remind newlyweds of two numbers: "1" vs. "9125." "1" is the number of days of your wedding. How much money did you spend? How much anxiety did you expend? How much time did you invest in preparing for that one day? Now think of the number "9125." That is the number of days in a 25 year marriage. How much are you going to invest in making those years wonderful? Think about it!

Time is probably our most precious commodity because we have a finite amount of it. There is nothing in life that we covet that can be obtained without spending time devoted to it.

Being educated, being wealthy, or being loved all require an investment of time in its pursuit. If you're spending time seeking pleasure you may not be making money; if you're making money you may not be having pleasure; and if you are absorbed seeking pleasure and making money, you may not be spending time making love.

The key to understanding these truths is the notion that we will trade up for something more valuable when we choose to sacrifice.

Sacrificing for others is literally a gift to oneself. We go to a higher, more virtuous plane. In the words of Charles Dubois, "The important thing is this: To be able at any moment to sacrifice what we are for what we could become."[2]

And what we're becoming is an abstract thing that others may not even see. Every day sacrifices of the heart and soul are never even noticed by others. Yet, each of these moments helps to define further the person we are becoming. When we tithe in our congregations, when we hug our children good bye as they leave for school each morning, when we take time to plan the evening meal, as we volunteer for Meals on Wheels, when we cancel a business meeting to watch our son sing in the school choir, we become more of who we were meant to be.

Achieving wealth in our concrete jungles does not in any way reflect a higher self. All thoughts centered on "being the most" or "having the most" suggest that we are off course in our journeys. Concrete possessions and wealth often feed more abstract notions about fame, reputation, and good fortune. The abstractions of possessions, power, and prestige that Richard Rohr talks about are not the abstractions that represent our greatest sacrifice. Only when we sacrifice in the name of love do we trade up for something more.

Where was the sacrifice for the two clients mentioned at the beginning of this chapter? Surely, smoking could be relegated to the back patio or mercifully relinquished completely for the sake of health. And, surely, children can be spared triangulation and the self-serving emotional ploys of divorcing parents – in the name of love! Where is the higher self in these individuals?

As I have belabored throughout this book, narcissism is a force which can alienate others, while compromising the greater well-being of all. It is in our own interest, as well as the interest of others, to promote the gift of sacrifice, as well as the other five gifts. Sacrifice is a gift because we release ourselves from the constant forces of narcissism which govern our lives.

Sacrifice reflects our goodness.

Why are we good? Are we merely good because we ply mind over impulse from time to time? Are we good because God inspires us to be so? Are we good because our very survival as a civilization requires that we be so? Perhaps all three! When we sacrifice for others we rise up from our slumber, from our denial that others have needs as important as our own. Even Sigmund Freud recognized that goodness is not the opposite of evil, but of self-centeredness. For every act of goodness, for every sacrifice made, we rise a little higher to find that more virtuous plane described by Charles Dubois.

Lifestyle choices and life crisis choices define our journey toward a higher self. By life-style choices, I mean the ongoing, everyday choices we make which serve not only our needs but those of others. I am referring to each of the small acts of service and devotion described already: each hug, each shared meal, each dollar put into savings, and each drug of choice bypassed. I am extolling the virtue of freedom as Sartre described it: an acceptance of respon-sibility – each day – for choice and a commitment to one's choice.

By life crisis choices I mean that tragedy awakens us from our benumbed sensitivities. When nature releases her fury in the form of earthquakes, cyclones, and floods we are remind-ed of innocent suffering. We rise up, even from our geographical boundaries, to give in such times. While the most devout among us might believe that all sinners will eventually suffer, it does not follow that every instance of suffering is retribution for sin. Perhaps if this were not a "fallen world" there would be no suffering; but since it is a fallen world, it does not follow that there is no innocent suffering. So we sacrifice our goods, our goodness, and our time to help victims.

We are most of service to others, however, when our own heart has been broken. Life crises teach us this in critical moments. When our family members lie flattened by illness in a hospital room, stand destitute in bankruptcy court – financially ruined, or left "hanging" by social oppres-sion or discrimination – we have a duty to respond, to sacrifice in the name of love.

A loving relationship is the universal higher journey into which we all may fit. So long as we view such bonds as imperfect tapestries or as quilts of many colors, we will spend our time well off. Varied patterns using a full spectrum of colors and design are the quilts my grand-mother used to piece together. She knew full well that each quilt was unique and that her gift was not intended to be perfect. She wished only that we be warm in the cold breath of night once the last fireplace ember lost its light. Every stitch reflected the everyday choice she made to love us deeply.

The kind of sacrifice I am describing herein is a deeply personal experience. It is an ex-perience that lifts us up from our self-centered lives and frees us to be far more than we ever thought we could be. This freedom to expand is perhaps best described in metaphors, as the English Romantic poet Shelley once wrote:

I can give not what men call love,
But wilt thou accept not what the heart lifts above and the heavens reject not
the desire of the moth for the star, of the night for the morrow;
A longing for something afar from the sphere of our sorrow.[3]

Sacrifice permits us to belong to something much greater than our own realm. It is a realm, I believe, best called love. As G. N. Devy describes, "The desire to belong to a dream realm far from the sphere of our animal world is the source of goodness that individuals display in every society and age. The creative freedom that their sacrifice and dedication bring in return is the intoxicating energy that fuels their resolve to change the human existence. At the heart of goodness is the limitless freedom which allows the human to be divine."[4]

Our Story

Children also teach us a profound lesson in sacrifice. Any loving parent knows that the loss of a child is life's cruelest blow. The sweet innocence of childhood is not intended to end prematurely. The rebellious spirit of adolescence is intended to morph into something more intelligible. And the promise of early adulthood ideals needs its own time on the vine to mature. On Father's Day, 2002, Claire and I began a journey of sacrifice that would bring us frighteningly close to this loss of innocence, spirit, and ideals – indeed, the potential loss of our child's life.

It began as a seemingly innocent trip to Nuevo Laredo on a Saturday morning June 15th. Our son Erik, and his girlfriend Terri, went to Nuevo Laredo for the evening. They drove across in Terri's car and stayed at a hotel on the Mexican side. After socializing awhile with some college friends at the Cadillac Bar, Erik and Terri were eager to check out Firenses, another club. After dancing the night away they eventually retired to their motel room.

Several hours later, at 3 a.m., Erik and Terri heard a loud knock on their hotel door. Naively Erik opened the door. It was one of the Mexicans they had met at Firenses just hours before. He implored Erik to give him a ride home since he supposedly got separated from his friend. When they were about a mile away the guy pulled a gun on Erik and threatened to shoot him if he did not get out of the car and give up the vehicle. As Erik frantically jumped out of his car he had the painful realization that this was a set up. Running as quickly as he could, he got back to the hotel only to find his worst fear realized.

Terri was gone.

While the car jacking was occurring at gun point, the second guy, who had been hiding in the shadows of the hotel, had convinced Terri to go with him – insisting that Erik was in trouble with the police. Terri was taken to a remote site, raped, and somehow escaped as the rapist was making calls on his cell phone. She was picked up, half naked, near one of the bridge crossings to the United States.

In the meantime, Erik was panic-stricken and called the Mexican police. When they arrived he was in a frenzy, fearing for Terri's life. There was no communication, given the language barrier. They threw him to the ground. Within minutes they found a prescription of Valium – which Terri had legally filled the day before. Refusing to address the car-jacking and abduction issues, the police focused entirely on what they had found on Erik. They wanted to know where the prescription was. When Erik repeatedly told them it was in his stolen vehicle, they asked for money. He had none since his wallet was in the vehicle as well.

He was then arrested and thrown in jail.

Prison can be a brutal place. El Penal de La Loma was such a place. We soon learned that the last man murdered by other prisoners at La Loma had been an American man one year before. I was tortured by the thought of Erik being knifed to death in this concrete jungle. Fear paralyzed me. As an uncertain future gripped us, Claire and I dropped to our knees in a God-forsaken hotel room in Laredo, where we prepared for battle in a war we didn't understand.

We prayed.

We also hired two attorneys: one attorney understood the Mexican jurisprudence system and would work in a legal system where a person can be detained on the presumption of guilt, with no evidence; a second Mexican attorney was also retained as a consultant in the case. The job of this second attorney was to work toward Erik's release "from the inside out!"

Our first visual impression of Erik at La Loma was his nubbled, unshaven face behind rusting iron rails of a chest-high window, where he came to greet us. We were in shock. After passing through numerous checkpoints along the way, we had been permitted entrance. Erik took us down darkened hallways to a central room where bedrolls were laid out along the bare perimeter of a hollow, poorly lit room. Expressionless faces with piercing, hollow eyes greeted us everywhere.

We were gringos, with money, in a foreign land.

He told us that he had slept on a concrete floor among 300 or so strangers, in this small section of the prison. He informed us that he had been given a choice by prison authorities. He could be transferred to the American unit where he would be in the company of nine others who lacked money for their own defense, or choose to stay within the Mexican unit where he currently was lodged. To our chagrin, he insisted on remaining on the Mexican side where he believed he could use his two years of Spanish and his survival skills much more effectively. He believed that his likelihood of survival was greater if he befriended some Mexican prisoners who had power within that environment! He concluded by telling us that three "senior" Mexican prisoners had offered one remaining spot in their separate nook – for the right price!

For the right price!

For the right price we were able to buy him a cot from the metal shop, blankets, fresh water, and fresh food served from private food vendors within the prison itself. Without financial support he would lie alone in the dark, maintain all-night vigils, and eat from large soup buckets filled with watered-down brine. For the right price Erik's health and safety could be "insured" – not assured. We paid with cash as well as with gratitude!

Those three men proved to be a blessing, and we are grateful to this day.

It was summertime in Texas now, and the temperature soared into the 100's in the border town of Nuevo Laredo. Each weekend Claire and I would leave promptly from work, drive three hours to Laredo, buy two foam ice chests, fill them with fruits and meat, and then make our way to a motel room where we would fill the chests with ice for the night. The next morning we would carry the heavy chests across the border into Mexico where we would hail a cab for the 20-minute drive to El Penal de La Loma. As this sweaty weekend ritual continued through July and August we soon realized that we did not have to hail a cab any longer on Saturday or Sunday mornings. These border town cabbies knew our every move – and they waited for us.

In addition to our weekend trips to Nuevo Laredo, I soon began a weekly ritual of Tuesdays with Erik. Each Tuesday I would rise at 5:00 am, grope my way to the car, and drive alone to Laredo. Knowing its value, I would carry an ice chest filled with food across a forsaken bridge, past beggars more forlorn than me, hail a cab, and arrive at the prison entrance by opening time – 9:00 am. Often I would find Erik depressed, simply lying still in his 6x9 cubicle. Often I would find myself depressed as well and simply lie next to him, just holding him until we both fell asleep. He would later tell me that these were precious times for him when the warmth of my body would comfort him without emasculating judgment from the other men in prison.

    Often I would read to him in English since he seldom heard our language spoken. At other times, we would watch VHS movies on a small television "smuggled" into their cubby hole. One day we watched *The Shawshank Redemption*, a painfully appropriate movie. I left before it concluded and asked Erik to listen for the special words left for Morgan Freeman by Timothy Robbins in a buried box, by a barren stone wall: "Hope is a good thing; maybe the best of all things; and good things never die."

    Leaving the prison at the end of the day was hell.

    My helplessness and profound sadness could not be measured on any Richter scale devised my humankind. I mourned very deeply. Each Tuesday evening, as I exited past two guards, I would steal one final glimpse of Erik's saddened face as he tried to accept his fate. He would wave goodbye and tell me that he loved me. Trying to ignore his sweat-sodden t-shirt so plainly evident, I would return these precious graces and move quickly to the front gate where I would break down and cry. I usually drove without stopping until I saw the Austin city limits sign approaching. Only then would I take a deep breath and begin to release my tightened grip on the steering wheel.

    Time and space within this chapter do not permit me to detail the rest of our story. I will say that there were countless legal delays, unexpected "vacations" by the judge, and seemingly meaningless testimony from Claire, Erik, and myself. We felt completely impotent in this murky "system of justice." Finally, in the early part of September – after nearly three months of agony – the judge had yet another 10 days to render a verdict. Our second attorney, the one needed for consultation, made it quite clear that more money would help the judge be more judicious! At 12:00 pm MIDNIGHT, the judge ruled.

    On Friday, September 13th, Erik was finally released from El Penal de La Loma.

    He was dropped off at the Mexican border, where we anxiously awaited him – not knowing for sure if he would be released. When he appeared in the darkness, we all hugged tightly, yet quietly, almost mutely. We sighed together as one. Then, as if drawn by some universal force, we briskly walked to the center of the bridge, to a point on a wall, which read, United States of America. As we stepped across that line, the shackles removed, freedom beneath our feet, we cried like we had never cried. These were the first tears that Erik had shed in the 16 weeks of captivity.

Sacrifice permits us to belong to something much greater than our own realm.

The creation of life is a miracle. Guardianship of that life is love. Erik's detention at La Loma was a life crisis for all of us, Jessica included. Our daughter lost her parents that summer. We were all thrown into an abyss. Looking into that frightening void has taught us to cherish our blessings as well as the price we pay to keep them. We sacrificed money and time for some greater treasure called love. As each of us held our breath that summer, we reached out to one another in love. Between parent and child, what more needs to be said?

    Material things mattered not in the summer of 2002. What mattered was the beating of a heart, the warmth of a smile, and the cosmic hope that there might be one more day to look into each other's eyes. We asked for little more than this, that summer:

Look into my eyes - you will see
What you mean to me
Search your heart - search your soul
And when you find me there you'll search no more
Don't tell me it's not worth tryin' for
You can't tell me it's not worth dyin' for
You know it's true
Everything I do - I do it for you[5]

Sacrifice and Personal Identity

Sacrifice implies that a relationship exists.

The relationship may be with a love partner, a child, a parent, a social cause, an alma mater, a country, Planet Earth, or the living God. When we choose to sacrifice we place a high value on the "other" that we sacrifice for. In the process we must give up something – perhaps something of extraordinary, personal value.

For theologians, sacrifice belongs in the realm of religion – in one's devoutness. For ancient Jews, the story of Abraham and Isaac underscores the ultimate sacrifice expected of God's servants. To willingly give up one's only son is certainly the ultimate sacrifice. For Christians, Jesus' crucifixion is regarded as the perfect sacrifice. He spilled his blood on the cross for the sins of the world. Eucharist practice today is a symbolic celebration of the body and blood of Christ. Devout Christians are called to give themselves to God as a living sacrifice. In the words of the Apostle Paul, in Romans 12:1-2, "I beseech you therefore, brethren, by the mercies of God, that you present your bodies a living sacrifice, holy, acceptable to God, which is your reasonable service."

Claire and I were willing to give up our time, our life's savings, our work commitments, our peace of mind, our physical health, and perhaps even our lives to get our son back to safety. Our commitment was resolute and unwavering. If we paused at all, it was to catch our breath after wretched, unpredictable blows would bring us to our knees. We would then rise up again to take on the unrelenting high tide we faced.

I know that our story is extreme and that sacrifice must be viewed along a much fuller continuum. While I viscerally poured myself into the life-threatening drama which encased our lives in 2002, I recognize that I fail miserably with more mundane examples of sacrifice. I protest when asked to go 10 minutes out of my way for an extra liter of water on the way home from work; I reluctantly groan when I must give up a photography weekend shooting wildflowers in the Hill Country just outside Austin; and I occasionally grimace when I must relinquish a Sunday football game for the sake of Claire's mother who prefers a late lunch on the weekends. Am I really very far removed from that fellow mentioned at the beginning of the chapter who wouldn't give up having his G-spot massaged and wouldn't stop smoking in the car or the house?

For the narcissist, mired in his own ego or pleasure needs, it is the relationship to one-self that must be relinquished.

For the narcissist, sacrifice may be the supreme gift offered in love. The narcissist, in order to survive in a love relationship, must give up something about her life which has become so valued that its partial loss seems catastrophic, or, at least, plainly unfair. To give up the glory of one's role at work, the glamour of one's status among friends, or the gratification of more power or posses-sions seems too much to bear for the narcissist. Being right, righteous, or self-righteous must go. These compromises are ego dystonic – alien to one's sense of self, for the narcissist. They contra-dict one's sense of identity – who one has become. If I see myself as a VIP or BMOC (Big Man on Campus), am I willing to forgo strokes at work for the sake of family time at home?

For the boyfriend described at the beginning of this chapter, his penis and cigarettes were Freudian extensions of his identity – phallic symbols he seldom lost touch with! This myopic, self-serving narcissism proved to be a disaster for his love partners in one relationship after another. This narcissist saw himself foremost as a sexual being, and secondarily as a man with strong will. These were two aspects of his identity he refused to give up, compromise, or relinquish. A former wife had once called him an "egomaniac, a self-absorbed loner," while he thought of himself as a "tower of power" and fell prey to a self-image with voracious tastes.

The ego can become a relentless force, an indomitable presence, in our lives. We often live for it; some even die for it. Sacrifice requires that we free ourselves from the entanglements of the ego and from the very "things" we get attached to – in the name of love. When the ego rules, when self-interest reigns, when we refuse to sacrifice, what is it that we are "controlling" or holding onto – status, recognition, knowledge, physical appearance, money, or special abili-ties? But are any of these things truly who we are!

Author Eckert Tolle reminds us that: "As long as the egoic mind is running your life, you cannot truly be at ease; you cannot be at peace or fulfilled except for brief intervals when you ob-tained what you wanted, when a craving has just been fulfilled. Since the ego is a derived sense of self, it needs to identify with external things. It needs to be both defended and fed constantly."[6]

When it comes to sacrifice, our challenge is two-fold: first, we must understand what we hold onto so dearly; second, we must be willing to forsake the very things we cherish – for the sake of love. These are not easy tasks and may well take a lifetime to figure out. But it is possible to take a snapshot picture of life through a simple but profound exercise that I learned over 35 years ago. It is called "Life Review."

Who Am I

I invite you to answer a simple question: Who am I? Over and over again, ten times, ask your-self: Who am I? You may choose to answer in terms of the roles and responsibilities you have in life, the groups you belong to, the beliefs you hold true, or certain qualities or traits you have as a person. Try to list those things which are really important to your sense of yourself – things that, if you lost them, would make a radical difference to your identity and meaning of life for you. Silent, individual reflection is necessary while doing this exercise.

(1) Corporate V.P. _____

(2) A sensitive man _____

(3) A mother _____

(4)_____

(5)_____

(6)_____

(7)_____

(8)_____

(9)_____

(10)_____

Consider each item in your "Who am I" list separately. Try to imagine how it would feel if that piece of you were no longer as important. For example, if you put "accountant" or "triathlete" as one of the items, what would less time spent at accounting or "working out" mean to you? How would you feel? What would you do? What would your life be like? Who would benefit from the available time you would now have since you would be working, or working out, less?

After reviewing each item in this way, rank order the items in the list by putting a number in front of each item. Put a **1** in front of the item which is most essential to your sense of yourself, the loss of which would require the greatest struggle to adjust to. Put a **10** beside the item which is least essential to your sense of yourself. Try to order all the items in this way, without any item tying for first place, second place, third place, etc. If some items in your list are aspects of your self that you dislike and would like to be rid of, they don't necessarily fall in the lower end of the rank order. The question for rank-ordering is how stressful would the adjustment struggle be if you lost that item? Some aspects of yourself that you dislike might be very hard to actually give up. I'll always remember the world-renowned researcher at the University of Texas who hated research but simply made too much money and got too many ego strokes to give it up – until he came to therapy.

Sacrifice is the only *Gift* that invites us to give up something that defines us in order to love another.

Sacrifice requires us to look inwardly in order to give outwardly. Along with *humility* and *acceptance*, sacrifice requires personal transformation so that we are free to love more fully. We now are ready for the final *Gift* – the *Gift* of "vision." With vision we see clearly the life we have been given as well as the life we intend to live. This vision becomes clear only when we look into our hearts: only then can we truly awaken. Without doing so, everything is but a dream.

CHAPTER **20**

The Gift of Vision

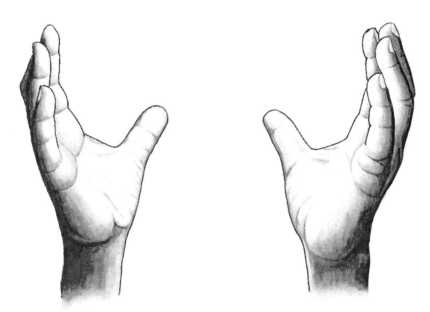

Your life is a sacred journey. And it is about change, growth, discovery, movement, transformation, continuously expanding your vision of what is possible, stretching your soul – learning to see clearly and deeply – listening to your intuition, taking courageous challenges at every step along the way. You are on the path... exactly where you are meant to be right now.... And from here, you can only go forward, shaping your life story into a magnificent tale of triumph, of healing, of courage, of beauty, of wisdom, of power, of dignity, and of love.[1]

More often than not, it is our children who teach us about relationship and vision.

Once upon a time, some years ago, I thought I was ready for Erik to go to Texas Christian University. More than ready! I was weary from over three years of mindless alcoholic escapades, academic conferences with exasperated teachers, humiliating tete-a-tetes with the high school principal, soccer coach or athletic director, and playing footsie in a minefield of legal problems which ranged from shoplifting to minor in possession charges. Along the way we also racked up four moving violations and two automobile accidents, one of which totaled a really sharp four-wheel drive Ford Bronco. Thankfully Erik escaped this high-speed drama in a cow pasture without even a scratch. Likewise there is no need to mention the countless "tardies" and unexcused absences at school. Oh, how Claire and I loved those calls!

"Dr. Bugen, this is the attendance office. Do you know that Erik has missed his first four classes today – just like he did yesterday and on Monday as well?"

"Uh, uh, no, but I'll check it out!!"

I was weary of that testosterone-driven peer group where the average social maturity level seemed to hover somewhere between fourth and fifth grade. I was weary of three years of beer cans and bottles scattered indiscreetly throughout the woods surrounding my house. I was weary of broken doors, shattered garage windows, smashed structural support beams, decimated basketball backboards, ravaged refrigerators, and sloth like scavengers in sleeping bags scattered scantily throughout our living room. I was weary of complaints from neighbors, calls from police stations, and applications for deferred adjudication. In short, it was time for Erik to find higher ground somewhere North of Austin. A new plateau, with a wide sweeping panorama, was in order. Texas Christian University, with its ratio of 2.6 women to every male specimen, would be the passageway to this new frontier, this personal transformation from ruffian moth to exhilarated butterfly.

Sunday, August 20, 1994 had finally come. True to form, Erik had done nothing to prepare for his departure. Claire, a friend named Barbara and I, had meticulously packed the car the night before. Girbaud shirts, slacks and assorted odds and ends hung impatiently from a rack strung firmly across the back seat of our Explorer. Desk lamp, toiletries, and underwear were ready for liftoff. All we needed was Erik's stereo dismantled and snuggly tucked into the remaining storage space behind the rear seat. This was to be Erik's only task on Sunday morning, his only rite of passage to the Big Show. All he had to do was arise at eight o'clock, as promised, to accomplish this one thing – hardly a Herculean task! Eight, eight-thirty, nine, nine-thirty came and went. Yes, we knew he had been out on the town till 3:30 a.m. No, we had not protested the night out or the overnight guests his last night home. Many rites of passage are often observed by novitiates! But there must be a time to start your engines.

Carpe diem. It was time to seize the day.

As Claire and I rushed to catch the second half of Jessica's semifinal tournament soccer game we knew that the stereo would be packed upon our return in one hour. After all, music emanating from 15-inch woofers is a tribal symbol for deliverance. Erik would certainly ensure safe passage of such integral symbols. We were right! They were packed, but not by Erik. Once again our friend, Barbara, had saved the day by grabbing a screwdriver with one hand and a threatening guillotine with the other. "Erik, you had better get your ass in gear or your parents with kill you when they get back from Jessica's game." To no avail, Barbara ended up doing the work while Erik schmoosed on the phone - saying goodbye to numerous young femme fatales who desired his 1-800 pager number. Some umbilical cords are indeed difficult to cut.

By 12:25 Sunday afternoon I was ready to lose my marbles. Totally frustrated by Erik's apparent denial that he was actually leaving Austin, Texas for Fort Worth, Texas I aimed my carcass for his vehicle where I presumed I would ride shotgun while he reluctantly drove away from our "Friends are always welcome!" watering hole. Aghast, I suddenly discovered that Erik was feverishly taking fenders off his car – a project that the devil had subliminally and maliciously placed on his agenda to create a mental breakdown on my part. As the devil worked his evil I responded appropriately.

"Erik, I've had it! Mom and I must drive all the way to Fort Worth and back today. We are getting a very, very, very late start. Give me that damn screwdriver, now! Get the hell in the car, now!" Claire, Barbara, Jessica and Alexis all came running to prevent a total system failure. Somehow the warm sentiment of this special moment – my son's departure for college – had been tainted by my pent up frustrations which seemed to yield to a deeper theme of discontent – a theme which echoed from the past, "ERIK, YOU ARE INCREDIBLY DISORGANIZED and a $#$###&!!"

As we pulled out of our Canon Wren Ponderosa, I imagined what a sight we were! Erik, who was behind the wheel, looked like Mario Andretti in his 400th mile of Indianapolis while I appeared to be in a guilt-laden, catatonic stupor following my outrageous emotional display just seconds earlier. Claire, haunted by her failure to prevent Mount Vesuvius from erupting, drafted closely and protectively behind in the now overstuffed Explorer, while Jessica, grief-stricken by this departure of her big brother, cried crocodile tears in the rear view mirror.

What would life be like for her now? After all, this is the same brother who just one month before had helped to construct a 12 foot ejaculating penis and single handedly – after jumping over a 14 foot railing in the Westlake High Commons – had carried this gigantic phallic symbol over his head to the cheers of hundreds of students during the last week of school. Among the well-wishers, of course, was his starry-eyed freshman sister. How could life in the Bugen family or at Westlake High School ever be the same?

As Erik drove his tension-filled Prelude northward along the IH-35 corridor to Fort Worth we fatefully found ourselves in a deluge of rain. The sky had opened up as if to wash away our pain. We both welcomed this cleansing and in the next hour we managed to hold hands and honor our love for one another through tender touch and unspoken devotion.

The message, after all, was quite clear: We must forgive in the name of love.

Like many travelers before us, we were taking only the most essential belongings and setting our sights on a distant land that beckoned us with an eerie sense of wonder and promise. What would become of my son who now had control of the car but knew not where he was heading? What would become of Jessica who would now be carving out her own high school niche with the fading presence of an older sibling silhouetting her journey? What would become of Claire and me? I wondered about all these things as I sunk more and more into the shadows of the bluish cloth of his passenger seat? A frightening sense of insignificance came over me. I suddenly felt alone and scared.

> *I wondered: Had the most important extensions of my life – my children – come into their own? Had the fruits of our labor matured abundantly on the resilient limbs of our humble lives?*

Erik's dormitory room resembled 10,000 other dormitory rooms. No larger than a cracker box, it possessed a simplicity required of youthful Spartan warriors about to launch themselves into academic battle. Their hovel consisted of four walls, two wooded desks, four bureau drawers, and a single unadorned window to ponder the heavens above for inspirational guidance. Yes, there were a few 20th Century accoutrements to complement this ascetic life style: (1) Stereo system with 15-inch woofers, (2) Refrigerator, (3) Computer with CD rom, (4) Clock radios, (5) Answering machine, and (6) Hi-tech stacking trays from the Container Store – a must for anxious parents who fear that the chaos of Freshman year might engulf their child unless these artificial life supports are available.

Claire even bought a shoe rack that was neatly placed in Erik's tiny two by two foot closet. The odds of Erik bending over at the end of each day to precisely place his shoes or high tops on two miniscule plastic tubes was as likely to occur as a July snowstorm in Austin, Texas! Yet, Erik endured these last attempts to parent on our part and smiled pleadingly as we headed for the Explorer to return home. We had packed his underwear, arranged his toothbrush and toothpaste by the sink, made his bed, and plugged in his radio.

It was now time to go.

As I walked from his room I glanced over my shoulder to notice the one picture Erik had intended for display – an image of the two of us surging through the powerful, threatening rapids of the Colorado River during a father/son raft trip a few years before. It was a lovely image of us yoked together in a common purpose, taking on a common foe. We both looked exhilarated and afraid. With telescopic wizardry I zoomed in to grasp a final sentimental view of that shared moment together – a fleeting moment in time – that seemed to mean something to Erik as well. Leaking a few tears I struggled to the car where final goodbyes and hugs were somehow endured.

I so desperately wanted to hold on to so many fleeting images: Feeding Erik cereal as his mouth jabbed hungrily and impatiently at the spoon; Telling nighttime stories as we played with transformers; Dipping in Barton Springs Pool; Patting his butt after a swimming or soccer match; or comforting him when he struggled, lost or was rejected by a friend.

The "storm clouds were clearing" in these tearful moments as we sluggishly headed home to Austin. There were no remnants of irritation, annoyance, disappointment, anger or frustration. I was not dwelling upon the siphoned off Johnny Walker or Chivas Regal which frequently seemed to fall below the indelible line I drew on the bottles in the liquor cabinet. There was no brooding about school attendance, lost homework, speeding tickets or court appearances. Instead I was overwhelmed by a profound sadness that I had not foreseen. I felt empty; like I had lost something very special – perhaps something I had not fully appreciated when I had it.

If two words could describe Erik – two words which underscore his soul – they would be *"inexpressible delight."* This quality alone accounts for more spontaneity than the whole of Yellowstone National Park could manifest through spontaneous offerings in one year! Knowing this, I wondered:

> *Had I been a good father?*
> *Had I spent enough time with Erik?*
> *Had I listened, hugged, and cherished him enough?*
> *Had I celebrated enough day-to-day moments with Erik?*
> *Where had 18 of 48 years of my life just gone?*

I would wonder these same thoughts three years hence when Jessica graduated. It had seemed so normal to get caught up in the routines of life, the day-to-day squabbles, the angry aftermaths, the Type A lifestyles, and the search for fame and glory. All of these essentials for the good life suddenly seemed frivolous – truly superficial – as I tried to sooth the empty hole in my gut. When these layers of distraction were removed I was left to see, once again, the deeper sentiment of love which is my true grounding in life. Yet, another life lesson: looking backwards often reveals the trailing gases of what we have created.

Do you continuously expand your vision, or do you just live life blindly?

To have vision requires that we see in different ways: We must see *within* ourselves – to find stable, core values, perhaps our essence, that supersede fleeting self interests. We must see *beyond* ourselves – to find some other person, cause, or thing more loved than ourselves. We must look *behind* ourselves – to bless the trailing gases that have shaped our lives for 14 billion years. And we must look *forward* and wonder how we might leave a lasting imprint in an immense, ever-expanding, black-holed universe – that we are part of a greater whole. The ability to see in these ways is true wisdom.

I have described five *Gifts* so far – *Humility, Forgiveness, Acceptance, Compassion,* and *Sacrifice.* Each of the six gifts affirms that we matter, we count, and that love – above all other earthly pursuits – allows us to see life clearly. I really don't think any relationship can endure without these gifts. This chapter's focus on Vision encourages each of us to see our place in a larger relational world – a cosmic universe. Our intimate connections to one another are being threatened by whirlwind lifestyles and technological advances these days. Often our vision only extends 12 inches or so to a cell phone or computer screen.

I fear that as we leave the fire pit of our ancestors further and further behind, we are going blind.

Nancy McCranie is director of volunteer and bereavement services for Hospice Austin. After traveling through 40 countries over a seven-year period of time with her husband Nancy described what a life-changing experience it was when complete strangers took the time to graciously welcome her. "The most striking thing about our years on the road was not the breathtaking beauty, or the incredible cultural diversity, or even the crippling poverty we witnessed. Rather, most memorable was how the simple lives of the people we met contrasted with an extravagant generosity of spirit. Time and time again virtual strangers, people with little to give by our standards, would open their homes and hearts to offer us shelter, friendship, a cup of tea, a piece of bread. These encounters were humbling, awakening in us a deep sense of gratitude."[2]

Our real challenge is to be astonished by the more ordinary visions of everyday life.

Each of us is awash in a daily tidal pool of wonder – if only we could value what we experience. Have you not found it wonderful to be forgiven after shattering trust, to receive a hug from a child as you return home at the end of the day, or to watch an early morning mist envelop a pond as you walk with friends or a loved one? We learn to see in these moments – beyond our reflected selves.

Elise, wife of Sean from the previous chapter on sacrifice, reflected on "Vision":

Dearest Sean: You mean the world to me. The word vision has many shades of meaning to me. When I think about the future I think about a future we would like to have. It is binocular vision: four eyes, two people, two views all blending into one. It is more than a goal or an objective; it encompasses our spirit and soul as a couple, not just what we individually want to accomplish. Personal goals mean far less to me than relationship goals. This vision goes well beyond where we live in our retirement years or how much money we might have saved. It seeks a life together that is the best of what we have to offer each other. There are no guarantees about our health or our wealth. What matters is a presence in each other's lives that enriches, enlivens, and nurtures.

I know that the full measure of our lives can only be measured by looking at the fullness of our journey together. No single chapter, no single event, or any moment in time can define us. A full journey for us means that we build on all that we've learned and experienced together in order to create a new beginning – one in which we not only comfort and support each other, but one in which we enjoy each other. This foundation has many pillars that include the love of family and friends, shared activities that strengthen our bodies and mind, and a spiritual life that takes us beyond our personal pleasure or pain. While I know that either of us could find ways to achieve a personal vision, this vision is for the two of us. We can achieve it only by seeking it together. Sean, I love you. Yours forever, Elise.

Elise wisely reflects the elements of *vision*:

✳ Affirm stable, core values which define your life. Choose to live them!
✳ Affirm that some other person, family, or cause is more loved than oneself.

* Affirm that past experiences serve as precious grist for a full life ahead.
* Affirm that abstract intangibles far exceed concrete tangibles in life.
* Describe the legacy or lasting imprint you intend to leave behind.
* Affirm that relationship goals far exceed personal goals in life.
* Affirm that we are not only *pushed* forward by our pasts, but *pulled* forward by vision.

My contention is simple enough: each of us is on a path that connects to an abundant world. Our life is a miraculous, astonishing, marvelous gift – a gift so precious that we must share it with others. A life without love is mournful; a love not shared, tragic. Life is love – let it snow, let it snow, let it snow! What does it mean to love and to be the only species on earth with the capacity to hold a broken heart, to yearn for a future nest, and to etch meaning out of ongoing life dramas? We are unique as a species and stand alone as the Human Element in an extraordinary Dow Chemical advertisement:

For each of us, there's a moment of discovery.
We turn a page, we raise a hand.
And just then, in the flash of a synapse
we learn that life is elemental -
And this knowledge changes everything.
We look around and see the grandness of the scheme...

The human element is the element of change.
It gives us our footing to stand fearlessly and face the future.
It is a way of seeing.
It gives us a way of touching.
Issues, ambitions, lives!
The human element;
Nothing is more fundamental.
Nothing more elemental![3]

We take so much for granted.

The human element is like stained-glass windows. It is that moment of discovery when we learn more about lasting love. We sparkle and shine when the sun is out, but when darkness sets in, our true beauty is revealed only if there is a light from within. We are torch lights which attract others to us. We are part of the light which gives this universe its life. And it is light which gives meaning to darkness. We are meaning-makers and vision-seekers who possess a gift no other species can acclaim: we can articulate a future with a defined purpose. Facing the darkness of an unknown future, each of us must take a bold step forward: "When we come to the edge of all the light we have – and we must take a step into the darkness of the unknown – we must believe one of two things: either we will find something firm to stand on, or we will be taught to fly."[4]

While we Homo sapiens have been around for maybe 300,000 years, the concept of love has existed for less than a 1,000! Take a moment to wonder along with writer John McPhee and David Brower. Brower, as I mentioned in Chapter Two, is one of the acclaimed heroes of the Sierra Club. Brower, in his Sermon, asks us to envision the six days of Genesis as merely a figure of speech for what in scientific fact has been four and one-half billion years. In this view, a day equals something like seven hundred and fifty million years, and thus "all day Monday and until Tuesday noon creation was busy getting the earth going." Think of life beginning on Tuesday noon, and the "beautiful, organic wholeness of it" developing over the next four days. McPhee goes on:

> At 4 p.m. Saturday, the big reptiles came on. Five hours later, when the redwoods appeared, there were no more big reptiles. Three minutes before midnight, Christ arrived. At one-fortieth of a second before midnight, the Industrial Revolution began. We are surrounded by people who think that what we have been doing for that one-fortieth of a second can go on indefinitely. They are considered normal, but they are stark raving mad.[5]

If this doesn't grab you consider a geological parallel. McPhee guides us again:

> In geological terms, the Precambrian runs from New Year's Day until well after Halloween. Dinosaurs appear in the middle of December and are gone the day after Christmas. The last ice sheet melts on December 31st at one minute before midnight, and the Roman Empire lasts five seconds. With your arms spread wide to represent all time on earth, look at one hand with its line of life. The Cambrian begins in the wrist, and the Permian Extinction is at the outer end of the palm. All of the Cenozoic is in a fingerprint, and in a single stroke with a medium-grained nail file you could eradicate human history.

A fraction of a millisecond! That's all we have. We can hope for more. We can pray for more. We can sacrifice for more. We can even kill each other in the name of more. But this is it, folks. Our time on earth is limited, and it's over in a flash. We can spend it being self-absorbed with golf balls, crystal balls, and evening balls or we can find each other in the mist. We can go to our church, mosque, or synagogue to find God, and if we are lucky, we find each other. Or, in the words of astrophysicist, Jeffrey Bennett, we must confront our narcissistic inclinations:

> We can continue to act as though we are the center of the universe, but in that case we will suffer the consequences of our ignorance. Or we can develop a true cosmic perspective and set our civilization on a course to a better future for all, a future that someday will take our descendents to the stars...[this] cosmic perspective should teach us some humility, because the central lesson of Galileo's discoveries is that we humans are no more central to the universe than our planet or star...Emotionally, and behaviorally, our species still acts as though the whole of creation somehow revolves around each of us personally.[6]

We must remember that only 400 years ago Galileo spent the dwindling days of his life under house arrest for daring to report his observations that Venus (as well as Earth) actually orbited the sun, and not, as previously believed, Earth. I know we want to feel special but we can't let our self-absorption blind us to a greater truth – a greater vision: not only does our precious planet Earth orbit the sun, but our sun is merely one sun among 100 billion stars within our Milky Way Galaxy; and our galaxy is but one within a cosmos of 100 billion galaxies in the observable universe. Somehow, we must wrestle with the notion that all these stars and all these galaxies probably far exceed all the grains of sand on all the beaches on Earth. Very humbling!

So, here we are! Let us breathe life into something, anything, larger than ourselves – if only for a fraction of a millisecond. But tell that to "stars" like Heidi Montag who shamelessly and unabashedly revealed to the world in 2010 that she underwent 10 plastic surgery procedures all at once to "feel perfect." At age 23, Ms. Montag asserted that she already had her third breast augmentation scheduled and is "just starting" out on her journey to plastic heaven.

Somehow, I don't think this is what Galileo had in mind!

We are here to complete ourselves, not just by reaching in, nor by reaching out for silicone implants. We are here to fill our empty space within, our dark holes, with mature love – not plastic surgery. Consumerism and materialism trivialize the gift of life. Our journeys are not about perfect bodies or idealized body-images as seen on *Dr. 90210*, *The Biggest Loser*, *The Swan*, *Look-a-Like*, *I Want a Famous Face*, and *Celebrity Fit Club*. Life is about exploring relationships and this is our time in history to see this clearly.

Jessica's Vision

Christmas morning, December 25th, 2007, was a special morning for the Bugen and Hutson families. For on this day, Ryan Hutson stole away from his Houston home at 6 a.m., drove two hours north to our home in Austin, and knocked on our door "unexpectedly!"

Our daughter Jessica had been hoping for some clothing, some jewelry, maybe even a surprise pug puppy for the holidays, but not Ryan at 10:00 am in the morning! So, as the ruse unfolded, Ryan marched into the house with a large dog crate filled with the cutest stuffed pug imaginable. Just under the white chin of this precious puppy was hung a blue box delicately draped with a bright red ribbon. As blurred and muted emotions became pregnant with meaning, Jessica somehow found her way to the crate, then the stuffed pug, then the gilded box, and finally to the diamond ring which had been brought to her, by this special man, on this special day.

On this Christmas morning, Ryan Earl Hutson proposed to Jessica Megan Bugen. Jessica's long-cherished vision to be engaged was, at last, honored. The splendor and magic of that moment released a volume of pent-up tears so titanic the Hoover Dam would have ruptured. For just a moment, time stood still. No other Christmas gifts mattered in this tear-stained moment of joy.

This was the moment that Jessica had been waiting for – for six years!

Jessica had vision. Even on those days when her patience was tested, her faith in doubt, she cherished Ryan and the vision of a life she would embrace with him – one day! A destination, out of sight, called to her. I reminded her of the words of Norman Vincent Peale who said "No matter how dark things seem to be, or actually are, raise your sights and see the possibilities – always see them, for they're always there."

We are pushed forward by our pasts but pulled forward by vision.

I had seen this strength of character in Jessica many times over the years. Jessica has always known how to hold the imaginary line – how to hold the rudder steady. This is what many women learn to do in their families. As Erik's younger sister, Jessica knew how to call out her older brother when he crossed some line of respectability. As a fullback on her state-ranked soccer team at Westlake High School she literally held the line. She tackled hard, blocked hard, and resolutely held the line. As a fullback, Jessica's role was to see the big picture unfolding before her, breathe deeply, and then commit.

While protecting her net or her family, Jessica's gaze was not on any particular spot on the field. Like the rest of us in life, Jessica often zigzagged from side to side, often falling, in pursuit of her dynamically moving goal. While impeding an attacking forward, blocking an attempted goal, or winning a game were on her radar screen, these "goals" were not here mainstay. These goals were within her sights, but they did not reflect her vision. It was the helping with, the belonging to, the caring for, and the loving of the game – all relationships – that mattered to Jessica much more than the winning. Jessica merely wanted to share a dream with her family or team.

Claire and I had known of the impending Christmas morning "surprise" for two weeks – but could not say a word. While celebrating a friend's birthday in a spiritual country setting two weekends before, Ryan had approached Claire and me with the exciting news. Ironically, he chose to tell us while the three of us were standing alone on an outdoor labyrinth, intricately made out of fine hardened woods. Because it was a surprise, the three of us were not free to hug – tearfully or otherwise – as Jessica was clearly within view. This could not have been scripted any better. We were standing in a circular labyrinth which is often viewed as a symbol of wholeness, the epitome of an archetypal journey.

The labyrinth symbolizes the cyclic journey that each of us must take daily and seasonally throughout our entire lives as we follow a path to our own unity and wholeness. While reaching the center of the labyrinth is one's intent, every participant in this glorious and ancient ritual will approach the center and then – when the center is just within reach – be taken back to an outer circuit that is far removed from his or her destination. Eventually, with patience and persistence, the center is reached. Often, when we are on a journey, the only sextant we have is the vision of a homecoming not yet seen.

Jessica understood that a vision is experienced twice.

She first created a spell-binding image in her mind. She imagined what life would look like with Ryan Earl Hutson. She would often talk about what kind of life they would have together – if only he would propose! She had a blueprint in her mind. She would often share her ideas on what being a wife, a mother or a daughter-in-law would be like. Now, after so many years of dreaming the dream, we all bore witness to Jessica experiencing her dream – living it.

At first glance, the lesson of the labyrinth appears to be clear: persist and you will reach your destination. Yet, there are many twists and turns along the way. Are we meant to discount or minimize each of these stops? Is it possible that each of these markers is intended to open our eyes – so we can see more clearly? Is each step taken a precious moment to reflect, to be aware, to feel pain, and then come to our senses?

Vision – a gutsy thing….is an expectation that what has already begun will be brought to its fullness.

This is vision's purpose. When we get lost in life's messiness or big spiritual questions, vision helps us find our way out. There was no right or wrong way for Jessica and Ryan to walk through their courtship. Unlike a maze, their labyrinth journey required only one choice. "Do I enter or not?" The choice is whether or not to walk a spiritual path. We'll never know how many gut checks, how many heart to hearts, or how many soul-searching, self talks occurred for both Jessica and Ryan. No doubt there were times when each reached the center of their labyrinth just long enough to pause, to face fears, to breathe deeply, and then to wonder not whether I'm on the right path, but what is this path teaching me. Surely, each of us in long-term relationships, have wondered the same. Jessica and Ryan had a picture of their unfolding life, an embedded image, which guided them. Happily, each of them reached beyond moments of doubt, into the conception of what can be! We all rejoice!

Jessica and Ryan married in a beautiful destination wedding on March 10, 2009.

Living in the Now

Eckhart Tolle has written two best sellers recently: *The Power of Now* and *A New Earth: Awakening to Your Life's Purpose*. Tolle emphasizes that "we are not our mind; we can find our way out of psychological pain; authentic power is found by surrendering to the Now… the present moment, where problems do not exist. It is here we find our joy and are able to embrace our true selves. It is here we discover that we are already complete and perfect."[7]

Tolle's books touch the lives of many and have inspired Oprah to place him high on her book club selection list. Much of what Tolle describes I think I get: first, that our over-analytic, ego-based minds can distort reality; second, that cravings are the ego mind's incessant seeking of fulfillment in external things; and third, that the pain we create now is usually some form of unacceptance. I particularly agree with his belief that we live too much in the past and the future, realms inhabited by an unforgiving mind and an overly ambitious ego. Time is a human concoction which blurs our vision of the present – of Now.

Imagine the Earth devoid of human life, inhabited only by plants and animals. Would it still have a past and a future? Could we still speak of time in any meaningful way? The question "What time is it?" or "What's the date today?" – If anybody were there to ask it – would be quite meaningless. The oak tree or the eagle would be bemused by such a question. "What time?" they would ask. "Well, of course, it's now. The time is now. What else is there?" [8]

So, I agree that our minds can be mischief-making, that our external cravings are superficial and distracting, and that we suffer more by being judgmental and resentful. All of that is fine. I even buy into the notion that we are so busy holding onto grievances and transforming our present lives into future dreams that we squander the Now while creating heartache and discontent each and every day. Acceptance, now, of our life givens is a necessity.

Tolle extols the virtue of looking inward, one of the characteristics of the *Gift* of vision. This reflects what we often call introspection and contemplative prayer; it is also the path of enlightenment which the Buddha, i.e. Siddhartha, described as an end to suffering. While the path to enlightenment is a worthy endeavor, it is time-consuming and most devout "experts" agree that it won't be achieved in this lifetime. Besides, the Buddha had more time to contemplate the eternal Being, the ever-present One, than we do. The Buddha did not have a mortgage to pay, a dual career marriage to balance, and college educations to fund. In fact, the Buddha left his son and wife behind in order to find enlightenment!

Here's the rub for me: if one is fully conscious – i.e. enlightened in the way described by New Age devotees – would we even need a relationship with one another? Is the journey inward, so revered by Tolle, yet another narcissistic pursuit which paradoxically blocks our vision of another? Is the pursuit of inner peace actually killing our relationships with one another?

Is enlightenment yet another self-absorbed entitlement which blinds us to the rest of humanity?

The truth is that both humanity and society have arrived at a tipping point. Our sheer brain size has evolved to a point where its massive cortex cannot be turned off by flicking a switch. If we only lived in the Now we'd have brains the size of salamanders with fewer synapses! The very time zones critiqued by Tolle – i.e. past and future – are the very morsels upon which our cerebral cortex feeds. Our associative neural pathways have exploded in growth. There is no turning back. Our neocortex is filled with accumulated knowledge built upon two unique human capacities: the capacity to reconstruct a past and the capacity to anticipate a future. Our societies have become so complex and demanding that we face emotional and financial bankruptcy if we are not suitably prepared in our life planning – a futuristic endeavor. Even our love relationships would go bankrupt if we did not problem-solve on a continual basis.

No wonder we seek self-fulfillment within! But self-reverie, self-absorption, and self-enlightenment are not the answers. We are losing the forest for the trees. In our desperate need to turn off our stressful spigots, we are turning away from each other.

Listen, as Tolle talks about relationships being but a ripple upon the ocean: "But in that state of inner connectedness, you feel this pull somewhere on the surface or periphery of your life. Anything that happens to you in that state feels somewhat like that. The whole world seems like waves or ripples on the surface of a vast and deep ocean. You are that ocean and, of course, you are also a ripple, but a ripple that has realized its true identity as the ocean, and compared to that vastness and depth, the world of waves and ripple is not all that important."[9] Relationships not that important! Eh?

That's a hard one for me. I certainly acknowledge that peace can be found momentarily by turning inward – but not as a life quest. So much that is meaningful about existence is the grandeur of a relationship beyond ourselves. Whether I am communing with nature, swimming luxuriously in our beautiful Barton Springs, mowing my lawn, donating to Hospice Austin, talking with a client, hugging a loved one, or praying to God – in all ways I am connected to a vastness far beyond me. In my best moments I am humbly reverent in regard to these bonds. I am in awe of them. In my worst moments, I can only hope that some unconscious part of me is being nourished by that which I experience.

Personally, the words of Oren Lyons ring truer to me that the words of Eckhart Tolle – words I became aware of as I prepared to deliver a marriage address at a friend's wedding. The groom approached me and asked that I include a very special reading that meant much to him as well as his bride-to-be. The few words the groom asked me to read aloud were selected from an interview conducted by Bill Moyers as he talked with Oren Lyons, an Onondaga Chief of one of our Native American tribes:

> *We are given these instructions by our forbearers; we are told that when we sit in council for the welfare of the people, we counsel for the welfare of that seventh generation to come. It should be foremost in our minds – not even our generation, not even ourselves, but those that are unborn. So that when their time comes, they may enjoy the same things that we're enjoying now. I'm sitting here as the seventh generation because seven generations ago, those people were looking out for me. Seven generations from now someone will be here, I know."* [10]

I believe that we should look out for one another – into our friendship and love circles. This vision of Oren Lyons is becoming more and more difficult as we drift more and more out of touch with one another. There is a battle going on between the pursuit of materialism and the pursuit of spiritualism. Both are distracting us. Neither should win. Both must find a way to live harmoniously with the other. This book has challenged the foolhardiness of those who pursue the egoistic, narcissistic world of materialism. Emptor: Buyers beware! The satisfactions we seek for materialism may become a problem more vexing for a society already in flux; however, a journey focused only inward may blind us to one another in even worse ways.

Both materialism and spiritualism can be narcissistic paths which remove us from society – from each other. In either case, vision has been lost.

This is precisely what happened in Greece when monks built monasteries high above the Plains of Thessaly in Meteora, so that they would not be disturbed on their paths to enlightenment. These monasteries could only be reached by parishioners if a rope were dropped down to them, whereupon they would be hoisted 1,500 feet upward to the monasteries above – awesome structures built during the 12th and 13th centuries.

One monastery, Athos, still survives today on a remote peninsula in the Aegean Sea. Ironically, Athos and its 100 or so Greek Orthodox monks are under attack: not by bands of marauding Mongols but by their very countrymen in Athens who want them evicted from their 1000-year-old reclusive habitat! Why? Because they are too removed from society! While the monks have sought refuge from a world of materialism and commercialism, Athens believes the monks have symbolically become a blight who bitterly oppose the reconciliation between orthodox Christians and the Roman Catholic church. Of course, Methodius, the monastery's abbot, declares that the monks of the Esphigmenou Monastery will challenge the eviction order in Greece's highest administrative court.

Lack of reconciliation, lack of communication, and lack of collaboration mark this standoff. The Greek word for idiot is *idiotes*. The etymology of this word implies that anyone who removes himself from the goings-on within a society risks being an out-lier – an idiot! Each of us who drifts too far outward into the world of materialism, into the world of pride, power, and possession is at risk of idiocy; likewise, any one who drifts too far inward, on a self-absorbed path toward enlightenment, is also at risk. Anyone in either scenario we have abandoned a love object, a person to love, or a society to nurture. Both are equally tragic. There's a wake up call here in the words of Bob Dylan:

> *Come gather 'round people*
> *Wherever you roam*
> *And admit that the waters*
> *Around you have grown*
> *And accept it that soon*
> *You'll be drenched to the bone.*
> *If your time to you*
> *Is worth savin'*
> *Then you better start swimmin'*
> *Or you'll sink like a stone*
> *For the times they are a-changin'.*[11]

I'm Here for Now, Not Forever

As each of us grapples with life's mysteries, we see the times they are a-changin'.

Irwin Yalom describes four "ultimate concerns" of life: [1] *Death* – of something – is just around the corner waiting for us. There is no escape. [2] *Freedom* to make life choices is an absolutely stunning burden at times. The responsibility to fill the vessel of our lives wisely is terrifying. [3] *Isolation* is a "final, unbearable gap" we must bear no matter how close or intimate we become with another. We enter this existence alone and must exit this paradise alone. [4] And, if we all must die, if we all must bear the consequences of our choices, if we must all live alone in a vast indifferent universe, then what *Meaning* does our life have for us?[12] Coincidentally, these "concerns" are quite similar to those which prompted Siddhartha to seek the Four Noble Truths.

Jungian psychoanalyst James Hollis, agreeing with the universality of these "ultimate concerns," also implores us to wonder why we are here, what is the meaning of existence, and what truly matters the most in life?

> *Our common existential condition is separation. We are traumatically separated from the Other at birth, live a life of estrangement from others, yet perpetually desire reconciliation, homecoming... We are all exiles, whether we know it or not, for who among us feels truly, vitally linked to the four great orders of mystery: the cosmos, nature, the tribe, and self?[13]*

A magnificent life force exists within us. Some, like James Hollis, call this dynamic force, Eros. This force reminds us that we are not quite dead yet. Though we are haunted by fears, Eros calls out to us reminding us that the perils of life journeys can be endured, that the Siren call seduces us into an adventure, and that somehow love, as the quintessential vision, summons us all to a better place. With Eros, we feel alive.

At this point in my life I have learned the importance of caring, of listening, of touching. I hug well. I have learned to appreciate what I have been given and not take anything for granted. My relationships with Claire, Erik, Jessica, and extended family and friends have taken on a new meaning for me. I see time differently and tend not to waste it. Most important of all, though, I have learned to cherish and value love.

The mysterious road ahead beckons me. No matter what the future brings my life has been worthwhile. I would have preferred not to have had a cancer diagnosis but it took the specter of death to further awaken me to life. Not surprisingly to those who know me, I still have my dreams – they just might be shorter!

What do we create and hold onto in this brief journey that can buffer us from a deep and tragic fear that our life has been but an insignificant spec in a vastness far greater than we can hope to imagine? As I have pondered these four ultimate concerns over the years, I have slowly generated a series of questions which have helped me and others. I would suggest that each of you – especially Heidi Montag – consider one thought per day during quiet reflection:

Meaning in Life: 20 Critical Questions

1) Life is…
2) The thing I want most during my life is…
3) The most important thing in life is…
4) My life up to now has been…
5) In the future I…
6) At the moment I feel…
7) I'm happiest when…
8) When I'm alone I….
9) I believe strongly that…

10) What really turns me on is...

11) Death is ...

12) What really frightens me about death is...

13) What really frightens me about life is...

14) My soul is...

15) I feel most alive when...

16) I contribute the most to others when I...

17) I contribute to my own growth and well-being the most by...

18) The one dream I've discarded that I should start dreaming about again is...

19) The one thing I should start doing now is...

20) The one thing I should stop doing now is...

Each of these incomplete statements reveals the incomplete visions of our lives.

Albert Camus, in his epic work *The Rebel*, knew this well: "Rebellion is a claim, motivated by the concept of complete unity, against the suffering of life and death and a protest against the human condition for its incompleteness!"[14] Camus knew that we do not notice the line of a circle that reflects 350 degrees; we notice, instead, the missing 10 degrees. The missing 10 degrees! Like a mountaineer hearing the faint calling in a far away valley, we live our lives responding to throbbing, incessant echoes – inescapable cries, an undeniable hunger that demands our attention consciously or unconsciously.

I know that the empty hole in my gut is very real yet I struggle to hold on – not just to the sweet, precious love I receive from Claire, Erik, and Jessica and so many others – but also to my fleeting life and dreams. I have learned enough to know that my imperfect life cannot always be full of happiness, but it can be full of love. I know, as well, my time is limited and that the unfolding of my children, and my children's children, is beyond my reach – though not beyond my imagination.

To be at peace with life's incompleteness is one of life's greatest gifts.

May we all be blessed with the humble notion that we are good enough, that our lives are good enough – and rest! May we each go forward with the humble wisdom to know that we are OK even when we are not! May we all rejoice in the knowledge that we breathed life into love and, gleefully, love returned the favor.

When we come to the edge of all the light we have been given may we pause long enough to see each other on lonely highways, to wonder who we truly are, and ask "Why am I here?" As Pulitzer prize-winning poet Mary Oliver captures in *Dreamwork*:

You do not have to be good.
You do not have to walk on your knees
for a hundred miles through the desert, repenting.
You only have to let the soft animal of your body love what it loves.

Tell me about your despair, yours, and I will tell you mine.
Meanwhile the world goes on.
Meanwhile the sun and the clear pebbles of the rain
Are moving across the landscapes,
over the prairies and the deep trees,
the mountains and the rivers.
Meanwhile the wild geese, high in the clean blue air,
are heading home again.
Whoever you are, no matter how lonely,
the world offers itself to your imagination,
calls to you like the wild geese, harsh and exciting –
Over and over announcing your place in the family of things.[15]

REFERENCES

Introduction

1. Nouwen, J. Henri (1972). "Help me open my clenched fists." *With Open Hands.* Notre Dame, Indiana: Ave Maria Press.

2. Rohr, Richard (1995). *Radical Grace: Daily Meditations.* Cincinnati, Ohio: St. Anthony Messenger Press.

3. Twenge, Jean (2006). *Generation Me.* New York, N.Y.: Free Press.

4. Johnson, Sue (2008). *Hold Me Tight: Seven Conversations for a Lifetime of Love.* New York, N.Y.: Little, Brown & Company.

5. Markham, Edwin (1915). "Outwitted." P. 1. *The Shoes of Happiness and Other Poems.* New York, N.Y.: Doubleday, Page and Company.

6. Hernandez, Wit (2006). *Henri Nouwen: A Spirituality of Imperfection.* P. 115. Mahwah, N.J.: Paulist Press.

7. Whitley, Keith. (1990). "I'm no stranger to the rain." *Greatest Hits by Keith Whitley.* RCA Records USA.

8) Hernandez, Wit (2006). *Henri Nouwen: A Spirituality of Imperfection.* P. 115. Mahwah, N.J.: Paulist Press.

9) Hernandez, Wit (2006). *Henri Nouwen: A Spirituality of Imperfection.* P. 77. Mahwah, N.J.: Paulist Press.

Chapter One

1) Simpson, James T. (2008). "The way it is." Internet Posting.

2) Bowles, Paul. (1995). *Morocco: Sahara to the Sea.* "Preface." New York, N.Y. Abbeville Press Publisher.

3) Hotchkiss, Sandy (2002) *Why Is It Always About You?* "Introduction xvii." New York, N.Y.: Free Press.

4) Hotchkiss, Sandy (2002) *Why Is It Always About You?* Pgs. 3-35. New York, N.Y.: Free Press.

Chapter Two

1) Andersen, Hans Christian; Tatar, Maria (Ed. and transl.); Allen, Julie K. (Transl.) (2008). "The Emperor's New Clothes." *The Annotated Hans Christian Andersen.* New York and London: W. W. Norton & Company, Inc.

2) Yalom, Irwin D. (1980). *Existential Psychotherapy.* New York, N.Y.: Basic Books.

3) Perls, Frederick S. (1969) *Gestalt Therapy Verbatim.* "The Gestalt Prayer." New York, N.Y.: Bantam Books.

4) Womack, Lee Ann. (2004). "I hope you dance." *Greatest Hits.* Nashville, Tennessee. MCA Records Inc.

5) Cohen, Leonard (1975). "Anthem." *Best of Leonard Cohen.* Columbia Records.

6) Alford, Henry (1844). In Lucy Adams (2000): *52 Hymn Story Devotions.* Nashville, Tennessee: United Methodist Publishing House.

7) Brower, David (1971). In John McPhee (1971): *Encounters With the Archdruid.* New York, N.Y.: Farrar, Straus, and Giroux.

Chapter Three

1) Pitts, Leonard (1999). "Are you famous and beautiful? Maybe you're qualified to run for president." In *Austin American Statesman.* October 18, 1999. Cox.

2) Harris, Emma Lou. (1979). "Beneath Still Waters." *Blue Kentucky Girl.* Rhino Records, USA.

3) Faludi, Susan (1999). *Stiffed: The Betrayal of the American Man.* P. 39. San Francisco, California: Harper perennial.

4) Horney, Karen (1939). *New Ways in Psychoanalysis.* P. 91. New York, N.Y.: W.W. Norton & Co.

5) Ali, Hameed (2004). *Diamond Heart and Training Center.* Berkeley, CA.: Ridhwan Foundation.

6) Solomon, Marion F. (1989). *Narcissism and Intimacy.* Pgs. 43-44. New York, N.Y.: W.W. Norton & Company, Inc.

7) Viorst, Judith. (1986). *Necessary Losses.* P. 59. New York, N.Y.: Fireside.

8) Kurtz, Ernest & Ketcham, Katherine (1992). *The Spirituality of Imperfection: Storytelling and the Journey to Wholeness.* P. 116. New York, N.Y.: Bantam Books.

Chapter Four

1) Peart, Niel (1978). "The Trees." Mapletrader.com.: Album Hemispheres.

2) Rosenberg, Josef (2002). "Deadly Sins." www.deadlysins.com/sins/history.html.

3) Fairlie, Henry (1978). *The Seven Deadly Sins Today.* P. 35. Washington, D.C.: New Republic Books.

4) MacLaine, Shirley (1977). In Henry Fairlie: *The Seven Deadly Sins Today.* (1978). P. 31. Washington. D.C.: New Republic Books.

5) Chesterton, G.K. (2009) "Quotations of G.K. Chesterton." *The American Chesterion Society.* http://chesterton.org/acs/quotes.htm.

6) Fairlie, Henry (1978). *The Seven Deadly Sins Today.* P. 35. Washington, D.C.: New Republic Books.

7) Tracy, Jessica & Robins, Rick (2006). "The Pride Expression." *Psychological Science,* Vol. 15, No. 3.

8) Dweck, C. S. (2006). *Mindset: The new psychology of success.* New York: Random House.

9) Mayer, Toby G. (2007). *Beverly Hills Institute of Aesthetic and Reconstructive Surgery.* Beverly Hills, California.

10) Fairlie, Henry (1978). *The Seven Deadly Sins Today.* Pgs. 64-65. Washington, D.C.: New Republic Books.

11) Goodall, Jane ((2007). *Cell Biology.* Vol. 17, March.

12) Fairlie, Henry (1978). *The Seven Deadly Sins Today.* Pg. 114. Washington, D. C.: New Republic Books.

13) Cohen, Richard (1997). "Titanic is rich with success and failure of technology and society." *Austin American Statesman.* December 27th, 2007.

14) Fairlie, Henry (1978). *The Seven Deadly Sins Today,* P. 131. Washington, D.C.: New Republic Books.

15) Park, Laura (2007). "Excessive concern over appearance can harm health." *Reuters.* Reuters.com/article/healthNews/idUSCOL February 15th, 2007.

16) Fairlie, Henry (1978). *The Seven Deadly Sins Today.* P. 175. Washington, D.C.: New Republic Books.

17) Dawkins, Richard (1976). *The Selfish Gene.* P. 11. New York, N.Y.: Oxford University Press.

Chapter Five

1) Dawkins, Richard (1976). *The Selfish Gene.* P. 3. New York, N.Y.: Oxford University Press.

2) Dawkins, Richard (1976). *The Selfish Gene.* P. 4. New York, N.Y.: Oxford University Press.

3) Fisher, Helen (1992). *Anatomy of Love.* New York, N.Y.: Ballantine Books.

4) Baker, Robin (1996). *Sperm Wars.* Introduction: xv. Toronto, Canada.: Harper Collins.

5) Goleman, Daniel (1996). "The secret of happiness: It's in the genes." *Austin American Statesman.* July 21st, 1996.

6) Diener, Edward (1996). In D. Goleman "The secret of happiness: It's in the genes." *Austin American Statesman.* July 21st, 1996.

7) Hamer, Dean (1997). In R. Pool: "Portrait of a gene guy." *Discover.* October, 1997.

8) Davidson, Richard (1989). In D. Goleman. "New research overturns a milestone of infancy." *The New York Times.* June 6, 1989.

9) Willour, Virginia (2007). "Genetic link to suicidal tendencies nailed down." *Austin American Statesman.* February 26, 2007.

10) de Waal, Frans B.M. (2001). In S. Carpenter: "Psychology is bound to become more Darwinian, says eminent primatologist." *Monitor.* April, 2001.

11) Tennyson, Alford Lord (1890). "The Princess." In Eugene Parsons: *Poems of Alfred Lord Tennyson.* New York: Thomas Y. Crowell Company, 1900.

12) de Waal, Frans B.M. (2001). In S. Carpenter: "Psychology is bound to become more Darwinian, says eminent primatologist." *Monitor.* April, 2001.

13) Lykken, David (1996). In D. Goleman "The secret of happiness: It's in the genes." *Austin American Statesman.* July 21st, 1996.

Chapter Six

1) Mclachlan, Sarah (1997). "Angel." *Mirrorball.* Arista Records. USA. 1997.

2) Marano, Hara Estroff (1996). "What killed Margaux Hemingway." *Psychology Today.* December 1, 1996.

3) Missildine, Hugh (1963). *Your Inner Child of the Past.* New York: Simon and Schuster.

4) Williams, Hank Jr. (1963). "Family tradition." *Greatest Hits.* MGM Records.

5) Kagan, Jerome (1998). In S. Begley: "The nurture assumption." *Newsweek,* p. 57. September 7,

1998.

6) Vachss, Andrew (1998). Safehouse. New York, N.Y.: Knoff Publishing.

7) Lykken, David (2000). "Reconstructing fathers." *American Psychologist*. P. 681. June, 2000.

8) Henshaw SK and Kost K. "Trends in the characteristics of women obtaining abortions, 1974 to 2004." New York: Guttmacher Institute, 2008.

9) Harris, J. R. (1998). *The nurture assumption: Why children turn out the way they do*. New York, N.Y.: Free Press.

10) Mike and the Mechanics (1988). "The living years." *Nobody's Perfect*. Atlantic Records, USA.

Chapter Seven — Leadership

1) Brooks, David (2007). "Democracy's full of private virtue, public vice." Editorial: *Austin American Statesman*, February 13, 2007.

2) Hightower, Jim & DeMarco, Susan (2008). *Swim against the current: Even a dead fish can go with the flow*. New York, N.Y.: John Wiley and Sons.

3) McCain, John (2004). "The search for courage." Yahoo Special Edition. Exerpted from: J. McCain: *Why Courage Matters*. http://biz.yahoo.com/special/courage04.html.

4) Pitts, Leonard. "Skipping the straight talk." Editorial: *Austin American Statesman*, April 21, 2010.

5) Golis, Andrew (2010). "Disillusioned Bayh advocates electoral "shock" to broken system." Yahoo News. February 16, 2010.

6) Bennis, Warren (2007). "The challenges of leadership in the modern world." *American Psychologist*. P. 3. Volume 62, Number 1.

7) McCain, John (2004). "The search for courage." Yahoo Special Edition. Exerpted from: J. McCain: *Why Courage Matters*. http:biz.yahoo.com/special/courage04.html.

8) Vroom, Victor and Jago, Arthur (2007). "The role of the situation in leadership." *American Psychologist*. Pg. 17-24. Volume 62, Number 1.

9) Ludeman, Kate (1989). *The Worth Ethic*. P. 4. New York, N.Y.: E. P. Dutton.

10) Will, George (2008). "McCain's closing argument." *Austin American Statesman*. September 18, 2008.

11) Meyerson, Harold (2004). "For Bush the believer, facts are for girlie men." Editorial: *Austin American Statesman*. October 22, 2004.

12) Pitts, Leonard (2004). "This nation bought what Bush was selling: a forgery of a war." Commentary: *Austin American Statesman*. October 23, 2004.

13) Jackson, Derrick (2004). "What I hope they'll say: We're a selfish nation." Editorial: *Austin American Statesman*. September 30, 2004.

14) Kaminer, Wendy (1997). "Why we love gurus." *Newsweek*. October 20, 1997.

15) Blais, Jacqueline (2005). "Vonnegut, on politics, presidents, and librarians." *USA Today*. October 5, 2005.

Chapter Eight — Psychotherapy

1) Craik, Dinah (1859). "A life for a life." In Sally Mitchell: *Dinah Mulock Craik*. (1883). Boston: Twayne Publishers.

2) Yalom, Irvin (1989). *Love's Executioner*. Prologue. P. 3. New York, N.Y.: Basic Books, Inc.

3) Yalom, Irvin (1989). *Love's Executioner*. Prologue. P. 13. New York, N.Y.: Basic Books, Inc.

4) Peck, M. Scott (1978). *The Road Less Traveled*. New York, N.Y.: Simon & Schuster.

5) Lamott, Anne (2007). *Grace (Eventually): Thoughts on Faith*. New York, N.Y.: Penguin.

6) Wistow, Fred (1997). "Confessions of a lifelong therapy addict." *Family Therapy Networker*. July 1, 1997.

7) O'Hara, Maureen. (1997) "Relational empathy: Beyond modernist egocentrism to postmodern

contextualism." In L. Greenberg and A. Bohart (Eds): *Empathy Reconsidered*. Washington, D.C.: American Psychological Association.

8) Yalom, Irvin (1989). *Love's Executioner*. Prologue. P. 11. New York, N.Y.: Basic Books, Inc.

Chapter Nine – Religion

1) Lennon, John (1971). "Imagine." *Imagine*. New York, N.Y.: Ascot Sound Studios

2) Goodman, Ellen (2003). "Might doesn't make right, even when you're talking about deities." *Austin American Statesman*. October 23, 2003.

3) Cable News Network (2001). "Falwell apologizes to gays, feminists, lesbians." *CNN.com/US.*, 2001.

4) Jung, C. G.; Adler, G. and Hull, R. F. C., eds. (1977) *Collected Works of C. G. Jung, Volume 18: The Symbolic Life: Miscellaneous Writings*, Princeton, NJ: Princeton University Press

5) Cross, F.L. (2005). "Sermon on the Mount." *Matthew* 5:1-12. In *The Oxford Dictionary of the Christian Church*. New York, N.Y.: Oxford University Press.

6) Lively, Bob (2006). "Following Jesus not about acquiring power or imposing your views." *Austin American Statesman*, June 10, 2006.

7) Taylor, Humphrey (2003). "The religious and other beliefs of Americans 2003." *The Harris Poll*, Number 11, February 26, 2003.

8) Rolheiser, Ronald (2004). *The Shattered Lantern*. P. 74. New York, N.Y.: The Crossroad Publishing Company.

9) Rolheiser, Ronald (2004). *The Shattered Lantern*. P. 90. New York, N.Y.: The Crossroad Publishing Company.

10) Kurtz, Ernest & Ketcham, Katherine (1992). *The Spirituality of Imperfection: Storytelling and the Journey to Wholeness*. P. 34. New York, N.Y.: Bantam Books.

11) Postman, Neil (1985). *Amusing Ourselves to Death: Public Discourse in the Age of Show Business*. New York, N.Y.: Penguin.

12) Peck, Scott (1987). *The Different Drum: Community Making and Peace*. P. 303. New York, N.Y.: Simon and Schuster.

13) Krakauer, John (2003). *Under the Banner of Faith: A Story of Violent Faith*. Prologue, P. 13. New York, N.Y.: Doubleday.

14) Meyer, Charles (2000). *Dying Church Living God: A Call to Begin Again*. Kelowna, BC.: Northstone Publishing.

15) Whitehurst, Emilee D. "Pentecost reminds us of the importance of diversity." Editorial: *Austin American Statesman*. June 10, 2006.

16) Kurtz, Ernest & Ketcham, Katherine (1992). *The Spirituality of Imperfection: Storytelling and the Journey to Wholeness*. P. 56. New York, N.Y.: Bantam Books.

17) Kurtz, Ernest & Ketcham, Katherine (1992). *The Spirituality of Imperfection: Storytelling and the Journey to Wholeness*. P. 25. New York, N.Y.: Bantam Books.

18) Borg, Marcus J. (2001). *Reading the Bible Again for the First Time*. P. 22. New York, N.Y.: Harper-Collins.

19) Borg, Marcus J. (2001). *Reading the Bible Again for the First Time*. P. 23. New York, N.Y.: Harper-Collins.

20) Peck, Scott (1987). *The Different Drum: Community Making and Peace*. Prologue. P. 13. New York, N.Y.: Simon and Schuster.

21) Obama, Barack (2006). http://obama.senate.gov/speech/060628-call_to_renewal_keynote_address/print.php.

22) Rohr, Richard (2010). "Emerging Christianity: A non-dual vision." *Radical Grace*. January-March. Volume 23, Number 1. P. 3.

Chapter Ten – Our Need for Attachment

1) Morris, Desmond (1971). *Intimate Behavior.* New York, N.Y.: Random House.

2) Nouwen, Henri (1992). *Mark 1:10-11* In: *The Return of the Prodigal Son: A Story of Homecoming.* New York, N.Y.: Image Books.

3) Schnarch, David (1997). *Passionate Marriage.* New York, N.Y.: Henry Holt and Company.

4) Bowlby, John (1969). *Attachment.* New York, N.Y.: Basic Books, Inc.

5) Ainsworth, Mary et al. (1978). *Patterns of Attachment: A Psychological Study of the Strange Situation.* Hillsdale, N.J.: Erlbaum.

6) Main, M & Solomon, J., (1990). In Greenberg, M. T., Cicchetti, D., & Cummings, M. (Eds.). *Attachment in the preschool years: Theory, research, and intervention* (pp. 121-160). The University of Chicago Press: Chicago.

7) Karen, Robert (1990). "Becoming attached." P. 35. *The Atlantic Monthly.* February, 1990.

8) Siegel, Daniel and Hartzell, Mary. (2003). *Parenting from the Inside Out.* New York, N.Y.: Tarcher.

9) Ornish, Dean (1998). *Love and Survival: 8 Pathways to Intimacy and Health.* New York, N.Y.: HarperCollins.

10) Robinson, Marnia and Wile, Douglas (2009). *Cupid's Poisoned Arrow: From Habit to Harmony.* Berkeley, California. North Atlantic Books.

11) APA, University of California, San Francisco (July 15, 1999). "Hormone involved in reproduction may have role in the maintenance of relationships." *Science Daily.* February 19, 2010, from http://www.sciencedaily.com//releases/1999/07/990715062344.htm.

12) Morris, Desmond (1971). *Intimate Behavior.* New York, N.Y.: Random House.

13) Horney, Karen (1939). *New Ways in Psychoanalysis.* New York, N.Y.: W. W. Norton.

Chapter Eleven – Romantic Love

1) Johnson, Robert (1986). *We.* Introduction: xi. San Francisco, California. Harper & Row, 1983.

2) Johnson, Robert (1986). *We.* P. 33. San Francisco, California. Harper & Row, 1983.

3) Stein, R. (1977). "When first we met." *San Francisco Chronicle,* February 14, 1977.

4) Langdon-Davies, J. (1927). *A Short History of Women.* Pgs. 266-267. New York, N.Y.: Literary Guild of America.

5) Johnson, Robert (1986). *We.* P. 108. San Francisco, California. Harper & Row, 1983.

6) Jackson, Don (1965). "Family rules – marital quid pro quo." *Archives of General Psychiatry,* 12, 589-594.

7) Fromm, Erich (1956). *The Art of Loving.* P. 36. New York, N.Y.: Harper & Row.

8) James, Muriel (1979). *Marriage is for Loving.* P. 38. Reading, Massachusetts: Addison-Wesley.

Chapter Twelve – Disenchantment

1) *Time Magazine*, April, 1989, P. 58.

2) Kopp, Sheldon (1978). *An End to Innocence.* New York, N.Y.: MacMillan.

3) Seligman, Martin E. (2002). *Authentic Happiness: Using the New Positive Psychology to Realize Your Potential for Lasting Fulfillment.* New York, N.Y.: Free Press.

4) Wensinger, A. (Ed.). (1984). *Paula Modersohn-Becker: The Letters and Journals.* New York, N.Y.: Taplinger Publishing.

Chapter Thirteen – Mature, Covenant Love

1) Frost, Robert (1949). "The road not taken." *Complete Poems of Robert Frost.* New York, N.Y. Henry Holt.

2) Maslow, Abraham (1970). *Motivation and Personality.* P. 156. New York, N.Y.: Harper & Row.

3) Kierkegaard, Soren (1954). *Fear and Trembling.* New York, N.Y.: Anchor.

4) Perls, Fritz (1971). *Gestalt Therapy Verbatim.* P. 30. New York, N.Y.: Bantam.

5) Gibran, Khalil (1923). "Marriage." *The Prophet.* In Biblioteca Universale Rizzoli of Milan, 1992.

6) Peck, M. Scott (1978). *The Road Less Traveled.* P. 98. New York, N.Y.: Simon and Schuster.

7) Hampden-Turner, Charles (1982). *Maps of the Mind.* P. 48. New York, N.Y.: MacMillan.

8) Guggenbuhl-Craig Adolph (1977). *Marriage: Dead or Alive.* New Orleans, Louisiana. Spring Publications.

Chapter Fourteen – Self Assessment

1) Moore, Thomas (1994). *Soulmates: Honoring the Mysteries of Love and Relationship.* P. 19. New York, N.Y.: HarperCollins.

Chapter Fifteen – Humility

1) Kurtz, Ernest & Ketcham, Katherine (1992). *The Spirituality of Imperfection: Storytelling and the Journey to Wholeness.* P. 185. New York, N.Y.: Bantam Books.

2) Kurtz, Ernest & Ketcham, Katherine (1992). *The Spirituality of Imperfection: Storytelling and the Journey to Wholeness.* P. 186. New York, N.Y.: Bantam Books.

3) Rowatt. Wade (2006). "The positive psychology of humility relative to arrogance." *Texas Psychologist.* Pgs. 24-27. Fall, 2006.

4) Kurtz, Ernest & Ketcham, Katherine (1992). *The Spirituality of Imperfection: Storytelling and the Journey to Wholeness.* P. 193. New York, N.Y.: Bantam Books.

5) Epstein, Mark (1999). *Going to Pieces Without Falling Apart.* P. 19. New York, N.Y.: Broadway Books.

6) Klinkenborg, Verlyn (2010). "The power of Patagonia." *National Geographic.* P. 88. February, 2010.

7) Biema, David (2006). "Mother Teresa's crisis of faith." *Time Magazine*, August 23, 2006.

8) Hampden-Turner, Charles (1982). *Maps of the Mind.* Pgs. 22-24. New York, N.Y.: MacMillan.

9) Gross, Ronald (2003). "Following Socrates' way everyday." *Spiritual and Health Magazine.* Spring, 2003.

10) Rowatt. Wade (2006). "The positive psychology of humility relative to arrogance." *Texas Psychologist.* Pgs. 24-27. Fall, 2006.

Chapter Sixteen – Forgiveness

1) Kurtz, Ernest & Ketcham, Katherine (1992). *The Spirituality of Imperfection: Storytelling and the Journey to Wholeness.* P. 225. New York, N.Y.: Bantam Books.

2) Anonymous (1976). *Alcoholics Anonymous: The Story of How Many Thousands of Men and Women Have Recovered from Alcoholism.* 3rd Edition. New York, N.Y.: Alcoholics Anonymous World Services.

3) Kurtz, Ernest & Ketcham, Katherine (1992). *The Spirituality of Imperfection: Storytelling and the Journey to Wholeness.* Pgs. 213-214. New York, N.Y.: Bantam Books.

4) McLachlin, Sarah (1999). "Building a mystery." *Mirrorball.* Arista Records. Nashville, Tennessee.

5) Spring, Janis Abrahms (2005). *How Can I Forgive You?: The Courage to Forgive or, the Freedom Not To.* New York, N.Y.: HarperCollins.

6) Kurtz, Ernest & Ketcham, Katherine (1992). *The Spirituality of Imperfection: Storytelling and the Journey to Wholeness.* P. 214. New York, N.Y.: Bantam Books.

7) Cohen, Leonard (1975). "Anthem." *Best of Leonard Cohen.* Columbia Records.

8) Agora (2008). "Wise message for the world from the late comedian George Carlin." *The Canadian.* www.agoracosmopolitan.com/home/Frontpage/2008/08/04/02504.html.

9) Nouwen, J. Henri (1972). "Help me open my clenched fists." *With Open Hands.* Notre Dame, Indiana: Ave Maria Press.

10) Nouwen, Henri (1992). *The Return of the Prodigal Son: A Story of Homecoming.* New York, N.Y.: Image Books.

11) Kurtz, Ernest & Ketcham, Katherine (1992). *The Spirituality of Imperfection: Storytelling and the Journey to Wholeness.* P. 222. New York, N.Y.: Bantam Books.

Chapter Seventeen — Acceptance

1) Byrne, Rhonda (2006). *The Secret.* P. 183. New York, N.Y.: Atria Books.

2) Henley, Don (2000). "For my wedding." *Inside Job.* Warner Brothers Records.

3) Henley, Don & Lynch, Stan (The Eagles) (1994). "Learn to be still." *Hell Freezes Over.* Digital Sound Recording.

4) Clark, James Midgely (1957). *Meister Eckhart: An Introduction to the Study of His Works with an Anthology of His Sermons,* Edinburgh: Thomas Nelson.

5) Henley, Don (2000). "My Thanksgiving." *Inside Job.* Warner Brothers Records.

6) Hawthorn, Nathaniel (1987). *King Midas and the Golden Touch.* New York, N.Y.: Houghton Mifflin Harcourt.

7) Ferrucci, Piero (1982). *What We May Be.* New York, N.Y.: Jeremy P. Tarcher/Putnam.

8) Haggard, Merle (2010). "I am what I am." *I Am What I Am.* Hog Records: Santa Monica.

9) Pitts, Leonard (2001). "Even Michael Jordan can't stop the clock." *Austin American Statesman.* April 20, 2001.

10) Seng-t'san (606). In Suzuki D.T. (1960). *Manual of Zen Buddhism,* New York, N.Y.: Evergreen Edition.

11) Womach, Lee Ann (2000). "I hope you dance." *I Hope You Dance.* MCA Nashville.

12) Keller, Helen (1988). *The Story of My Life.* New York, N.Y.: Random House, Inc.

13) Oliver, Mary (1986). "The journey." *Dreamwork.* New York, N.Y.: Atlantic Monthly Press.

14) Evans, Nicholas (1995). *The Horse Whisperer.* New York, N.Y.: Random House, Inc.

15) Hollis, James (2009). *What Matters Most.* P. 234. New York, N.Y.: Gotham Books, Inc.

16) Ayres, Robert (2004). "Downpour." *San Antonio Express News.* November 21, 2004.

17) Seligman, Martin (2002). *Authentic Happiness: Using the New Positive Psychology to Realize Your Potential for Lasting Fulfillment.* New York: Free Press. (Paperback edition, Free Press, 2004.)

Chapter Eighteen — Compassion

1) Blake, William (1976). In A. Kazin (Ed.) *The Portable William Blake.* P. 97. New York, N.Y.: Penguin Books.

2) de Waal, Frans (2005). "A century of getting to know the chimpanzee." *Nature* 437, Pgs. 56-59.

3) Fromm, Erich (1956). *The Art of Loving.* New York, N.Y.: Harper & Row, Inc.

4) Keltner, Dacher (2009). *Born to be Good.* New York, N.Y.: W. W. Norton & Co., Inc.

5) Zen Center of San Diego (2010). wwwzencentersandiego.org/ppr/

6) Becker, Ernest (1973). *The Denial of Death.* New York, N.Y.: Simon & Schuster.

7) Edwards, Tilden (1994). *Living in the Presence: Spiritual Exercises to Open Our Living to the Awareness of God.* San Francisco, California. HarperCollins.

8) Kluger, Jeffrey (2007). "What makes us moral." *Time CNN.* November 21, 2007.

9) Trivers, R.L. (1971). "The evolution of reciprocal altruism." *Quarterly Review of Biology.* Volume 46, Pgs. 35-57.

10) Fowler, James & Christakis, Nicholas (2010). "Acts of kindness spread surprisingly easily: Just a few people can make a difference." *Science Daily.* http://www.sciencedaily.com/releases/2010/03/100308151049.htm

11) Babauta, Leo (2007). "A guide to cultivating compassion in your life, with 7 practices." http://zenhabits.net/2007/06/a-guide-to-cultivating-compassion-in-your-life-with-7-practices/

Chapter Nineteen – Sacrifice

1) Adams, Bryan (1971). "(Everything I do) I do it for you." *Robin Hood: Prince of Thieves*. Santa Monica, Ca., A & M Records.
2) DuBois, Charles (1804-1867). *The Quotations Page*. www.quotationspage.com.
3) Shelley, Percy Bysshe (1892-1922). In Devy, G. N. (2001). "Reaching out." THE HINDU, April 8, 2001. www.hinduonnet.com/folio/fo0104/01040060.htm.
4) Devy, G. N. (2001). "Reaching out." THE HINDU, April 8, 2001. www.hinduonnet.com/folio/fo0104/01040060.htm.
5) Adams, Bryan (1971). "(Everything I do) I do it for you." *Robin Hood: Prince of Thieves*. Santa Monica, Ca., A & M Records.
6) Tolle, Eckert (1997). *The Power of Now*. P. 37. Vancouver, B.C. Canada. Namaste Publishing Inc.

Chapter Twenty – Vision

1) Adams, Caroline (2010). "Your life is a sacred journey." *The Butler Brothers: Creative Communication*. www.thebutlerbrothers.com/blog//your-life-is-a-sacred-journey/
2) McCranie, Nancy (2010). "Practicing gratitude." *Hospice Austin Volunteer Voice*. Winter 2010.
3) The Dow Chemical Company (2007). "The human element." Midland, Michigan. www.dow.com.
4) Serenity (2010). "Introduction." www.webmaze.com/adult/rooms/serenity.html.
5) Brower, David (1971). "The sermon." In John McPhee (1971): *Encounters with the Archdruid*. New York, N.Y.: Farrar, Straus, and Giroux.
6) Bennett, Jeffrey (2009). "Jeffrey Bennett: A bit of perspective for the universe 'we.'" *Star Tribune*. Minneapolis, Minnesota. February 12, 2009.
7) Tolle, Eckert (1997). *The Power of Now*. P. 23. Vancouver, B.C. Canada. Namaste Publishing Inc.
8) Tolle, Eckert (1997). *The Power of Now*. P. 27. Vancouver, B.C. Canada. Namaste Publishing Inc.
9) Tolle, Eckert (1997). *The Power of Now*. P. 143. Vancouver, B.C. Canada. Namaste Publishing Inc.
10) Lyons, Oren and Moyers, Bill (1991). "Oren Lyons – The faithkeeper." Public Affairs Television, Inc., July 3, 1991.
11) Dylan, Bob (1964). "The times they are a-changin'" *The Times They are A-Changin'*. New York, N.Y.: Columbia Records.
12) Yalom, Irvin (1980). *Existential Psychotherapy*, New York, N.Y.: Basic Books.
13) Hollis, James (2009). *What Matters Most: Living a More Considered Life*. P. 46. New York, N.Y.: Gotham Books.
14) Camus, Albert (1951). *The Rebel*. New York, N.Y.: Vintage Books.
15) Oliver, Mary (1986). "Wild geese." *Dreamwork*. New York, N.Y.: Atlantic Monthly Press.

CPSIA information can be obtained at www.ICGtesting.com
Printed in the USA
LVOW110231130712

289911LV00003B/5/P